PENGUIN

THE PENGUIN

T0357745

'Poignant . . . memorable . . . impressively fresh and compelling . . . the reader is bound to come away from a collection like this asking what the poetry of lament might help to teach us about the task of grieving for the threatened loss of an entire world'
Rowan Williams, *New Statesman*

'If you have any weakness for poetry at all this book will draw you in then devastate you' *The Times*

'A magnificent reminder of the permanence of love' *Daily Mail*

'The giants of the genre are well represented . . . there are discoveries aplenty . . . so monumental is this anthology that one can imagine it pillowing a knight's head on an elaborately carved marble tomb' *Tablet*

'Funny, angry and provocative . . . the anthology is a success . . . the editors' introduction is excellent – clear, informative and thought-provoking' *Daily Telegraph*

ABOUT THE EDITORS

Andrew Motion's most recent collection is *New and Selected Poems 1977–2022* (2023). He was UK Poet Laureate from 1999 to 2009, is co-founder of The Poetry Archive and Poetry by Heart, and since 2015 has lived in Baltimore, where he is Homewood Professor of the Arts at Johns Hopkins University.

Stephen Regan's books include *Irish Writing: An Anthology of Irish Literature in English 1789–1939* (2004) and *The Sonnet* (2019). He has taught at Ruskin College, Oxford; Royal Holloway, University of London; and Durham University, where he is Professor Emeritus. He is currently a Research Associate at the University of Melbourne.

THE PENGUIN BOOK OF ELEGY

Poems of Memory, Mourning and Consolation

Edited by
ANDREW MOTION *and* STEPHEN REGAN

PENGUIN CLASSICS
an imprint of
PENGUIN BOOKS

PENGUIN CLASSICS

UK | USA | Canada | Ireland | Australia
India | New Zealand | South Africa

Penguin Classics is part of the Penguin Random House group of companies
whose addresses can be found at global.penguinrandomhouse.com

First published in Penguin Classics 2023
This edition published 2024
002

Editorial matter and selection copyright © Andrew Motion and Stephen Regan, 2023

The acknowledgements on pp. 615–21 constitute an extension of this copyright page

The moral rights of the editors have been asserted

Typeset by Jouve (UK), Milton Keynes
Printed and bound in Great Britain by Clays Ltd, Elcograf S.p.A.

The authorized representative in the EEA is Penguin Random House Ireland,
Morrison Chambers, 32 Nassau Street, Dublin DO2 YH68

A CIP catalogue record for this book is available from the British Library

ISBN: 978–0–241–26962–6

Contents

CONTENTS

CONTENTS

CONTENTS

CONTENTS

CONTENTS

CONTENTS

Introduction

All poetry exists as a record of life snatched from the destructive flow of time, and so to some extent all poetry is elegiac. Whatever the ostensible subject of a poem, readers can always intuit the voice of the poet saying: 'I saw this, and I felt this, and tomorrow or the day after tomorrow, I won't.' This means that any collection of poems could, in a slightly devious sense, be called a book of elegies. But this *Penguin Book of Elegy* has a more particular purpose: we have brought together the best and most varied examples we can find of poems of loss and mourning written in English (and translated into English) between Classical antiquity and the present day. All of them respond to bereavement with some combination of sorrow, shock, rage, emptiness, bewilderment or hauntedness. Many of the poems additionally express a longing for consolation, giving voice at the same time to the wonder and incredulity that can arise from a sense of renewal. John Milton's vision of his dead wife, for instance – 'Methought I saw my late espousèd saint' – contains a similar experience of ghostly revelation to that which occurs in Seamus Heaney's meeting with his murdered cousin in 'The Strand at Lough Beg': 'I turn because the sweeping of your feet / Has stopped behind me'.

Marvellous encounters with the dead require a more than usually willing 'suspension of disbelief'.[1] But while this often produces work of sublime eloquence, it also tends to bring poets to the limits of language's ability to measure up to the richness and strangeness of human experience, where words either seem inadequate, or falter and break down altogether.[2] Faced with this likely disappointment, it is not surprising that elegiac poetry should often be characterized by a high degree of self-consciousness. Even while striving to become a lasting memorial, elegies often leave their creators and their audience in a troubled state where thoughts and feelings fall short of the resolution they desire.

Paradoxically, this sense of disappointment gives elegiac poetry much of the energy its readers most admire, often allowing it to speak across boundaries of time and nationality, and to extend the sense of personal bereavement to include the loss of ideas, homeland, identity and opportunity. This kind of broadening is strikingly evident in much of the modern and contemporary poetry we have chosen, where individual grief and widespread cultural deprivation are both closely entwined and explicitly announced. Even in much earlier poetry, however, the broadening of perspective from personal mourning to communal loss is clearly apparent. A strong sense of communal sorrow flows through the poems by anonymous authors included here, and in keeping with the enlargement of perspective from solitary to shared endeavour, these poems frequently mix genres such as the ballad, song, epitaph, valediction and obsequy. The amplification of sorrow is also deeply felt in the examples we have included of poems in translation – mostly from mid-twentieth century European poets whose experience of war means that their work frequently combines personal with national lamentation.

✛

Our aim has been to collect poems that face and surmount loss in ways that are captivating and moving, while also mapping the large landscape of poetic mourning and exploring its traditions. Many of the poems included here, whether they acknowledge it or not, reach back centuries to Classical models and draw on well-established conventions of elegiac writing. The word elegy derives from the Greek *elogos*, a term that was originally used for a particular metrical structure of verse – the elegiac couplet – which consisted of alternating hexameter and pentameter lines. The poems written in these elegiac couplets drew on a wide variety of subject matter; in time, however, *elegos* came to be used as the word to describe the singing of sad or mournful songs, usually accompanied by a wind instrument – and it is this idea of lament, rather than metrical arrangement, that has come to define elegy in the sense that we understand it now. As early as Roman times the word *elegia* had come to indicate a prevailing tone of loss and sorrow in line with our own understanding of the terms, although the poems of Catullus and Ovid show that its original focus had been enlarged to include poems of disappointed love, which in turn gave birth to a parallel tradition of 'erotic elegies' or lovers' complaints.

The most decisive Classical influence on the evolution of elegy in the Western tradition was the pastoral or bucolic poetry of Theocritus and Virgil: the way in which their poetry brought together commemorations of landscape and sacrificial fertility rituals – enacted to ensure the well-being of shepherds and their animals – led to the creation of a new form of pastoral elegy, which was initially associated with commemorative rites dedicated to the mythical shepherd-poet Daphnis. The first 'idyll' of Theocritus, for instance, is a lament by the shepherd Thyrsis for the death of Daphnis, tormented by the love-goddess Aphrodite. In later elegies such as Bion's 'Lament for Adonis' (an important influence on Shelley's *Adonais*), the figure of Daphnis is substituted by Adonis, the legendary favourite of Aphrodite, but the preoccupation with mythical shepherds continues. Classical pastoral elegy of this kind provides a potent model for later lamentations, as well as establishing a set of codes and conventions that survive to the present day. Although the term 'pastoral' has come to be associated in a general way with rural scenery, it has its etymology in the Latin 'pastor' (meaning shepherd), and both this and the related suggestion of 'pastoral' as caring and nurturing greatly enabled the transition from Classical to Christian models of elegy.

Typically, early pastoral elegy opens with an invocation to the Muses, calls on listeners to mourn the death of a young shepherd, registers the effects of his death on the surrounding landscape, summons a procession of mourners (usually nymphs or other kinds of guardians), and then embarks on elaborate funeral rituals including the offering of tributes and the laying of flowers on a grave. Stylistically, this structure includes a good deal of repetition (particularly in the form of refrains), as well as antiphony or the use of multiple voices. Rhetorically, it relies on a language of appeal and interrogation, with occasional outbursts of anger or complaint, before moving towards reconciliation and consolation. Very often these final stages of the poem anticipate new life in the changing seasons, in the revitalizing movement of water in streams, in returning sources of light, and in emblems of sexual power and rebirth that are drawn from the natural world.

Although the dissemination of Classical pastoral elegy throughout

Renaissance Europe is generally seen to herald the foundation of elegy as a distinct poetic genre, the influence of the Old English elegy also played an important role. As many as nine such poems exist in the manuscript of the so-called Exeter Book, one of the most significant verse manuscripts to have survived from the Anglo-Saxon period (now held in Exeter Cathedral Library). These include 'The Wanderer', 'The Seafarer' and 'The Wife's Lament', all of which frame descriptions of exile and longing in a time of tumultuous change. J. R. R. Tolkien claimed that the Old English epic *Beowulf* was elegiac as well as heroic, a poem infused with sorrow and lament. The voice of mourning can often be found, as well, in medieval poetry – in Chaucer's *Book of the Duchess*, for instance, and in the plangent dream vision of the anonymous *Pearl*. Given the long and well-established history of the genre, it is not surprising to find in modern elegies a strong and self-conscious sense of legacy and dialogue, but the very subject of mourning also generates among poets a strong sense of shared endeavour which manifests itself in a high incidence of echo and allusion.

These various forms of pastoral provided a poetic blueprint for the development of English elegy that began to take a coherent shape in the 1570s, most notably in the 'November' eclogue of Edmund Spenser's *Shepheardes Calender*, with its clear echoes of Theocritus. Building on this example, English poets swiftly became adept at mingling mythological and familiar characters, adapting Classical settings to English landscape, and converting pagan figures such as Orpheus and Pan into Christian archetypes. The best-known distillation of these syncretic tendencies is Milton's 'Lycidas', which was first published in 1638 as part of a volume of elegies commemorating the death of Edward King, Milton's contemporary at the University of Cambridge, who had drowned in a shipwreck in the Irish Sea in August of the previous year. But if this makes 'Lycidas' the prime example of the influence of Classical pastoral on English Renaissance poetry, the poem also determines the course of much that follows in English elegiac writing. Its masterful, calm artistry, its large and comprehensively integrated patterns of imagery, and the sheer ambition of its vision make it not only the first great English elegy, but the first great elegy of the Christian era.

'Lycidas' begins by mourning in a mood that seems almost dutiful, perhaps even a little sullen, as it registers 'once more' the solemn task of recording a premature death. It calls upon the Muses ('Begin then, sisters of the sacred well'), it questions the custodians of the dead ('Where were ye, nymphs, when the remorseless deep / Closed o'er the head of your loved Lycidas?'), and it organizes the procession of mourners and the ritual of wreath-laying with a knowing acknowledgement of traditional practice ('Bid amaranthus all his beauty shed, / And daffadillies fill their cups with tears'). But this initial sense of obligation soon gives way to more genuine-seeming grief, which brings with it a revitalized poetic authority that is clinched in the poem's conclusion. Here the 'forced fingers rude' that previously threatened to 'shatter' the leaves of laurel, myrtle and ivy are said to have sensitively 'touched the tender stops of various quills'. More dramatic still, the speaker's formerly insistent pronouncement that 'Lycidas is dead' is now revoked: 'Weep no more, woeful shepherds, weep no more, / For Lycidas your sorrow is not dead.' The imperative mood here is vital (gently instructing rather than commanding), as in later elegies, because it signifies that the speaker is prepared to take on the task of managing the experience of loss and of reordering the world that survives after it. It also prepares us for the magnificent apotheosis at the end of the poem, in which the dead youth, now under the tutelary guidance of Saint Michael, is transported from earth to heaven: 'Look homeward angel now, and melt with ruth: / And, O ye dolphins, waft the hapless youth.'

In his influential study of the genre, *The English Elegy* (1985), Peter Sacks presents a largely Freudian reading of elegy that acknowledges the complex psychological processes at work in each poem of mourning. Sacks is surely right to detect in the driving rhythmical power of 'Lycidas' not only a desire for the resurrection of its subject, Edward King, but a yearning on Milton's part for poetic immortality.[3] The poem does, after all, reflect on the speaker's own 'destined urn' and 'sable shroud' in its invocation of the Muses, even suggesting poetic rivalry between the dead man and his successor. In writing a personal elegy, one addressed to another poet rather than a mythological figure, Milton established an important precedent. 'Lycidas' became the prototype for a grand series of later elegies that mourn dead poets while also brooding on notions of poetic rivalry and inheritance: Shelley's *Adonais* (for John Keats), Matthew Arnold's 'Memorial Verses' (for William Wordsworth),

Tennyson's *In Memoriam* (for Arthur Henry Hallam), Swinburne's 'Ave atque Vale' (for Charles Baudelaire), and Elizabeth Bishop's 'North Haven' (for Robert Lowell).

The lively and varied critical reception of 'Lycidas' in its own time and since has been influential in shaping how other elegies are regarded. In this respect, the questions asked about Milton's poem serve as an index for how later elegies are appreciated and understood. Can such a high degree of artifice and invention, readers have often wondered, be consistent with genuine sorrow? To appreciate the poem fully, do we have to possess the same kind and degree of religious faith as the author? Some critics have shifted the debate away from these questions of sincerity, sympathy and belief by claiming that the success of any poem depends primarily on its rhetorical performance: that is, on whether or not we find its language persuasive. This, in turn, has led to an intensive study of the complex ways in which the resources of language are stretched in the process of trying to represent absence and loss. 'Lycidas' and other elegies that live in its wake persistently draw attention to their own materiality, their own substance as words on the page, as if to dispel any questions about absence and the failure of representation that might be at their heart. The proof of this tendency lies in the highly sensuous language often found in elegies, a prominent example in 'Lycidas' being the passage of floral tributes to the dead subject, in which we are shown valleys that 'purple all the ground with vernal flowers'. Similarly, a final glimpse of the speaker emphasizing the colour of his clothing confirms his physical survival: 'At last he rose, and twitched his mantle blue: / Tomorrow to fresh woods, and pastures new'.

✣

As the traditions of English elegy continued to develop, their emotional and psychological complexities became more often and more deeply aligned with the representation of a real or imaginary place – usually a landscape of some kind. One of the best-known examples from any period, Thomas Gray's 'Elegy Written in a Country Churchyard' (1751) conforms to this pattern, but it also marks a crucial turning point in the history of the genre by switching its attention away from privileged subjects towards the rural poor, and by presenting them in a demythologized context. The tone of the poem, too, aspires less towards grandeur than it does towards stability and repose, focusing not on the familiar pastoral figure of the shepherd but on the more earthy and 'weary' ploughman. In the process, it supplies many of the imaginative resources that are developed in subsequent grief-landscapes, which (especially in the nineteenth century) regularly feature such details as the 'ivy-mantled tower' and the 'yew tree's shade'.

In creating this effect, Gray combines the Classical tradition of elegy with popular eighteenth-century poems that feature a rural prospect, creating what is in effect a group elegy rather than the commemoration of a single individual. This, despite the fact that the poem's consideration of lost potential is attached to the ideal of the exceptional person, in this case (and conventionally) another poet: 'Some mute inglorious Milton here may rest'. Other elements in the poem confirm its ambivalent politics. In what looks like a bold critique of 'the boast of heraldry, the pomp of power', for instance, differences of rank and status are obliterated by death the great leveller, and yet, as William Empson argued, the poem also wants to persuade us that 'we ought to accept the injustice of society as we do the inevitability of death'.[4] In the same sort of way, the speaker-poet's appended epigraph, which closes the poem, appears to banish a desire for lasting recognition while simultaneously declaring a need for it.

The elegant compromises of Gray's poem were challenged by the Romantic poets in general, but in particular by William Wordsworth, and in a way that can be said to develop Gray's project rather than reject it. Not only does Wordsworth's extensive poetry of loss more obviously use the language of common speech than Gray manages to do, it is also more definitely inclined to address the hardships of the rural poor. Given his distrust of ostentatious poetic figuration, which he clearly signals in the Preface to *Lyrical Ballads* (1800), it's no wonder that he avoided writing conventional elegies in the style of 'Lycidas', despite his great admiration for Milton. Wordsworth writes emphatically in the famous Preface about his preference for 'simple and unelaborated expressions' over the more extravagant and ornamental verses of some of his contemporaries.[5] One of his major achievements was to give a new and striking prominence to the obscure figure of Lucy who had been sung about in English ballads, and to elevate the values of the local and ordinary in lyric form:

> She lived unknown, and few could know
> When Lucy ceased to be;
> But she is in her Grave, and, oh
> The difference to me!

In lines such as these, the elaborate conventions associated with pastoral elegy are stripped away and replaced with something apparently very simple. Yet the longer we contemplate the poem, the more we realize that its plain diction is deployed to release complex thoughts: about the degree of Lucy's unknownness and the reasons for it, and about the characteristics we're meant to deduce from her being 'Fair, as a star when only one / Is shining in the sky!' (the reference is to Hesper, a star appearing early in the evening and remaining until dawn). Wordsworth seems to invite incredulity or even mockery, given that Lucy's obscurity and singularity might be read as backhanded compliments. The details of her being like a flower half hidden and a star shining on its own have a sly sort of humour that is at once unusual in elegy, and, in its mixture of bathos and bafflement, reflective of the poem's truth to life – and death.[6]

The closest that Wordsworth comes to writing a formal elegy is in his 'Elegiac Stanzas, suggested by a Picture of Peele Castle in a Storm, Painted by Sir George Beaumont', which he wrote following the death of his brother John at sea in 1805. The painting, which shows a dark and overcast castle on a threatening coast, and a ship heaving through tumultuous waves, displaces Wordsworth's previously bright memories of Peele Castle, with images that are now taken to represent his turbulent state of mind. Associating grief with the place itself in a way that anticipates the later elegies of Tennyson and Thomas Hardy, Wordsworth sees in the 'rugged Pile' an emblem of strength and resilience, buttressed by 'the unfeeling armour of old time'. The purpose of this 'armour', however, is not to suppress or deny feeling but to reorganize it into an acceptance of what cannot be altered: 'A power is gone, which nothing can restore; / A deep distress hath humanised my Soul.' The ending of the poem is subdued and might even be read mistakenly as platitudinous (like the end of 'She dwelt among the untrodden ways', which was written not long before). In fact it is final proof of the value that lies in the stoical acceptance of our earthly condition: 'Not without hope we suffer and we mourn.'

The major elegy of the romantic period is undoubtedly Shelley's *Adonais*, inspired by the death of Keats in Rome in February 1821. Unlike Wordsworth, Shelley had no qualms about seizing on the conventions of Greek pastoral elegy, clearly signaling his indebtedness to Theocritus, Bion and Moschus. The example of 'Lycidas' is equally clear: like Milton, Shelley starkly announces the reasons for his grief – 'I weep for Adonais – he is dead' – then moves towards a revocation: 'Peace, peace! He is not dead, he doth not sleep –'. Similarly, he calls on tutelary spirits and other guardians, charging them with neglect much as Milton did, while also summoning a procession of mourners (a strange congregation of 'Desires and Adorations, Winged Persuasions and veiled Destinies'). But the poem repeatedly animates these conventions by combining them with striking innovations. Most remarkable of all of them, the poet-speaker includes himself in the mourning procession, appearing as 'one frail Form, / A phantom among men' who furiously directs his anger at those who have (as he sees it) hastened the death of the young poet by attacking his work. In the process, Shelley helped to establish the myth that Keats was mortally wounded by the savage reviews of his work in *Blackwood's Magazine* and the *Quarterly Review*: 'the curse of Cain / Light on his head who pierced thy innocent breast, / And scared the angel soul that was its earthly guest!'.

Another notable disruption of convention is the setting of *Adonais*, which is part mythological and part nineteenth-century Mediterranean, populated by 'the green lizard' and 'the golden snake'. The mourning itself proceeds while Keats lies beneath 'the vault of blue Italian day', with 'that high Capital' of Rome providing a fitting backdrop of 'ages, empires, and religions', and in the closing stages of the poem Shelley rejects Milton's Christian consolations to move uneasily through the realm of Platonic idealism, before eventually inclining towards 'Heaven' and 'Eternity': 'The One remains, the many change and pass; / Heaven's light forever shines, Earth's shadows fly'. In the end, the Eternity that Shelley secures for Keats is poetic immortality – but this is not achieved without a continuing sense of compromise: 'I am borne darkly, fearfully, afar', Shelley writes, conceding his eventual loss of control as he glances ahead to the time of his own death. Many readers have noticed how, in the closing lines of the poem, it seems that 'the soul of Adonais, like a star', not only 'Beacons' but *beckons* 'from the abode where the Eternal are'.

✠

One of the first readers of *Adonais* was Arthur Henry Hallam, whom Tennyson would later elegize in *In Memoriam*. Hallam died in Vienna on 15 September 1833 and his body was transported by sea from Trieste, delaying his burial until 3 January 1834. Tennyson appears to have started writing the series of lyrics that would eventually comprise his poem shortly after receiving news of Hallam's death in October 1833, although the poem was not completed and published in book form until 1850, the same year that Tennyson became Poet Laureate. In its Section 11, the speaker imagines Hallam's body on the journey to its burial ground in Clevedon, Somerset, punctuating a meditation on the surrounding rural landscape with recurring thoughts of the sea:

> Calm and deep peace in this wide air,
>   These leaves that redden to the fall;
>   And in my heart, if calm at all,
> If any calm, a calm despair:
>
> Calm on the seas, and silver sleep,
>   And waves that sway themselves in rest,
>   And dead calm in that noble breast
> Which heaves but with the heaving deep.

What looks like simple repetition in these lines works in complex ways to create delicate adjustments of thought and feeling, registered throughout the poem in a habitual contrast of inner and outer landscapes. The tight *abba* rhymes in each quatrain, reminiscent of the opening quatrains of Petrarch's love sonnets, mimetically capture the rhythms of grief, subtly articulating both a continual longing for intimate union and a repeated dispersal of that imagined possibility.

In Memoriam is a poem replete with traditions, strewn with flowers and flocks, and even featuring an 'Old Yew' that reminds us of the yew in Gray's 'Elegy'. In several ways, though, it departs from its predecessors and discovers in grief a network of psychological and emotional difficulties previously unmapped in elegiac poetry. Writing about that yew tree, for instance, Tennyson says that his speaker lacks the tree's powers of endurance ('Sick for thy stubborn hardihood') and attributes his failure to human weakness. Here and elsewhere the language of the poem is at once intimate and visceral, often transporting us from familiar pastoral terrain to new urban landscapes – most memorably in Section 7, where the speaker revisits the empty house of his dead friend: 'Dark house, by which once more I stand / Here in the long unlovely street'. The passage is a powerful demonstration of Tennyson's uncanny ability to convey feelings of desolation through the simple but precise notation of external phenomena, as in the famously bleak alliterative monosyllables of the final line: 'On the bald street breaks the blank day.'

All these features of *In Memoriam* make it one of the most moving poems in the tradition. Equally striking is the way it explores its own work of mourning. Time and again Tennyson recognizes the urge to speak of loss while also harbouring deep reservations about the value of doing so, since he expects his words to fall short of their purpose; 'I sometimes hold it half a sin,' he says at one point, 'To put in words the grief I feel', and elsewhere he admits that his desire for spiritual reunion with Hallam exceeds what language is able to convey. In all these respects *In Memoriam* manifests the deeply ambivalent nature of elegy: at every turn it proves that the need to remember is inseparable from the need to forget, and the longing to hold on is indivisible from the contrary need to let go: 'I cannot think the thing farewell'.

In Memoriam found immense popularity in the second half of the nineteenth century. Queen Victoria included extracts in her *album consolativum*, compiled after the death of Prince Albert in 1861, and she later confided to Tennyson that she had been comforted by reading the poem. In the early twentieth century, however, with the emergence of a new modernist spirit in poetry, its reputation began to pale. Thomas Hardy wrote to Henry Newbolt in 1909 saying that although he had done his duty to the poem by 'adoring it in years past', he now found it unsatisfactory: 'While the details of its expression are perfect, the form as a whole is defective, & much of the content has grown commonplace nowadays.' In particular, Hardy objected to 'the awful anticlimax of finishing off such a poem with a highly respectable middleclass wedding' when 'it ought to have ended with something like an earthquake'.[7]

Hardy no doubt had *In Memoriam* in mind when he began to compose his own 'Poems of 1912–13' shortly after the death of his first wife Emma Gifford on 27 November 1912. Decisively breaking with the solemn metrical and stanzaic regularity of Tennyson's poem and its predecessors, Hardy embarked on a series of elegies (eventually completing twenty-one of them), all written in different forms. Although some readers have tried to order the sequence so that it describes a movement from sudden grief to psychological recovery, none of the attempts is convincing – because the aim of the poems is not resolution but protracted and intense uncertainty. As Michael Millgate points out in his biography of Hardy, they were written in a mood of guilty remorse and reawakened love, with Hardy often returning in his imagination to the happy scenes of courtship that he had enjoyed with Emma in the early days of their marriage.[8]

The variety of forms used in 'Poems 1912–13' gives Hardy the opportunity to view his loss from a wide range of mental and emotional points of view. Ever the versatile craftsman, he modulates his voice to sound by turns indignant, bitter, defiant, distraught, bemused and tender. 'The Going', for instance, draws on the familiar euphemism of death as a departure, but the poem's confrontational tone and brisk idiom are strikingly modern: 'Why do you make me leave the house / And think for a breath it is you I see'. Even more arresting is the speaker's imagined sense of sinking in the dislocated and heavily punctuated phrasing of the final stanza, where the dead woman is lovingly rebuked by the poet-speaker, who imagines himself becoming her partner in the shades: 'I seem but a dead man held on end / To sink down soon'. The same sense of simultaneous connection and separation appears at the end of 'The Voice', which after evoking lost love in a series of waltz-like rhythms (dactylic tetrameter), ends in physical and psychological collapse, 'faltering forward'.

Hardy's sequence powerfully contends with the established conventions of elegiac poetry and registers his complicated sense of loss in highly original and often idiosyncratic ways. Despite these innovations, it was immediately widely admired and immediately influential. This was partly because the book in which 'Poems 1912–13' originally appeared, *Satires of Circumstance*, was published in 1914, and therefore became an unavoidable example for poets who would soon want to write elegies on a scale never previously seen, on the battlefields of the Western Front. Wilfred Owen, who planned to call a volume of his poems *English Elegies* (but was killed before completing the manuscript) was the greatest of many who built on Hardy's foundations. His first successful war poem, for instance, 'Anthem for Doomed Youth', mixes the response of a distinctly modern sensibility with emblems of conventional mourning – bells and flowers and prayers – in ways that remind us of Hardy's tactics. And their influence persists to the present day, in terms of tone as well as structure: Christopher Reid's 'A Scattering' is one of several recent elegies which adopt the loosely linked shape of Hardy's sequence.

W. B. Yeats, who professed a strong dislike for 'certain poems written in the midst of the great war', on the grounds that 'passive suffering is not a theme for poetry', nevertheless wrote one of the great elegies of the twentieth century in response to a casualty of that war.[9] 'In Memory of Major Robert Gregory' honours the death of a young Irish soldier (the son of Yeats's friend and patron, Lady Augusta Gregory) who was killed when his aircraft crashed on the Italian front in 1918. Yeats adds significantly to the traditions of elegy in his tribute, reinvigorating it with images drawn from Irish art and culture. Although Robert Gregory is repeatedly praised as if he were an English Renaissance courtier ('Our Sidney and our perfect man'), he is also identified as a specifically Irish artist, whose potential was still to be realized: 'We dreamed that a great painter had been born / To cold Clare rock and Galway rock and thorn'. Furthermore, as Yeats's early nationalist aspirations turned to disappointment, he composed several other political elegies that combined the patriotic, commemorative mode of Irish songs and ballads with the more personal and introspective mode of lyric poetry, and blended elements of irony and sarcasm with more familiar mourning gestures (in 'September 1913', for instance, and 'Easter 1916').

When Yeats died in 1939, Auden had just left England for America, and the elegy that he wrote for his great predecessor soon afterwards is remarkable not just for the liberties it takes with the conventions of the genre, but for the directness with which it seeks to explain the role of poetry in the modern world. This is clear from the flatly documentary opening lines – 'He disappeared in the dead of winter: / The brooks were frozen, the airports almost deserted' – where we get a reference to global transport systems rather than mythological landscapes, and a simple but effective cliché rather than rhetorical grandeur. It is an apt introduction to a poem in which Auden recognizes common human fallibility in his subject, as well as abundant talent: 'You were silly like us; your gift survived it all.'

+

Auden's elegy, written by an English poet in America about an Irish poet who died in France, reminds us that genres travel. At one level, elegy might be said to have an obvious universal application: everyone dies. At another level, though, elegy has national characteristics that often derive from particular religious and social structures. American elegy is a case in point, being less inclined to draw on the traditions of Classical myth and landscape that underpin the European model, and instead drawing its own cultural and spatial boundaries. Peter Sacks speculates that the 'severe repression and rationalization of grief' in early Puritan America helped to create a 'nakedly expressive style' of writing that persists right through to the work of the 'confessional' poets of the 1950s and '60s.[10] One might add that different kinds of repression have helped to create the no less 'nakedly expressive' but powerfully committed work of Black writers such as Gwendolyn Brooks and more recent poets such as Jericho Brown, in whose poetry the commemoration of personal loss is often inseparable from the losses caused by racial injustice.

Walt Whitman's great elegy for Abraham Lincoln, 'When Lilacs Last in the Dooryard Bloom'd' is in many respects the foundational American elegy, being as much a lament for the dead of the Civil War as it is for Lincoln himself, and observing decorum while also following its own bold path among swamps and cedar trees. As Whitman imagines Lincoln's coffin being carried 'Through day and night . . . with the cities draped in black', we see it borne on a series of images taken from the entire country's vast and variegated landscape, ranging from his own 'Manhattan with spires' to 'the far-spreading prairies cover'd with grass and corn'. Many succeeding poets have chosen to adopt the same kind of expansiveness in their elegies – Allen Ginsberg in *Kaddish* is one obvious example – but in the process they have also adapted it to catch a greater sense of volatility than their European counterparts. Jahan Ramazani has argued convincingly that modern American elegy often expresses grief in ways that are remarkably violent, traumatized and unresolved, focusing his attention on mid-twentieth century work by poets such as John Berryman, Sylvia Plath, Anne Sexton and Robert Lowell.[11] Lowell is perhaps best remembered now for the troubled elegies of *Life Studies* that focus on family loss: 'My Last Afternoon with Uncle Devereux Winslow', for instance, and 'Sailing Home from Rapallo'. But his stature as an elegist also rests on the achievement of more obviously public and political poems not included here – poems such as 'The Quaker Graveyard at Nantucket' (1946) and 'For the Union Dead' (1960). In both these poems Lowell's personal losses are imbued with a deep sense of betrayed idealism – a note which is amplified in the work of contemporary African American poets such as Terrance Hayes, whose *American Sonnets for My Past and Future Assassin* are at once intimate self-portraits and indictments of the abuse of state and political power.

Lowell was himself the subject of the fine elegy 'North Haven', which Elizabeth Bishop wrote soon after his death in September 1977. Its lines return to an island off the coast of Maine where they had previously spent time together and speak affectionately of Lowell while meditating on loss and renewal. In these respects, her island pastoral observes the traditional tropes of elegy, being 'full of flowers' and populated by goldfinches and other birds that seem not only to guarantee nature's benevolent return but also to mirror the artistic urge for perfection and permanence: 'Nature repeats herself, or almost does: / repeat, repeat, repeat; revise, revise, revise'. That careful qualification 'almost does' is a troubling reminder of what cannot be recovered, despite the best efforts of art and nature. Even so, the gentle remonstrance and encouragement in the poem contrast markedly with the more explosive responses to death in the work of other American poets at this time. 'North Haven' is the final, subtle maturing of the mourning note that Bishop had already sounded in 'Sestina' and 'First Death in Nova Scotia' (collected in *Questions of Travel*, 1965), and also in 'One Art' (1976), a villanelle that seeks to impose order on a lifetime's experience of contingency and loss.

✛

Compared to Bishop, recent American elegists might seem exceptionally interested in the expression of forms of violation – and in the violation of forms of expression – rather than in restraint. But it's worth emphasizing that the focus on disruption has been noticeable from the earliest days of American poetry – in poems written by Phillis Wheatley in the eighteenth century, through the work of Harlem Renaissance poets such as Countee Cullen and Langston Hughes in the 1920s, and into the present day. Cullen, for instance, opens his 'Threnody for a Brown Girl' with an echo of conventional European forms of lament – 'Weep not, you who loved her' – only to end it by demanding: 'Lay upon her no white stone / From a foreign quarry'. With the same need for independence in mind, his near-contemporary Langston Hughes crosses European models with jazz and blues and gospel songs. A more recent African-American poet Margaret Walker elegizes Malcolm X, and Jericho Brown writes an elegiac sonnet opening with the names of flowers and closing with the names of fellow Black Americans unjustly 'cut down'.

It's clear from these examples that American political elegy has its own distinctive strategies – and the same goes for its more personal counterparts. Poems written by daughters for their parents make an interesting case in point. In the poetry of Amy Clampitt, familial grief is blended with reflections on the deprivations of history, the losses experienced by marginalized communities, and ecological threat. 'A Procession at Candlemas' records a daughter's journey by bus along Route 60 to visit her dying mother in hospital. For all its modern imagery of highways and filling stations, the poem is steeped in myth and history, and the feast of Candlemas, which is associated with rites of purification, gives Clampitt the chance to reassert the figure of the mother in a genre often dominated by patriarchal figures of authority. Deploying powerful symbols drawn from Classical and biblical myth (from the worship of Athena as well as from that of the Virgin Mary), the poem roots its sorrow in the larger losses of American history, alluding to both the sufferings of Native American people and the violent destruction caused by modern warfare. Most forcefully of all, Clampitt brings her search for origin and meaning back to the image of the female body and the physical realities of childbirth.

✛

In contrast to these modern American elegies, a good deal of British and Irish poetry of the post-war period is less inclined to disrupt tradition than to treat it with irony and modest circumspection. Michael Longley, for instance, has written several poems about sectarian violence and the Holocaust that temper grief by various kinds of ethical and emotional reserve. And Geoffrey Hill's poems, which are fundamentally drawn to an elegiac mode, also express resistance to it as they seek to make sense of history and its atrocities. Hill is acutely conscious of the ethical complications of mourning for the victims of history, distant from him in so many ways, and is troubled by the potential for impertinence and vulgarity that lies in seeming to assume that his work is equal to the tasks he sets it. 'September Song', an elegy for an un-named ten-year-old victim of the Holocaust, is a well-known example: a parenthetical insertion at the centre of the poem draws attention to the culpabilities of self-interest, while simultaneously undercutting them: '(I have made / an elegy for myself / it is true)'.

Other recent British and Irish elegists may share Hill's sense that the form carries a risk of self-aggrandizement, but most have shared his trust in traditional lyric structures and sought to modify conventions rather than reject them. The sonnet seems to have had a particular appeal – partly, no doubt, because it has a longstanding reputation as the pre-eminent poetic form of love and devotion, and partly because it licenses the intensity that is essential to elegy. In addition, sonnets have the advantage of being available for use in sequences, or as waystations among other literary forms. Tony Harrison's *from The School of Eloquence* (1978), Douglas Dunn's *Elegies* (1985) and Seamus Heaney's 'Clearances', in *The Haw Lantern* (1987), all mobilize the technical resources of the form to concentrate their expressions of grief. It's also noticeable that many recent British and Irish poets have pursued the same goal of intensity by invoking the language of religious ceremony and prayer in their elegies, even when their poems have no intention of looking for religious consolation. Dunn's 'The Kaleidoscope' is notable for its simultaneous invocation and denial of sacramental rites, both seeking transcendence and candidly confessing to feelings of absurdity and bewilderment.

These religious elements are all survivals of the ancient pastoral mode, which is even more obviously refurbished by Ted Hughes, especially in those poems written from the perspective of one who works on the land and tends to animals. In 'Sheep' and other poems concerned with lambing (see, for instance, 'February 17th'), Hughes writes movingly and unsentimentally about the death of animals, reinvigorating the pastoral tradition by writing unflinchingly about the harshness of farming. A more modest but powerful reworking of the pastoral tradition occurs in Heaney's 'The Strand at Lough Beg', written in memory of his second cousin Colum McCartney, a farm worker and the victim of a random sectarian assassination in Northern Ireland in 1975. Here the liminal 'strand' where 'cattle graze / Up to their bellies in an early mist' provides a benign pastoral setting for an imagined encounter between the poet and his dead relation. Remarkably, Heaney has McCartney's shade reprimand him in the later penitential *Station Island* (1984) for having 'saccharined' his death with 'morning dew'. Here, and in many other contemporary elegies, ranging from Linton Kwesi Johnson's 'Reggae fi Dada' through Paul Muldoon's 'Incantata' to Jackie Kay's 'Burying My African Father', there is evidence of a continuing need to break boundaries. In each case, the poet's purpose is not simply to re-work conventions in ways that suit the changed social and political circumstances of the modern world, but to withstand the scepticism of its ironical gaze, and to avoid the pitfalls of cliché and sentimentality.

This need to contend with scepticism and the related tendency of modern elegy to question its own verbal adequacy are reflective of changes in our contemporary attitudes to death and the afterlife, and recent elegies suggest that poets are increasingly attracted to ironies of one kind or another. Claims made by the imagination on behalf of the deceased are more likely than before to be exposed to self-questioning, and doubts about the value of ritual – even of those which are intended to sustain belief – are more prominently a part of the mourning process. Where nature once provided some reassurance about the possibility of renewal, if not return, now it is more likely to remind us of ecological fragility and even extinction. Yet for all this, the urge to confront the mystery of death, and to find ways to make the dead live again, remains undiminished. One of the finest modern elegies, Denise Riley's poem for her son Jacob, 'A Part Song', is testament to this. Here, a mother speaks to her dead son while apparently suspecting that the conventions of the elegiac form might be exhausted, and that her own expressions of grief are likely to seem stilted and contrived. 'She do the bereaved in different voices',

Riley says, adapting the phrase that T. S. Eliot considered as a title for *The Waste Land*.[12] The echo is both dramatic and sadly self-ironising. Yet even as it chides itself, her poem cuts through such aesthetic reservations, determined to establish connection: 'By finding any device to hack through / the thickening shades to you, you now / Strangely unresponsive son'. By virtue of this imaginative struggle, the poem earns its response – which at the close of the poem arrives in a voice that belongs to the long history of the form as well as to the poet's immediate present: '*My sisters and my mother / Weep dark tears for me . . .*'

Such adaptations and inclusions remind us that elegy has proved to be an exceptionally versatile form of poetry, deeply implicated in literary history by virtue of its self-conscious invocation of echo and allusion. Every example is aware that what purports to be a unique expression of sorrow in fact takes its place as part of a tradition, and by some means or other borrows from the past while seeking to establish itself as the inaugural voice. This spirit of dialogue and inheritance has helped to consolidate the achievements of elegy as a poetic form over the centuries and has also ensured its continuing force in contemporary culture. Despite cynicism and despair, elegy continues to allow the imagination to contend with what Wallace Stevens called 'death's own supremest images',[13] while simultaneously commemorating what has been lost, and even celebrating what remains.

Andrew Motion and Stephen Regan

Notes

1 Samuel Taylor Coleridge, *Biographia Literaria; Or Biographical Sketches of My Literary Life and Opinions* (London: Rest Fenner, 1817), volume 2, p. 2.

2 Gregory Nagy, 'Ancient Greek Elegy', in *The Oxford Handbook of Elegy*, ed. Karen Weisman (Oxford: Oxford University Press, 2010), p. 13.

3 Peter Sacks, *The English Elegy: Studies in the Genre from Spenser to Yeats* (Baltimore: Johns Hopkins University Press, 1985), p. 90.

4 William Empson, *Some Versions of Pastoral* (New York: New Directions, 1974), p. 4.

5 *The Prose Works of William Wordsworth*, ed. W. J. B. Owen and Jane Worthington Smyser (Oxford: Oxford University Press, 1974), volume 1, p. 124.

6 For a larger discussion of Wordsworth and comedy, see Matthew Bevis, *Wordsworth's Fun* (Chicago and London: Chicago University Press, 2019).

7 Thomas Hardy, *The Collected Letters*, ed. Richard L. Purdy and Michael Millgate (Oxford: Oxford University Press, 1984), volume 4, p. 5.

8 Michael Millgate, *Thomas Hardy: A Biography Revisited* (Oxford: Oxford University Press, 2006), pp. 429–47.

9 W. B. Yeats (ed.), *The Oxford Book of Modern Verse 1892-1935* (Oxford: Clarendon Press, 1936), p. xxxiv.

10 Sacks, *The English Elegy*, p. 313.

11 Jahan Ramazani, *Poetry of Mourning: The Modern Elegy from Hardy to Heaney* (Chicago and London: University of Chicago Press, 1994), p. 4.

12 'He do the police in different voices' was a line originally used by Charles Dickens in *Our Mutual Friend* (1865) and adopted by T. S. Eliot as a working title for the poem that would become *The Waste Land*. See *The Waste Land: A Facsimile and Transcript*, ed. Valerie Eliot (London: Faber, 2011).

13 Wallace Stevens, 'The Owl in the Sarcophagus', in *The Collected Poems* (New York: Random House, 1982), p. 436.

A Note on the Text

It might seem strange to follow an Introduction which gives a chronological history of elegy with an arrangement of Contents that is alphabetical. But to us it makes sense for at least two reasons. Firstly, and as our Introduction makes plain, elegies of all periods are constantly in dialogue with one another, and an alphabetic arrangement highlights this reciprocity. Secondly, while offering readers the satisfaction of finding authors they already admire, we also want to give them the surprise and delight of finding poems previously unknown – and we think the plan we've adopted will increase the chances of that happening. Death itself might be as predictable as taxation, but the way poets have responded to it is infinitely various.

ANONYMOUS

Cock Robin

Who killed Cock Robin?
I, said the Sparrow,
With my bow and arrow,
I killed Cock Robin.

Who saw him die?
I, said the Fly,
With my little eye,
I saw him die.

Who caught his blood?
I, said the Fish,
With my little dish,
I caught his blood.

Who'll make the shroud?
I, said the Beetle,
With my thread and needle,
I'll make the shroud.

Who'll dig his grave?
I, said the Owl,
With my pick and shovel,
I'll dig his grave.

Who'll be the parson?
I, said the Rook,
With my little book,
I'll be the parson.

Who'll be the clerk?
I, said the Lark,
If it's not in the dark,
I'll be the clerk.

Who'll carry the link?
I, said the Linnet,
I'll fetch it in a minute,
I'll carry the link.

Who'll be chief mourner?
I, said the Dove,
I mourn for my love,
I'll be chief mourner.

Who'll carry the coffin?
I, said the Kite,
If it's not through the night,
I'll carry the coffin.

Who'll bear the pall?
We, said the Wren,
Both the cock and the hen,
We'll bear the pall.

Who'll sing a psalm?
I, said the Thrush,
As she sat on a bush,
I'll sing a psalm.

Who'll toll the bell?
I, said the Bull,
Because I can pull,
I'll toll the bell.

All the birds of the air
Fell a-sighing and a-sobbing,
When they heard the bell toll
For poor Cock Robin.

The Corpus Christi Carol

He bore him up, he bore him down,
He bore him into an orchard brown.
Lully, lullay, lully, lullay!
The falcon has borne my mate away.

In that orchard there was a hall
That was hanged with purple and pall;
Lully, lullay, lully, lullay!
The falcon has borne my mate away.

And in that hall there was a bed:
It was hanged with gold so red;
Lully, lullay, lully, lullay!
The falcon has borne my mate away.

And in that bed there lies a knight,
His wounds bleeding day and night;
Lully, lullay, lully, lullay!
The falcon has borne my mate away.

By that bed's side there kneels a maid,
And she weeps both night and day;
Lully, lullay, lully, lullay!
The falcon has borne my mate away.

And by that bed's side there stands a stone,
'The Body of Christ' written thereon.
Lully, lullay, lully, lullay!
The falcon has borne my mate away.

The Three Ravens

There were three ravens sat on a tree,
    Downe a downe, hay down, hay downe.
There were three ravens sat on a tree,
    With a downe;
There were three ravens sat on a tree,
They were as blacke as they might be.
    With a downe dery downe.

The one of them said to his mate,
Where shall we our breakfast take?

Downe in yonder greene field,
There lies a knight slain under his shield.

His hounds they lie downe at his feete,
So well they their master keepe.

His hawkes they flie so eagerly,
There's no fowle dare him come nie.

Downe there comes a fallow doe,
As great with yong as she might goe.

She lift up his bloudy hed,
And kist his wounds that were so red.

She got him up upon her backe,
And carried him to earthen lake.

She buried him before the prime,
She was dead herselfe ere even-song time.

God send every gentleman,
Such hawkes, such hounds, and such a leman.

Sir Patrick Spens

The King sits in Dunferline toun,
Drinkin the blude-reid wine
'O whaur will A get a skeely skipper
Tae sail this new ship o mine?'

O up and spak an eldern knight,
Sat at the king's richt knee;
'Sir Patrick Spens is the best sailor
That ever sailt the sea.'

Our king has written a braid letter
And sealed it wi his hand,
And sent it to Sir Patrick Spens,
Wis walkin on the strand.

'Tae Noroway, to Noroway,
Tae Noroway ower the faem;
The King's dauchter o Noroway,
Tis thou maun bring her hame.'

The first word that Sir Patrick read
Sae loud, loud laucht he;
The neist word that Sir Patrick read
The tear blindit his ee.

'O wha is this has duin this deed
An tauld the king o me,
Tae send us out, at this time o year,
Tae sail abuin the sea?'

'Be it wind, be it weet, be it hail, be it sleet,
Our ship maun sail the faem;
The King's dauchter o Noroway,
Tis we maun fetch her hame.'

They hoystit their sails on Monenday morn,
Wi aw the speed they may;
They hae landit in Noroway
Upon a Wodensday.

'Mak ready, mak ready, my merry men aw!
Our gude ship sails the morn.'
'Nou eer alack, ma maister dear,
I fear a deadly storm.'

'A saw the new muin late yestreen
Wi the auld muin in her airm
And gif we gang tae sea, maister,
A fear we'll cam tae hairm.'

They hadnae sailt a league, a league,
A league but barely three,
When the lift grew dark, an the wind blew loud
An gurly grew the sea.

The ankers brak, an the topmaist lap,
It was sic a deadly storm.
An the waves cam ower the broken ship
Til aw her sides were torn.

'Go fetch a web o silken claith,
Anither o the twine,
An wap them into our ship's side,
An let nae the sea cam in.'

They fetcht a web o the silken claith,
Anither o the twine,
An they wappp'd them roun that gude ship's side,
But still the sea cam in.

O laith, laith were our gude Scots lords
Tae weet their cork-heelt shuin;
But lang or aw the play wis playd
They wat their hats abuin.

And mony wis the feather bed
That flattert on the faem;
And mony wis the gude lord's son
That never mair cam hame.

O lang, lang may the ladies sit,
Wi their fans intae their hand,
Afore they see Sir Patrick Spens
Come sailin tae the strand!

And lang, lang may the maidens sit
Wi their gowd kames in their hair,
A-waitin for their ane dear loes!
For them they'll see nae mair.

Half-ower, half-ower to Aberdour,
Tis fifty fathoms deep;
An there lies gude Sir Patrick Spens,
Wi the Scots lords at his feet!

The Wife of Usher's Well

There lived a wife at Usher's Well,
And a wealthy wife was she;
She had three stout and stalwart sons,
And sent them oer the sea.

They hadna been a week from her,
A week but barely ane,
Whan word came to the carline wife
That her three sons were gane.

They hadna been a week from her,
A week but barely three,
Whan word came to the carlin wife
That her sons she'd never see.

'I wish the wind may never cease,
Nor fashes in the flood,
Till my three sons come hame to me,
In earthly flesh and blood.'

It fell about the Martinmas,
When nights are lang and mirk.
The carline wife's three sons came hame,
And their hats were o' the birk.

It neither grew in syke nor ditch,
Nor yet in ony sheugh;
But at the gates o' Paradise,
That birk grew fair eneugh.

'Blow up the fire, my maidens,
Bring water from the well;
For a' my house shall feast this night,
Since my three sons are well.'

And she has made to them a bed,
She's made it large and wide;
And she's ta'en her mantle her about,
Sat down at the bed-side.

Up then crew the red, red cock,
And up and crew the gray;
The eldest to the youngest said,
'Tis time we were away.'

The cock he hadna craw'd but once,
And clapp'd his wings at a',
When the youngest to the eldest said,
'Brother, we must awa'.

'The cock doth craw, the day doth daw,
The channerin' worm doth chide;
Gin we be miss'd out o' our place,
A sair pain we maun bide.'

'Lie still, lie still but a little wee while,
Lie still but if we may;
Gin my mother should miss us when she wakes,
She'll go mad ere it be day.'

'Fare ye weel, my mother dear!
Fareweel to barn and byre!
And fare ye weel, the bonny lass
That kindles my mother's fire!'

from *Pearl*

14

More marvels then did daunt my soul;
I saw beyond that merry mere
A crystal cliff that shone full bright,
Many a noble ray stood forth;
At the foot thereof there sat a child, –
So debonair, – a maid of grace;
Glistening white was her array, –
I knew her well, I had seen her ere.
As gleaming gold, refin'd and pure,
So shone that glory' neath the cliff;
Long toward her there I look'd, –
The longer, I knew her more and more.

15

The more I scann'd her face so fair,
Her beauteous form when I had found,
Such gladd'ning glory came to me,
As rarely had been mine before.
Longing me seized to call her name,
But wonder dealt my heart a blow;

I saw her in *so* strange a place,
Well might the shock mine heart appal.
Then lifted she *her* visage fair,
As ivory pure her face was white;
It thrill'd mine heart, struck all astray,
And ever the longer, more and more.

16

More than my longing was now my dread;
I stood full still; I dared not speak;
With open eyes and fast-closed mouth,
I stood as meek as hawk in hall.
I took it for a ghostly vision;
I dreaded what might there betide,
Lest what I saw should me escape
Ere I it held within my reach;
When, lo! that spotless child of grace,
So smooth, so small, so sweetly slight,
Arose in all her royal array, –
A precious piece, bedight with pearls.

Dahn the Plug'ole

A muvver was barfin' 'er biby one night,
The youngest of ten and a tiny young mite,
The muvver was poor an' the biby was thin,
Only a skelington covered in skin;
The muvver turned rahnd for the soap off the rack,
She was but a moment, but when she turned back,
The biby was gorn; and in anguish she cried,
'Oh, where is my biby?' – The angels replied:

'Your biby 'as fell dahn the plug'ole,
Your biby 'as gorn dahn the plug;

The poor little thing was so skinny an' thin
'E oughter been barfed in a jug;
Your biby is perfekly 'appy,
'E won't need a barf any more,
Your biby 'as fell dahn the plug'ole,
Not lorst, but gorn before.'

RAYMOND ANTROBUS
(1986–)

Sound Machine

'My mirth can laugh and talk, but cannot sing;
My grief finds harmonies in everything.'
James Thomson

And what comes out if it isn't the wires
Dad welds to his homemade sound system,
which I accidently knock loose
while he is recording Talk-Over dubs, killing
the bass, flattening the mood and his muses,
making Dad blow his fuses and beat me.
But it wasn't my fault; the things he made
could be undone so easily –
and we would keep losing connection.
But praise my Dad's mechanical hands.
Even though he couldn't fix my deafness
I still channel him. My sound system plays
on Father's Day in Manor Park Cemetery
where I find his grave, and for the first time
see his middle name, OSBERT, derived from Old English
meaning *God* and *bright*. Which may
have been a way to bleach him, darkest
of his five brothers, the only one sent away
from the country to live up-town
with his light skin aunt. She protected him
from police, who didn't believe he belonged
unless they heard his English,
which was smooth as some up-town roads.
His aunt loved him and taught him
to recite Wordsworth and Coleridge – rhythms
that wouldn't save him. He would become

Rasta and never tell a soul about the name
that undid his blackness. It is his grave
that tells me the name his black
body, even in death, could not move or mute.

MATTHEW ARNOLD

(1822–1892)

Memorial Verses

April, 1850

Goethe in Weimar sleeps, and Greece,
Long since, saw Byron's struggle cease.
But one such death remain'd to come;
The last poetic voice is dumb –
We stand to-day by Wordsworth's tomb.

When Byron's eyes were shut in death,
We bow'd our head and held our breath.
He taught us little; but our soul
Had *felt* him like the thunder's roll.
With shivering heart the strife we saw
Of passion with eternal law;
And yet with reverential awe
We watch'd the fount of fiery life
Which served for that Titanic strife.

When Goethe's death was told, we said:
Sunk, then, is Europe's sagest head.
Physician of the iron age,
Goethe has done his pilgrimage.
He took the suffering human race,
He read each wound, each weakness clear;
And struck his finger on the place,
And said: *Thou ailest here, and here!*
He look'd on Europe's dying hour
Of fitful dream and feverish power;
His eye plunged down the weltering strife,
The turmoil of expiring life –
He said: *The end is everywhere,*

Art still has truth, take refuge there!
And he was happy, if to know
Causes of things, and far below
His feet to see the lurid flow
Of terror, and insane distress,
And headlong fate, be happiness.

And Wordsworth! – Ah, pale ghosts, rejoice!
For never has such soothing voice
Been to your shadowy world convey'd,
Since erst, at morn, some wandering shade
Heard the clear song of Orpheus come
Through Hades, and the mournful gloom.
Wordsworth has gone from us – and ye,
Ah, may ye feel his voice as we!
He too upon a wintry clime
Had fallen – on this iron time
Of doubts, disputes, distractions, fears.
He found us when the age had bound
Our souls in its benumbing round;
He spoke, and loosed our heart in tears.
He laid us as we lay at birth
On the cool flowery lap of earth,
Smiles broke from us and we had ease;
The hills were round us, and the breeze
Went o'er the sun-lit fields again;
Our foreheads felt the wind and rain.
Our youth return'd; for there was shed
On spirits that had long been dead,
Spirits dried up and closely furl'd,
The freshness of the early world.

Ah! since dark days still bring to light
Man's prudence and man's fiery might,
Time may restore us in his course
Goethe's sage mind and Byron's force;
But where will Europe's latter hour
Again find Wordsworth's healing power?
Others will teach us how to dare,

And against fear our breast to steel;
Others will strengthen us to bear –
But who, ah! who, will make us feel?
The cloud of mortal destiny,
Others will front it fearlessly –
But who, like him, will put it by?
Keep fresh the grass upon his grave,
O Rotha, with thy living wave!
Sing him thy best! for few or none
Hears thy voice right, now he is gone.

W. H. AUDEN
(1907–1973)

In Memory of W. B. Yeats
(d. Jan. 1939)

I

He disappeared in the dead of winter:
The brooks were frozen, the airports almost deserted,
And snow disfigured the public statues;
The mercury sank in the mouth of the dying day.
What instruments we have agree
The day of his death was a dark cold day.

Far from his illness
The wolves ran on through the evergreen forests,
The peasant river was untempted by the fashionable quays;
By mourning tongues
The death of the poet was kept from his poems.

But for him it was his last afternoon as himself,
An afternoon of nurses and rumours;
The provinces of his body revolted,
The squares of his mind were empty,
Silence invaded the suburbs,
The current of his feeling failed; he became his admirers.

Now he is scattered among a hundred cities
And wholly given over to unfamiliar affections,
To find his happiness in another kind of wood
And be punished under a foreign code of conscience.
The words of a dead man
Are modified in the guts of the living.

But in the importance and noise of to-morrow
When the brokers are roaring like beasts on the floor of the Bourse,
And the poor have the sufferings to which they are fairly
    accustomed,
And each in the cell of himself is almost convinced of his freedom,
A few thousand will think of this day
As one thinks of a day when one did something slightly unusual.
What instruments we have agree
The day of his death was a dark cold day.

2

You were silly like us; your gift survived it all:
The parish of rich women, physical decay,
Yourself. Mad Ireland hurt you into poetry.
Now Ireland has her madness and her weather still,
For poetry makes nothing happen: it survives
In the valley of its making where executives
Would never want to tamper, flows on south
From ranches of isolation and the busy griefs,
Raw towns that we believe and die in; it survives,
A way of happening, a mouth.

3

Earth, receive an honoured guest:
William Yeats is laid to rest.
Let the Irish vessel lie
Emptied of its poetry.

In the nightmare of the dark
All the dogs of Europe bark,
And the living nations wait,
Each sequestered in its hate;

Intellectual disgrace
Stares from every human face,
And the seas of pity lie
Locked and frozen in each eye.

Follow, poet, follow right
To the bottom of the night,
With your unconstraining voice
Still persuade us to rejoice;

With the farming of a verse
Make a vineyard of the curse,
Sing of human unsuccess
In a rapture of distress;

In the deserts of the heart
Let the healing fountain start,
In the prison of his days
Teach the free man how to praise.

WILLIAM BARNES
(1801–1886)

The Music o' the Dead

When music, in a heart that's true,
Do kindle up wold loves anew,
An' dim wet eyes, in feäirest lights,
Do zee but inward fancy's zights;
When creepèn years, wi' with'rèn blights,
   'V a-took off them that wer so dear,
    How touchèn 'tis if we do hear
      The tuèns o' the dead, John.

When I, a-stannèn in the lew
O' trees a storm's a-beätèn drough,
Do zee the slantèn mist a-drove
By spitevul winds along the grove,
An' hear their hollow sounds above
   My shelter'd head, do seem, as I
    Do think o' zunny days gone by,
      Lik' music vor the dead, John.

Last night, as I wer gwaïn along
The brook, I heärd the milk-maïd's zong
A-ringèn out so clear an' shrill
Along the meäds an' roun' the hill.
I catch'd the tuèn, an' stood still
   To hear't; 'twer woone that Jeäne did zing
    A-vield a-milkèn in the spring,–
      Sweet music o' the dead, John.

Don't tell o' zongs that be a-zung
By young chaps now, wi' sheämeless tongue:
Zing me wold ditties, that would start
The maïdens' tears, or stir my heart

To teäke in life a manly peärt, –
  The wold vo'k's zongs that twold a teäle,
  An' vollow'd round their mugs o' eäle,
  The music o' the dead, John.

The Wife a-Lost

Since I noo mwore do zee your feäce,
  Up steäirs or down below,
I'll zit me in the lwonesome pleäce,
  Where flat-bough'd beech do grow;
Below the beeches' bough, my love,
  Where you did never come,
An' I don't look to meet ye now,
  As I do look at hwome.

Since you noo mwore be at my zide,
  In walks in zummer het,
I'll goo alwone where mist do ride,
  Drough trees a-drippèn wet;
Below the raïn-wet bough, my love,
  Where you did never come,
An' I don't grieve to miss ye now,
  As I do grieve at hwome.

Since now bezide my dinner-bwoard
  Your vaïce do never sound,
I'll eat the bit I can avword
  A-vield upon the ground;
Below the darksome bough, my love,
  Where you did never dine,
An' I don't grieve to miss ye now,
  As I at hwome do pine.

Since I do miss your vaïce an' feäce
  In praÿer at eventide,
I'll praÿ wi' woone sad vaïce vor greäce
  To goo where you do bide;
Above the tree an' bough, my love,
  Where you be gone avore,
An' be a-waïtèn vor me now,
  To come vor evermwore.

Woak Hill

When sycamore leaves wer a-spreadèn,
  Green-ruddy, in hedges,
Bezide the red doust o' the ridges,
  A-dried at Woak Hill;

I packed up my goods all a-sheenèn
  Wi' long years o' handlèn,
On dousty red wheels ov a waggon,
  To ride at Woak Hill.

The brown thatchen ruf o' the dwellèn
  I then wer a-leävèn,
Had shelter'd the sleek head o' Meäry,
  My bride at Woak Hill.

But now vor zome years, her light voot-vall
  'S a-lost vrom the vloorèn.
Too soon vor my jaÿ an' my childern,
  She died at Woak Hill.

But still I do think that, in soul,
  She do hover about us;
To ho vor her motherless childern,
  Her pride at Woak Hill.

Zoo – lest she should tell me hereafter
    I stole off 'ithout her,
An' left her, uncall'd at house-riddèn,
    To bide at Woak Hill –

I call'd her so fondly, wi' lippèns
    All soundless to others,
An' took her wi' aïr-reachèn hand,
    To my zide at Woak Hill.

On the road I did look round, a-talkèn
    To light at my shoulder,
An' then led her in at the door-way,
    Miles wide vrom Woak Hill.

An' that's why vo'k thought, vor a season,
    My mind wer a-wandrèn
Wi' sorrow, when I wer so sorely
    A-tried at Woak Hill.

But no; that my Meäry mid never
    Behold herzelf slighted,
I wanted to think that I guided
    My guide vrom Woak Hill.

PAUL BATCHELOR

(1977–)

Pit Ponies

'But what is that clinking in the darkness?'
Louis MacNeice

Listen. They're singing in your other life:
'Faith of our Fathers' sounding clear as day
from the pit-head where half the village has turned out
to hear the latest news from underground,
news that will be brought to them by the caged ponies
hauled up and loosed in Raff Smiths field.

Could that have been you in Raff Smiths field,
mouthing the words and listening to the cages lift,
watching sunlight break on dirty ponies,
noting the way, unshoed for their big day,
each one flinches on the treacherous ground,
pauses and sniffs, then rears and blunders about?

As at a starting pistol they gallop out
and a roll of thunder takes hold of the field –
thunder, or else an endless round
of cannon fire. Hooves plunge and lift.
They pitch themselves headlong into the day:
runty, fabulously stubborn pit ponies.

But they seem to have a sense, the ponies,
a sidelong kind of sense about
getting called in at last light on the fifth day:
they seem to know the strike has failed,
as though they felt the tug of their old lives.
They shy and shake their heads. They paw the ground.

Let's leave them there for now, holding their ground
for all it's worth, and say the ponies
might maintain their stand-off, as the livid
shades of miners might yet stagger out
of history into the pitched field
dotted with cannonballs you see today.

Let's pretend you might come back some day
to wait a lifetime on this scrap of ground
until the silence – like the silence of a field
after battle – breaks, and you hear ponies
buck and whinny as the chains pay out
and once again the rusty cages lift . . .

As though the day was won, as though the ground
was given, the ponies gallop out
to claim their piece of field, their only life.

HILAIRE BELLOC

(1870–1953)

Matilda

Who Told Lies, and was Burned to Death

Matilda told such Dreadful Lies,
It made one Gasp and Stretch one's Eyes;
Her Aunt, who, from her Earliest Youth,
Had kept a Strict Regard for Truth,
Attempted to Believe Matilda:
The effort very nearly killed her,
And would have done so, had not She
Discovered this Infirmity.
For once, towards the Close of Day,
Matilda, growing tired of play,
And finding she was left alone,
Went tiptoe to the Telephone
And summoned the Immediate Aid
Of London's Noble Fire-Brigade.
Within an hour the Gallant Band
Were pouring in on every hand,
From Putney, Hackney Downs, and Bow.
With Courage high and Hearts a-glow,
They galloped, roaring through the Town,
'Matilda's House is Burning Down!'
Inspired by British Cheers and Loud
Proceeding from the Frenzied Crowd,
They ran their ladders through a score
Of windows on the Ball Room Floor;
And took Peculiar Pains to Souse
The Pictures up and down the House,
Until Matilda's Aunt succeeded
In showing them they were not needed;

And even then she had to pay
To get the Men to go away!

It happened that a few Weeks later
Her Aunt was off to the Theatre
To see that Interesting Play
The Second Mrs Tanqueray.
She had refused to take her Niece
To hear this Entertaining Piece:
A Deprivation Just and Wise
To Punish her for Telling Lies.
That Night a Fire did break out –
You should have heard Matilda Shout!
You should have heard her Scream and Bawl,
And throw the window up and call
To People passing in the Street –
(The rapidly increasing Heat
Encouraging her to obtain
Their confidence) – but all in vain!
For every time she shouted 'Fire!'
They only answered 'Little Liar!'
And therefore when her Aunt returned,
Matilda, and the House, were Burned.

GWENDOLYN BENNETT

(1902–1981)

Epitaph

When I am dead, carve this upon my stone:
Here lies a woman, fit root for flower and tree,
Whose living flesh, now mouldering round the bone,
Wants nothing more than this for immortality,
That in her heart, where love so long unfruited lay
A seed for grass or weed shall grow,
And push to light and air its heedless way;
That she who lies here dead may know
Through all the putrid marrow of her bones
The searing pangs of birth,
While none may know the pains nor hear the groans
Of she who lived with barrenness upon the earth.

JOHN BERRYMAN

(1914–1972)

Dream Song 155

I can't get him out of my mind, out of my mind,
He was out of his own mind for years,
in police stations & Bellevue.
He drove up to my house in Providence
ho ho at 8 a.m. in a Cambridge taxi
and told it to wait.

He walked my living-room, & did not want breakfast
or even coffee, or even even a drink.
He paced, I'd say Sit down,
it makes me nervous, for a moment he'd sit down,
then pace. After an hour or so *I* had a drink.
He took it back to Cambridge,

we never learnt why he came, or what he wanted.
His mission was obscure. His mission was real,
but obscure.
I remember his electrical insight as the young man,
his wit & passion, gift, the whole young man
alive with surplus love.

THE KING JAMES BIBLE

(1611)

2 Samuel 1

The beauty of Israel is slain upon thy high places: how are the
mighty fallen!

Tell it not in Gath, publish it not in the streets of Askelon; lest the
daughters of the Philistines rejoice, lest the daughters of the
uncircumcised triumph.

Ye mountains of Gilboa, let there be no dew, neither let there be
rain, upon you, nor fields of offerings: for there the shield of
the mighty is vilely cast away, the shield of Saul, as though he
had not been anointed with oil.

From the blood of the slain, from the fat of the mighty, the bow
of Jonathan turned not back, and the sword of Saul returned
not empty.

Saul and Jonathan were lovely and pleasant in their lives, and in
their death they were not divided: they were swifter than
eagles, they were stronger than lions.

Ye daughters of Israel, weep over Saul, who clothed you in
scarlet, with other delights, who put on ornaments of gold
upon your apparel.

How are the mighty fallen in the midst of the battle! O Jonathan,
thou wast slain in thine high places.

I am distressed for thee, my brother Jonathan: very pleasant hast
thou been unto me: thy love to me was wonderful, passing
the love of women.

How are the mighty fallen, and the weapons of war perished!

Ecclesiastes 3

To every thing there is a season, and a time to every purpose
under the heaven:

A time to be born, and a time to die; a time to plant, and a time
to pluck up that which is planted;

A time to kill, and a time to heal; a time to break down, and a
time to build up;

A time to weep, and a time to laugh; a time to mourn, and a time
to dance;

A time to cast away stones, and a time to gather stones
together; a time to embrace, and a time to refrain from
embracing;

A time to get, and a time to lose; a time to keep, and a time to
cast away;

A time to rend, and a time to sew; a time to keep silence, and a
time to speak;

A time to love, and a time to hate; a time of war, and a time of
peace.

What profit hath he that worketh in that wherein he laboureth?

I have seen the travail, which God hath given to the sons of men
to be exercised in it.

He hath made every thing beautiful in his time: also he hath set
the world in their heart, so that no man can find out the work
that God maketh from the beginning to the end.

I know that there is no good in them, but for a man to rejoice,
and to do good in his life.

And also that every man should eat and drink, and enjoy the
good of all his labour, it is the gift of God.

I know that, whatsoever God doeth, it shall be for ever: nothing
can be put to it, nor any thing taken from it: and God doeth
it, that men should fear before him.

That which hath been is now; and that which is to be hath
already been; and God requireth that which is past.

And moreover I saw under the sun the place of judgment, that
wickedness was there; and the place of righteousness, that
iniquity was there.

I said in mine heart, God shall judge the righteous and the
wicked: for there is a time there for every purpose and for
every work.

I said in mine heart concerning the estate of the sons of men, that
God might manifest them, and that they might see that they
themselves are beasts.

For that which befalleth the sons of men befalleth beasts; even
    one thing befalleth them: as the one dieth, so dieth the other;
    yea, they have all one breath; so that a man hath no
    preeminence above a beast: for all is vanity.
All go unto one place; all are of the dust, and all turn to dust
    again.

LAURENCE BINYON

(1869–1943)

For the Fallen

With proud thanksgiving, a mother for her children,
England mourns for her dead across the sea.
Flesh of her flesh they were, spirit of her spirit,
Fallen in the cause of the free.

Solemn the drums thrill: Death august and royal
Sings sorrow up into immortal spheres.
There is music in the midst of desolation
And a glory that shines upon our tears.

They went with songs to the battle, they were young,
Straight of limb, true of eye, steady and aglow.
They were staunch to the end against odds uncounted,
They fell with their faces to the foe.

They shall not grow old, as we that are left grow old:
Age shall not weary them, nor the years condemn.
At the going down of the sun and in the morning
We will remember them.

They mingle not with their laughing comrades again;
They sit no more at familiar tables of home;
They have no lot in our labour of the day-time;
They sleep beyond England's foam.

But where our desires are and our hopes profound,
Felt as a well-spring that is hidden from sight,
To the innermost heart of their own land they are known
As the stars are known to the Night;

As the stars that shall be bright when we are dust
Moving in marches upon the heavenly plain,
As the stars that are starry in the time of our darkness,
To the end, to the end, they remain.

BION

(c. 120–57 BCE)

Lament for Adonis

I weep for Adonis, cry, 'Fair Adonis is dead';
'Fair Adonis is dead,' the Loves echo my grief.
Sleep no more, Cypris, shrouded in purple,
awake to this grief, and put on mourning,
beat your breast and tell all mankind:
'Fair Adonis is dead.'

I weep for Adonis; the Loves echo my grief.

Fair Adonis lies high in the hills, his thigh
holed by a tusk, white into white.
Cypris despairs as his breathing grows softer;
the blood flows red down his snow-white flesh,
the eyes beneath his brow grow dark,
the rose flies from his lip, and on it dies
the kiss that Cypris shall never know again.
Now the goddess longs for the kiss of the dead,
and he cannot feel the live touch of her lips.

I weep for Adonis; the Loves echo my grief.

Cruel, cruel was the wound in his thigh,
but crueller still the wound in her heart.
Loud is the baying of his faithful dogs,
loud the weeping of the Nymphs on the hill.
Aphrodite unbraids her hair, goes barefoot,
in tears, around the wood, her curls in tatters.
The undergrowth tears at her sacred flesh,
the brambles spill her holy blood, but on she runs,
her cries the louder, the length of the glades,
screaming for her Assyrian boy,

35

forever calling on her lover's name.
A dark pool of blood congeals round his navel,
the purple spreads up his breast from the thighs,
discolouring the nipples, once white as snow.

'Alas, Cytherea,' the Loves cry again.

Her gracious man has perished, and with him
her beauty. When Adonis lived,
Cypris was fair; her looks died when he did.
'Alas, poor Cypris,' from every summit;
from all the woods, 'Alas, poor Adonis.'
The rivers weep for Aphrodite's grief,
Adonis is mourned by the mountain streams;
all nature's flowers grow red with sorrow.
Cythera's island is everywhere filled,
its ridges, its glens, with songs of lament:
'Alas, Cytherea. Fair Adonis is dead,'
and Echo replies, 'Fair Adonis is dead.'
Who would not weep for Cypris' luckless love?

She saw, she took in Adonis' mortal wound.
It was not to be checked; she saw his thigh
drowning in blood, flung up her arms, crying,
'Wait, Adonis, my lost love, wait,
stay till I am with you one short last time,
till I have you in my arms, pressing lip on lip.
Awake, Adonis, just one brief moment,
for a kiss, last kiss, a kiss to live
as long as you have breath; breathe your last
into my mouth, breathe your soul into my heart,
till I've sipped the sweetness of your poison
to the dregs, drunk the lees of your love.
That kiss I will cherish as I would
the man himself, now fate takes you,
Adonis, takes you into exile,
distant exile on Acheron's shore,
within the domain of that harshest of kings:
while I, a god, live on behind you,

a wretched god, unable to follow.
Take him, Persephone, take my lover;
you have far greater powers than I,
and all that is loveliest falls to you.
For me all that's worst, all that's saddest,
unending; again I weep for my dead Adonis,
and I live, Persephone, in fear of you.
You are dead, my one love, dearest of men,
you are gone like a dream. Cytherea is widowed;
her girdle of love lost its magic with you;
Love is lying idle and stays indoors.
Why were you rash? Oh, why went hunting?
How, oh how was so perfect a man
enticed to take on the wildest of beasts?'
So Cypris lamented; Love echoes her grief:
'Alas, Cytherea. Fair Adonis is dead.'

Aphrodite sheds tears as Adonis blood,
drop matches drop; on the ground
they mingle, and bring forth flowers.
From the blood grows a rose,
from the tears an anemone.

I weep for Adonis; fair Adonis is dead.

Enough tears now, Cypris, enough for your man
as he lies in the woods. But it isn't right
to leave him there, alone among the leaves;
give him your bed, in death as in life.
For in death, Cytherea, he still has his beauty,
a beauty in death as a beauty in sleep.
So lay him now where he used to lie
on those same soft sheets, in that same gold bed,
where he shared your sacred sleep all those nights;
it is longing to bear his weight again.
Strew him with garlands, with flowers,
then leave them to die. Let all nature die,
now Adonis is dead. Anoint him
with Syrian perfumes, with oils;

let all fragrance fade, let perfumes all die,
for he was your perfume, and he now is dead.
There lies Adonis, wreathed in purple,
graceful Adonis. Love mourns; Love weeps;
the Loves have cut off their hair in sorrow.
Here someone has laid his bow at his side,
another his arrows, another his quiver.
One lays a feather. One looses his shoe.
Some bring water in a golden pail,
and bathe his thigh. One stands behind
and fans fair Adonis with his feather wings.

'Alas, Cytherea,' the Loves echo their grief.

Hymen has lit every torch at the door,
and sprinkled marriage garlands around it.
He sings no longer of wedding joys
but rather of grief, of Adonis' death.
The Graces weep over Cinyras' child,
saying one to the other, 'Adonis is dead.'
Their cries of sorrow have a sharper note
than their songs of praise. Even the Fates
weep for Adonis, and call out his name.
In their songs they weave him a life-giving spell
but it falls on deaf ears. Not by his own wish;
Persephone has him, and won't let him go.

Enough tears, Cytherea, enough for today.
No more wailing now or beating your breast.
There is time enough to come for your grief,
time to weep, time to sorrow, as year succeeds year.

Translated by Anthony Holden

ELIZABETH BISHOP

(1911–1979)

North Haven

In Memoriam: Robert Lowell

I can make out the rigging of a schooner
a mile off; I can count
the new cones on the spruce. It is so still
the pale bay wears a milky skin, the sky
no clouds, except for one long, carded horse's-tail.

The islands haven't shifted since last summer,
even if I like to pretend they have
– drifting, in a dreamy sort of way,
a little north, a little south or sidewise,
and that they're free within the blue frontiers of bay.

This month, our favorite one is full of flowers:
Buttercups, Red Clover, Purple Vetch,
Hawkweed still burning, Daisies pied, Eyebright,
the Fragrant Bedstraw's incandescent stars,
and more, returned, to paint the meadows with delight.

The Goldfinches are back, or others like them,
and the White-throated Sparrow's five-note song,
pleading and pleading, brings tears to the eyes.
Nature repeats herself, or almost does:
repeat, repeat, repeat; revise, revise, revise.

Years ago, you told me it was here
(in 1932?) you first 'discovered *girls*'
and learned to sail, and learned to kiss.
You had 'such fun,' you said, that classic summer.
('Fun' – it always seemed to leave you at a loss ...)

You left North Haven, anchored in its rock,
afloat in mystic blue . . . And now – you've left
for good. You can't derange, or re-arrange,
your poems again. (But the Sparrows can their song.)
The words won't change again. Sad friend, you cannot change.

WILLIAM BLAKE

(1757–1827)

Nurse's Song
(Songs of Innocence)

When the voices of children are heard on the green,
And laughing is heard on the hill,
My heart is at rest within my breast,
And everything else is still.

'Then come home, my children, the sun is gone down
And the dews of night arise;
Come, come, leave off play, and let us away
Till the morning appears in the skies.'

'No, no, let us play, for it is yet day,
And we cannot go to sleep;
Besides, in the sky the little birds fly,
And the hills are all covered with sheep.'

'Well, well, go and play till the light fades away,
And then go home to bed.'
The little ones leaped and shouted and laughed
And all the hills echoèd.

Nurse's Song
(Songs of Experience)

When the voices of children are heard on the green,
And whisperings are in the dale,
The days of my youth rise fresh in my mind,
My face turns green and pale.

Then come home, my children, the sun is gone down,
And the dews of night arise;
Your spring and your day are wasted in play,
And your winter and night in disguise.

The Chimney Sweeper
(Songs of Innocence)

When my mother died I was very young,
And my father sold me while yet my tongue
Could scarcely cry *'weep 'weep, 'weep 'weep!*
So your chimneys I sweep, and in soot I sleep.

There's little Tom Dacre, who cried when his head,
That curled like a lamb's back, was shaved: so I said,
'Hush, Tom! never mind it, for when your head's bare,
You know that the soot cannot spoil your white hair.'

And so he was quiet, and that very night,
As Tom was a-sleeping he had such a sight!
That thousands of sweepers, Dick, Joe, Ned, and Jack,
Were all of them locked up in coffins of black;

And by came an Angel who had a bright key,
And he opened the coffins and set them all free;
Then down a green plain, leaping, laughing they run,
And wash in a river and shine in the sun.

Then naked and white, all their bags left behind,
They rise upon clouds, and sport in the wind.
And the Angel told Tom, if he'd be a good boy,
He'd have God for his father and never want joy.

And so Tom awoke; and we rose in the dark
And got with our bags and our brushes to work.
Though the morning was cold, Tom was happy and warm;
So if all do their duty, they need not fear harm.

The Chimney Sweeper
(Songs of Experience)

A little black thing among the snow,
Crying 'weep, 'weep, in notes of woe!
Where are thy father and mother? say?
'They are both gone up to the church to pray.

'Because I was happy upon the heath,
And smiled among the winter's snow,
They clothed me in the clothes of death,
And taught me to sing the notes of woe.

'And because I am happy and dance and sing,
They think they have done me no injury,
And are gone to praise God and his priest and king,
Who make up a heaven of our misery.'

MALIKA BOOKER
(1970–)

Death of an Overseer

(c. 1815–1817)

1

The overseer dead and he whip sprout
scarlet lilies. Whole cane fields bowed
and weeds run riot,
mosquitoes stop suck blood
and fireflies lose their light.
Yea, he who wield whip with skill, dead;
he who hit them roped bodies wearing blindfold,
he who lash don't miss, dead.

He who sing, *This job is too sweet,* as he fleck,
bloody raindrops from blistering skin, gone,
causing women to raise up they red petticoats
and dance, trampling he grave,
while machetes pound stone, lips drown rum,
and burn on highwine.

2

He disappeared from their thoughts
in a finger click. There was one-piece of no funeral
where Angie wrap that long skirt tight
so she could sway to leaves clapping
on the trees where she used to hang and swing,
licks raining on her skin

making marks like scattered rice.
Oh the splek and splak of that rope!

Now she prays to God to pelt him
with hard rock, to peel he skin
from he bones, make he crawl like swine,
this day when the mosquitoes strike
and the fireflies cease to glow.

3

Who beat drum and chant themselves into trance?
Who plant flower seed with light heart? Who talk
to jumbie, begging them to whip he hard down there,
beat he with bamboo, make he body bear red hibiscus,
he face turn ripe tomato, make he seed dry and burn?

Oh now he dead, life sweet like ripe sugar cane
and children's laughter fresh like spring water.

ELIZABETH BOYD

(c. 1710–1745)

On the Death of an Infant of Five Days Old

How frail is human life! How fleet our breath,
Born with the symptoms of approaching death!
What dire convulsions rend a mother's breast,
When by a first-born son's decease distressed.
Although an embryo, an abortive boy,
Thy wond'rous beauties give a wond'rous joy:
Still flattering Hope a flattering idea gives,
And, whilst the birth can breathe, we say it lives.
With what kind warmth the dear-loved babe was pressed:
The darling man was with less love caressed!
How dear, how innocent, the fond embrace!
The father's form all o'er, the father's face,
The sparkling eye, gay with a cherub smile,
Some flying hours the mother-pangs beguile;
The pretty mouth a Cupid's tale expressed,
In amorous murmurs, to the full-swoll'n breast.
If angel infancy can so endear,
Dear angel-infants must command a tear.
Oh! could the stern-souled sex but know the pain,
Or the soft mother's agonies sustain,
With tenderest love the obdurate heart would burn,
And the shocked father tear for tear return.

ANNE BRADSTREET

(1612–1672)

In Memory of My Dear Grandchild, Elizabeth Bradstreet

Farewell dear babe, my heart's too much content,
Farewell sweet babe, the pleasure of mine eye,
Farewell fair flower that for a space was lent,
Then ta'en away unto eternity.
Blest babe why should I once bewail thy fate,
Or sigh the days so soon were terminate;
Sith thou art settled in an everlasting state. Since
By nature trees do rot when they are grown.
And plums and apples thoroughly ripe do fall,
And corn and grass are in their season mown,
And time brings down what is both strong and tall.
But plants new set to be eradicate,
And buds new blown, to have so short a date,
Is by His hand alone that guides nature and fate.

KAMAU BRATHWAITE

(1930–2020)

Elegy for Rosita

That she is suddenly still
with her stillness her mourning
i cannot think

i cannot know
the anxious pilgrimage of blood
that only finds a doctor's watered consolation
and so returns in crisis to the helpless life
brinked on the precipice of her heart's rending

That she is suddenly come
to the door of her pain's ending
i cannot think

Nor can i pray that morning will
not raise the mourning from her head
nor hoist the suns back to her eyes

to say she is not dead

ROBERT BRIDGES

(1844–1930)

On a Dead Child

Perfect little body, without fault or stain on thee,
With promise of strength and manhood full and fair!
Though cold and stark and bare,
The bloom and the charm of life doth awhile remain on thee.

Thy mother's treasure wert thou; – alas! no longer
To visit her heart with wondrous joy; to be
Thy father's pride; – ah, he
Must gather his faith together, and his strength make stronger.

To me, as I move thee now in the last duty,
Dost thou with a turn or gesture anon respond;
Startling my fancy fond
With a chance attitude of the head, a freak of beauty.

Thy hand clasps, as 'twas wont, my finger, and holds it:
But the grasp is the clasp of Death, heartbreaking and stiff;
Yet feels to my hand as if
'Twas still thy will, thy pleasure and trust that enfolds it.

So I lay thee there, thy sunken eyelids closing, –
Go lie thou there in thy coffin, thy last little bed! –
Propping thy wise, sad head,
Thy firm, pale hands across thy chest disposing.

So quiet! doth the change content thee? – Death, whither hath he
    taken thee?
To a world, do I think, that rights the disaster of this?
The vision of which I miss,
Who weep for the body, and wish but to warm thee and awaken
    thee?

Ah! little at best can all our hopes avail us
To lift this sorrow, or cheer us, when in the dark,
Unwilling, alone we embark,
And the things we have seen and have known and have heard of,
    fail us.

CHARLOTTE BRONTË
(1816–1855)

On the Death of Emily Jane Brontë

My darling, thou wilt never know
The grinding agony of woe
   That we have borne for thee.
Thus may we consolation tear
E'en from the depth of our despair
   And wasting misery.

The nightly anguish thou art spared
When all the crushing truth is bared
   To the awakening mind,
When the galled heart is pierced with grief,
Till wildly it implores relief,
   But small relief can find.

Nor know'st thou what it is to lie
Looking forth with streaming eye
   On life's lone wilderness.
'Weary, weary, dark and drear,
How shall I the journey bear,
   The burden and distress?'

EMILY BRONTË
(1818–1848)

Remembrance

Cold in the earth – and the deep snow piled above thee,
Far, far removed, cold in the dreary grave!
Have I forgot, my only Love, to love thee,
Severed at last by Time's all-severing wave?

Now, when alone, do my thoughts no longer hover
Over the mountains, on that northern shore,
Resting their wings where heath and fern-leaves cover
Thy noble heart forever, ever more?

Cold in the earth – and fifteen wild Decembers,
From those brown hills, have melted into spring:
Faithful, indeed, is the spirit that remembers
After such years of change and suffering!

Sweet Love of youth, forgive, if I forget thee,
While the world's tide is bearing me along;
Other desires and other hopes beset me,
Hopes which obscure, but cannot do thee wrong!

No later light has lightened up my heaven,
No second morn has ever shone for me;
All my life's bliss from thy dear life was given,
All my life's bliss is in the grave with thee.

But, when the days of golden dreams had perished,
And even Despair was powerless to destroy,
Then did I learn how existence could be cherished,
Strengthened, and fed without the aid of joy.

Then did I check the tears of useless passion –
Weaned my young soul from yearning after thine;
Sternly denied its burning wish to hasten
Down to that tomb already more than mine.

And, even yet, I dare not let it languish,
Dare not indulge in memory's rapturous pain;
Once drinking deep of that divinest anguish,
How could I seek the empty world again?

RUPERT BROOKE

(1887–1915)

The Soldier

If I should die, think only this of me:
    That there's some corner of a foreign field
That is for ever England. There shall be
    In that rich earth a richer dust concealed;
A dust whom England bore, shaped, made aware,
    Gave, once, her flowers to love, her ways to roam,
A body of England's, breathing English air,
    Washed by the rivers, blest by suns of home.

And think, this heart, all evil shed away,
    A pulse in the eternal mind, no less
        Gives somewhere back the thoughts by England given;
Her sights and sounds; dreams happy as her day;
    And laughter, learnt of friends; and gentleness,
        In hearts at peace, under an English heaven.

JERICHO BROWN

(1976–)

The Tradition

Aster. Nasturtium. Delphinium. We thought
Fingers in dirt meant it was our dirt, learning
Names in heat, in elements classical
Philosophers said could change us. *Stargazer.*
Foxglove. Summer seemed to bloom against the will
Of the sun, which news reports claimed flamed hotter
On this planet than when our dead fathers
Wiped sweat from their necks. *Cosmos. Baby's Breath.*
Men like me and my brothers filmed what we
Planted for proof we existed before
Too late, sped the video to see blossoms
Brought in seconds, colors you expect in poems
Where the world ends, everything cut down.
John Crawford. Eric Garner. Mike Brown.

WILLIAM BROWNE

(c. 1590–1645)

On the Countess Dowager of Pembroke

Underneath this sable herse
Lies the subject of all verse:
Sidney's sister, Pembroke's mother:
Death, ere thou hast slain another
Fair and learn'd and good as she,
Time shall throw a dart at thee.

ELIZABETH BARRETT BROWNING
(1806–1861)

Felicia Hemans

To L. E. L., Referring to Her Monody on that Poetess.

1

Thou bay-crowned living One, that o'er the bay-crowned Dead
    art bowing,
And, o'er the shadeless moveless brow, the vital shadow throwing;
And, o'er the sighless songless lips, the wail and music wedding;
Dropping above the tranquil eyes, the tears not of their shedding! –

2

Take music from the silent Dead, whose meaning is completer;
Reserve thy tears for living brows, where all such tears are meeter;
And leave the violets in the grass, to brighten where thou treadest!
No flowers for her! no need of flowers – albeit 'bring flowers,'
    thou saidest.

3

Yes, flowers, to crown the 'cup and lute!' since both may come to
    breaking:
Or flowers, to greet the 'bride!' the heart's own beating works its
    aching:
Or flowers, to soothe the 'captive's' sight, from earth's free bosom
    gathered,
Reminding of his earthly hope, then withering as it withered!

4

But bring not near her solemn corse, the type of human seeming!
Lay only dust's stern verity upon her dust undreaming.
And while the calm perpetual stars shall look upon it solely,
Her spherèd soul shall look on *them,* with eyes more bright and
    holy.

5

Nor mourn, O living One, because her part in life was mourning.
Would she have lost the poet's fire, for anguish of the burning? –
The minstrel harp, for the strained string? the tripod, for the afflated
Woe? or the vision, for those tears, in which it shone dilated?

6

Perhaps she shuddered, while the world's cold hand her brow
    was wreathing,
But never wronged that mystic breath, which breathed in all her
    breathing;
Which drew from rocky earth and man, abstractions high and
    moving –
Beauty, if not the beautiful, and love, if not the loving.

7

Such visionings have paled in sight: the Saviour she descrieth,
And little recks *who* wreathed the brow which on His bosom lieth.
The whiteness of His innocence o'er all her garments, flowing, –
There, learneth she the sweet 'new song,' she will not mourn in
    knowing.

8

Be happy, crowned and living One! and, as thy dust decayeth,
May thine own England say for thee, what now for Her it sayeth –
'Albeit softly in our ears her silver song was ringing,
The footfall of her parting soul is softer than her singing!'

L. E. L.'S Last Question

'Do you think of me as I think of you?'
*From her poem written during
the voyage to the Cape*

I

'Do you think of me as I think of you,
My friends, my friends?' – She said it from the sea,
The English minstrel in her minstrelsy;
While, under brighter skies than erst she knew,
Her heart grew dark, – and groped there, as the blind,
To reach, across the waves, friends left behind –
'Do you think of me as I think of you?'

2

It seemed not much to ask – As *I* of *you?* –
We all do ask the same. No eyelids cover
Within the meekest eyes, that question over, –
And little, in the world, the Loving do,
But sit (among the rocks?) and listen for
The echo of their own love evermore –
'Do you think of me as I think of you?'

3

Love-learned, she had sung of love and love, –
And, like a child, that, sleeping with dropt head
Upon the fairy book he lately read,
Whatever household noises round him move,
Hears in his dream some elfin turbulence, –
Even so, suggestive to her inward sense,
All sounds of life assumed one tune of love.

4

And when the glory of her dream withdrew, –
When knightly gestes and courtly pageantries
Were broken in her visionary eyes,
By tears the solemn seas attested true, –
Forgetting that sweet lute beside her hand,
She asked not, – Do you praise me, O my land? –
But, – 'Think ye of me, friends, as I of you?'

5

Hers was the hand that played for many a year,
Love's silver phrase for England, – smooth and well!
Would God, her heart's more inward oracle,
In that lone moment, might confirm her dear!
For when her questioned friends in agony
Made passionate response, – 'We think of *thee*,' –
Her place was in the dust, too deep to hear.

6

Could she not wait to catch their answering breath?
Was she content – content – with ocean's sound,
Which dashed its mocking infinite around
One thirsty for a little love? – beneath

Those stars, content, – where last her song had gone, –
They, mute and cold in radiant life, – as soon
Their singer was to be, in darksome death?

7

Bring your vain answers – cry, 'We think of *thee!*'
How think ye of her? warm in long ago
Delights? – or crowned with budding bays? Not so.
None smile and none are crowned where lieth she, –
With all her visions unfulfilled, save one –
Her childhood's – of the palm-trees in the sun –
And lo! their shadow on her sepulchre!

8

'Do ye think of me as I think of you?' –
O friends, – O kindred, – O dear brotherhood
Of all the world! what are we, that we should
For covenants of long affection sue?
Why press so near each other, when the touch
Is barred by graves? Not much, and yet too much,
Is this 'Think of me as I think of you.'

9

But while on mortal lips I shape anew
A sigh to mortal issues, – verily
Above the unshaken stars that see us die,
A vocal pathos rolls! and HE who drew
All life from dust, and for all, tasted death,
By death and life and love, appealing, saith,
Do you think of me as I think of you?

Mother and Poet

(Turin, after News from Gaeta, 1861)

1

Dead! One of them shot by the sea in the east,
  And one of them shot in the west by the sea.
Dead! both my boys! When you sit at the feast
  And are wanting a great song for Italy free,
    Let none look at *me!*

2

Yet I was a poetess only last year,
  And good at my art, for a woman, men said;
But *this* woman, *this,* who is agonized here,
  – The east sea and west sea rhyme on in her head
    For ever instead.

3

What art can a woman be good at? Oh, vain!
  What art *is* she good at, but hurting her breast
With the milk-teeth of babes, and a smile at the pain?
  Ah boys, how you hurt! you were strong as you pressed,
    And I proud, by that test.

4

What art's for a woman? To hold on her knees
  Both darlings! to feel all their arms round her throat,
Cling, strangle a little! to sew by degrees
  And 'broider the long-clothes and neat little coat;
    To dream and to doat.

5

To teach them . . . It stings there! *I* made them indeed
  Speak plain the word *country*. I taught them, no doubt,
That a country's a thing men should die for at need.
  I prated of liberty, rights, and about
      The tyrant cast out.

6

And when their eyes flashed . . . O my beautiful eyes! . . .
  I exulted; nay, let them go forth at the wheels
Of the guns, and denied not. But then the surprise
  When one sits quite alone! Then one weeps, then one kneels!
      God, how the house feels!

7

At first, happy news came, in gay letters moiled
  With my kisses, – of camp-life and glory, and how
They both loved me; and, soon coming home to be spoiled
  In return would fan off every fly from my brow
      With their green laurel-bough.

8

Then was triumph at Turin: 'Ancona was free!'
  And some one came out of the cheers in the street,
With a face pale as stone, to say something to me.
  My Guido was dead! I fell down at his feet,
      While they cheered in the street.

9

I bore it; friends soothed me; my grief looked sublime
  As the ransom of Italy. One boy remained
To be leant on and walked with, recalling the time
  When the first grew immortal, while both of us strained
    To the height he had gained.

10

And letters still came, shorter, sadder, more strong,
  Writ now but in one hand, 'I was not to faint, –
One loved me for two – would be with me ere long:
  And *Viva l' Italia!* – *he* died for, our saint,
    Who forbids our complaint.'

11

My Nanni would add, 'he was safe, and aware
  Of a presence that turned off the balls, – was imprest
It was Guido himself, who knew what I could bear,
  And how 'twas impossible, quite dispossessed,
    To live on for the rest.'

12

On which, without pause, up the telegraph line
  Swept smoothly the next news from Gaeta: – *Shot.*
Tell his mother. Ah, ah, 'his,' 'their' mother, – not 'mine,'
  No voice says '*My* mother' again to me. What!
    You think Guido forgot?

13

Are souls straight so happy that, dizzy with Heaven,
 They drop earth's affections, conceive not of woe?
I think not. Themselves were too lately forgiven
  Through THAT Love and Sorrow which reconciled so
  The Above and Below.

14

O Christ of the five wounds, who look'dst through the dark
 To the face of Thy mother! consider, I pray,
How we common mothers stand desolate, mark,
  Whose sons, not being Christs, die with eyes turned away,
  And no last word to say!

15

Both boys dead? but that's out of nature. We all
 Have been patriots, yet each house must always keep one.
'Twere imbecile, hewing out roads to a wall;
  And, when Italy's made, for what end is it done
  If we have not a son?

16

Ah, ah, ah! when Gaeta's taken, what then?
 When the fair wicked queen sits no more at her sport
Of the fire-balls of death crashing souls out of men?
  When the guns of Cavalli with final retort
  Have cut the game short?

17

When Venice and Rome keep their new jubilee,
  When your flag takes all heaven for its white, green, and red,
When *you* have your country from mountain to sea,
  When King Victor has Italy's crown on his head,
    (And *I* have my Dead) –

18

What then? Do not mock me. Ah, ring your bells low,
  And burn your lights faintly! *My* country is *there*,
Above the star pricked by the last peak of snow:
  My Italy's THERE, with my brave civic Pair,
    To disfranchise despair!

19

Forgive me. Some women bear children in strength,
  And bite back the cry of their pain in self-scorn;
But the birth-pangs of nations will wring us at length
  Into wail such as this – and we sit on forlorn
    When the man-child is born.

20

Dead! One of them shot by the sea in the east,
  And one of them shot in the west by the sea.
Both! both my boys! If in keeping the feast
  You want a great song for your Italy free,
    Let none look at *me*!

BASIL BUNTING

(1900–1985)

from *Briggflatts*

I

Brag, sweet tenor bull,
descant on Rawthey's madrigal,
each pebble its part
for the fells' late spring.
Dance tiptoe, bull,
black against may.
Ridiculous and lovely
chase hurdling shadows
morning into noon.
May on the bull's hide
and through the dale
furrows fill with may,
paving the slowworm's way.

A mason times his mallet
to a lark's twitter,
listening while the marble rests,
lays his rule
at a letter's edge,
fingertips checking,
till the stone spells a name
naming none,
a man abolished.
Painful lark, labouring to rise!
The solemn mallet says:
In the grave's slot
he lies. We rot.

Decay thrusts the blade,
wheat stands in excrement
trembling. Rawthey trembles.
Tongue stumbles, ears err
for fear of spring.
Rub the stone with sand,
wet sandstone rending
roughness away. Fingers
ache on the rubbing stone.
The mason says: Rocks
happen by chance.
No one here bolts the door,
love is so sore.

Stone smooth as skin,
cold as the dead they load
on a low lorry by night.
The moon sits on the fell
but it will rain.
Under sacks on the stone
two children lie,
hear the horse stale,
the mason whistle,
harness mutter to shaft,
felloe to axle squeak,
rut thud the rim,
crushed grit.

Stocking to stocking, jersey to jersey,
head to a hard arm,
they kiss under the rain,
bruised by their marble bed.
In Garsdale, dawn;
at Hawes, tea from the can.
Rain stops, sacks
steam in the sun, they sit up.
Copper-wire moustache,
sea-reflecting eyes

and Baltic plainsong speech
declare: By such rocks
men killed Bloodaxe.

Fierce blood throbs in his tongue,
lean words.
Skulls cropped for steel caps
huddle round Stainmore.
Their becks ring on limestone,
whisper to peat.
The clogged cart pushes the horse downhill.
In such soft air
they trudge and sing,
laying the tune frankly on the air.
All sounds fall still,
fellside bleat,
hide-and-seek peewit.

Her pulse their pace,
palm countering palm,
till a trench is filled,
stone white as cheese
jeers at the dale.
Knotty wood, hard to rive,
smoulders to ash;
smell of October apples.
The road again,
at a trot.
Wetter, warmed, they watch
the mason meditate
on name and date.

Rain rinses the road,
the bull streams and laments.
Sour rye porridge from the hob
with cream and black tea,
meat, crust and crumb.
Her parents in bed
the children dry their clothes.

He has untied the tape
of her striped flannel drawers
before the range. Naked
on the pricked rag mat
his fingers comb
thatch of his manhood's home.

Gentle generous voices weave
over bare night
words to confirm and delight
till bird dawn.
Rainwater from the butt
she fetches and flannel
to wash him inch by inch,
kissing the pebbles.
Shining slowworm part of the marvel.
The mason stirs:
Words!
Pens are too light.
Take a chisel to write.

Every birth a crime,
every sentence life.
Wiped of mould and mites
would the ball run true?
No hope of going back.
Hounds falter and stray,
shame deflects the pen.
Love murdered neither bleeds nor stifles
but jogs the draftsman's elbow.
What can he, changed, tell
her, changed, perhaps dead?
Delight dwindles. Blame
stays the same.

Brief words are hard to find,
shapes to carve and discard:
Bloodaxe, king of York,
king of Dublin, king of Orkney.

Take no notice of tears;
letter the stone to stand
over love laid aside lest
insufferable happiness impede
flight to Stainmore,
to trace
lark, mallet,
becks, flocks
and axe knocks.

Dung will not soil the slowworm's
mosaic. Breathless lark
drops to nest in sodden trash;
Rawthey truculent, dingy.
Drudge at the mallet, the may is down,
fog on fells. Guilty of spring
and spring's ending
amputated years ache after
the bull is beef, love a convenience.
It is easier to die than to remember.
Name and date
split in soft slate
a few months obliterate.

ROBERT BURNS
(1759–1796)

Epitaph for James Smith

Lament him, Mauchline husbands a',
 He aften did assist ye;
For had ye staid hale weeks awa,
 Your wives they ne'er had miss'd ye.

Ye Mauchline bairns, as on ye press
 To school in bands thegither,
O tread ye lightly on his grass, –
 Perhaps he was your father!

Lament for James, Earl of Glencairn

The wind blew hollow frae the hills,
By fits the sun's departing beam
Look'd on the fading yellow woods,
That wav'd o'er Lugar's winding stream:
Beneath a craigy steep, a Bard,
Laden with years and meikle pain,
In loud lament bewail'd his lord,
Whom Death had all untimely ta'en.

He lean'd him to an ancient aik,
Whose trunk was mould'ring down with years;
His locks were bleached white with time,
His hoary cheek was wet wi' tears!
And as he touch'd his trembling harp,
And as he tun'd his doleful sang,
The winds, lamenting thro' their caves,
To Echo bore the notes alang.

'Ye scatter'd birds that faintly sing,
The reliques o' the vernal queir!
Ye woods that shed on a' the winds
The honours of the agèd year!
A few short months, and glad and gay,
Again ye'll charm the ear and e'e;
But nocht in all-revolving time
Can gladness bring again to me.

'I am a bending agèd tree,
That long has stood the wind and rain;
But now has come a cruel blast,
And my last hald of earth is gane;
Nae leaf o' mine shall greet the spring,
Nae simmer sun exalt my bloom;
But I maun lie before the storm,
And ithers plant them in my room.

'I've seen sae mony changefu' years,
On earth I am a stranger grown:
I wander in the ways of men,
Alike unknowing, and unknown:
Unheard, unpitied, unreliev'd,
I bear alane my lade o' care,
For silent, low, on beds of dust,
Lie a' that would my sorrows share.

'And last, (the sum of a' my griefs!)
My noble master lies in clay;
The flow'r amang our barons bold,
His country's pride, his country's stay:
In weary being now I pine,
For a' the life of life is dead,
And hope has left may aged ken,
On forward wing for ever fled.

'Awake thy last sad voice, my harp!
The voice of woe and wild despair!
Awake, resound thy latest lay,
Then sleep in silence evermair!
And thou, my last, best, only, friend,
That fillest an untimely tomb,
Accept this tribute from the Bard
Thou brought from Fortune's mirkest gloom.

'In Poverty's low barren vale,
Thick mists obscure involv'd me round;
Though oft I turn'd the wistful eye,
Nae ray of fame was to be found:
Thou found'st me, like the morning sun
That melts the fogs in limpid air,
The friendless bard and rustic song
Became alike thy fostering care.

'O! why has worth so short a date,
While villains ripen grey with time?
Must thou, the noble, gen'rous, great,
Fall in bold manhood's hardy prim
Why did I live to see that day –
A day to me so full of woe?
O! had I met the mortal shaft
That laid my benefactor low!

'The bridegroom may forget the bride
Was made his wedded wife yestreen;
The monarch may forget the crown
That on his head an hour has been;
The mother may forget the child
That smiles sae sweetly on her knee;
But I'll remember thee, Glencairn,
And a' that thou hast done for me!'

GEORGE GORDON, LORD BYRON
(1788–1824)

Stanzas for Music

I

Bright be the place of thy soul!
    No lovelier spirit than thine
E'er burst from its mortal control,
    In the orbs of the blessed to shine.
On earth thou wert all but divine,
    As thy soul shall immortally be;
And our sorrow may cease to repine
    When we know that thy God is with thee.

2

Light be the turf of thy tomb!
    May its verdure like emeralds be!
There should not be the shadow of gloom
    In aught that reminds us of thee.
Young flowers and an evergreen tree
    May spring from the spot of thy rest:
But not cypress nor yew let us see;
    For why should we mourn for the blest?

Remember thee! Remember thee!

Remember thee! remember thee!
  Till Lethe quench life's burning stream
Remorse and shame shall cling to thee,
  And haunt thee like a feverish dream!

Remember thee! Ay, doubt it not.
  Thy husband too shall think of thee!
By neither shalt thou be forgot,
  Thou *false* to him, thou *fiend* to me!

On This Day I Complete My Thirty-Sixth Year

Missolonghi, Jan. 22, 1824

'Tis time this heart should be unmoved,
  Since others it hath ceased to move:
Yet, though I cannot be beloved,
  Still let me love!

My days are in the yellow leaf;
  The flowers and fruits of love are gone;
The worm, the canker, and the grief
  Are mine alone!

The fire that on my bosom preys
  Is lone as some volcanic isle;
No torch is kindled at its blaze –
  A funeral pile.

The hope, the fear, the jealous care,
  The exalted portion of the pain
And power of love, I cannot share,
  But wear the chain.

But 'tis not *thus* – and 'tis not *here* –
   Such thoughts should shake my soul, nor *now*,
Where glory decks the hero's bier,
     Or binds his brow.

The sword, the banner, and the field,
   Glory and Greece, around me see!
The Spartan, borne upon his shield,
     Was not more free.

Awake! (not Greece – she is awake!)
   Awake, my spirit! Think through *whom*
Thy life-blood tracks its parent lake,
     And then strike home!

Tread those reviving passions down,
   Unworthy manhood! – unto thee
Indifferent should the smile or frown
     Of beauty be.

If thou regrett'st thy youth, *why live?*
   The land of honourable death
Is here: – up to the field, and give
     Away thy breath!

Seek out – less often sought than found –
   A soldier's grave, for thee the best;
Then look around, and choose thy ground,
     And take thy rest.

Elegy on Thyrza

And thou art dead, as young and fair
　　As aught of mortal birth;
And form so soft and charms so rare
　　Too soon return'd to Earth!
Though Earth received them in her bed,
And o'er the spot the crowd may tread
　　In carelessness or mirth,
There is an eye which could not brook
A moment on that grave to look.

I will not ask where thou liest low,
　　Nor gaze upon the spot;
There flowers or weeds at will may grow,
　　So I behold them not:
It is enough for me to prove
That what I loved, and long must love,
　　Like common earth can rot;
To me there needs no stone to tell
'Tis Nothing that I loved so well.

Yet did I love thee to the last,
　　As fervently as thou
Who didst not change through all the past,
　　And canst not alter now.
The love where Death has set his seal
Nor age can chill, nor rival steal,
　　Nor falsehood disavow;
And, what were worse, thou canst not see
Or wrong, or change, or fault in me.

The better days of life were ours,
　　The worst can be but mine;
The sun that cheers, the storm that lours,
　　Shall never more be thine.
The silence of that dreamless sleep
I envy now too much to weep;

Nor need I to repine
That all those charms have pass'd away
I might have watch'd through long decay.

The flower in ripen'd bloom unmatch'd
  Must fall the earliest prey;
Though by no hand untimely snatch'd.
The leaves must drop away.
And yet it were a greater grief
To watch it withering, leaf by leaf,
  Than see it pluck'd to-day;
Since earthly eye but ill can bear
To trace the change to foul from fair.

I know not if I could have borne
  To see thy beauties fade;
The night that follow'd such a morn
  Had worn a deeper shade.
Thy day without a cloud hath pass'd,
And thou wert lovely to the last,
  Extinguish'd, not decay'd;
As stars that shoot along the sky
Shine brightest as they fall from high.

As once I wept, if I could weep,
  My tears might well be shed
To think I was not near, to keep
  One vigil o'er thy bed –
To gaze, how fondly! on thy face,
To fold thee in a faint embrace,
  Uphold thy drooping head,
And show that love, however vain,
Nor thou nor I can feel again.

Yet how much less it were to gain,
  Though thou hast left me free,
The loveliest things that still remain
  Than thus remember thee!
The all of thine that cannot die
Through dark and dread eternity
  Returns again to me,
And more thy buried love endears
Than aught except its living years.

CHRISTIAN CAMPBELL
(1979–)

Rudical
(*Derek Bennett, killed by the police*)

After Matisse's Icare (Jazz), *1943*

I who born
Thirty-one years
Since *The Windrush* come
Thirty-one years
Life of a man
I who born
Forty-one bullets
Amadou Diallo
Life of a man
Seven kill me
I who born

    & because we suck the neon marrow of the streets
    & because we tote a solar plexus of islands (*for true*)
    & because we yuck out the blue heart of night (*right*)
    & because our heads gather thick as a blood (*teach them*)
    & because we eat out the honey of mad laughter (*everytime*)
    & because we outrun the delirium of streetlights (*ok*)
    & because we are gray bugs scuttling from the lifted rock
    & because & because & &
    & because high street skeets a thousand niggers
    & because my eyehole grows iridescent with the moon
    & because we holler for the bloodclad sun
    & because we mourn the burst testes of the stars
    & because we skank cross rivers of blood

Mine New Cross mine Oldham Notting Hill Bradford Brixton mine
too Nassau Laventille Bridgetown Kingston Britain has branded an
x in my flesh this rolled throat of killings this septic eye this urge of
maggotry this seed of Mars this blasted plot this hurt hissing realm
this ogly island this England

THOMAS CAMPION

(1567–1620)

O Come Quickly!

Never weather-beaten sail more willing bent to shore,
   Never tired pilgrim's limbs affected slumber more,
Than my weary spright now longs to fly out of my troubled breast.
   O! come quickly, sweetest Lord, and take my soul to rest.

Ever blooming are the joys of Heaven's high Paradise.
   Cold age deafs not there our ears, nor vapour dims our eyes;
Glory there the sun outshines, whose beams the blessed only see.
   O! come quickly, glorious Lord, and raise my spright to thee.

THOMAS CAREW

(c. 1595–1640)

An Elegy upon the Death of the Dean of Paul's, Dr John Donne

Can we not force from widow'd poetry,
Now thou art dead, great Donne, one elegy,
To crown thy hearse? Why yet did we not trust,
Though with unkneaded dough-baked prose, thy dust,
Such as the unscissor'd lecturer, from the flower
Of fading rhetoric, short-lived as his hour,
Dry as the sand that measures it, might lay
Upon the ashes on the funeral day?
Have we nor tune nor voice? Didst thou dispense
Through all our language both the words and sense?
'Tis a sad truth. The pulpit may her plain
And sober Christian precepts still retain;
Doctrines it may, and wholesome uses, frame,
Grave homilies and lectures; but the flame
Of thy brave soul, that shot such heat and light,
As burn'd our earth, and made our darkness bright,
Committed holy rapes upon the will,
Did through the eye the melting heart distil,
And the deep knowledge of dark truths so teach,
As sense might judge what fancy could not reach,
Must be desired for ever. So the fire,
That fills with spirit and heat the Delphic choir,
Which, kindled first by thy Promethean breath,
Glow'd here awhile, lies quench'd now in thy death.
The Muses' garden, with pedantic weeds
O'erspread, was purg'd by thee; the lazy seeds
Of servile imitation thrown away,
And fresh invention planted; thou didst pay
The debts of our penurious bankrupt age;
Licentious thefts, that make poetic rage

A mimic fury, when our souls must be
Possess'd, or with Anacreon's ecstacy,
Or Pindar's, not their own; the subtle cheat
Of sly exchanges, and the juggling feat
Of two-edged words, or whatsoever wrong
By ours was done the Greek or Latin tongue,
Thou hast redeem'd, and open'd us a mine
Of rich and pregnant fancy; drawn a line
Of masculine expression, which, had good
Old Orpheus seen, or all the ancient brood
Our superstitious fools admire, and hold
Their lead more precious than thy burnish'd gold,
Thou hadst been their exchequer, and no more
They each in other's dung had search'd for ore.
Thou shalt yield no precedence, but of time,
And the blind fate of language, whose tuned chime
More charms the outward sense: yet thou mayst claim
From so great disadvantage greater fame,
Since to the awe of thy imperious wit
Our troublesome language bends, made only fit
With her tough thick-ribb'd hoops to gird about
Thy giant fancy, which had proved too stout
For their soft melting phrases. As in time
They had the start, so did they cull the prime
Buds of invention many a hundred year,
And left the rifled fields, besides the fear
To touch their harvest; yet from those bare lands,
Of what was only thine, thy only hands
(And that their smallest work,) have gleaned more
Than all those times and tongues could reap before.
    But thou art gone, and thy strict laws will be
Too hard for libertines in poetry;
They will recall the goodly exiled train
Of gods and goddesses, which in thy just reign
Was banish'd nobler poems; now with these,
The silenced tales i' th' *Metamorphoses*,
Shall stuff their lines, and swell the windy page,
Till verse, refined by thee in this last age,
Turn ballad-rhyme, or those old idols be

Adored again with new apostacy.
  O pardon me, that break with untuned verse
The reverend silence that attends thy hearse,
Whose solemn awful murmurs were to thee,
More than these rude lines, a loud elegy,
That did proclaim in a dumb eloquence
The death of all the arts: whose influence,
Grown feeble, in these panting numbers lies,
Gasping short-winded accents, and so dies.
So doth the swiftly-turning wheel not stand
In th' instant we withdraw the moving hand,
But some short time retain a faint weak course,
By virtue of the first impulsive force:
And so, whilst I cast on thy funeral pile
Thy crown of bays, oh let it crack awhile,
And spit disdain, till the devouring flashes
Suck all the moisture up, then turn to ashes.
  I will not draw the envy to engross
All thy perfections, or weep all the loss;
Those are too numerous for one elegy,
And this too great to be express'd by me.
Let others carve the rest; it shall suffice
I on thy grave this epitaph incise: –
Here lies a king that ruled, as he thought fit,
The universal monarchy of wit;
Here lies two flamens, and both those the best:
Apollo's first, at last the true God's priest.

Epitaph for Maria Wentworth

And here the precious dust is laid;
Whose purely-temper'd clay was made
So fine that it the guest betray'd.

Else the soul grew so fast within,
It broke the outward shell of sin,
And so was hatch'd a cherubin.

In height, it soar'd to God above;
In depth, it did to knowledge move,
And spread in breadth to general love.

Before, a pious duty shin'd
To parents, courtesy behind;
On either side an equal mind.

Good to the poor, to kindred dear,
To servants kind, to friendship clear,
To nothing but herself severe.

So, though a virgin, yet a bride
To ev'ry grace, she justified
A chaste polygamy, and died.

Learn from hence, reader, what small trust
We owe this world, where virtue must,
Frail as our flesh, crumble to dust.

CIARAN CARSON

(1948–2019)

In Memory

As he told it
when the boy
he was stumbled
on the well
in the derelict brickyard
deep as a brick mill chimney
leaning over the rim
he shouted
the two syllables
of his name
deep down into it
to hear his echo.
Now that the man
he would become
is dead
that unfathomable
darkness
echoes
still.

ELIZABETH CARTER

(1717–1806)

On the Death of Mrs Rowe

Accept, much honoured shade! the artless lays
The Muse a tribute to thy memory pays.
The sad relation of thy loss to hear,
What friend to virtue can refrain a tear?
A loss to no one private breast confined,
But claims the general sorrow of mankind.

Since here, alas, thy longer life's denied,
Farewell, our sex's ornament and pride!
Born with a genius fitted to excel,
And blessed with sense t' apply that genius well.
Long did romance o'er female wits prevail,
Th' intriguing novel and the wanton tale.
What different subjects in thy pages shine!
How chaste the style, how generous the design!
Thy better purpose was, with lenient art,
To charm the fancy, and amend the heart;
From trifling follies to withdraw the mind,
To relish pleasures of a nobler kind.
No lawless freedoms e'er profaned thy lays,
To virtue sacred and thy maker's praise.
This still shall last, when every meaner theme
In death must quit the memory like a dream.
In the bright regions of unfading joy,
This forms the happy spirit's blest employ:
To God each raptured seraph tunes his tongue,
The inexhausted subject of their song;
Where human minds the same glad concert raise,
And spend their blest eternity in praise.

CATULLUS

(c. 84–54 BCE)

Elegy on the Sparrow

Each Love, each Venus, mourn with me!
Mourn, every son of gallantry!
The Sparrow, my own nymph's delight,
The joy and apple of her sight;
The honey-bird, the darling dies,
To Lesbia dearer than her eyes.
As the fair-one knew her mother,
So he knew her from another.
With his gentle lady wrestling;
In her snowy bosom nestling;
With a flutter, and a bound,
Quivering round her and around;
Chirping, twittering, ever near,
Notes meant only for her ear.
Now he skims the shadowy way,
Whence none return to cheerful day.
Beshrew the shades! that thus devour
All that's pretty in an hour.

Translated by Charles Abraham Elton

Catullus 101

By ways remote and distant waters sped,
Brother, to thy sad grave-side am I come,
That I may give the last gifts to the dead,
And vainly parley with thine ashes dumb:
Since she who now bestows and now denies
Hath taken thee, hapless brother, from mine eyes.

But lo! these gifts, the heirlooms of past years,
Are made sad things to grace thy coffin shell,
Take them, all drenchèd with a brother's tears,
And, brother, for all time, hail and farewell!

Translated by Aubrey Beardsley

Catullus 101

Many the peoples many the oceans I crossed –
I arrive at these poor, brother, burials
so I could give you the last gift owed to death
and talk (why?) with mute ash.
Now that Fortune tore you from me, you
oh poor (wrongly) brother (wrongly) taken from me,
now still anyway this – what a distant mood of parents
handed down as the sad gift for burials –
accept! Soaked with tears of a brother
and into forever, brother, farewell and farewell.

Translated by Anne Carson

CHARLES CAUSLEY

(1917–2003)

Eden Rock

They are waiting for me somewhere beyond Eden Rock:
My father, twenty-five, in the same suit
Of Genuine Irish Tweed, his terrier Jack
Still two years old and trembling at his feet.

My mother, twenty-three, in a sprigged dress
Drawn at the waist, ribbon in her straw hat,
Has spread the stiff white cloth over the grass.
Her hair, the colour of wheat, takes on the light.

She pours tea from a Thermos, the milk straight
From an old H.P. sauce-bottle, a screw
Of paper for a cork; slowly sets out
The same three plates, the tin cups painted blue.

The sky whitens as if lit by three suns.
My mother shades her eyes and looks my way
Over the drifted stream. My father spins
A stone along the water. Leisurely,

They beckon to me from the other bank.
I hear them call, 'See where the stream-path is!
Crossing is not as hard as you might think.'

I had not thought that it would be like this.

C. P. CAVAFY

(1863–1933)

For Ammonis, Who Died Aged 29 in 610

Raphael, they are asking you to write some words,
an epitaph for the poet Ammonis,
something stylish and refined. You can do it,
you are just the man to write it down
for Ammonis, our very own.

Of course, you'll speak about his poems –
but talk about his beauty too,
his subtle beauty that we loved.

Your Greek is always lyrical and fine,
but now we need your artistry.
Our love and sorrow pass into a stranger's tongue.
Pour your Egyptian into that foreign voice.

Raphael your verses should be written down
so, you know, they capture something of our life,
so that every stress and every phrase will show
an Alexandrian is writing of an Alexandrian.

Translated by Stephen Regan

JANE CAVE

(1754–1812)

An Elegy on a Maiden Name

Adieu, dear name, which birth and Nature gave –
Lo! at the altar I've interr'd dear Cave,
For there it fell, expir'd, and found a grave.

Forgive, dear spouse, this ill-tim'd tear or two,
They are not meant in disrespect to you.
I hope the name, which you have lately giv'n,
Was kindly meant, and sent to me by heav'n,
But, ah! the loss of Cave I must deplore,
For that dear name the tend'rest mother bore.
With that she pass'd full forty years of life,
Adorn'd th' important character of wife:
Then meet for bliss, from earth to heav'n retir'd,
With holy zeal, and true devotion fir'd.

In me, what blest my father, may you find,
A wife domestic, virtuous, meek and kind.
What blest my mother may I meet in you,
A friend, and husband – faithful, wise, and true.

Then be our voyage prosp'rous, or adverse,
No keen upbraidings shall our tongues rehearse;
But mutually we'll brave against the storm,
Remembering still, for help-mates we were born.
Then let rough torrents roar, or skies look dark,
If love commands the helm which guides our bark,
No shipwreck will we fear, but to the end,
Each find in each, a just, unshaken friend.

PAUL CELAN

(1920–1970)

Deathfugue

Black milk of daybreak we drink it at evening
we drink it at midday and morning we drink it at night
we drink and we drink
we shovel a grave in the air where you won't lie too cramped
A man lives in the house he plays with his vipers he writes
he writes when it grows dark to Deutschland your golden hair
    Margarete
he writes it and steps out of doors and the stars are all sparkling
    he whistles his hounds to stay close
he whistles his Jews into rows has them shovel a grave in the ground
he commands us play up for the dance

Black milk of daybreak we drink you at night
we drink you at morning and midday we drink you at evening
we drink and we drink
A man lives in the house he plays with his vipers he writes
he writes when it grows dark to Deutschland your golden hair
    Margarete
Your ashen hair Sulamith we shovel a grave in the air where you
    won't lie too cramped

He shouts dig this earth deeper you lot there you others sing up
    and play
he grabs for the rod in his belt he swings it his eyes are so blue
stick your spades deeper you lot there you others play on for the
    dancing

Black milk of daybreak we drink you at night
we drink you at midday and morning we drink you at evening
we drink and we drink
a man lives in the house your goldenes Haar Margarete
your aschenes Haar Sulamith he plays with his vipers

He shouts play death more sweetly this Death is a master from
Deutschland
he shouts scrape your strings darker you'll rise up as smoke to
the sky
you'll then have a grave in the clouds where you won't lie too
cramped

Black milk of daybreak we drink you at night
we drink you at midday Death is a master aus Deutschland
we drink you at evening and morning we drink and we drink
this Death is ein Meister aus Deutschland his eye it is blue
he shoots you with shot made of lead shoots you level and true
a man lives in the house your goldenes Haar Margarete
he looses his hounds on us grants us a grave in the air
he plays with his vipers and daydreams der Tod ist ein Meister aus
Deutschland

dein goldenes Haar Margarete
dein aschenes Haar Sulamith

Translated by John Felstiner

AMY CLAMPITT

(1920–1994)

A Procession at Candlemas

I

Moving on or going back to where you came from,
bad news is what you mainly travel with:
a breakup or a breakdown, someone running off

or walking out, called up or called home:
death in the family. Nudged from their stanchions
outside the terminal, anonymous of purpose

as a flock of birds, the bison of the highway
funnel westward onto Route 80, mirroring
an entity that cannot look into itself and know

what makes it what it is. Sooner or later
every trek becomes a funeral procession.
The mother curtained in Intensive Care –

a scene the mind leaves blank, fleeing instead
toward scenes of transhumance, the belled sheep
moving up the Pyrenees, red-tasseled pack llamas

footing velvet-green precipices, the Kurdish
women, jingling with bangles, gorgeous
on their rug-piled mounts – already lying dead,

bereavement altering the moving lights
to a processional, a feast of Candlemas.
Change as child-bearing, birth as a kind

of shucking off: out of what began
as a Mosaic insult – such a loathing
of the common origin, even a virgin,

having given birth, needs purifying –
to carry fire as though it were a flower,
the terror and the loveliness entrusted

into naked hands, supposing God might have,
might actually need a mother: people have
at times found this a way of being happy.

A Candlemas of moving lights along Route 80;
lighted candles in a corridor from Arlington
over the Potomac, for every carried flame

the name of a dead soldier: an element
fragile as ego, frightening as parturition,
necessary and intractable as dreaming.

The lapped, wheelborne integument, layer
within layer, at the core a dream of
something precious, ripped: Where are we?

The sleepers groan, stir, rewrap themselves
about the self's imponderable substance,
or clamber down, numb-footed, half in a drowse

of freezing dark, through a Stonehenge
of fuel pumps, the bison hulks slantwise
beside them, drinking. What is real except

what's fabricated? The jellies glitter
cream-capped in the cafeteria showcase;
gumball globes, Life Savers cinctured

in parcel gilt, plop from their housings
perfect, like miracles. Comb, nail clipper,
lip rouge, mirrors and emollients embody,

niched into the washroom wall case,
the pristine seductiveness of money.
Absently, without inhabitants, this

nowhere oasis wears the place name
of Indian Meadows. The westward-trekking
transhumance, once only, of a people who,

in losing everything they had, lost even
the names they went by, stumbling past
like caribou, perhaps camped here. Who

can assign a trade-in value to that sorrow?
The monk in sheepskin over tucked-up saffron
intoning to a drum becomes the metronome

of one more straggle up Pennsylvania Avenue
in falling snow, a whirl of tenderly
remorseless corpuscles, street gangs

amok among magnolias' pregnant wands,
a stillness at the heart of so much whirling:
beyond the torn integument of childbirth,

sometimes, wrapped like a papoose into a grief
not merely of the ego, you rediscover almost
the rest-in-peace of the placental coracle.

2

Of what the dead were, living, one knows
so little as barely to recognize
the fabric of the backward-ramifying

antecedents, half-noted presences
in darkened rooms: the old, the feared,
the hallowed. Never the same river

drowns the unalterable doorsill. An effigy
in olive wood or pear wood, dank
with the sweat of age, walled in the dark

at Brauron, Argos, Samos: even the unwed
Athene, who had no mother, born – it's declared –
of some man's brain like every other pure idea,

had her own wizened cult object, kept
out of sight like the incontinent whimperer
in the backstairs bedroom, where no child

ever goes – to whom, year after year,
the fair linen of the sacred peplos
was brought in ceremonial procession –

flutes and stringed instruments, wildflower-
hung cattle, nubile Athenian girls, young men
praised for the beauty of their bodies. Who

can unpeel the layers of that seasonal
returning to the dark where memory fails,
as birds re-enter the ancestral flyway?

Daylight, snow falling, knotting of gears:
Chicago. Soot, the rotting backsides
of tenements, grimed trollshapes of ice

underneath the bridges, the tunnel heaving
like a birth canal. Disgorged, the infant
howling in the restroom; steam-table cereal,

pale coffee; wall-eyed TV receivers, armchairs
of molded plastic: the squalor of the day
resumed, the orphaned litter taken up again

unloved, the spawn of botched intentions,
grief a mere hardening of the gut,
a set piece of what can't be avoided:

parents by the tens of thousands living
unthanked, unpaid but in the sour coin
of resentment. Midmorning gray as zinc

along Route 80, corn-stubble quilting
the underside of snowdrifts, the cadaverous
belvedere of windmills, the sullen stare

of feedlot cattle; black creeks puncturing
white terrain, the frozen bottomland
a mush of willow tops; dragnetted in ice,

the Mississippi. Westward toward the dark,
the undertow of scenes come back to, fright
riddling the structures of interior history:

Where is it? Where, in the shucked-off
bundle, the hampered obscurity that has been
for centuries the mumbling lot of women,

did the thread of fire, too frail
ever to discover what it meant, to risk
even the taking of a shape, relinquish

the seed of possibility, unguessed-at
as a dream of something precious? Memory,
that exquisite blunderer, stumbling

like a migrant bird that finds the flyway
it hardly knew it knew except by instinct,
down the long-unentered nave of childhood,

late on a midwinter afternoon, alone
among the snow-hung hollows of the windbreak
on the far side of the orchard, encounters

sheltering among the evergreens, a small
stilled bird, its cap of clear yellow
slit by a thread of scarlet – the untouched

nucleus of fire, the lost connection
hallowing the wizened effigy, the mother
curtained in Intensive Care: a Candlemas

of moving lights along Route 80, at nightfall,
in falling snow, the stillness and the sorrow
of things moving back to where they came from.

JOHN CLARE
(1793–1864)

The Lament of Swordy Well

Petitioners are full of prayers
To fall in pitys way
But if her hand the gift forbears
Theyll sooner swear then pray
They're not the worst to want who lurch
On plenty with complaints
No more then those who go to church
Are eer the better saints

I hold no hat to beg a mite
Nor pick it up when thrown
No limping leg I hold in sight
But pray to keep my own
Where profit gets his clutches in
Theres little he will leave
Gain stooping for a single pin
Will stick it on his sleeve

For passers bye I never pin
No troubles to my breast
Nor carry round some names to win
More money from the rest
Im swordy well a piece of land
Thats fell upon the town
Who worked me till I couldnt stand
& crush me now Im down

In parish bonds I well may wail
Reduced to every shift
Pity may grieve at troubles tale
But cunning shares the gift
Harvests with plenty on his brow
Leaves losses taunts with me
Yet gain comes yearly with the plough
& will not let me be

Alas dependance thou'rt a brute
Want only understands
His feelings wither branch & root
That falls in parish hands
The muck that clouts the ploughmans shoe
The moss that hides the stone
Now Im become the parish due
Is more then I can own

Though Im no man yet any wrong
Some sort of right may seek
& I am glad if een a song
Gives me the room to speak
Ive got among such grubbling geer
& such a hungry pack
If I brought harvests twice a year
They'd bring me nothing back

When war their tyrant prices got
I trembled with alarms
They fell & saved my little spot
Or towns had turned to farms
Let profit keep an humble place
That gentry may be known
Let pedigrees their honours trace
& toil enjoy its own

The silver springs grown naked dykes
Scarce own a bunch of rushes
When grain got high the tasteless tykes
Grubbed up trees banks & bushes
& me they turned me inside out
For sand & grit & stones
& turned my old green hills about
& pickt my very bones

These things that claim my own as theirs
Where born but yesterday
But ere I fell to town affairs
I were as proud as they
I kept my horses cows & sheep
& built the town below
Ere they had cat or dog to keep
& then to use me so

Parish allowance gaunt & dread
Had it the earth to keep
Would even pine the bees to dead
To save an extra keep
Prides workhouse is a place that yields
From poverty its gains
& mines a workhouse for the fields
A starving the remains

The bees flye round in feeble rings
& find no blossom bye
Then thrum their almost weary wings
Upon the moss & die
Rabbits that find my hills turned oer
Forsake my poor abode
They dread a workhouse like the poor
& nibble on the road

If with a clover bottle now
Spring dares to lift her head
The next day brings the hasty plough
& makes me miserys bed
The butterflyes may wir & come
I cannot keep em now
Nor can they bear my parish home
That withers on my brow

No now not een a stone can lie
Im just what eer they like
My hedges like the winter flye
& leave me but the dyke
My gates are thrown from off the hooks
The parish thoroughfare
Lord he thats in the parish books
Has little wealth to spare

I couldnt keep a dust of grit
Nor scarce a grain of sand
But bags & carts claimed every bit
& now theyve got the land
I used to bring the summers life
To many a butterflye
But in oppressions iron strife
Dead tussocks bow & sigh

Ive scarce a nook to call my own
For things that creep or flye
The beetle hiding neath a stone
Does well to hurry bye
Stock eats my struggles every day
As bare as any road
He's sure to be in somthings way
If eer he stirs abroad

I am no man to whine & beg
But fond of freedom still
I hang no lies on pitys peg
To bring a grist to mill
On pitys back I neednt jump
My looks speak loud alone
My only tree they've left a stump
& nought remains my own

My mossy hills gains greedy hand
& more then greedy mind
Levels into a russet land
Nor leaves a bent behind
In summers gone I bloomed in pride
Folks came for miles to prize
My flowers that bloomed no where beside
& scarce believed their eyes

Yet worried with a greedy pack
They rend & delve & tear
The very grass from off my back
Ive scarce a rag to wear

Im fain to shun the greedy pack
That now so tear & brag
They strip my coat from off my back
& scarcely leave a rag
That like the parish hurt & hurt
While gains new suit I wear
Then swear I never pay 'em for't
& add to my despair

Though now I seem so full of clack
Yet when yer' riding bye
The very birds upon my back
Are not more fain to flye
I feel so lorn in this disgrace
God send the grains to fall
I am the oldest in the place
& the worst served of all

Lord bless ye I was kind to all
& poverty in me
Could always find a humble stall
A rest & lodging free
Poor bodys with an hungry ass
I welcomed many a day
& gave him tether room & grass
& never said him nay

There was a time my bit of ground
Made freemen of the slave
The ass no pindard dare to pound
When I his supper gave
The gipseys camp was not affraid
I made his dwelling free
Till vile enclosure came & made
A parish slave of me

The gipseys further on sojourn
No parish bonds they like
No sticks I own & would earth burn
I shouldnt own a dyke
I am no friend to lawless work
Nor would a rebel be
& why I call a christian turk
Is they are turks to me

& if I could but find a friend
With no deciet to sham
Who'd send me some few sheep to tend
& leave me as I am
To keep my hills from cart & plough
& strife of mongerel men
& as spring found me find me now
I should look up agen

& save his Lordships woods that past
The day of danger dwell
Of all the fields I am the last
That my own face can tell
Yet what with stone pits delving holes
& strife to buy & sell
My name will quickly be the whole
Thats left of swordy well

I Am

I am – yet what I am, none cares or knows;
   My friends forsake me like a memory lost:
I am the self-consumer of my woes –
   They rise and vanish in oblivion's host
Like shadows in love-frenzied stifled throes
   And yet I am, and live – like vapours tost

Into the nothingness of scorn and noise,
   Into the living sea of waking dreams,
Where there is neither sense of life or joys,
   But the vast shipwreck of my life's esteems;
Even the dearest that I love the best
   Are strange – nay, rather, stranger than the rest.

I long for scenes where man hath never trod
    A place where woman never smiled or wept
There to abide with my Creator, God,
    And sleep as I in childhood sweetly slept,
Untroubling and untroubled where I lie
    The grass below – above, the vaulted sky.

LUCILLE CLIFTON

(1936–2010)

the lost baby poem

the time i dropped your almost body down
down to meet the waters under the city
and run one with the sewage to the sea
what did i know about waters rushing back
what did i know about drowning
or being drowned

you would have been born into winter
in the year of the disconnected gas
and no car   we would have made the thin
walk over genesee hill into the canada wind
to watch you slip like ice into strangers' hands
you would have fallen naked as snow into winter
if you were here i could tell you these
and some other things

if i am ever less than a mountain
for your definite brothers and sisters
let the rivers pour over my head
let the sea take me for a spiller
of seas   let black men call me stranger
always   for your never named sake

SAMUEL TAYLOR COLERIDGE

(1772–1834)

Epitaph

Stop, Christian Passer-by! – Stop, child of God,
And read with gentle breast. Beneath this sod
A poet lies, or that which once seem'd he.
O, lift one thought in prayer for S. T. C.;
That he who many a year with toil of breath
Found death in life, may here find life in death!
Mercy for praise – to be forgiven for fame
He ask'd, and hoped, through Christ. Do thou the same!

TONY CONNOR

(1930–)

Elegy for Alfred Hubbard

Hubbard is dead, the old plumber:
who will mend our burst pipes now,
the tap that has dripped all the summer,
testing the sink's overflow?

No other like him. Young men with knowledge
of new techniques and theories from books
may better his work, straight from college,
but who will challenge his squint-eyed looks

in kitchen, bathroom, under floorboards,
rules of thumb which were often wrong;
seek as erringly stopcocks in cupboards,
or make a job last half as long?

He was a man who knew the ginnels
alleyways, streets – the whole district:
family secrets, minor annals,
time-honoured fictions fused to fact.

Seventy years of gossip muttered
under his cap, his tufty thatch,
so that his talk was slow and clotted,
hard to follow, and too much.

As though nothing fell, none vanished,
and time were the maze of Cheetham Hill,
in which the dead – with jobs unfinished
waited to hear him ring the bell.

For much he never got round to doing,
but meant to, when weather bucked up,
or worsened, or when his pipe was drawing,
or when he'd finished this cup.

I thought time, he forgot so often,
had forgotten him; but here's Death's pomp
over his house, and by the coffin
the son who will inherit his blowlamp,

tools, workshop, cart, and cornet
(pride of Cheetham Prize Brass Band),
and there's his mourning widow, Janet,
stood at the gate he'd promised to mend.

Soon he will make his final journey:
shaved and silent, strangely trim,
with never a pause to talk to any-
body: how arrow-like, for him!

In St Mark's Church, whose dismal tower
he pointed and painted when a lad,
they will sing his praises amidst flowers
while, somewhere, a cellar starts to flood,

and the housewife banging his front-door knocker
is not surprised to find him gone,
and runs for Thwaite, who's a better worker,
and sticks at a job until it's done.

ABRAHAM COWLEY

(1618–1667)

On the Death of Mr William Hervey

It was a dismal and a fearful night:
Scarce could the Morn drive on th' unwilling Light,
When Sleep, Death's image, left my troubled breast
 By something liker Death possest.
My eyes with tears did uncommanded flow,
 And on my soul hung the dull weight
 Of some intolerable fate.
What bell was that? Ah me! too much I know!

My sweet companion and my gentle peer,
Why hast thou left me thus unkindly here,
Thy end for ever and my life to moan?
 O, thou hast left me all alone!
Thy soul and body, when death's agony
 Besieged around thy noble heart,
 Did not with more reluctance part
Than I, my dearest Friend, do part from thee.

My dearest Friend, would I had died for thee!
Life and this world henceforth will tedious be:
Nor shall I know hereafter what to do
 If once my griefs prove tedious too.
Silent and sad I walk about all day,
 As sullen ghosts stalk speechless by
 Where their hid treasures lie;
Alas! my treasure's gone; why do I stay?

Say, for you saw us, ye immortal lights,
How oft unwearied have we spent the nights,
Till the Ledæan stars, so famed for love,
    Wonder'd at us from above!
We spent them not in toys, in lusts, or wine;
      But search of deep Philosophy,
        Wit, Eloquence, and Poetry –
Arts which I loved, for they, my Friend, were thine.

Ye fields of Cambridge, our dear Cambridge, say
Have ye not seen us walking every day?
Was there a tree about which did not know
    The love betwixt us two?
      Henceforth, ye gentle trees, for ever fade;
Or your sad branches thicker join
      And into darksome shades combine,
Dark as the grave wherein my Friend is laid!

Large was his soul: as large a soul as e'er
Submitted to inform a body here;
High as the place 'twas shortly in Heaven to have,
    But low and humble as his grave.
So high that all the virtues there did come,
      As to their chiefest seat
      Conspicuous and great;
So low, that for me too it made a room.

Knowledge he only sought, and so soon caught
As if for him Knowledge had rather sought;
Nor did more learning ever crowded lie
    In such a short mortality.
Whene'er the skilful youth discoursed or writ,
      Still did the notions throng
      About his eloquent tongue;
Nor could his ink flow faster than his wit.

His mirth was the pure spirits of various wit,
Yet never did his God or friends forget;
And when deep talk and wisdom came in view,
    Retired, and gave to them their due.
For the rich help of books he always took,
    Though his own searching mind before
    Was so with notions written o'er,
As if wise Nature had made that her book.

With as much zeal, devotion, piety,
He always lived, as other saints do die.
Still with his soul severe account he kept,
    Weeping all debts out ere he slept.
Then down in peace and innocence he lay,
    Like the Sun's laborious light,
    Which still in water sets at night,
Unsullied with his journey of the day.

But happy Thou, ta'en from this frantic age,
Where ignorance and hypocrisy does rage!
A fitter time for Heaven no soul e'er chose –
    The place now only free from those.
There 'mong the blest thou dost for ever shine;
    And wheresoe'er thou casts thy view
    Upon that white and radiant crew,
See'st not a soul clothed with more light than thine.

WILLIAM COWPER

(1731–1800)

Epitaph on a Hare

Here lies, whom hound did ne'er pursue,
    Nor swifter greyhound follow,
Whose foot ne'er tainted morning dew,
    Nor ear heard huntsman's hallo',

Old Tiney, surliest of his kind,
    Who, nursed with tender care,
And to domesticate bounds confined,
    Was still a wild jack-hare.

Though duly from my hand he took
    His pittance every night,
He did it with a jealous look,
    And, when he could, would bite.

His diet was of wheaten bread,
    And milk, and oats, and straw,
Thistles, or lettuces instead,
    With sand to scour his maw.

On twigs of hawthorn he regaled,
    On pippins' russet peel;
And, when his juicy salads failed,
    Sliced carrot pleased him well.

A Turkey carpet was his lawn,
    Whereon he loved to bound,
To skip and gambol like a fawn,
    And swing his rump around.

His frisking was at evening hours,
    For then he lost his fear;
But most before approaching showers,
    Or when a storm drew near.

Eight years and five round-rolling moons
    He thus saw steal away,
Dozing out all his idle noons,
    And every night at play.

I kept him for his humor's sake,
    For he would oft beguile
My heart of thoughts that made it ache,
    And force me to a smile.

But now, beneath this walnut-shade
    He finds his long, last home,
And waits in snug concealment laid,
    Till gentler Puss shall come.

He, still more agèd, feels the shocks
    From which no care can save,
And, partner once of Tiney's box,
    Must soon partake his grave.

The Poplar Field

The poplars are felled, farewell to the shade
And the whispering sound of the cool colonnade:
The winds play no longer and sing in the leaves,
Nor Ouse on his bosom their image receives.

Twelve years have elapsed since I first took a view
Of my favourite field, and the bank where they grew,
And now in the grass behold they are laid,
And the tree is my seat that once lent me a shade.

The blackbird has fled to another retreat
Where the hazels afford him a screen from the heat;
And the scene where his melody charmed me before
Resounds with his sweet-flowing ditty no more.

My fugitive years are all hasting away,
And I must ere long lie as lowly as they,
With a turf on my breast and a stone at my head,
Ere another such grove shall arise in its stead.

'Tis a sight to engage me, if anything can,
To muse on the perishing pleasures of man;
Short-lived as we are, our enjoyments, I see,
Have a still shorter date, and die sooner than we.

HART CRANE

(1899–1932)

At Melville's Tomb

Often beneath the wave, wide from this ledge
The dice of drowned men's bones he saw bequeath
An embassy. Their numbers as he watched,
Beat on the dusty shore and were obscured.

And wrecks passed without sound of bells,
The calyx of death's bounty giving back
A scattered chapter, livid hieroglyph,
The portent wound in corridors of shells.

Then in the circuit calm of one vast coil,
Its lashings charmed and malice reconciled,
Frosted eyes there were that lifted altars;
And silent answers crept across the stars.

Compass, quadrant and sextant contrive
No farther tides . . . High in the azure steeps
Monody shall not wake the mariner.
This fabulous shadow only the sea keeps.

RICHARD CRASHAW

(1613–1649)

A Hymn to the Name and Honour of the Admirable Saint Teresa

Love, thou are absolute, sole Lord
Of life and death. To prove the word,
We'll now appeal to none of all
Those thy old soldiers, great and tall,
Ripe men of martyrdom, that could reach down
With strong arms their triumphant crown:
Such as could with lusty breath
Speak loud, unto the face of death,
Their great Lord's glorious name; to none
Of those whose spacious bosoms spread a throne
For love at large to fill. Spare blood and sweat:
We'll see Him take a private seat,
And make His mansion in the mild
And milky soul of a soft child.
Scarce has she learnt to lisp a name
Of martyr, yet she thinks it shame
Life should so long play with that breath
Which spent can buy so brave a death.
She never undertook to know
What death with love should have to do.
Nor has she e'er yet understood
Why, to show love, she should shed blood;
Yet, though she cannot tell you why,
She can love, and she can die.
Scarce has she blood enough to make
A guilty sword blush for her sake;
Yet has a heart dares hope to prove
How much less strong is death than love . . .

Since 'tis not to be had at home,
She'll travel for a martyrdom.
No home for her, confesses she,
But where she may a martyr be.
She'll to the Moors, and trade with them
For this unvalued diadem;
She offers them her dearest breath,
With Christ's name in't, in charge for death:
She'll bargain with them, and will give
Them God, and teach them how to live
In Him; or, if they this deny,
For Him she'll teach them how to die.
So shall she leave amongst them sown
Her Lord's blood, or at least her own.

Farewell then, all the world, adieu!
Teresa is no more for you.
Farewell all pleasures, sports, and joys,
Never till now esteemèd toys!

Farewell whatever dear may be –
Mother's arms, or father's knee!
Farewell house, and farewell home!
She's for the Moors and Martyrdom.

Sweet, not so fast; lo! thy fair spouse,
Whom thou seek'st with so swift vows,
Calls thee back, and bids thee come
T' embrace a milder martyrdom . . .

O how oft shalt thou complain
Of a sweet and subtle pain!
Of intolerable joys!
Of a death, in which who dies
Loves his death, and dies again,
And would for ever so be slain;
And lives and dies, and knows not why
To live, but that he still may die!
How kindly will thy gentle heart

Kiss the sweetly-killing dart!
And close in his embraces keep
Those delicious wounds, that weep
Balsam, to heal themselves with thus,
When these thy deaths, so numerous,
Shall all at once die into one,
And melt thy soul's sweet mansion;
Like a soft lump of incense, hasted
By too hot a fire, and wasted
Into perfuming clouds, so fast
Shalt thou exhale to heaven at last
In a resolving sigh, and then, –
O what? Ask not the tongues of men.

Angels cannot tell; suffice,
Thyself shalt feel thine own full joys,
And hold them fast for ever there.
So soon as thou shalt first appear,
The moon of maiden stars, thy white
Mistress, attended by such bright
Souls as thy shining self, shall come,
And in her first ranks make thee room;
Where, 'mongst her snowy family,
Immortal welcomes wait for thee.
O what delight, when she shall stand
And teach thy lips heaven, with her hand,
On which thou now may'st to thy wishes
Heap up thy consecrated kisses!
What joy shall seize thy soul, when she,
Bending her blessèd eyes on thee,
Those second smiles of heaven, shall dart
Her mild rays through thy melting heart!

Angels, thy old friends, there shall greet thee,
Glad at their own home now to meet thee.
All thy good works which went before,
And waited for thee at the door,
Shall own thee there; and all in one
Weave a constellation

Of crowns, with which the King, thy spouse,
Shall build up thy triumphant brows.
All thy old woes shall now smile on thee,
And thy pains sit bright upon thee:
All thy sorrows here shall shine,
And thy sufferings be divine.
Tears shall take comfort, and turn gems,
And wrongs repent to diadems.
Even thy deaths shall live, and new
Dress the soul which late they slew.
Thy wounds shall blush to such bright scars
As keep account of the Lamb's wars.

Those rare works, where thou shalt leave writ
Love's noble history, with wit
Taught thee by none but Him, while here
They feed our souls, shall clothe thine there.
Each heavenly word by whose hid flame
Our hard hearts shall strike fire, the same
Shall flourish on thy brows, and be
Both fire to us and flame to thee;
Whose light shall live bright in thy face
By glory, in our hearts by grace.
Thou shalt look round about, and see
Thousands of crown'd souls throng to be
Themselves thy crown, sons of thy vows,
The virgin-births with which thy spouse
Made fruitful thy fair soul; go now,
And with them all about thee bow
To Him; put on, He'll say, put on,
My rosy Love, that thy rich zone,
Sparkling with the sacred flames
Of thousand souls, whose happy names
Heaven keeps upon thy score: thy bright
Life brought them first to kiss the light
That kindled them to stars; and so
Thou with the Lamb, thy Lord, shalt go.

And, wheresoe'er He sets His white
Steps, walk with Him those ways of light,
Which who in death would live to see,
Must learn in life to die like thee.

An Epitaph upon Husband and Wife

(Who Died and Were Buried Together)

To these whom death again did wed
This grave's the second marriage-bed.
For though the hand of Fate could force
'Twixt soul and body a divorce,
It could not sever man and wife,
Because they both lived but one life.
Peace, good reader, do not weep;
Peace, the lovers are asleep.
They, sweet turtles, folded lie
In the last knot that love could tie.
Let them sleep, let them sleep on,
Till the stormy night be gone,
And the eternal morrow dawn;
Then the curtains will be drawn,
And they wake into a light
Whose day shall never die in night.

COUNTEE CULLEN
(1903–1946)

Colored Blues Singer

Some weep to find the Golden Pear
Feeds maggots at the core,
And some grow cold as ice, and bear
Them prouder than before.

But you go singing like the sea
Whose lover turns to land;
You make your grief a melody
And take it by the hand.

Such songs the mellow-bosomed maids
Of Africa intone
For lovers dead in hidden glades,
Slow rotting flesh and bone.

Such keenings tremble from the kraal,
Where sullen-browed abides
The second wife whose dark tears fail
To draw him to her sides.

Somewhere Jeritza breaks her heart
On symbols Verdi wrote;
You tear the strings of your soul apart,
Blood dripping note by note.

Threnody for a Brown Girl

Weep not, you who love her –
What rebellious flow
Grief undams shall recover
Whom the gods bid go?
Sorrow rising like a wall,
Bitter, blasphemous –
What avails it to recall
Beauty back to us?

Think not this grave shall keep her,
This marriage-bed confine;
Death may dig it deep and deeper –
She shall climb it like a vine.
Body that was quick and sentient,
Dear as thought or speech,
Death could not, with one trenchant
Blow, snatch out of reach!

She is nearer than the word
Wasted on her now,
Nearer than the swaying bird
On its rhythmic bough.
Only were our faith as much
As a mustard seed,
Aching hungry hands might touch
Her as they touch a reed.

Life, who was not loth to trade
Her unto death, has done
Better than he planned, has made
Her wise as Solomon.
Now she knows the Why and Wherefore,
Troublous Whence and Whither;
Why men strive and sweat, and care for
Bays that droop and wither.

All the stars she knows by name,
End and origin thereof,
Knows if love be kin to shame,
If shame be less than love.
What was crooked now is straight,
What was rough is plain;
Grief and sorrow have no weight
Now to cause her pain.

One to her are flame and frost;
Silence is her singing lark.
We alone are children – lost,
Crying in the dark.
Varied features now, and form
Change has bred upon her;
Crush no bug or nauseous worm
Lest you tread upon her.

Pluck no flower lest she scream;
Bruise no slender reed
Lest it prove more than it seem,
Lest she groan and bleed.
More than ever trust your brother,
Read him golden, pure –
It may be she finds no other
House so safe and sure.

Set no poet carving
Rhymes to make her laugh;
Only live hearts starving
Need an epitaph.
Lay upon her no white stone
From a foreign quarry;
Earth and sky, be these alone
Her obituary.

Swift as startled fawn or swallow,
Silence all her sound,
She has fled; we cannot follow
Further than this mound.
We who take the beaten track,
Trying to appease
Hearts near breaking with their lack,
We need elegies.

WALTER DE LA MARE
(1873–1956)

Fare Well

When I lie where shades of darkness
Shall no more assail mine eyes,
Nor the rain make lamentation
    When the wind sighs;
How will fare the world whose wonder
Was the very proof of me?
Memory fades, must the remembered
    Perishing be?

Oh, when this my dust surrenders
Hand, foot, lip, to dust again,
May these loved and loving faces
    Please other men!
May the rusting harvest hedgerow
Still the Traveller's Joy entwine,
And as happy children gather
    Posies once mine.

Look thy last on all things lovely,
Every hour. Let no night
Seal thy sense in deathly slumber
    Till to delight
Thou have paid thy utmost blessing;
Since that all things thou wouldst praise
Beauty took from those who loved them
    In other days.

TOI DERRICOTTE

(1941–)

Elegy for my Husband

Bruce Derricotte, June 22, 1928–June 21, 2011

What was there is no longer there:
Not the blood running its wires of flame through the whole length
Not the memories, the texts written in the language of the flat hills
No, not the memories, the porch swing and the father crying
The genteel and elegant aunt bleeding out on the highway
(Too black for the white ambulance to pick up)
Who had sent back lacquered plates from China
Who had given away her best ivory comb that one time she was
    angry
Not the muscles, the ones the white girls longed to touch
But must not (for your mother warned
You would be lynched in that all-white Ohio town you grew up in)
Not that same town where you were the only, the one good
    black boy
All that is gone
Not the muscles running, the baseball flying into your mitt
Not the hand that laid itself over my heart and saved me
Not the eyes that held the long gold tunnel I believed in
Not the restrained hand in love and in anger
Not the holding back
Not the taut holding

EMILY DICKINSON
(1830–1886)

'Because I could not stop for Death'

Because I could not stop for Death –
He kindly stopped for me –
The Carriage held but just Ourselves –
And Immortality.

We slowly drove – He knew no haste
And I had put away
My labor and my leisure too,
For His Civility –

We passed the School, where Children strove
At Recess – in the Ring –
We passed the Fields of Gazing Grain –
We passed the Setting Sun –

Or rather – He passed Us –
The Dews drew quivering and chill –
For only Gossamer, my Gown –
My Tippet – only Tulle –

We paused before a House that seemed
A Swelling of the Ground –
The Roof was scarcely visible –
The Cornice – in the Ground –

Since then –'tis Centuries – and yet
Feels shorter than the Day
I first surmised the Horses' Heads
Were toward Eternity –

'Safe in their Alabaster Chambers'

Safe in their Alabaster Chambers –
Untouched by Morning –
And untouched by Noon –
Lie the meek members of the Resurrection –
Rafter of Satin – and Roof of Stone!

Grand go the Years – in the Crescent – above them –
Worlds scoop their Arcs –
And Firmaments – row –
Diadems – drop – and Doges – surrender –
Soundless as dots – on a Disc of Snow –

'I felt a Funeral, in my Brain'

I felt a Funeral, in my Brain,
And Mourners to and fro
Kept treading – treading – till it seemed
That Sense was breaking through –

And when they all were seated,
A Service, like a Drum –
Kept beating – beating – till I thought
My Mind was going numb –

And then I heard them lift a Box
And creak across my Soul
With those same Boots of Lead, again,
Then Space – began to toll,

As all the Heavens were a Bell,
And Being, but an Ear,
And I, and Silence, some strange Race
Wrecked, solitary, here –

And then a Plank in Reason, broke,
And I dropped down, and down –
And hit a World, at every plunge,
And Finished knowing – then –

MAURA DOOLEY

(1957–)

I've Been Thinking a Lot About Heaven

I watched him tidy up his sorrow,
tuck it into his pocket, slide it into a pit
cleared for the bulb of a snowdrop
but grief is slippery, ungainly, ugly.
O chokey, noisy, bullying grief!

I'm thinking a lot about Heaven
while this train cuts a line from
Doncaster to Retford, through a blur
of mist on the meadows and towns.
Last night's rain and morning dew

and the suddenness of swifts is a curlicue
on blue, blue which I know
is a matter of wavelength and molecule
but which is also distance, *blue-remembered,*
and an unknown spire piercing the heart.

JOHN DONNE
(1572–1631)

A Funeral Elegy

'Tis lost, to trust a tomb with such a guest,
  Or to confine her in a marble chest.
Alas, what's marble, jet, or porphyry,
  Prized with the chrysolite of either eye,
Or with those pearls, and rubies which she was?
  Join the two Indies in one tomb, 'tis glass;
And so is all to her materials,
  Though every inch were ten Escurials,
Yet she's demolished: can we keep her then
  In works of hands, or of the wits of men?
Can these memorials, rags of paper, give
  Life to that name, by which name they must live?
Sickly, alas, short-lived, aborted be
  Those carcase verses, whose soul is not she.
And can she, who no longer would be she,
  Being such a tabernacle, stoop to be
In paper wrapped; or, when she would not lie
  In such a house, dwell in an elegy?
But 'tis no matter; we may well allow
  Verse to live so long as the world will now.
For her death wounded it. The world contains
  Princes for arms, and counsellors for brains,
Lawyers for tongues, divines for hearts, and more,
  The rich for stomachs, and for backs, the poor;
The officers for hands, merchants for feet
  By which remote and distant countries meet.
But those fine spirits which do tune and set
  This organ, are those pieces which beget
Wonder and love; and these were she; and she
  Being spent, the world must needs decrepit be.
For since death will proceed to triumph still,

He can find nothing, after her, to kill,
Except the world itself, so great as she.
  Thus brave and confident may Nature be,
Death cannot give her such another blow,
  Because she cannot such another show.
But must we say she's dead? may't not be said
  That as a sundered clock is piecemeal laid,
Not to be lost, but by the maker's hand
  Repolished, without error then to stand,
Or as the Afric Niger stream enwombs
  Itself into the earth, and after comes
(Having first made a natural bridge, to pass
  For many leagues) far greater than it was,
May't not be said, that her grave shall restore
  Her, greater, purer, firmer, than before?
Heaven may say this, and joy in't; but can we
  Who live, and lack her, here this vantage see?
What is't to us, alas, if there have been
  An Angel made a Throne, or Cherubin?
We lose by't: and as aged men are glad
  Being tasteless grown, to joy in joys they had,
So now the sick starved world must feed upon
  This joy, that we had her, who now is gone.
Rejoice then Nature, and this world, that you,
  Fearing the last fires hastening to subdue
Your force and vigour, ere it were near gone,
  Wisely bestowed and laid it all on one.
One, whose clear body was so pure, and thin,
  Because it need disguise no thought within.
'Twas but a through-light scarf, her mind to enrol,
  Or exhalation breathed out from her soul.
One, whom all men who durst no more, admired,
  And whom, whoe'er had worth enough, desired;
As when a temple's built, saints emulate
  To which of them, it shall be consecrate.
But as when heaven looks on us with new eyes,
  Those new stars every artist exercise,
What place they should assign to them they doubt,
  Argue, and agree not till those stars go out:

So the world studied whose this piece should be,
   Till she can be nobody's else, nor she:
But like a lamp of balsamum, desired
   Rather to adorn than last, she soon expired,
Clothed in her virgin white integrity;
   For marriage, though it do not stain, doth dye.
To 'scape th' infirmities which wait upon
   Woman, she went away, before she was one;
And the world's busy noise to overcome,
   Took so much death, as served for opium.
For though she could not, nor could choose to die,
   She hath yielded to too long an ecstasy.
He which not knowing her sad history,
   Should come to read the book of destiny,
How fair and chaste, humble and high she had been,
   Much promised, much performed, at not fifteen,
And measuring future things by things before,
   Should turn the leaf to read, and read no more,
Would think that either destiny mistook,
   Or that some leaves were torn out of the book.
But 'tis not so; Fate did but usher her
   To years of reason's use, and then infer
Her destiny to herself; which liberty
   She took but for thus much, thus much to die.
Her modesty not suffering her to be
   Fellow-commissioner with Destiny,
She did no more but die; if after her
   Any shall live, which dare true good prefer,
Every such person is her delegate,
   T' accomplish that which should have been her fate.
They shall make up that book, and shall have thanks
   Of Fate, and her, for filling up their blanks.
For future virtuous deeds are legacies,
   Which from the gift of her example rise;
And 'tis in heaven part of spiritual mirth,
   To see how well the good play her, on earth.

LORD ALFRED DOUGLAS

(1870–1945)

The Dead Poet

I dreamed of him last night, I saw his face
All radiant and unshadowed of distress,
And as of old, in music measureless,
I heard his golden voice and marked him trace
Under the common thing the hidden grace,
And conjure wonder out of emptiness,
Till mean things put on beauty like a dress
And all the world was an enchanted place.

And then methought outside a fast locked gate
I mourned the loss of unrecorded words,
Forgotten tales and mysteries half said,
Wonders that might have been articulate,
And voiceless thoughts like murdered singing birds.
And so I woke and knew that he was dead.

KEITH DOUGLAS

(1920–1944)

Simplify Me When I'm Dead

Remember me when I am dead
and simplify me when I'm dead.

As the processes of earth
strip off the colour and the skin
take the brown hair and blue eye

and leave me simpler than at birth,
when hairless I came howling in
as the moon came in the cold sky.

Of my skeleton perhaps
so stripped, a learned man will say
'He was of such a type and intelligence,' no more.

Thus when in a year collapse
particular memories, you may
deduce, from the long pain I bore

the opinions I held, who was my foe
and what I left, even my appearance
but incidents will be no guide.

Time's wrong-way telescope will show
a minute man ten years hence
and by distance simplified.

Through that lens see if I seem
substance or nothing: of the world
deserving mention or charitable oblivion

not by momentary spleen
or love into decision hurled,
leisurely arrive at an opinion.

Remember me when I am dead
and simplify me when I'm dead.

Vergissmeinnicht

Three weeks gone and the combatants gone
returning over the nightmare ground
we found the place again, and found
the soldier sprawling in the sun.

The frowning barrel of his gun
overshadowing. As we came on
that day, he hit my tank with one
like the entry of a demon.

Look. Here in the gunpit spoil
the dishonoured picture of his girl
who has put: *Steffi. Vergissmeinnicht*
in a copybook gothic script.

We see him almost with content,
abased, and seeming to have paid
and mocked at by his own equipment
that's hard and good when he's decayed.

But she would weep to see today
how on his skin the swart flies move;
the dust upon the paper eye
and the burst stomach like a cave.

For here the lover and killer are mingled
who had one body and one heart.
And death who had the soldier singled
has done the lover mortal hurt.

JOHN DRYDEN
(1631–1700)

Upon the Death of the Lord Hastings

Must noble Hastings immaturely die,
The honour of his ancient family,
Beauty and learning thus together meet,
To bring a winding for a wedding sheet?
Must virtue prove death's harbinger? must she,
With him expiring, feel mortality?
Is death, sin's wages, grace's now? shall art
Make us more learned, only to depart?
If merit be disease; if virtue, death;
To be good, not to be; who'd then bequeath
Himself to discipline? who'd not esteem
Labour a crime? study self-murder deem?
Our noble youth now have pretence to be
Dunces securely, ignorant healthfully.
Rare linguist, whose worth speaks itself, whose praise,
Though not his own, all tongues besides do raise:
Than whom great Alexander may seem less,
Who conquered men, but not their languages.
In his mouth nations speak; his tongue might be
Interpreter to Greece, France, Italy.
His native soil was the four parts o' the earth;
All Europe was too narrow for his birth.
A young apostle; and, – with reverence may
I speak't, – inspired with gift of tongues, as they.
Nature gave him, a child, what men in vain
Oft strive, by art though furthered, to obtain.
His body was an orb, his sublime soul
Did move on virtue's and on learning's pole;
Whose regular motions better to our view,
Than Archimedes' sphere, the heavens did shew.
Graces and virtues, languages and arts,

Beauty and learning, filled up all the parts.
Heaven's gifts, which do like falling stars appear
Scattered in others, all, as in their sphere,
Were fixed, and conglobate in's soul, and thence
Shone through his body, with sweet influence;
Letting their glories so on each limb fall,
The whole frame rendered was celestial.
Come, learned Ptolemy, and trial make,
If thou this hero's altitude can'st take:
But that transcends thy skill; thrice happy all,
Could we but prove thus astronomical.
Lived Tycho now, struck with this ray which shone
More bright i' the morn, than others beam at noon,
He'd take his astrolabe, and seek out here
What new star 'twas did gild our hemisphere.
Replenished then with such rare gifts as these,
Where was room left for such a foul disease?
The nation's sin hath drawn that veil, which shrouds
Our day-spring in so sad benighting clouds.
Heaven would no longer trust its pledge, but thus
Recalled it, – rapt its Ganymede from us.
Was there no milder way but the small-pox,
The very filthiness of Pandora's box?
So many spots, like næves, our Venus soil?
One jewel set off with so many a foil;
Blisters with pride swelled, which through's flesh did sprout
Like rosebuds, stuck i' the lily-skin about.
Each little pimple had a tear in it,
To wail the fault its rising did commit;
Which, rebel-like, with its own lord at strife,
Thus made an insurrection 'gainst his life.
Or were these gems sent to adorn his skin,
The cabinet of a richer soul within?
No comet need foretell his change drew on,
Whose corpse might seem a constellation.
Oh had he died of old, how great a strife
Had been, who from his death should draw their life;
Who should, by one rich draught, become whate'er
Seneca, Cato, Numa, Cæsar, were!

Learned, virtuous, pious, great; and have by this
An universal metempsychosis.
Must all these aged sires in one funeral
Expire? all die in one so young, so small?
Who, had he lived his life out, his great fame
Had swoln 'bove any Greek or Roman name.
But hasty winter, with one blast, hath brought
The hopes of autumn, summer, spring, to nought.
Thus fades the oak i' the sprig, i' the blade the corn;
Thus without young, this Phœnix dies, newborn.
Must then old three-legged grey-beards with their gout,
Catarrhs, rheums, aches, live three ages out?
Time's offals, only fit for the hospital!
Or to hang an antiquary's rooms withal!
Must drunkards, lechers, spent with sinning, live
With such helps as broths, possets, physic give?
None live, but such as should die? shall we meet
With none but ghostly fathers in the street?
Grief makes me rail, sorrow will force its way,
And showers of tears tempestuous sighs best lay.
The tongue may fail; but overflowing eyes
Will weep out lasting streams of elegies.
But thou, O virgin-widow, left alone,
Now thy beloved, heaven-ravished spouse is gone,
Whose skilful sire in vain strove to apply
Med'cines, when thy balm was no remedy;
With greater than Platonic love, O wed
His soul, though not his body, to thy bed:
Let that make thee a mother; bring thou forth
The ideas of his virtue, knowledge, worth;
Transcribe the original in new copies; give
Hastings o' the better part: so shall he live
In's nobler half; and the great grandsire be
Of an heroic divine progeny:
An issue which to eternity shall last,
Yet but the irradiations which he cast.
Erect no mausoleums; for his best
Monument is his spouse's marble breast.

To the Memory of Mr Oldham

Farewell, too little and too lately known,
Whom I began to think and call my own;
For sure our souls were near allied; and thine
Cast in the same poetic mould with mine.
One common note on either lyre did strike,
And knaves and fools we both abhorred alike:
To the same goal did both our studies drive,
The last set out the soonest did arrive.
Thus Nisus fell upon the slippery place,
While his young friend performed and won the race.
O early ripe – to thy abundant store
What could advancing age have added more?
It might (what nature never gives the young)
Have taught the numbers of thy native tongue.
But satire needs not those, and wit will shine
Through the harsh cadence of a rugged line:
A noble error, and but seldom made,
When poets are by too much force betrayed.
Thy generous fruits, though gathered ere their prime
Still showed a quickness; and maturing time
But mellows what we write to the dull sweets of rhyme.
Once more, hail and farewell; farewell thou young
But ah too short, Marcellus of our tongue;
Thy brows with ivy, and with laurels bound;
But fate and gloomy night encompass thee around.

PAUL LAURENCE DUNBAR

(1872–1906)

A Death Song

Lay me down beneaf de willers in de grass,
Whah de branch 'll go a-singin' as it pass.
　　An' w'en I 's a-layin' low,
　　I kin hyeah it as it go
Singin', 'Sleep, my honey, tek yo' res' at las'.'

Lay me nigh to whah hit meks a little pool,
An' de watah stan's so quiet lak an' cool,
　　Whah de little birds in spring,
　　Ust to come an' drink an' sing,
An' de chillen waded on dey way to school.

Let me settle w'en my shouldahs draps dey load
Nigh enough to hyeah de noises in de road;
　　Fu' I t'ink de las' long res'
　　Gwine to soothe my sperrit bes'
Ef I 's layin' 'mong de t'ings I 's allus knowed.

WILLIAM DUNBAR

(1459–1520)

Lament for the Makaris

I that in heill wes and gladnes,
Am trublit now with gret seiknes,
And feblit with infermite;
Timor mortis conturbat me.

Our plesance heir is all vane glory,
This fals warld is bot transitory,
The flesche is brukle, the Fend is sle;
Timor mortis conturbat me.

The stait of man dois change and vary,
Now sound, now seik, now blith, now sary,
Now dansand mery, now like to dee;
Timor mortis conturbat me.

No stait in erd heir standis sickir;
As with the wynd wavis the wickir,
Wavis this warldis vanite.
Timor mortis conturbat me.

On to the ded gois all estatis,
Princis, prelotis, and potestatis,
Baith riche and pur of al degre;
Timor mortis conturbat me.

He takis the knychtis in to feild,
Anarmit under helme and scheild;
Victour he is at all mellie;
Timor mortis conturbat me.

That strang unmercifull tyrand
Takis, on the moderis breist sowkand,
The bab full of benignite;
Timor mortis conturbat me.

He takis the campion in the stour,
The capitane closit in the tour,
The lady in bour full of bewte;
Timor mortis conturbat me.

He sparis no lord for his piscence,
Na clerk for his intelligence;
His awfull strak may no man fle;
Timor mortis conturbat me.

Art-magicianis, and astrologgis,
Rethoris, logicianis, and theologgis,
Thame helpis no conclusionis sle;
Timor mortis conturbat me.

In medicyne the most practicianis,
Lechis, surrigianis, and phisicianis,
Thame self fra ded may not supple;
Timor mortis conturbat me.

I se that makaris amang the laif
Playis heir ther pageant, syne gois to graif;
Sparit is nocht ther faculte;
Timor mortis conturbat me.

He hes done petuously devour,
The noble Chaucer, of makaris flour,
The Monk of Bery, and Gower, all thre;
Timor mortis conturbat me.

The gude Syr Hew of Eglintoun,
And eik Heryot, and Wyntoun,
He hes tane out of this cuntre;
Timor mortis conturbat me.

That scorpion fell hes done infek
Maister Johne Clerk, and Jame Afflek,
Fra balat making and tragidie;
Timor mortis conturbat me.

Holland and Barbour he hes berevit;
Allace! that he nocht with us levit
Schir Mungo Lokert of the Le;
Timor mortis conturbat me.

Clerk of Tranent eik he has tane,
That maid the Anteris of Gawane;
Schir Gilbert Hay endit hes he;
Timor mortis conturbat me.

He hes Blind Hary and Sandy Traill
Slaine with his schour of mortall haill,
Quhilk Patrik Johnestoun myght nocht fle;
Timor mortis conturbat me.

He hes reft Merseir his endite,
That did in luf so lifly write,
So schort, so quyk, of sentence hie;
Timor mortis conturbat me.

He hes tane Roull of Aberdene,
And gentill Roull of Corstorphin;
Two bettir fallowis did no man se;
Timor mortis conturbat me.

In Dumfermelyne he hes done roune
With Maister Robert Henrisoun;
Schir Johne the Ros enbrast hes he;
Timor mortis conturbat me.

And he hes now tane, last of aw,
Gud gentill Stobo and Quintyne Schaw,
Of quham all wichtis hes pete:
Timor mortis conturbat me.

Gud Maister Walter Kennedy
In poynt of dede lyis veraly,
Gret reuth it wer that so suld be;
Timor mortis conturbat me.

Sen he hes all my brether tane,
He will nocht lat me lif alane,
On forse I man his nyxt pray be;
Timor mortis conturbat me.

Sen for the deid remeid is none,
Best is that we for dede dispone,
Eftir our deid that lif may we;
Timor mortis conturbat me.

DOUGLAS DUNN

(1942–)

The Kaleidoscope

To climb these stairs again, bearing a tray,
Might be to find you pillowed with your books,
Your inventories listing gowns and frocks
As if preparing for a holiday.
Or, turning from the landing, I might find
My presence watched through your kaleidoscope,
A symmetry of husbands, each redesigned
In lovely forms of foresight, prayer and hope.
I climb these stairs a dozen times a day
And, by that open door, wait, looking in
At where you died. My hands become a tray
Offering me, my flesh, my soul, my skin.
Grief wrongs us so. I stand, and wait, and cry
For the absurd forgiveness, not knowing why.

LADY KATHERINE DYER

(c. 1585–1654)

'My dearest dust could not thy hasty day . . .'

My dearest dust, could not thy hasty day
Afford thy drowzy patience leave to stay
One hower longer: so that we might either
Sate up, or gone to bedd together?
But since thy finisht labor hath possest
Thy weary limbs with early rest,
Enjoy it sweetly: and thy widdowe bride
Shall soone repose her by thy slumbering side.
Whose business, now, is only to prepare
My nightly dress, and call to prayre:
Mine eyes wax heavy and ye day growes old.
The dew falls thick, my beloved growes cold.
Draw, draw ye closed curtaynes: and make room:
My dear, my dearest dust; I come, I come.

T. S. ELIOT
(1888–1965)

from *The Waste Land*

Death by Water

Phlebas the Phoenician, a fortnight dead,
Forgot the cry of gulls, and the deep sea swell
And the profit and loss.

                    A current under sea
Picked his bones in whispers. As he rose and fell
He passed the stages of his age and youth
Entering the whirlpool.

                    Gentile or Jew
O you who turn the wheel and look to windward,
Consider Phlebas, who was once handsome and tall as you.

RALPH WALDO EMERSON
(1803–1882)

from *Threnody*

The South-wind brings
Life, sunshine, and desire,
And on every mount and meadow
Breathes aromatic fire;
But over the dead he has no power.
The lost, the lost, he cannot restore;
And, looking over the hills, I mourn
The darling who shall not return.

I see my empty house,
I see my trees repair their boughs;
And he, the wondrous child,
Whose silver warble wild
Outvalued every pulsing sound
Within the air's cerulean round, –
The hyacinthine boy, for whom
Morn well might break and April bloom, –
The gracious boy, who did adorn
The world whereinto he was born,
And by his countenance repay
The favor of the loving Day, –
Has disappeared from the Day's eye;
Far and wide she cannot find him;
My hopes pursue, they cannot bind him.
Returned this day, the south wind searches,
And finds young pines and budding birches;
But finds not the budding man;
Nature, who lost him, cannot remake him;
Fate let him fall, Fate can't retake him;
Nature, Fate, Men, him seek in vain.

And whither now, my truant wise and sweet,
O, whither rend thy feet?
I had the right, few days ago,
Thy steps to watch, thy place to know;
How have I forfeited the right?
Hast thou forgot me in a new delight?

VICKI FEAVER

(1943–)

Gorilla

He was my first love.
Why else would I cycle, every Saturday,
to the museum in the park?

It wasn't the working model
of a coal mine, or specimen jars
of seasonal wild flowers,

or the families of striped snails
and black and white plaster mice
demonstrating the Laws of Mendel.

I headed straight past the jigsaw-
coated giraffe (its head peering
over the balcony) to a case

stuck away in a gloomy corner;
but not so dark I couldn't see
the glossy pouch of his penis and balls.

He was posed against a backdrop of jungle,
one arm grasping a vine,
standing on two legs like a man.

The boys at the dancing class
(I always got the spotty or fat ones)
gripped me with clammy paws.

His hands were like padded gloves
stitched from smooth black leather.
He could swing me off the floor.

I looked up at his lolling tongue;
at his jaw of ferocious teeth.
I gazed into his yellow eyes:

and he gazed back, as if to say,
*if you loved me enough
you could bring me back to life.*

CALEB FEMI

(1990–)

The Story of Damilola Taylor

A happy boy lived and his warmth filled the corridors of the block.
Go well where you go, boy with a smile like a burning chariot.

JAMES FENTON

(1949–)

At the Kerb

i.m. Mick Imlah

Grief to bestow, where once they bestowed their beauty,
Who are these mourners processing to the grave,
Each bearing a history like a precious ointment
And tender on their sleeves the wounds of love?

Brutal disease has numbered him a victim,
As if some unmarked car had appeared one day
And snatched him off to torture and confinement,
Then dumped him by the kerbside and sped away;

As if they stooped now at the kerb to lift the body,
As if they broke the jars and the unguent flowed,
Flowed down the sleeves and wounds, ran down the kerbstones,
Grief to bestow what beauty once bestowed.

SARAH LOUISA FORTEN
(1814–1883)

The Grave of the Slave

The cold storms of winter shall chill him no more,
His woes and his sorrows, his pains are all o'er, –

The sod of the valley now covers his form,
He is safe in his last home, and fears not the storm.

The poor slave is laid all unheeded and lone,
Where the rich and the poor find a permanent home;
No master can raise him, with voice of command,
He knows not, he hears not, his cruel demand.

Not a tear, not a sigh, to embalm his cold tomb,
No friend to lament him, no child to bemoan;
Not a stone marks the place, where he peacefully lies,
The earth for his pillow, his curtain the skies.

Poor slave! shall we sorrow that death was thy friend?
The last, and the kindest, that Heaven could send: –
The grave to the weary is welcomed and blest;
And death, to the captive, is freedom and rest.

ROBERT FROST
(1874–1963)

Nothing Gold Can Stay

Nature's first green is gold,
Her hardest hue to hold.
Her early leaf's a flower;
But only so an hour.
Then leaf subsides to leaf,
So Eden sank to grief,
So dawn goes down to day.
Nothing gold can stay.

ROBERT GARIOCH

(1909–1981)

Elegy

They are lang deid, folk that I used to ken
their firm set lips aa mowdert and agley,
sherp-tempert een rusty amang the cley:
they are baith deid, thae wycelike, bienlie men,

heidmaisters, that had been in pouer for ten
or twenty year afore fate's taiglie wey
brocht me, a young, weill-harnit, blate and fey
new-cleckit dominie, intill their den.

Ane tellt me it was time I learnt to write –
round-haund, he meant – and saw about my hair:
I mind of him, beld-heidit, wi a kyte.
Ane sneerit quarterly – I cuidna square
my savings bank – and sniftert in his spite.
Weill, gin they arena deid, it's time they were.

JOHN GAY
(1685–1732)

My Own Epitaph

Life is a jest; and all things show it.
I thought so once; but now I know it.

ALLEN GINSBERG

(1926–1997)

from *Kaddish*

For Naomi Ginsberg, 1894–1956

5

Caw caw caw crows shriek in the white sun over grave stones in
    Long Island
Lord Lord Lord Naomi underneath this grass my halflife and my
    own as hers
caw caw my eye be buried in the same Ground where I stand in
    Angel
Lord Lord great Eye that stares on All and moves in a black cloud
caw caw strange cry of Beings flung up into sky over the waving
    trees
Lord Lord O Grinder of giant Beyonds my voice in a boundless
    field in Sheol
Caw caw the call of Time rent out of foot and wing an instant in
    the universe
Lord Lord an echo in the sky the wind through ragged leaves the
    roar of memory
caw caw all years my birth a dream caw caw New York the bus
    the broken shoe the vast highschool caw caw all Visions of
    the Lord
Lord Lord Lord caw caw caw Lord Lord Lord caw caw caw Lord

OLIVER GOLDSMITH

(1728–1774)

Retaliation

Of old, when Scarron his companions invited,
Each guest brought his dish, and the feast was united;
If our landlord supplies us with beef, and with fish,
Let each guest bring himself, and he brings the best dish:
Our Dean shall be venison, just fresh from the plains;
Our Burke shall be tongue, with a garnish of brains;
Our Will shall be wild fowl, of excellent flavour,
And Dick with his pepper, shall heighten their savour:
Our Cumberland's sweet-bread its place shall obtain,
And Douglass's pudding, substantial and plain:
Our Garrick's a sallad, for in him we see
Oil, vinegar, sugar, and saltness agree:
To make out the dinner, full certain I am,
That Ridge is anchovy, and Reynolds is lamb;
That Hickey's a capon, and by the same rule,
Magnanimous Goldsmith, a goosberry fool:
At a dinner so various, at such a repast,
Who'd not be a glutton, and stick to the last:
Here, waiter, more wine, let me sit while I'm able,
'Till all my companions sink under the table;
Then with chaos and blunders encircling my head,
Let me ponder, and tell what I think of the dead.

Here lies the good Dean, re-united to earth,
Who mixt reason with pleasure, and wisdom with mirth:
If he had any faults, he has left us in doubt,
At least, in six weeks, I could not find 'em out;
Yet some have declar'd, and it can't be denied 'em,
That sly-boots was cursedly cunning to hide 'em.

Here lies our good Edmund, whose genius was such,
We scarcely can praise it, or blame it too much;
Who, born for the Universe, narrow'd his mind,
And to party gave up, what was meant for mankind.
Tho' fraught with all learning, kept straining his throat,
To persuade Tommy Townsend to lend him a vote;
Who, too deep for his hearers, still went on refining,
And thought of convincing, while they thought of dining;
Tho' equal to all things, for all things unfit,
Too nice for a statesman, too proud for a wit:
For a patriot too cool; for a drudge, disobedient,
And too fond of the *right* to pursue the *expedient*.
In short, 'twas his fate, unemploy'd, or in place, Sir,
To eat mutton cold, and cut blocks with a razor.

Here lies honest William, whose heart was a mint,
While the owner ne'er knew half the good that was in't;
The pupil of impulse, it forc'd him along,
His conduct still right, with his argument wrong;
Still aiming at honour, yet fearing to roam,
The coachman was tipsy, the chariot drove home;
Would you ask for his merits, alas! he had none,
What was good was spontaneous, his faults were his own.

Here lies honest Richard, whose fate I must sigh at,
Alas, that such frolic should now be so quiet!
What spirits were his, what wit and what whim,
Now breaking a jest, and now breaking a limb;
Now rangling and grumbling to keep up the ball,
Now teazing and vexing, yet laughing at all?
In short so provoking a Devil was Dick,
That we wish'd him full ten times a day at Old Nick,
But missing his mirth and agreeable vein,
As often we wish'd to have Dick back again.

Here Cumberland lies having acted his parts,
The Terence of England, the mender of hearts;
A flattering painter, who made it his care
To draw men as they ought to be, not as they are.

His gallants are all faultless, his women divine,
And comedy wonders at being so fine;
Like a tragedy queen he has dizen'd her out,
Or rather like tragedy giving a rout.
His fools have their follies so lost in a croud
Of virtues and feelings, that folly grows proud,
And coxcombs alike in their failings alone,
Adopting his portraits are pleas'd with their own.
Say, where has our poet this malady caught,
Or wherefore his characters thus without fault?
Say was it that vainly directing his view,
To find out mens virtues and finding them few,
Quite sick of pursuing each troublesome elf,
He grew lazy at last and drew from himself?

Here Douglas retires from his toils to relax,
The scourge of impostors, the terror of quacks:
Come all ye quack bards, and ye quacking divines,
Come and dance on the spot where your tyrant reclines,
When Satire and Censure encircl'd his throne,
I fear'd for your safety, I fear'd for my own;
But now he is gone, and we want a detector,
Our Dodds shall be pious, our Kenricks shall lecture;
Macpherson write bombast, and call it a style,
Our Townshend make speeches, and I shall compile;
New Lauders and Bowers the Tweed shall cross over,
No countryman living their tricks to discover;
Detection her taper shall quench to a spark,
And Scotchman meet Scotchman and cheat in the dark.

Here lies David Garrick, describe me who can,
An abridgment of all that was pleasant in man;
As an actor, confest without rival to shine,
As a wit, if not first, in the very first line,
Yet with talents like these, and an excellent heart,
The man had his failings, a dupe to his art;
Like an ill judging beauty, his colours he spread,
And beplaister'd, with rouge, his own natural red.
On the stage he was natural, simple, affecting,

'Twas only that, when he was off, he was acting:
With no reason on earth to go out of his way,
He turn'd and be varied full ten times a day;
Tho' secure of our hearts, yet confoundedly sick,
If they were not his own by finessing and trick,
He cast off his friends, as a huntsman his pack;
For he knew when he pleased he could whistle them back.
Of praise, a mere glutton, he swallowed what came,
And the puff of a dunce, he mistook it for fame;
'Till his relish grown callous, almost to disease,
Who pepper'd the highest, was surest to please.
But let us be candid, and speak out our mind,
If dunces applauded, he paid them in kind.
Ye Kenricks, ye Kellys, and Woodfalls so grave,
What a commerce was yours, while you got and you gave?
How did Grub-street re-echo the shouts that you rais'd,
While he was be-Rosciused, and you were beprais'd?
But peace to his spirit, wherever it flies,
To act as an angel, and mix with the skies:
Those poets, who owe their best fame to his skill,
Shall still be his flatterers, go where he will.
Old Shakespeare receive him with praise and with love,
And Beaumonts and Bens be his Kellys above.

Here Hickey reclines, a most blunt, pleasant creature,
And slander itself must allow him good-nature:
He cherish'd his friend, and he relish'd a bumper;
Yet one fault he had, and that one was a thumper;
Perhaps you may ask if that man was a miser?
I answer, no, no, for he always was wiser;
Too courteous, perhaps, or obligingly flat;
His very worst foe can't accuse him of that.
Perhaps he confided in men as they go,
And so was too foolishly honest; ah, no.
Then what was his failing? come tell it, and burn ye,
He was, could he help it? a special attorney.

Here Reynolds is laid, and to tell you my mind,
He has not left a better or wiser behind;
His pencil was striking, resistless and grand,
His manners were gentle, complying and bland;
Still born to improve us in every part,
His pencil our faces, his manners our heart:
To coxcombs averse, yet most civilly staring,
When they judged without skill he was still hard of hearing:
When they talk'd of their Raphaels, Corregios and stuff,
He shifted his trumpet, and only took snuff.

LORNA GOODISON

(1947–)

For My Mother
(May I Inherit Half Her Strength)

My mother loved my father
I write this as an absolute
in this my thirtieth year
the year to discard absolutes

he appeared, her fate disguised,
as a sunday player in a cricket match,
he had ridden from a country
one hundred miles south of hers.

She tells he dressed the part,
visiting dandy, maroon blazer
cream serge pants, seam like razor,
and the beret and the two-tone shoes.

My father stopped to speak to her sister,
till he looked and saw her by the oleander,
sure in the kingdom of my blue-eyed grandmother.
He never played the cricket match that day.

He wooed her with words and he won her.
He had nothing but words to woo her,
On a visit to distant Kingston he wrote,

'I stood on the corner of King Street and looked,
and not one woman in that town was lovely as you'.

My mother was a child of the petite bourgeoisie
studying to be a teacher, she oiled her hands
to hold pens.
My father barely knew his father, his mother died young,
he was a boy who grew with his granny.

My mother's trousseau came by steamer through the snows
of Montreal
where her sisters Albertha of the cheekbones and the
perennial Rose, combed Jewlit backstreets with French-
turned names for Doris' wedding things.

Such a wedding Harvey River, Hanover, had never seen
Who anywhere had seen a veil fifteen chantilly yards long?
and a crepe de chine dress with inlets of silk godettes
and a neck-line clasped with jewelled pins!

And on her wedding day she wept. For it was a brazen bride in
    those days
who smiled
and her bouquet looked for the world like a sheaf of wheat
against the unknown of her belly,
a sheaf of wheat backed by maidenhair fern, representing
    Harvey River
her face washed by something other than river water.

My father made one assertive move, he took the imported cherub
    down
from the heights of the cake and dropped it in the soft territory
between her breasts . . . and she cried.

When I came to know my mother many years later, I knew her as
    the figure
who sat at the first thing I learned to read: 'SINGER', and she
    breast-fed
my brother while she sewed; and she taught us to read while she
    sewed and

she sat in judgement over all our disputes as she sewed.

She could work miracles, she would make a garment from a
    square of cloth
in a span that defied time. Or feed twenty people on a stew made
    from
fallen-from-the-head cabbage leaves and a carrot and a cho-cho
    and a palmfill
of meat.

And she rose early and sent us clean into the world and she went
    to bed in
the dark, for my father came in always last.

There is a place somewhere where my mother never took the
    younger ones
a country where my father with the always smile
my father whom all women loved, who had the perpetual quality
    of wonder
given only to a child . . . hurt his bride.

Even at his death there was this 'Friend' who stood at her side,
but my mother is adamant that that has no place in the memory of
my father.

When he died, she sewed dark dresses for the women amongst us
and she summoned that walk, straight-backed, that she gave to us
and buried him dry-eyed.

Just that morning, weeks after
she stood delivering bananas from their skin
singing in that flat hill country voice

she fell down a note to the realisation that she did
not have to be brave, just this once,
and she cried.

For her hands grown coarse with raising nine children
for her body for twenty years permanently fat
for the time she pawned her machine for my sister's
Senior Cambridge fees
and for the pain she bore with the eyes of a queen

and she cried also because she loved him.

BARNABE GOOGE

(1540–1594)

An Epytaphe of the Death of Nicolas Grimoald

Beholde this fle-
tyng world how al things fade
Howe every thyng
doth passe and weare awaye,
Eche state of lyfe,
by comon course and trade,
Abydes no ryme,
but hath a passyng daye.
For looke as lyfe,
that pleasaunt Dame hath brought,
The pleasaunt yeares,
and dayes of lustynes.
So Death our Foe,
consumeth all to nought,
Envyeng thefe,
with Darte doth us oppresse,
And that whiche is,
the greatest gryfe of all,
The gredye Grype,
doth no estate respect,
But wher he comes,
he makes them down to fall,
Ne stayes he at,
the hie sharpe wytted sect,
For if that wytt,
or worthy Eloquens,
Or learnyng deape,
coulde move hym to forbeare,
O *Grimoald* then,
thou hadste not yet gon hence
But heare hadest sene,

full many an aged yeare.
Ne had the Mu-
ses loste so fyne a Floure,
Nor had *Miner-*
va wept to leave the so,
If wysdome myght
have fled the fatall howre,
Thou hadste not yet
ben suffred for to go,
A thousande doltysh
Geese we myght have sparde,
A thousande wytles
heads, death might have found
And taken them,
for whom no man had carde,
And layde them lowe,
in deepe oblivious grounde,
But Fortune fa-
vours Fooles as old men saye
And lets them lyve,
and take the wyse awaye.

W. S. GRAHAM

(1918–1986)

Lines on Roger Hilton's Watch

Which I was given because
I loved him and we had
Terrible times together.

O tarnished ticking time
Piece with your bent hand,
You must be used to being
Looked at suddenly
In the middle of the night
When he switched the light on
Beside his bed. I hope
You told him the best time
When he lifted you up
To meet the Hilton gaze.

I lift you up from the mantel
Piece here in my house
Wearing your verdigris.
At least I keep you wound
And put my ear to you
To hear Botallack tick.

You realise your master
Has relinquished you
And gone to lie under
The ground at St Just.

Tell me the time. The time
Is Botallack o'clock.
This is the dead of night.

He switches the light on
To find a cigarette
And pours himself a Teachers.
He picks me up and holds me
Near his lonely face
To see my hands. He thinks
He is not being watched.

The images of his dream
Are still about his face
As he spits and tries not
To remember where he was.

I am only a watch
And pray time hastes away.
I think I am running down.

Watch, it is time I wound
You up again. I am
Very much not your dear
Last master but we had
Terrible times together.

ROBERT GRAVES
(1895–1985)

The Untidy Man

There was a man, a very untidy man,
  Whose fingers could nowhere be found to put in his tomb.
He had rolled his head far underneath the bed:
  He had left his legs and arms lying all over the room.

THOMAS GRAY

(1716–1771)

On the Death of Richard West

In vain to me the smiling mornings shine,
And reddening Phoebus lifts his golden fire:
The birds in vain their amorous descant join,
Or cheerful fields resume their green attire:
These ears, alas! for other notes repine,
A different object do these eyes require.
My lonely anguish melts no heart but mine;
And in my breast the imperfect joys expire.
Yet morning smiles the busy race to cheer,
And new-born pleasure brings to happier men:
The fields to all their wonted tribute bear;
To warm their little loves the birds complain.
I fruitless mourn to him that cannot hear,
And weep the more because I weep in vain.

Elegy Written in a Country Churchyard

The curfew tolls the knell of parting day,
    The lowing herd wind slowly o'er the lea,
The plowman homeward plods his weary way,
    And leaves the world to darkness and to me.

Now fades the glimmering landscape on the sight,
    And all the air a solemn stillness holds,
Save where the beetle wheels his droning flight,
    And drowsy tinklings lull the distant folds;

Save that from yonder ivy-mantled tower
   The moping owl does to the moon complain
Of such, as wandering near her secret bower,
   Molest her ancient solitary reign.

Beneath those rugged elms, that yew tree's shade,
   Where heaves the turf in many a moldering heap,
Each in his narrow cell forever laid,
   The rude forefathers of the hamlet sleep.

The breezy call of incense-breathing Morn,
   The swallow twittering from the straw-built shed,
The cock's shrill clarion, or the echoing horn,
   No more shall rouse them from their lowly bed.

For them no more the blazing hearth shall burn,
   Or busy housewife ply her evening care;
No children run to lisp their sire's return,
   Or climb his knees the envied kiss to share.

Oft did the harvest to their sickle yield,
   Their furrow oft the stubborn glebe has broke;
How jocund did they drive their team afield!
   How bowed the woods beneath their sturdy stroke!

Let not Ambition mock their useful toil,
   Their homely joys, and destiny obscure;
Nor Grandeur hear with a disdainful smile
   The short and simple annals of the poor.

The boast of heraldry, the pomp of power,
   And all that beauty, all that wealth e'er gave,
Awaits alike the inevitable hour.
   The paths of glory lead but to the grave.

Nor you, ye proud, impute to these the fault,
   If Memory o'er their tomb no trophies raise,
Where through the long-drawn aisle and fretted vault
   The pealing anthem swells the note of praise.

Can storied urn or animated bust
   Back to its mansion call the fleeting breath?
Can Honor's voice provoke the silent dust,
   Or Flattery soothe the dull cold ear of Death?

Perhaps in this neglected spot is laid
   Some heart once pregnant with celestial fire;
Hands that the rod of empire might have swayed,
   Or waked to ecstasy the living lyre.

But Knowledge to their eyes her ample page
   Rich with the spoils of time did ne'er unroll;
Chill Penury repressed their noble rage,
   And froze the genial current of the soul.

Full many a gem of purest ray serene,
   The dark unfathomed caves of ocean bear:
Full many a flower is born to blush unseen,
   And waste its sweetness on the desert air.

Some village Hampden, that with dauntless breast
   The little tyrant of his fields withstood;
Some mute inglorious Milton here may rest,
   Some Cromwell guiltless of his country's blood.

The applause of listening senates to command,
   The threats of pain and ruin to despise,
To scatter plenty o'er a smiling land,
   And read their history in a nation's eyes,

Their lot forbade: nor circumscribed alone
   Their growing virtues, but their crimes confined;
Forbade to wade through slaughter to a throne,
   And shut the gates of mercy on mankind,

The struggling pangs of conscious truth to hide,
   To quench the blushes of ingenuous shame,
Or heap the shrine of Luxury and Pride
   With incense kindled at the Muse's flame.

Far from the madding crowd's ignoble strife,
    Their sober wishes never learned to stray;
Along the cool sequestered vale of life
    They kept the noiseless tenor of their way.

Yet even these bones from insult to protect
    Some frail memorial still erected nigh,
With uncouth rhymes and shapeless sculpture decked,
    Implores the passing tribute of a sigh.

Their name, their years, spelt by the unlettered Muse,
    The place of fame and elegy supply:
And many a holy text around she strews,
    That teach the rustic moralist to die.

For who to dumb Forgetfulness a prey,
    This pleasing anxious being e'er resigned,
Left the warm precincts of the cheerful day,
    Nor cast one longing lingering look behind?

On some fond breast the parting soul relies,
    Some pious drops the closing eye requires;
Even from the tomb the voice of Nature cries,
    Even in our ashes live their wonted fires.

For thee, who mindful of the unhonored dead
    Dost in these lines their artless tale relate;
If chance, by lonely contemplation led,
    Some kindred spirit shall inquire thy fate,

Haply some hoary-headed swain may say,
    'Oft have we seen him at the peep of dawn
Brushing with hasty steps the dews away
    To meet the sun upon the upland lawn.

'There at the foot of yonder nodding beech
    That wreathes its old fantastic roots so high,
His listless length at noontide would he stretch,
    And pore upon the brook that babbles by.

'Hard by yon wood, now smiling as in scorn,
  Muttering his wayward fancies he would rove,
Now drooping, woeful wan, like one forlorn,
  Or crazed with care, or crossed in hopeless love.

'One morn I missed him on the customed hill,
  Along the heath and near his favorite tree;
Another came; nor yet beside the rill,
  Nor up the lawn, nor at the wood was he;

'The next with dirges due in sad array
  Slow through the churchway path we saw him borne.
Approach and read (for thou canst read) the lay,
  Graved on the stone beneath yon aged thorn.'

THE EPITAPH

Here rests his head upon the lap of Earth
  A youth to Fortune and to Fame unknown.
Fair Science frowned not on his humble birth,
  And Melancholy marked him for her own.

Large was his bounty, and his soul sincere,
  Heaven did a recompense as largely send:
He gave to Misery all he had, a tear,
  He gained from Heaven ('twas all he wished) a friend.

No farther seek his merits to disclose,
  Or draw his frailties from their dread abode
(There they alike in trembling hope repose),
  The bosom of his Father and his God.

Ode on the Death of a Favourite
Cat Drowned in a Tub of Goldfishes

'Twas on a lofty vase's side,
Where China's gayest art had dyed
The azure flowers that blow;
Demurest of the tabby kind,
The pensive Selima, reclined,
Gazed on the lake below.

Her conscious tail her joy declared;
The fair round face, the snowy beard,
The velvet of her paws,
Her coat, that with the tortoise vies,
Her ears of jet, and emerald eyes,
She saw; and purred applause.

Still had she gazed; but 'midst the tide
Two angel forms were seen to glide,
The genii of the stream;
Their scaly armour's Tyrian hue
Through richest purple to the view
Betrayed a golden gleam.

The hapless nymph with wonder saw;
A whisker first and then a claw,
With many an ardent wish,
She stretched in vain to reach the prize.
What female heart can gold despise?
What cat's averse to fish?

Presumptuous maid! with looks intent
Again she stretch'd, again she bent,
Nor knew the gulf between.
(Malignant Fate sat by, and smiled)
The slippery verge her feet beguiled,
She tumbled headlong in.

Eight times emerging from the flood
She mewed to every watery god,
Some speedy aid to send.
No dolphin came, no Nereid stirred;
Nor cruel Tom, nor Susan heard;
A Favourite has no friend!

From hence, ye beauties, undeceived,
Know, one false step is ne'er retrieved,
And be with caution bold.
Not all that tempts your wandering eyes
And heedless hearts, is lawful prize;
Nor all that glisters, gold.

THOM GUNN

(1929–2004)

Lament

Your dying was a difficult enterprise.
First, petty things took up your energies,
The small but clustering duties of the sick,
Irritant as the cough's dry rhetoric.
Those hours of waiting for pills, shot, X-ray
Or test (while you read novels two a day)
Already with a kind of clumsy stealth
Distanced you from the habits of your health.
  In hope still, courteous still, but tired and thin,
You tried to stay the man that you had been,
Treating each symptom as a mere mishap
Without import. But then the spinal tap.
It brought a hard headache, and when night came
I heard you wake up from the same bad dream
Every half-hour with the same short cry
Of mild outrage, before immediately
Slipping into the nightmare once again
Empty of content but the drip of pain.
No respite followed: though the nightmare ceased,
Your cough grew thick and rich, its strength increased.
Four nights, and on the fifth we drove you down
To the Emergency Room. That frown, that frown:
I'd never seen such rage in you before
As when they wheeled you through the swinging door.
For you knew, rightly, they conveyed you from
Those normal pleasures of the sun's kingdom
The hedonistic body basks within
And takes for granted – summer on the skin,
Sleep without break, the moderate taste of tea
In a dry mouth. You had gone on from me
As if your body sought out martyrdom

In the far Canada of a hospital room.
Once there, you entered fully the distress
And long pale rigours of the wilderness.
A gust of morphine hid you. Back in sight
You breathed through a segmented tube, fat, white,
Jammed down your throat so that you could not speak.
　　How thin the distance made you. In your cheek
One day, appeared the true shape of your bone
No longer padded. Still your mind, alone,
Explored this emptying intermediate
State for what holds and rests were hidden in it.
　　You wrote us messages on a pad, amused
At one time that you had your nurse confused
Who, seeing you reconciled after four years
With your grey father, both of you in tears,
Asked if this was at last your 'special friend'
(The one you waited for until the end).
'She sings,' you wrote, 'a Philippine folk song
To wake me in the morning . . . It is long
And very pretty.' Grabbing at detail
To furnish this bare ledge toured by the gale,
On which you lay, bed restful as a knife,
You tried, tried hard, to make of it a life
Thick with the complicating circumstance
Your thoughts might fasten on. It had been chance
Always till now that had filled up the moment
With live specifics your hilarious comment
Discovered as it went along; and fed,
Laconic, quick, wherever it was led.
You improvised upon your own delight.
I think back to the scented summer night
We talked between our sleeping bags, below
A molten field of stars five years ago:
I was so tickled by your mind's light touch
I couldn't sleep, you made me laugh too much,
Though I was tired and begged you to leave off.

Now you were tired, and yet not tired enough
– Still hungry for the great world you were losing

Steadily in no season of your choosing –
And when at last the whole death was assured,
Drugs having failed, and when you had endured
Two weeks of an abominable constraint,
You faced it equably, without complaint,
Unwhimpering, but not at peace with it.
You'd lived as if your time was infinite:
You were not ready and not reconciled,
Feeling as uncompleted as a child
Till you had shown the world what you could do
In some ambitious role to be worked through,
A role your need for it had half-defined,
But never wholly, even in your mind.
You lacked the necessary ruthlessness,
The soaring meanness that pinpoints success.
We loved that lack of self-love, and your smile,
Rueful, at your own silliness.

                                 Meanwhile,
Your lungs collapsed, and the machine, unstrained,
Did all your breathing now. Nothing remained
But death by drowning on an inland sea
Of your own fluids, which it seemed could be
Kindly forestalled by drugs. Both could and would:
Nothing was said, everything understood,
At least by us. Your own concerns were not
Long-term, precisely, when they gave the shot
– You made local arrangements to the bed
And pulled a pillow round beside your head.
And so you slept, and died, your skin gone grey,
Achieving your completeness, in a way.

Outdoors next day, I was dizzy from a sense
Of being ejected with some violence
From vigil in a white and distant spot
Where I was numb, into this garden plot
Too warm, too close, and not enough like pain.
I was delivered into time again
– The variations that I live among
Where your long body too used to belong

And where the still bush is minutely active.
You never thought your body was attractive,
Though others did, and yet you trusted it
And must have loved its fickleness a bit
Since it was yours and gave you what it could,
Till near the end it let you down for good,
Its blood hospitable to those guests who
Took over by betraying it into
The greatest of its inconsistencies
This difficult, tedious, painful enterprise.

IVOR GURNEY

(1890–1937)

To His Love

He's gone, and all our plans
    Are useless indeed.
We'll walk no more on Cotswold
    Where the sheep feed
    Quietly and take no heed.

His body that was so quick
    Is not as you
Knew it, on Severn river
    Under the blue
    Driving our small boat through.

You would not know him now . . .
    But still he died
Nobly, so cover him over
    With violets of pride
    Purple from Severn side.

Cover him, cover him soon!
    And with thick-set
Masses of memoried flowers –
    Hide that red wet
    Thing I must somehow forget.

Song

Only the wanderer
   Knows England's graces,
Or can anew see clear
   Familiar faces.

And who loves joy as he
   That dwells in shadows?
Do not forget me quite,
   O Severn meadows.

Cotswold Ways

One comes across the strangest things in walks:
Fragments of Abbey tithe-barns fixed in modern
And Dutch-sort houses where the water baulks
Weired up, and brick kilns broken among fern,
Old troughs, great stone cisterns bishops might have blessed
Ceremonially, and worthy mounting-stones;
Black timber in red brick, queerly placed
Where Hill stone was looked for – and a manor's bones
Spied in the frame of some wisteria'd house
And mill-falls and sedge pools and Saxon faces;
Stream-sources happened upon in unlikely places,
And Roman-looking hills of small degree
And the surprise of dignity of poplars
At a road end, or the white Cotswold scars,

Or sheets spread white against the hazel tree.
Strange the large difference of up-Cotswold ways;
Birdlip climbs bold and treeless to a bend,
Portway to dim wood-lengths without end,
And Crickley goes to cliffs are the crown of days.

Strange Hells

There are strange hells within the minds war made
Not so often, not so humiliatingly afraid
As one would have expected – the racket and fear guns made.
One hell the Gloucester soldiers they quite put out;
Their first bombardment, when in combined black shout

Of fury, guns aligned, they ducked lower their heads
And sang with diaphragms fixed beyond all dreads,
That tin and stretched-wire tinkle, that blither of tune;
'Après la guerre fini', till hell all had come down,
Twelve-inch, six-inch, and eighteen pounders hammering
    hell's thunders.

Where are they now, on state-doles, or showing shop-patterns
Or walking town to town sore in borrowed tatterns
Or begged. Some civic routine one never learns.
The heart burns – but has to keep out of face how heart burns.

THOMAS HARDY
(1840–1928)

Drummer Hodge

1

They throw in Drummer Hodge, to rest
    Uncoffined – just as found:
His landmark is a kopje-crest
    That breaks the veldt around;
And foreign constellations west
    Each night above his mound.

2

Young Hodge the Drummer never knew –
    Fresh from his Wessex home –
The meaning of the broad Karoo,
    The Bush, the dusty loam,
And why uprose to nightly view
    Strange stars amid the gloam.

3

Yet portion of that unknown plain
    Will Hodge for ever be;
His homely Northern breast and brain
    Grow to some Southern tree,
And strange-eyed constellations reign
    His stars eternally.

Thoughts of Phena

At news of her death

Not a line of her writing have I,
　　Not a thread of her hair,
No mark of her late time as dame in her dwelling, whereby
　　I may picture her there;
　　And in vain do I urge my unsight
　　　To conceive my lost prize
At her close, whom I knew when her dreams were upbrimming
　　　　　　　　　　　　　　　with light,
　　And with laughter her eyes.

What scenes spread around her last days,
　　Sad, shining, or dim?
Did her gifts and compassions enray and enarch her sweet ways
　　With an aureate nimb?
　　Or did life-light decline from her years,
　　　And mischances control
　　Her full day-star; unease, or regret, or forebodings, or fears
　　Disennoble her soul?

Thus I do but the phantom retain
　　Of the maiden of yore
As my relic; yet haply the best of her – fined in my brain
　　It may be the more
　　That no line of her writing have I,
　　　Nor a thread of her hair,
No mark of her late time as dame in her dwelling, whereby
　　I may picture her there.

　　　　　　　　　　　　　　　March 1890

A Singer Asleep

Algernon Charles Swinburne
1837–1909

1

In this fair niche above the unslumbering sea,
That sentrys up and down all night, all day,
From cove to promontory, from ness to bay,
The Fates have fitly bidden that he should be
    Pillowed eternally.

2

– It was as though a garland of red roses
Had fallen about the hood of some smug nun
When irresponsibly dropped as from the sun,
In fulth of numbers freaked with musical closes,
Upon Victoria's formal middle time
    His leaves of rhythm and rhyme.

3

O that far morning of a summer day
When, down a terraced street whose pavements lay
Glassing the sunshine into my bent eyes,
I walked and read with a quick glad surprise
    New words, in classic guise, –

4

The passionate pages of his earlier years,
Fraught with hot sighs, sad laughters, kisses, tears;
Fresh-fluted notes, yet from a minstrel who
Blew them not naïvely, but as one who knew
     Full well why thus he blew.

5

I still can hear the brabble and the roar
At those thy tunes, O still one, now passed through
That fitful fire of tongues then entered new!
Their power is spent like spindrift on this shore;
     Thine swells yet more and more.

6

– His singing-mistress verily was no other
Than she the Lesbian, she the music-mother
Of all the tribe that feel in melodies;
Who leapt, love-anguished, from the Leucadian steep
Into the rambling world-encircling deep
     Which hides her where none sees.

7

And one can hold in thought that nightly here
His phantom may draw down to the water's brim,
And hers come up to meet it, as a dim
Lone shine upon the heaving hydrosphere,
And mariners wonder as they traverse near,
     Unknowing of her and him.

8

One dreams him sighing to her spectral form:
'O teacher, where lies hid thy burning line;
Where are those songs, O poetess divine
Whose very orts are love incarnadine?'
And her smile back: 'Disciple true and warm,
  Sufficient now are thine.' ...

9

So here, beneath the waking constellations,
Where the waves peal their everlasting strains,
And their dull subterrene reverberations
Shake him when storms make mountains of their plains –
Him once their peer in sad improvisations,
And deft as wind to cleave their frothy manes –
I leave him, while the daylight gleam declines
  Upon the capes and chines.

        Bonchurch
        1910

The Going

Why did you give no hint that night
That quickly after the morrow's dawn,
And calmly, as if indifferent quite,
You would close your term here, up and be gone
  Where I could not follow
  With wing of swallow
To gain one glimpse of you ever anon!

  Never to bid good-bye,
  Or lip me the softest call,

Or utter a wish for a word, while I
Saw morning harden upon the wall,
    Unmoved, unknowing
    That your great going
Had place that moment, and altered all.

Why do you make me leave the house
And think for a breath it is you I see
At the end of the alley of bending boughs
Where so often at dusk you used to be;
    Till in darkening dankness
    The yawning blankness
Of the perspective sickens me!

    You were she who abode
    By those red-veined rocks far West,
You were the swan-necked one who rode
Along the beetling Beeny Crest,
    And, reining nigh me,
    Would muse and eye me,
While Life unrolled us its very best.

Why, then, latterly did we not speak,
Did we not think of those days long dead,
And ere your vanishing strive to seek
That time's renewal? We might have said,
    'In this bright spring weather
    We'll visit together
Those places that once we visited.'

    Well, well! All's past amend,
    Unchangeable. It must go.
I seem but a dead man held on end
To sink down soon. . . . O you could not know
    That such swift fleeing
    No soul foreseeing –
Not even I – would undo me so!

December 1912

The Voice

Woman much missed, how you call to me, call to me,
Saying that now you are not as you were
When you had changed from the one who was all to me,
But as at first, when our day was fair.

Can it be you that I hear? Let me view you, then,
Standing as when I drew near to the town
Where you would wait for me: yes, as I knew you then,
Even to the original air-blue gown!

Or is it only the breeze, in its listlessness
Travelling across the wet mead to me here,
You being ever dissolved to wan wistlessness,
Heard no more again far or near?

    Thus I; faltering forward,
    Leaves around me falling,
Wind oozing thin through the thorn from norward,
    And the woman calling.

December 1912

At Castle Boterel

As I drive to the junction of lane and highway,
    And the drizzle bedrenches the waggonette,
I look behind at the fading byway,
    And see on its slope, now glistening wet,
        Distinctly yet

Myself and a girlish form benighted
    In dry March weather. We climb the road

Beside a chaise. We had just alighted
  To ease the sturdy pony's load
    When he sighed and slowed.

What we did as we climbed, and what we talked of
  Matters not much, nor to what it led, –
Something that life will not be balked of
  Without rude reason till hope is dead,
    And feeling fled.

It filled but a minute. But was there ever
  A time of such quality, since or before,
In that hill's story? To one mind never,
  Though it has been climbed, foot-swift, foot-sore,
    By thousands more.

Primaeval rocks form the road's steep border.
  And much have they faced there, first and last,
Of the transitory in Earth's long order;
  But what they record in colour and cast
    Is – that we two passed.

And to me, though Time's unflinching rigour,
  In mindless rote, has ruled from sight
The substance now, one phantom figure
  Remains on the slope, as when that night
    Saw us alight.

I look and see it there, shrinking, shrinking,
  I look back at it amid the rain
For the very last time; for my sand is sinking,
  And I shall traverse old love's domain
    Never again.

March 1913

After a Journey

Hereto I come to view a voiceless ghost;
   Whither, O whither will its whim now draw me?
Up the cliff, down, till I'm lonely, lost,
   And the unseen waters' ejaculations awe me.
Where you will next be there's no knowing,
    Facing round about me everywhere,
      With your nut-coloured hair,
And grey eyes, and rose-flush coming and going.

Yes: I have re-entered your olden haunts at last;
   Through the years, through the dead scenes I have tracked you;
What have you now found to say of our past –
   Scanned across the dark space wherein I have lacked you?
Summer gave us sweets, but autumn wrought division?
    Things were not lastly as firstly well
      With us twain, you tell?
But all's closed now, despite Time's derision.

I see what you are doing: you are leading me on
   To the spots we knew when we haunted here together,
The waterfall, above which the mist-bow shone
   At the then fair hour in the then fair weather,
And the cave just under, with a voice still so hollow
    That it seems to call out to me from forty years ago,
      When you were all aglow,
And not the thin ghost that I now frailly follow!

Ignorant of what there is flitting here to see,
   The waked birds preen and the seals flop lazily;
Soon you will have, Dear, to vanish from me,
   For the stars close their shutters and the dawn whitens hazily.

Trust me, I mind not, though Life lours,
    The bringing me here; nay, bring me here again!
        I am just the same as when
Our days were a joy, and our paths through flowers.

Pentargan Bay

During Wind and Rain

They sing their dearest songs –
He, she, all of them – yea,
Treble and tenor and bass,
    And one to play;
With the candles mooning each face . . .
    Ah, no; the years O!
How the sick leaves reel down in throngs!

They clear the creeping moss –
Elders and juniors – aye,
Making the pathways neat
    And the garden gay;
And they build a shady seat . . .
    Ah, no; the years, the years;
See, the white storm-birds wing across!

They are blithely breakfasting all –
Men and maidens – yea,
Under the summer tree,
    With a glimpse of the bay,
While pet fowl come to the knee . . .
    Ah, no; the years O!
And the rotten rose is ript from the wall.

They change to a high new house,
He, she, all of them – aye,
Clocks and carpets and chairs
    On the lawn all day,
And brightest things that are theirs . . .
    Ah, no; the years, the years;
Down their carved names the rain-drop ploughs.

Lying Awake

You, Morningtide Star, now are steady-eyed, over the east,
    I know it as if I saw you;
You, Beeches, engrave on the sky your thin twigs, even the least;
    Had I paper and pencil I'd draw you.
You, Meadow, are white with your counterpane cover of dew,
    I see it as if I were there;
You, Churchyard, are lightening faint from the shade of the yew,
    The names creeping out everywhere.

TONY HARRISON

(1937-)

Book Ends

I

Baked the day she suddenly dropped dead
we chew it slowly that last apple pie.

Shocked into sleeplessness you're scared of bed.
We never could talk much, and now don't try.

You're like book ends, the pair of you, she'd say,
Hog that grate, say nothing, sit, sleep, stare . . .

The 'scholar' me, you, worn out on poor pay,
only our silence made us seem a pair.

Not as good for staring in, blue gas,
too regular each bud, each yellow spike.

A night you need my company to pass
and she not here to tell us we're alike!

Your life's all shattered into smithereens.

Back in our silences and sullen looks,
for all the Scotch we drink, what's still between's
not the thirty or so years, but books, books, books.

2

The stone's too full. The wording must be terse.
There's scarcely room to carve the FLORENCE on it –

Come on, it's not as if we're wanting verse.
It's not as if we're wanting a whole sonnet!

After tumblers of neat *Johnny Walker*
(I think that both of us were on our third)
you said you'd always been a clumsy talker
and couldn't find another, shorter word
for 'beloved' or for 'wife' in the inscription,
but not too clumsy that you can't still cut:

You're supposed to be the bright boy at description
and you can't tell them what the fuck to put!

I've got to find the right words on my own.

I've got the envelope that he'd been scrawling,
mis-spelt, mawkish, stylistically appalling
but I can't squeeze more love into their stone.

TERRANCE HAYES
(1971–)

American Sonnet for My Past and Future Assassin

Seven of the ten things I love in the face
Of James Baldwin concern the spiritual
Elasticity of his expressions. The sashay
Between left & right eyebrow, for example.
The crease between his eyes like a tuning
Fork or furrow, like a riverbed branching
Into tributaries like lines of rapturous sentences
Searching for a period. The dimple in his chin
Narrows & expands like a pupil. Most of all,
I love all of his eyes. And those wrinkles
The feel & color of wet driftwood in the mud
Around those eyes. Mud is made of
Simple rain & earth, the same baptismal
Spills & hills of dirt James Baldwin is made of.

SEAMUS HEANEY

(1939–2013)

The Strand at Lough Beg

In memory of Colum McCartney

'All round this little island, on the strand
Far down below there, where the breakers strive,
Grow the tall rushes from the oozy sand.'
            Dante, Purgatorio, *1, 100–103*

Leaving the white glow of filling stations
And a few lonely streetlamps among fields
You climbed the hills towards Newtownhamilton
Past the Fews Forest, out beneath the stars –
Along that road, a high, bare pilgrim's track
Where Sweeney fled before the bloodied heads,
Goat-beards and dogs' eyes in a demon pack
Blazing out of the ground, snapping and squealing.
What blazed ahead of you? A faked roadblock?
The red lamp swung, the sudden brakes and stalling
Engine, voices, heads hooded and the cold-nosed gun?
Or in your driving mirror, tailing headlights
That pulled out suddenly and flagged you down
Where you weren't known and far from what you knew:
The lowland clays and waters of Lough Beg,
Church Island's spire, its soft treeline of yew.

There you once heard guns fired behind the house
Long before rising time, when duck shooters
Haunted the marigolds and bulrushes,
But still were scared to find spent cartridges,
Acrid, brassy, genital, ejected,
On your way across the strand to fetch the cows.
For you and yours and yours and mine fought shy,

Spoke an old language of conspirators
And could not crack the whip or seize the day:
Big-voiced scullions, herders, feelers round
Haycocks and hindquarters, talkers in byres,
Slow arbitrators of the burial ground.

Across that strand of yours the cattle graze
Up to their bellies in an early mist
And now they turn their unbewildered gaze
To where we work our way through squeaking sedge
Drowning in dew. Like a dull blade with its edge
Honed bright, Lough Beg half-shines under the haze.
I turn because the sweeping of your feet
Has stopped behind me, to find you on your knees
With blood and roadside muck in your hair and eyes,
Then kneel in front of you in brimming grass
And gather up cold handfuls of the dew
To wash you, cousin. I dab you clean with moss
Fine as the drizzle out of a low cloud.
I lift you under the arms and lay you flat.
With rushes that shoot green again, I plait
Green scapulars to wear over your shroud.

FELICIA HEMANS

(1793–1835)

The Grave of a Poetess

I stood beside thy lowly grave;
Spring-odours breath'd around,
And music, in the river-wave,
Pass'd with a lulling sound.

All happy things that love the sun,
In the bright air glanc'd by,
And a glad murmur seem'd to run
Thro' the soft azure sky.

Fresh leaves were on the ivy-bough
That fring'd the ruins near;
Young voices were abroad – but thou
Their sweetness couldst not hear.

And mournful grew my heart for thee,
Thou in whose woman's mind
The ray that brightens earth and sea,
The light of song was shrined.

Mournful, that thou wert slumbering low,
With a dread curtain drawn
Between thee and the golden glow
Of this world's vernal dawn.

Parted from all the song and bloom
Thou wouldst have lov'd so well,
To thee the sunshine round thy tomb
Was but a broken spell.

The bird, the insect on the wing,
In their bright reckless play,
Might feel the flush and life of spring,–
And thou wert pass'd away!

But then, ev'n then, a nobler thought
O'er my vain sadness came;
Th' immortal spirit woke, and wrought
Within my thrilling frame.

Surely on lovelier things, I said,
Thou must have look'd ere now,
Than all that round our pathway shed
Odours and hues below.

The shadows of the tomb are here,
Yet beautiful is earth!
What see'st thou then where no dim fear,
No haunting dream hath birth?

Here a vain love to passing flowers
Thou gav'st – but where thou art,
The sway is not with changeful hours,
There love and death must part.

Thou hast left sorrow in thy song,
A voice not loud, but deep!
The glorious bowers of earth among,
How often didst thou weep!

Where couldst thou fix on mortal ground
Thy tender thoughts and high?–
Now peace the woman's heart hath found,
And joy the poet's eye.

EDWARD, LORD HERBERT
OF CHERBURY
(1587–1648)

Elegy Over a Tomb

Must I then see, alas, eternal night
Sitting upon those fairest eyes,
And closing all those beams, which once did rise
So radiant and bright
That light and heat in them to us did prove
Knowledge and love?

Oh, if you did delight no more to stay
Upon this low and earthly stage,
But rather chose an endless heritage,
Tell us at least, we pray,
Where all the beauties that those ashes ow'd
Are now bestow'd.

Doth the sun now his light with yours renew?
Have waves the curling of your hair?
Did you restore unto the sky and air
The red, and white, and blue?
Have you vouchsaf'd to flowers since your death
That sweetest breath?

Had not heav'n's lights else in their houses slept,
Or to some private life retir'd?
Must not the sky and air have else conspir'd,
And in their regions wept?
Must not each flower else the earth could breed,
Have been a weed?

But thus enrich'd may we not yield some cause
Why they themselves lament no more?
That must have chang'd the course they held before,
And broke their proper laws,
Had not your beauties giv'n this second birth
To heaven and earth.

Tell us, for oracles must still ascend
For those that crave them at your tomb,
Tell us where are those beauties now become,
And what they now intend;
Tell us, alas, that cannot tell our grief,
Or hope relief.

GEORGE HERBERT
(1593–1633)

Virtue

Sweet day, so cool, so calm, so bright,
The bridal of the earth and sky;
The dew shall weep thy fall to-night,
For thou must die.

Sweet rose, whose hue angry and brave
Bids the rash gazer wipe his eye;
Thy root is ever in its grave,
And thou must die.

Sweet spring, full of sweet days and roses,
A box where sweets compacted lie;
My music shows ye have your closes,
And all must die.

Only a sweet and virtuous soul,
Like season'd timber, never gives;
But though the whole world turn to coal,
Then chiefly lives.

MARY SIDNEY HERBERT, COUNTESS OF PEMBROKE
(1561–1621)

If Ever Hapless Woman Had a Cause

If ever hapless woman had a cause
   To breathe her plaints into the open air,
And never suffer inward grief to pause.
   Or seek her sorrow-shaken soul's repair;
Then I, for I have lost my only brother,
Whose like this age can scarcely yield another.

Come therefore, mournful Muses, and lament;
   Forsake all wanton pleasing motions;
Bedew your cheeks. Still shall my tears be spent,
   Yet still increased with inundations.
For I must weep, since I have lost my brother,
Whose like this age can scarcely yield another.

The cruel hand of murder cloyed with blood
   Lewdly deprived him of his mortal life.
Woe the death-attended blades that stood
   In opposition 'gainst him in the strife
Wherein he fell, and where I lost a brother,
Whose like this age can scarcely yield another.

Then unto Grief let me a temple make,
   And, mourning, daily enter Sorrow's ports,
Knock on my breast, sweet brother, for thy sake,
   Nature and love will both be my consorts,
And help me aye to wail my only brother,
Whose like this age can scarcely yield another.

ROBERT HERRICK
(1591–1674)

Upon Himself

Thou shalt not all die; for while Love's fire shines
Upon his Altar, men shall read thy lines;
And learn'd musicians shall to honour *Herricks*
Fame, and his name, both set, and sing his Lyricks.

GEOFFREY HILL

(1932–2016)

September Song

Born 19.6.32 – Deported 24.9.42

Undesirable you may have been, untouchable
you were not. Not forgotten
or passed over at the proper time.

As estimated, you died. Things marched,
sufficient, to that end.
Just so much Zyklon and leather, patented
terror, so many routine cries.

(I have made
an elegy for myself it
is true)

September fattens on vines. Roses
flake from the wall. The smoke
of harmless fires drifts to my eyes.

This is plenty. This is more than enough.

MICHAEL HOFMANN

(1957–)

For Gert Hofmann, died 1 July 1993

The window atilt, the blinds at half-mast,
the straw star swinging in the draught, and my father
for once not at his post, not in the penumbra
frowning up from his manuscript at the world.

Water comes running to the kitchen to separate
the lettuce for supper from the greenflies who lived there.
The sill clock ticks from its quartz heart, the everlasting radio
has its antenna bent where it pinked his eye once.

Ink, tincture of bees, the chair for him,
the chair for my mother, the white wastepaper basket
empty and abraded by so much balled-up paper,
nosebleeds and peach-pits.

The same books as for years, the only additions by himself,
an African mask over the door to keep out evil spirits,
a seventeenth-century genre scene – the children
little adults – varnished almost to blackness.

Outside, the onetime pond packed with nettles,
the cut-down-we-stand of bamboo, the berries
on the mountain ash already orange and reddening, although
the inscrutable blackbirds will scorn them months more.

THOMAS HOOD

(1799–1845)

I Remember, I Remember

I remember, I remember,
The house where I was born,
The little window where the sun
Came peeping in at morn;
He never came a wink too soon,
Nor brought too long a day,
But now, I often wish the night
Had borne my breath away!

I remember, I remember,
The roses, red and white,
The violets, and the lily-cups,
Those flowers made of light!
The lilacs where the robin built,
And where my brother set
The laburnum on his birthday, –
The tree is living yet!

I remember, I remember,
Where I was used to swing,
And thought the air must rush as fresh
To swallows on the wing;
My spirit flew in feathers then,
That is so heavy now,
And summer pools could hardly cool
The fever on my brow!

I remember, I remember,
The fir trees dark and high;
I used to think their slender tops
Were close against the sky:
It was a childish ignorance,
But now 'tis little joy
To know I'm farther off from heaven
Than when I was a boy.

GERARD MANLEY HOPKINS

(1844–1889)

Binsey Poplars

Felled 1879

My aspens dear, whose airy cages quelled,
  Quelled or quenched in leaves the leaping sun,
   Áll félled, félled, are áll félled;
    Of a fresh and following folded rank
        Not spared, not one
        That dandled a sandalled
     Shadow that swam or sank
On meadow and river and wind-wandering weed-winding bank.

  O if we but knew what we do
     When we delve or hew –
    Hack and rack the growing green!
      Since country is so tender
    To tóuch, her béing só slénder,
    That, like this sleek and seeing ball
    But a prick will make no eye at all,
    Where we, even where we mean
         To mend her we end her,
    When we hew or delve:
After-comers cannot guess the beauty been.
  Ten or twelve, only ten or twelve
    Strokes of havoc unselve
     The sweet especial scene,
    Rural scene, a rural scene,
    Sweet especial rural scene.

Spring and Fall

To a young child

Márgarét, áre you gríeving
Over Goldengrove unleaving?
Léaves, like the things of man, you
With your fresh thoughts care for, can you?
Ah! ás the heart grows older
It will come to such sights colder
By and by, nor spare a sigh
Though worlds of wanwood leafmeal lie,
And yet you *will* weep and know why.
Now no matter, child, the name:
Sórrow's springs áre the same.
Nor mouth had, no nor mind, expressed
What heart heard of, ghost guessed:
It ís the blight man was born for,
It is Margaret you mourn for.

Felix Randal

Felix Randal the farrier, O is he dead then? my duty all ended.
Who have watched his mould of man, big-boned and
    hardy-handsome
Pining, pining, till time when reason rambled in it and some
Fatal four disorders, fleshed there, all contended?

Sickness broke him. Impatient, he cursed at first, but mended
Being anointed and all; though a heavenlier heart began some
Months earlier, since I had our sweet reprieve and ransom
Tendered to him. Ah well, God rest him all road ever he offended!

This seeing the sick endears them to us, us too it endears.
My tongue had taught thee comfort, touch had quenched thy tears,
Thy tears that touched my heart, child, Felix, poor Felix Randal;

How far from then forethought of, all thy more boisterous years,
When thou at the random grim forge, powerful amidst peers,
Didst fettle for the great grey drayhorse his bright and battering
    sandal!

HORACE

(c. 67–8 BCE)

Odes 3.30

I have made a monument more lasting than bronze
and higher even than the pyramids of kings.
It will never be destroyed by wasting rain
or wild north winds, or by remorseless time

as days and years fly by and fade away.
I won't just die and disappear. Part of me
remains untouched by Libitina. I'll go on
and on, renewed in praise for what I've done.

So as priest and vestal climb the Capitol,
I will now ascend in hearts and minds,
a lowly one from near the roaring Aufidus,
where Daunus ruled a parched, impoverished land.

They will remember me and say I was the first
to bring Aeolian music to Italian verse.
So take the honour well earned by you, Melpomene,
And proudly crown my locks with Delphic bays.

Translated by Stephen Regan

A. E. HOUSMAN
(1859–1936)

To an Athlete Dying Young

The time you won your town the race
We chaired you through the market-place;
Man and boy stood cheering by,
And home we brought you shoulder-high.

To-day, the road all runners come,
Shoulder-high we bring you home,
And set you at your threshold down,
Townsman of a stiller town.

Smart lad, to slip betimes away
From fields where glory does not stay
And early though the laurel grows
It withers quicker than the rose.

Eyes the shady night has shut
Cannot see the record cut,
And silence sounds no worse than cheers
After earth has stopped the ears:

Now you will not swell the rout
Of lads that wore their honours out,
Runners whom renown outran
And the name died before the man.

So set, before its echoes fade,
The fleet foot on the sill of shade,
And hold to the low lintel up
The still-defended challenge-cup.

And round that early-laurelled head
Will flock to gaze the strengthless dead,
And find unwithered on its curls
The garland briefer than a girl's.

'Is my team ploughing'

'Is my team ploughing,
    That I was used to drive
And hear the harness jingle
    When I was man alive?'

Ay, the horses trample,
    The harness jingles now;
No change though you lie under
    The land you used to plough.

'Is football playing
    Along the river shore,
With lads to chase the leather,
    Now I stand up no more?'

Ay, the ball is flying,
    The lads play heart and soul;
The goal stands up, the keeper
    Stands up to keep the goal.

'Is my girl happy,
    That I thought hard to leave,
And has she tired of weeping
    As she lies down at eve?'

Ay, she lies down lightly,
    She lies not down to weep:
Your girl is well contented.
    Be still, my lad, and sleep.

'Is my friend hearty,
    Now I am thin and pine,
And has he found to sleep in
    A better bed than mine?'

Yes, lad, I lie easy,
    I lie as lads would choose;
I cheer a dead man's sweetheart,
    Never ask me whose.

'Far in a western brookland'

Far in a western brookland
    That bred me long ago
The poplars stand and tremble
    By pools I used to know.

There, in the windless night-time,
    The wanderer, marvelling why,
Halts on the bridge to hearken
    How soft the poplars sigh.

He hears: no more remembered
    In fields where I was known,
Here I lie down in London
    And turn to rest alone.

There, by the starlit fences,
    The wanderer halts and hears
My soul that lingers sighing
    About the glimmering weirs.

Epitaph on an Army of Mercenaries

These, in the day when heaven was falling,
  The hour when earth's foundations fled,
Followed their mercenary calling
  And took their wages and are dead.

Their shoulders held the sky suspended;
  They stood, and earth's foundations stay;
What God abandoned, these defended,
  And saved the sum of things for pay.

'Crossing alone the nighted ferry'

Crossing alone the nighted ferry
  With the one coin for fee,
Whom, on the far quayside in waiting,
  Count you to find? Not me.

The fond lackey to fetch and carry,
  The true, sick-hearted slave,
Expect him not in the just city
  And free land of the grave.

HENRY HOWARD, EARL OF SURREY
(1517–1547)

An Excellent Epitaph of Sir Thomas Wyatt

Wyatt resteth here, that quick could never rest;
Whose heavenly gifts increased by disdain,
And virtue sank the deeper in his breast;
Such profit he of envy could obtain.

A head, where wisdom mysteries did frame,
Whose hammers beat still in that lively brain
As on a stith, where some work of fame
Was daily wrought, to turn to Britain's gain.

A visage, stern and mild; where both did grow,
Vice to condemn, in virtues to rejoice;
Amid great storms whom grace assured so,
To live upright and smile at fortune's choice.

A hand that taught what might be said in rhyme;
That reft Chaucer the glory of his wit;
A mark the which (unperfited, for time)
Some may approach, but never none shall hit.

A tongue that served in foreign realms his king;
Whose courteous talk to virtue did enflame
Each noble heart; a worthy guide to bring
Our English youth, by travail unto fame.

An eye whose judgment no affect could blind,
Friends to allure, and foes to reconcile;
Whose piercing look did represent a mind
With virtue fraught, reposed, void of guile.

A heart where dread yet never so impressed
To hide the thought that might the truth avaunce;
In neither fortune lift, nor so repressed,
To swell in wealth, nor yield unto mischance.

A valiant corps, where force and beauty met,
Happy, alas! too happy, but for foes,
Lived, and ran the race that nature set;
Of manhood's shape, where she the mold did lose.

But to the heavens that simple soul is fled,
Which left with such, as covet Christ to know
Witness of faith that never shall be dead:
Sent for our health, but not received so.

Thus, for our guilt, this jewel have we lost;
The earth his bones, the heavens possess his ghost.

'Norfolk sprung thee, Lambeth holds thee dead'

Norfolk sprung thee, Lambeth holds thee dead;
Clere, of the Count of Cleremont, though hight
Within the womb of Ormond's race thou bred,
And saw'st thy cousin crowned in thy sight.
Shelton for love, Surrey for Lord thou chase;
(Aye, me! whilst life did last that league was tender)
Tracing whose steps thou sawest Kelsal blaze,
Landrecy burnt, and batter'd Boulogne render.
At Montreuil gates, hopeless of all recure,
Thine Earl, half dead, gave in thy hand his will;
Which cause did thee this pining death procure,
Ere summers four times seven thou couldst fulfill.
  Ah! Clere! if love had booted, care, or cost,
  Heaven had not won, nor earth so timely lost.

LANGSTON HUGHES
(1902–1967)

Silhouette

Southern gentle lady,
Do not swoon.
They've just hung a black man
In the dark of the moon.

They've hung a black man
To a roadside tree
In the dark of the moon
For the world to see
How Dixie protects
Its white womanhood.

Southern gentle lady
Be good!
Be good!

TED HUGHES

(1930–1998)

Sheep

I

The sheep has stopped crying.
All morning in her wire-mesh compound
On the lawn, she has been crying
For her vanished lamb. Yesterday they came.
Then her lamb could stand, in a fashion,
And make some tiptoe cringing steps.
Now he has disappeared.
He was only half the proper size,
And his cry was wrong. It was not
A dry little hard bleat, a baby-cry
Over a flat tongue, it was human,
It was a despairing human smooth Oh!
Like no lamb I ever heard. Its hindlegs
Cowered in under its lumped spine,
Its feeble hips leaned towards
Its shoulders for support. Its stubby
White wool pyramid head, on a tottery neck,
Had sad and defeated eyes, pinched, pathetic,
Too small, and it cried all the time
Oh! Oh! staggering towards
Its alert, baffled, stamping, storming mother
Who feared our intentions. He was too weak
To find her teats, or to nuzzle up in under,
He hadn't the gumption. He was fully
Occupied just standing, then shuffling
Towards where she'd removed to. She knew
He wasn't right, she couldn't
Make him out. Then his rough-curl legs,

So stoutly built, and hooved
With real quality tips,
Just got in the way, like a loose bundle
Of firewood he was cursed to manage,
Too heavy for him, lending sometimes
Some support, but no strength, no real help.
When we sat his mother on her tail, he mouthed her teat,
Slobbering a little, but after a minute
Lost aim and interest, his muzzle wandered,
He was managing a difficulty
Much more urgent and important. By evening
He could not stand. It was not
That he could not thrive, he was born
With everything but the will –
That can be deformed, just like a limb.
Death was more interesting to him.
Life could not get his attention.
So he died, with the yellow birth-mucus
Still in his cardigan.
He did not survive a warm summer night.
Now his mother has started crying again.
The wind is oceanic in the elms
And the blossom is all set.

2

What is it this time the dark barn again
Where men jerk me off my feet
And shout over me with murder voices
And do something painful to somewhere on my body

Why am I grabbed by the leg and dragged from my friends
Where I was hidden safe though it was hot
Why am I dragged into the light and whirled onto my back
Why am I sat up on my rear end with my legs splayed

A man grips me helpless his knees grip me helpless
What is that buzzer what is it coming
Buzzing like a big fierce insect on a long tangling of snake
What is the man doing to me with his buzzing thing

That I cannot see he is pressing it into me
I surrender I let my legs kick I let myself be killed

I let him hoist me about he twists me flat
In a leverage of arms and legs my neck pinned under his ankle

While he does something dreadful down the whole length of
    my belly
My little teats stand helpless and terrified as he buzzes around
    them

Poor old ewe! She peers around from her ridiculous position.
Cool intelligent eyes, of grey-banded agate and amber,

Eyes deep and clear with feeling and understanding
While her monster hooves dangle helpless
And a groan like no bleat vibrates in her squashed windpipe
And the cutter buzzes at her groin and her fleece piles away

Now it buzzes at her throat and she emerges whitely
More and more grotesquely female and nude
Paunchy and skinny, while her old rug, with its foul tassels
Heaps from her as a foam-stiff, foam-soft, yoke-yellow robe

Numbed all over she suddenly feels much lighter
She feels herself free, her legs are her own and she scrambles up
Waiting for that grapple of hands to fling her down again
She stands in the opened arch of his knees she is facing a bright
    doorway

With a real bleat to comfort the lamb in herself
She trots across the threshold and makes one high clearing bound
To break from the cramp of her fright
And surprised by her new lightness and delighted

She trots away, noble-nosed, her pride unsmirched.
Her greasy winter-weight stays coiled on the foul floor,
    for somebody else to bother about.
She has a beautiful wet green brand on her bobbing
    brand-new backside,
She baas, she has come off best.

3

The mothers have come back
From the shearing, and behind the hedge
The woe of sheep is like a battlefield
In the evening, when the fighting is over,
And the cold begins, and the dew falls,
And bowed women move with water.
Mother mother mother the lambs
Are crying, and the mothers are crying.
Nothing can resist that probe, that cry
Of a lamb for its mother, or an ewe's crying
For its lamb. The lambs cannot find
Their mothers among those shorn strangers.
A half-hour they have lamented,
Shaking their voices in desperation.
Bald brutal-voiced mothers braying out,
Flat-tongued lambs chopping off hopelessness.
Their hearts are in panic, their bodies
Are a mess of woe, woe they cry,
They mingle their trouble, a music
Of worse and worse distress, a worse entangling,
They hurry out little notes
With all their strength, cries searching this way and that.
The mothers force out sudden despair, blaaa!
On restless feet, with wild heads.

Their anguish goes on and on, in the June heat.
Only slowly their hurt dies, cry by cry,
As they fit themselves to what has happened.

LEIGH HUNT

(1784–1859)

On the Death of His Son Vincent

Waking at morn, with the accustomed sigh
For what no morn could ever bring me more,
And again sighing, while collecting strength
To meet the pangs that waited me, like one
Whose sleep the rack hath watched: I tried to feel
How good for me had been strange griefs of old,
That for long days, months, years, inured my wits
To bear the dreadful burden of one thought.
One thought with woeful need turned many ways,
Which, shunned at first, and scaring me, as wounds
Thrusting in wound, became, oh! almost clasped
And blest, as saviours from the one dire pang
That mocked the will to move it.

MICK IMLAH

(1956–2008)

Stephen Boyd (1957–95)

'And on thai went, talkand of play and sport . . .'
Henryson, Orpheus and Eurydice

I can't drive, and I dreamt that I was driving
Unstoppably through a succession of red lights
Till I hit that slow-moving Transit amidships –
A crash that must elsewhere have killed somebody.
So I was doubly relieved, when the smoke cleared,
To see it was you who climbed unhurt from the van,
Fuming: you, who I knew to be dead already;
For though the SALTIRE overlaid your face,
The funeral mask of Scotland's Everyman,
Those specs and spry moustache gave you away –
Those, and the warmth in your abuse of me –
And it seemed from how your empty trousers scissored
And slipped through the ground, the dream after all
Was benign; they'd made you a sort of wizard.

I first ran into you in '82,
In Oxford, when you came over the road
From a rival college, to do graduate work
In Magdalen MCR: four pints a night,
Electric-thin, brimful of mimicry,
With a laugh that stopped unnervingly – .
We might have kept suspiciously apart:
You a Glaswegian from the Irish side;
Me, from the softer suburbs of the Kirk,
Who hadn't knowingly met a Catholic boy
Till I was sent to have my tonsils out
In the Ear, Nose and Throat on the Paisley Road
Aged seven, where the alien ward was full

Of green favours, Celtic scarfs and scruffs;
And years of a Southern education since
Had trimmed my Scottishness to a tartan phrase
Brought out on match days and Remembrance Days.

So football, I'd assumed, would be your game –
Not the perversion I was public-schooled in;
Until, one evening's ending at the bar,
Jocking it up, I 'prophesied' aloud
The 'greatness' of some teenage Border prospect,
Saviour of Scottish rugby and so on –
And you stepped out of the wan group you'd adopted,
With that particular look you had, half doubt,
Half reckless allegiance; the look, in fact,
Of the early Christian in the film *The Robe*,
Patrolling Nero's streets, when his ear catches
In a slave's whistle from the sewer beneath
A Hebrew melody gone underground:
The trace-note of some fellow in the faith.

Those days, the Scots lost more games than they won,
But the playing parts were mightier than the sum:
The last sparks of the cherub Andy Irvine,
My mother's favourite, 'out of Heriot's';
The hooker, Deans, pent-up, belligerent;
The steep kicks of our fly-half, Rutherford
('That one's come down with snow on it, I'll tell you');
Paxton the number eight, who on the box
Was always 'thumping on' or 'smashing on';
And Leslie, the deadly flanker from Dundee.
You also liked that Catholic lump from Hawick,
Shonnie McGaughey, who in the national side
Revelled in having bridged the great divide.

This is a long poem for a friendship based
On little more than aping Bill McLaren,
And spelling out again that sport matters
Because it doesn't matter; by such a ruse,
If not for long, worse things could be postponed. –

Meanwhile, two prigs, we liked to disapprove
Of those who showed their fears or bared their heart;
As when, in one of your fancier flights,
You said of the social posture of a scholar
Whose girlfriend had gone off with someone other,
That he 'expects the whole community
To circulate his sorrow, open-mouthed,
Like the wee Marys in Giotto's *Crucifixion*!'

The problem was, that day in late November,
When flu had scrubbed out half of Magdalen's strength,
To get fifteen of any ability out
To take on Balliol; when you piped up
Unhelpfully, 'I'll play' – yet there was no one else.
So we put you at full-back, farthest away
From the kick-off, at least; you had arrived
In a pair of khaki shorts (we played in black),
Which in a private reference to the kilt
You wore with nothing underneath, and kept
Your heavy-duty glasses on as well;
I'm sorry, but you looked ridiculous.
Ten minutes in, nil-nil, my hamstring went,
And we were down to fourteen – or, thirteen
Plus you. And yet, although you couldn't 'catch
To save your life', today you rescued Magdalen.
You pouched their box-kick with a booming 'Mark!',
Tackled and got to your feet and tackled again,
Swearing in Scots, and in attack made one
Comedian's charge through their amazed three-quarters.
I thought you'd crack in the second half; you didn't;
Not when a bonfire spread the field with smoke,
Or the light faded, towards the final whistle.
Six-three to us: a try by David Gearing.
Now I pull muscles sprinting in my sleep
And you make probing runs from the deeper deep.

Two white diagonals on a field of blue:
The Saltire, or the *crux decussata*,
Banner of *Braveheart* and the Glasgow Kiss,

Is said to represent the wooden X
To which, one morning by the harbourfront
At Patras, they attached our patron saint,
The first disciple, Andrew of Galilee,
Fisher of Men, called 'Manly' in the Greek:
Then seventy, a good age for a martyr.
We see it in the struts of a hurdle gate;
We saw it in the angles on the blackboard
Of the attacking full-back and his wing
When scissoring or dummy-scissoring.

A warm deceptive spring followed the March
Of David Sole's Grand Slam in 1990;
I flew up to St Andrews, where you'd won
A fellowship in English, and got married
To Sue the musician; since somehow you'd fixed it
For the powers-that-be up there to pay me
To do a poetry reading with Kathleen Jamie.
Our lives had changed, or yours had changed especially,
But still we had our taste for the old routine;
In the Indian afterwards, you leant forward
To murmur, like an arch-conspirator,
'I predict greatness for Damian Cronin' –
A good hard lock, though frequently overweight,
In and out of the side till his knee gave way
In '98 – and never quite as good as great.

Of all your flawed predictions, this was the last,
That I remember. Soon we'd got the bus
Back to the pretty house you'd bought in Crail,
A fishing village with a postcard harbour,
And hit the whisky, you harmlessly hammered
In front of your wife; till the turning point
The pleasure ended, or pretending did.
You'd put a record on, of Monteverdi,
Or something even earlier, singing yourself
In a passionate, reedy voice – and weeping, lots,
Then weeping more; and Sue had arms around you,
Stroking and shooshing, but without surprise –

So this was not the first time, nor the last.
She made you steady, and I went to bed,
And slept; but it resumed – whispers, breaking –
You exclaiming – she hushing you down –
And when she brought my morning tea, you'd gone.

I heard you had two boys ('just thirteen more . . .'),
But didn't write; and then your colleague phoned
To say he understood that we'd been close
(I heard you bristle back, 'We were *not close*'),
And that he was afraid you'd 'Taken Your Life' –
Preferring not to say in which specific
Knock-kneed, hurtful, individual style.
It doesn't matter. And I wouldn't force the door
For one cartoon, Body with rocks, bottles,
Or railway track, to blot out what you were;
But while we're at it, I'd be pleased to know
Your standpoint on the new Cronin, Scott Murray,
Whose jumping in the line-out begs comparison
With the Spey salmon; and to square with you
The lessons I was meant to take away
From our phantom collision: not to let die
The memory of your glorious afternoon
V. Balliol; and not to dwell on loss
If your sons' path and mine should ever cross.

MAJOR JACKSON
(1968–)

Ferguson

Once there was a boy who thought it a noble idea to lie down in the middle of the street and sleep. For four hours, no one bothered him, but let him lie on the road as though he were an enchantment. This became newsworthy and soon helicopters hovered above, hosing his curled torso and thick legs in spotlights televised the world over. Foreign correspondents focused on the neighborhood and its relative poverty as recognized by the plethora of low-hanging jeans worn by shirtless men and loud music issuing from passing cars, which had the effect of drowning out everyone's already bottled-up thoughts about the boy sleeping in the middle of the street; others jumped in front of cameras seizing an opportunity to be seen by their relatives on the other side of town because they had run out of minutes on prepaid cellphones.

The roadkill in the neighborhood, and some on that very block, rodents, cats, and possums, feeling equal amounts of jealousy and futility, each began to rise and return to their den holes, cursing the boy sleeping in the street beneath their breaths for his virtuosic performance of stillness and tribulation in the city. The drug-addicted men and women leaning into doorways like art installations were used to being ignored, but they, too, felt affronted by the boy sleeping in the street and folded their cardboard homes.

For the first hour, he practiced not breathing. For ten seconds, he would hold his breath. And then, he practiced longer sets of minutes during the next three hours until he was able to stretch out his non-breathing for whole hunks at a time. When his breathing returned, it was so faint, his chest and shoulders barely moved; infinitesimal amounts of life poured out of him, but no one noticed. The police cordoned off his body, and after some time, declared him dead because they had only seen black men lying prone on the street as corpses, but never as sleeping humans.

The whole world, eager and hungry for a Lazarus moment,

watched and waited to see when he would awaken and rise to his
feet, especially his neighbors with minutes remaining on cellphones
who filmed and animatedly discoursed behind yellow tape the
ecstasies and muted sorrows of watching a boy sleep in the middle
of the street.

LINTON KWESI JOHNSON
(1952–)

Reggae fi Dada

galang dada
galang gwaan yaw sah
yu nevah ad noh life fi live
jus di wan life fi give
yu did yu time pan ert
yu nevah get yu just dizert
galang goh smile inna di sun
galang goh satta inna di palace af peace
o di waatah
it soh deep
di waatah
it soh daak
an it full a hawbah shaak

di lan is like a rack
slowly shattahrin to san
sinkin in a sea af calimity
where fear breed shadows
dat lurks in di daak
where people fraid fi waak
fraid fi tink fraid fi taak
where di present is haunted by di paas

a deh soh mi bawn
get fi know bout staam
learn fi cling to di dawn
an wen mi hear mi daddy sick
mi quickly pack mi grip an tek a trip

mi nevah have noh time
wen mi reach
fi si noh sunny beach
wen mi reach
jus people a live in shack
people livin back-to-back
mongst cackroach an rat
mongst dirt an dizeez
subjek to terrorist attack
political intrigue
kanstant grief
an noh sign af relief

o di grass
turn brown
soh many trees
cut doun
an di lan is ovahgrown

fram country to town
is jus thistle an tawn
inna di woun a di poor
is a miracle ow dem endure
di pain nite an day
di stench af decay
di glarin sights
di guarded affluence
di arrogant vices
cole eyes af kantemp
di mackin symbals af independence

a deh soh mi bawn
get fi know bout staam
learn fi cling to di dawn
an wen di news reach mi
seh mi wan daddy ded
mi ketch a plane quick

an wen mi reach mi sunny isle
it woz di same ole style
di money well dry
di bullits dem a fly
plenty innocent a die
many rivahs run dry
ganja plane flyin high
di poor man im a try
yu tink a lickle try im try
holdin awn bye an bye
wen a dallah cant buy
a lickle dinnah fi a fly

galang dada
galang gwaan yaw sah
yu nevah ad noh life fi live
just di wan life fi give
yu did yu time pan ert
yu nevah get yu jus dizert
galang goh smile inna di sun
galang goh satta inna di palace af peace

mi know yu couldn tek it dada
di anguish an di pain
di suffahrin di prablems di strain
di strugglin in vain
fi mek two ens meet
soh dat dem pickney coulda get

a lickle someting fi eat
fi put cloaz pan dem back
fi put shoes pan dem feet
wen a dallah cant buy
a lickle dinnah fi a fly

mi know yu try dada
yu fite a good fite
but di dice dem did loaded
an di card pack fix
yet still yu reach fifty-six
before yu lose yu leg wicket
'a noh yu bawn grung here'
soh wi bury yu a Stranger's Burying Groun
near to mhum an cousin Daris
nat far fram di quarry
doun a August Town

SAMUEL JOHNSON
(1709–1784)

An Epitaph on Claudy Phillips, a Musician

Phillips! whose touch harmonious could remove
The pangs of guilty pow'r, and hapless love,
Rest here distrest by poverty no more,
Find here that calm thou gav'st so oft before;
Sleep undisturb'd within this peaceful shrine,
Till angels wake thee with a note like thine.

On the Death of Dr Robert Levet

Condemned to Hope's delusive mine,
　As on we toil from day to day,
By sudden blasts, or slow decline,
　Our social comforts drop away.

Well tried through many a varying year,
　See Levet to the grave descend;
Officious, innocent, sincere,
　Of every friendless name the friend.

Yet still he fills Affection's eye,
　Obscurely wise, and coarsely kind;
Nor, lettered Arrogance, deny
　Thy praise to merit unrefined.

When fainting Nature called for aid,
　And hovering Death prepared the blow,
His vigorous remedy displayed
　The power of art without the show.

In Misery's darkest cavern known,
    His useful care was ever nigh,
Where hopeless Anguish poured his groan,
    And lonely Want retired to die.

No summons mocked by chill delay,
    No petty gain disdained by pride,
The modest wants of every day
    The toil of every day supplied.

His virtues walked their narrow round,
    Nor made a pause, nor left a void;
And sure the Eternal Master found
    The single talent well employed.

The busy day, the peaceful night,
    Unfelt, uncounted, glided by;
His frame was firm, his powers were bright,
    Though now his eightieth year was nigh.

Then with no throbbing fiery pain,
    No cold gradations of decay,
Death broke at once the vital chain,
    And freed his soul the nearest way.

EBENEZER JONES

(1820–1860)

The Poet's Death

Now the Poet's death was certain, and the leech had left the room;
Only those who fondly loved him, waited to receive the doom;
And the sister he loved best, whiter than hemlock did veer;
And she bent, and 'life is going' faintly whispered in his ear.

Though her fingers clasped his fingers, though her cheek by his
    did lay;
Though she whispered 'I am dying; with thee, death hath no
    dismay';
Fiercely sprang the startled Poet, and his eye did fight through
    space;
While dark agony did thicken his drawn lips, and wrench his face.

Sister arms did wind around him, knelt his sire beside the bed;
And his mother busied round him, love extinguishing her dread;
But the Poet heeded nothing, fixing still his fighting eye,
Gathering, gathering, gathering inward, that he was that hour
    to die.

Now the sound of smothered sobbings smote upon his distant
    mind,
And he turned a glance around him, that each gazer's love divined;
The torture in his face did stagger once before his mother's look;
Then came back more whiteningly, while his neck did downward
    crook.

From his crook'd down neck, his visage struggled love back
    through its pain,
First to one, and then to another, and then left them all again;
As the sister wept against him, shudderingly to her he turned;
And his lips did open at her, and his eyes for language yearned.

Quick at her his lips did open, strivingly his eyelids rose,
But no sound, no word, no murmur, their fast gesturings did
    disclose;
Straightly pointed he his arm then, where his poet-desk was lain;
To his grasp the sister brought it, while the stillness throbbed
    amain.

From his desk the Poet tore the unformed scriptures of his soul;
And to them he fiercely pointed, while his eyes large tears did roll;
'Perfected, my memory earth to endless time would love and bless;
I must die, and these will live not!' through his lips at last did press.

Whiter grew the gazing faces, as the cliffs that sunshine smites,
When they found no aid could come from earthly loves, or
    priestly rites;
O'er his scriptures he fell forward, and they all did trust and say,
That the last wild pang was on him, for as still as stone he lay.

But than lightning's flash more sudden, he did spurn the
    abhorred bed;
And a moment he stood tottering, tossed defyingly his head;
Ere one reached him, he was fallen, lifeless, and his wide dulled eye
Rigid with the fierce defiance that had just refused to die.

To the gloomy troop of Atheists, gibberingly the sister ran;
While the praying father kneeling, hurled at her his pious ban;
In the churchyard lies the Poet, and his scent the air depraves;
And ten thousand thousand like him, stuff the earth with such
    like graves.

BEN JONSON

(1572–1637)

Epitaphs

1 ON MY FIRST DAUGHTER

Here lies to each her parents' ruth
Mary, the daughter of their youth:
Yet, all Heaven's gifts being Heaven's due,
It makes the father less to rue.
At six months' end she parted hence
With safety of her innocence;
Whose soul Heaven's Queen (whose name she bears)
In comfort of her mother's tears,
Hath placed amongst her virgin-train;
Where, while that severed doth remain,
This grave partakes the fleshly birth,
Which cover lightly, gentle earth.

2 ON MY SON

Farewell, thou child of my right hand, and joy;
  My sin was too much hope of thee, loved boy.
Seven years thou wert lent to me, and I thee pay,
  Exacted by thy fate, on the just day.
O, could I lose all father now! For why
  Will man lament the state he should envy?
To have so soon 'scaped world's and flesh's rage,
  And, if no other misery, yet age?
Rest in soft peace, and, asked, say here doth lie
  Ben Jonson, his best piece of poetry.
For whose sake, henceforth, all his vows be such
  As what he loves may never like too much.

To the Memory of My Beloved,
the Author Mr William Shakespeare

To draw no envy (Shakespeare) on thy name,
Am I thus ample to thy book, and fame:
While I confess thy writings to be such,
As neither man, nor muse, can praise too much.
'Tis true, and all men's suffrage. But these ways
Were not the paths I meant unto thy praise:
For seeliest ignorance on these may light,
Which, when it sounds at best, but echoes right;
Or blind affection, which doth ne'er advance
The truth, but gropes, and urgeth all by chance;
Or crafty malice, might pretend this praise,
And think to ruin, where it seemed to raise.
These are, as some infamous bawd, or whore,
Should praise a matron. What could hurt her more?
But thou art proof against them, and indeed
Above the ill fortune of them, or the need.
I therefore will begin. Soul of the age!
The applause, delight, the wonder of our stage!
My Shakespeare, rise; I will not lodge thee by
Chaucer, or Spenser, or bid Beaumont lie
A little further, to make thee a room:
Thou art a monument, without a tomb,
And art alive still, while thy book doth live,
And we have wits to read, and praise to give.
That I not mix thee so, my brain excuses;
I mean with great, but disproportioned muses:
For, if I thought my judgement were of years,
I should commit thee surely with thy peers,
And tell, how far thou didst our Lyly outshine,
Or sporting Kyd, or Marlowe's mighty line.
And though thou hadst small Latin, and less Greek,
From thence to honour thee, I would not seek
For names; but call forth thundering Aeschylus,

Euripides, and Sophocles to us,
Pacuvius, Accius, him of Cordova dead,
To life again, to hear thy buskin tread,
And shake a stage: or, when thy socks were on,
Leave thee alone, for the comparison
Of all that insolent Greece, or haughty Rome
Sent forth, or since did from their ashes come.
Triumph, my Britain, thou hast one to show,
To whom all scenes of Europe homage owe.
He was not of an age, but for all time!
And all the muses still were in their prime,
When like Apollo he came forth to warm
Our ears, or like a Mercury to charm!
Nature herself was proud of his designs,
And joyed to wear the dressing of his lines!
Which were so richly spun, and woven so fit,
As, since, she will vouchsafe no other wit.
The merry Greek, tart Aristophanes,
Neat Terence, witty Plautus, now not please;
But antiquated, and deserted lie
As they were not of nature's family.
Yet must I not give nature all: thy art,
My gentle Shakespeare, must enjoy a part.
For though the poet's matter, nature be,
His art doth give the fashion. And, that he,
Who casts to write a living line, must sweat,
(Such as thine are) and strike the second heat
Upon the muses' anvil: turn the same,
(And himself with it) that he thinks to frame;
Or for the laurel, he may gain a scorn,
For a good poet's made, as well as born.
And such wert thou. Look how the father's face
Lives in his issue, even so, the race
Of Shakespeare's mind, and manners brightly shines
In his well-turnéd, and true-filéd lines:
In each of which, he seems to shake a lance,
As brandished at the eyes of ignorance.
Sweet swan of Avon, what a sight it were
To see thee in our waters yet appear,

And make those flights upon the banks of Thames,
That so did take Eliza, and our James!
But stay, I see thee in the hemisphere
Advanced, and made a constellation there!
Shine forth, thou star of poets, and with rage,
Or influence, chide, or cheer the drooping stage;
Which, since thy flight from hence, hath mourned like night.
And despairs day, but for thy volume's light.

JACKIE KAY
(1961–)

Burying My African Father

Now that I have walked all the way down
the red dust road and into Nzagha

and seen the lizards and geckos
and goats and all God's creatures

and walked beside the elephant grasses
the plantain, banana and cassava

through the gate of your compound
past the sign that read *Barbing Saloon here*

and held the tiny two-week-old baby
of your second cousin, and said *Odimma*

to her shy *Kedu*, and stood outside
your house and peered through the shutters,

and in the hotel room, I remembered you well
spinning and praying years ago in Abuja

when you told me you wouldn't reveal
the name of your village, your sons or your daughter.

Now that I have finally arrived, without you,
to the home of the ancestors, I can bid you farewell, *Adieu.*

For I must, with my own black pen – instead of a spade
ashes to ashes and dust to dust,

and years before you are actually dead,
bury you right here in my head.

JOHN KEATS

(1795–1821)

When I Have Fears That I May Cease to Be

When I have fears that I may cease to be
   Before my pen has gleaned my teeming brain,
Before high-pilèd books, in charactery,
   Hold like rich garners the full ripened grain;
When I behold, upon the night's starred face,
   Huge cloudy symbols of a high romance,
And think that I may never live to trace
   Their shadows with the magic hand of chance;
And when I feel, fair creature of an hour,
   That I shall never look upon thee more,
Never have relish in the faery power
   Of unreflecting love – then on the shore
Of the wide world I stand alone, and think
Till love and fame to nothingness do sink.

HENRY KING
(1592–1669)

Exequy on His Wife

Accept, thou shrine of my dead saint,
Instead of dirges this complaint;
And for sweet flowers to crown thy hearse,
Receive a strew of weeping verse
From thy grieved friend, whom thou mightst see
Quite melted into tears for thee.
   Dear loss! since thy untimely fate
My task hath been to meditate
On thee, on thee! Thou art the book,
The library, whereon I look
Though almost blind. For thee, loved clay,
I languish out, not live, the day,
Using no other exercise
But what I practise with mine eyes.
By which wet glasses I find out
How lazily time creeps about
To one that mourns. This, only this,
My exercise and business is:
So I compute the weary hours
With sighs dissolved into showers.
   Nor wonder if my time go thus
Backward and most preposterous:
Thou hast benighted me. Thy set
This eve of blackness did beget,
Who wast my day (though overcast
Before thou hadst thy noon-tide past)
And I remember must in tears
Thou scarce hadst seen so many years
As day tells hours. By thy clear sun
My love and fortune first did run;
But thou wilt never more appear

Folded within my hemisphere,
Since both thy light and motion,
Like a fled star, is fallen and gone,
And 'twixt me and my soul's dear wish
The earth now interposèd is,
Which such a strange eclipse doth make
As ne'er was read in almanac.

   I could allow thee for a time
To darken me and my sad clime;
Were it a month, a year, or ten,
I would thy exile live till then;
And all that space my mirth adjourn,
So thou wouldst promise to return
And, putting off thy ashy shroud,
At length disperse this sorrow's cloud.

   But woe is me! the longest date
Too narrow is to calculate
These empty hopes. Never shall I
Be so much blest as to descry
A glimpse of thee, till that day come
Which shall the earth to cinders doom,
And a fierce fever must calcine
The body of this world, like thine,
My little world! That fit of fire
Once off, our bodies shall aspire
To our souls' bliss: then we shall rise,
And view ourselves with clearer eyes
In that calm region where no night
Can hide us from each other's sight.

   Meantime thou hast her, Earth: much good
May my harm do thee. Since it stood
With Heaven's will I might not call
Her longer mine, I give thee all
My short-lived right and interest
In her, whom living I loved best:
With a most free and bounteous grief,
I give thee what I could not keep.
Be kind to her, and prithee look
Thou write into thy Doomsday book

Each parcel of this rarity,
Which in thy casket shrined doth lie.
See that thou make thy reckoning straight,
And yield her back again by weight;
For thou must audit on thy trust
Each grain and atom of this dust,
As thou wilt answer him that lent,
Not gave thee, my dear monument.

   So close the ground, and 'bout her shade
Black curtains draw: my bride is laid.

   Sleep on, my Love, in thy cold bed
Never to be disquieted.
My last good night! Thou wilt not wake
Till I thy fate shall overtake:
Till age, or grief, or sickness must
Marry my body to that dust
It so much loves; and fill the room
My heart keeps empty in thy tomb.
Stay for me there: I will not fail
To meet thee in that hollow vale.
And think not much of my delay;
I am already on the way,
And follow thee with all the speed
Desire can make, or sorrows breed.
Each minute is a short degree
And every hour a step towards thee.
At night when I betake to rest,
Next morn I rise nearer my west
Of life, almost by eight hours sail
Than when sleep breathed his drowsy gale.

   Thus from the sun my bottom steers,
And my day's compass downward bears.
Nor labour I to stem the tide
Through which to thee I swiftly glide.

   'Tis true, with shame and grief I yield;
Thou, like the van, first took'st the field
And gotten hast the victory
In thus adventuring to die
Before me, whose more years might crave

A just precedence in the grave.
But hark! my pulse, like a soft drum,
Beats my approach, tells thee I come;
And slow howe'er my marches be
I shall at last sit down by thee.

    The thought of this bids me go on
And wait my dissolution
With hope and comfort. Dear, (forgive
The crime) I am content to live
Divided, with but half a heart,
Till we shall meet and never part.

RUDYARD KIPLING

(1865–1936)

The Appeal

If I have given you delight
  By aught that I have done,
Let me lie quiet in that night
  Which shall be yours anon:

And for the little, little, span
  The dead are borne in mind,
Seek not to question other than
  The books I leave behind.

YUSEF KOMUNYAKAA

(1947–)

Elegy for Thelonious

Damn the snow.
Its senseless beauty
pours a hard light
through the hemlock.
Thelonious is dead. Winter
drifts in the hourglass;
notes pour from the brain cup.
Damn the alley cat
wailing a muted dirge
off Lenox Ave.
Thelonious is dead.
Tonight's a lazy rhapsody of shadows
swaying to blue vertigo
& metaphysical funk.
Black trees in the wind.
Crepuscule with Nellie
plays inside the bowed head.
'Dig the Man Ray of piano!'
O Satisfaction,
hot fingers blur
on those white rib keys.
Coming on the Hudson.
Monk's Dream.
The ghost of bebop
from 52nd Street,
footprints in the snow.
Damn February.
Let's go to Minton's
& play 'modern malice'

till daybreak. Lord,
there's Thelonious
wearing that old funky hat
pulled down over his eyes.

CHARLES LAMB

(1775–1834)

The Old Familiar Faces

I have had playmates, I have had companions,
In my days of childhood, in my joyful school-days,
All, all are gone, the old familiar faces.

I have been laughing, I have been carousing,
Drinking late, sitting late, with my bosom cronies,
All, all are gone, the old familiar faces.

I loved a Love once, fairest among women;
Closed are her doors on me, I must not see her –
All, all are gone, the old familiar faces.

I have a friend, a kinder friend has no man;
Like an ingrate, I left my friend abruptly;
Left him, to muse on the old familiar faces.

Ghost-like, I paced round the haunts of my childhood.
Earth seem'd a desert I was bound to traverse,
Seeking to find the old familiar faces.

Friend of my bosom, thou more than a brother,
Why wert not thou born in my father's dwelling?
So might we talk of the old familiar faces –

How some they have died, and some they have left me,
And some are taken from me; all are departed;
All, all are gone, the old familiar faces.

LETITIA ELIZABETH LANDON
(1802–1838)

Stanzas on the Death of Mrs Hemans

Bring flowers to crown the cup and lute,
Bring flowers, the bride is near;
Bring flowers to soothe the captive's cell,
Bring flowers to strew the bier!
Bring flowers! – thus said the lovely song;
And shall they not be brought
To her who linked the offering
With feeling and with thought?

Bring flowers, the perfumed and the pure,
Those with the morning dew,
A sigh in every fragrant leaf,
A tear on every hue.
So pure, so sweet thy life has been,
So filling earth and air
With odours and with loveliness
Till common scenes grew fair.

Thy song around our daily path
Flung beauty born of dreams,
That shadows on the actual world
The spirit's sunny gleams.
Mysterious influence, that to earth
Brings down the heaven above,
And fills the universal heart
With universal love.

Such gifts were thine – as from the block,
The unformed and the cold,
The sculptor calls to breathing life
Some shape of perfect mould;
So thou from common thoughts and things
Didst call a charmed song,
Which on a sweet and swelling tide
Bore the full soul along.

And thou from far and foreign lands
Didst bring back many a tone,
And giving such new music still,
A music of thine own.
A lofty strain of generous thoughts,
And yet subdued and sweet –
An angel's song, who sings of earth,
Whose cares are at his feet.

And yet thy song is sorrowful,
Its beauty is not bloom;
The hopes of which it breathes are hopes
That look beyond the tomb.
Thy song is sorrowful as winds
That wander o'er the plain,
And ask for summer's vanished flowers,
And ask for them in vain.

Ah, dearly purchased is the gift,
The gift of song like thine;
A fated doom is hers who stands
The priestess of the shrine.
The crowd – they only see the crown,
They only hear the hymn –
They mark not that the cheek is pale,
And that the eye is dim.

Wound to a pitch too exquisite,
The soul's fine chords are wrung;
With misery and melody
They are too highly strung.
The heart is made too sensitive
Life's daily pain to bear;
It beats in music, but it beats
Beneath a deep despair.

It never meets the love it paints,
The love for which it pines;
Too much of heaven is in the faith
That such a heart enshrines.
The meteor wreath the poet wears
Must make a lonely lot;
It dazzles only to divide
From those who wear it not.

Didst thou not tremble at thy fame
And loathe its bitter prize,
While what to others triumph seemed,
To thee was sacrifice?
Oh flower brought from paradise
To this cold world of ours,
Shadows of beauty such as thine
Recall thy native bowers.

Let others thank thee – 'twas for them
Thy soft leaves thou didst wreathe;
The red rose wastes itself in sighs
Whose sweetness others breathe!
And they have thanked thee – many a lip
Has asked of thine for words,
When thoughts, life's finer thoughts, have touched
The spirit's inmost chords.

How many loved and honoured thee
Who only knew thy name;
Which o'er the weary working world

Like starry music came!
With what still hours of calm delight
Thy songs and image blend;
I cannot choose but think thou wert
An old familiar friend.

The charm that dwelt in songs of thine
My inmost spirit moved;
And yet I feel as thou hadst been
Not half enough beloved.
They say that thou wert faint and worn
With suffering and with care;
What music must have filled the soul
That had so much to spare!

Oh weary one! since thou art laid
Within thy mother's breast –
The green, the quiet mother earth –
Thrice blessed be thy rest!
Thy heart is left within our hearts
Although life's pang is o'er;
But the quick tears are in my eyes,
And I can write no more.

Felicia Hemans

No more, no more – O, never more returning,
   Will thy beloved presence gladden earth;
No more wilt thou with sad, yet anxious, yearning
   Cling to those hopes which have no mortal birth.
Thou art gone from us, and with thee departed,
   How many lovely things have vanish'd too:
Deep thoughts that at thy will to being started,
   And feelings, teaching us our own were true.
Thou hast been round us, like a viewless spirit,
   Known only by the music on the air;

The leaf or flowers which thou hast named inherit
    A beauty known but from thy breathing there:
For thou didst on them fling thy strong emotion,
    The likeness from itself the fond heart gave;
As planets from afar look down on ocean,
    And give their own sweet image to the wave.

And thou didst bring from foreign lands their treasures,
    As floats thy various melody along;
We know the softness of Italian measures,
    And the grave cadence of Castilian song.
A general bond of union is the poet,
    By its immortal verse is language known,
And for the sake of song do others know it –
    One glorious poet makes the world his own.
And thou—how far thy gentle sway extended !
    The heart's sweet empire over land and sea;
Many a stranger and far flower was blended
    In the soft wreath that glory bound for thee.
The echoes of the Susquehanna's waters
    Paused in the pine woods words of thine to hear; –
And to the wide Atlantic's younger daughters
    Thy name was lovely, and thy song was dear.

Was not this purchased all too dearly! – never
    Can fame atone for all that fame hath cost.
We see the goal, but know not the endeavour,
    Nor what fond hopes have on the way been lost.
What do we know of the unquiet pillow,
    By the worn cheek and tearful eyelid prest,
When thoughts chase thoughts, like the tumultuous billow,
    Whose very light and foam reveals unrest?
We say, the song is sorrowful, but know not
    What may have left that sorrow on the song;
However mournful words may be, they show not
    The whole extent of wretchedness and wrong.
They cannot paint the long sad hours, pass'd only
    In vain regrets o'er what we feel we are.

Alas! the kingdom of the lute is lonely –
   Cold is the worship coming from afar.

Yet what is mind in woman but revealing
   In sweet clear light the hidden world below,
By quicker fancies and a keener feeling
   Than those around, the cold and careless, knew
What is to feed such feeling, but to culture
   A soil whence pain will never more depart?
The fable of Prometheus and the vulture,
   Reveals the poet's and the woman's heart.
Unkindly are they judged – unkindly treated –
   By careless tongues and by ungenerous words;
While cruel sneer, and hard reproach, repeated,
   Jar the fine music of the spirit's chords.
Wert thou not weary – thou whose soothing numbers
   Gave other lips the joy thine own had not?
Didst thou not welcome thankfully the slumbers
   Which closed around thy mourning human lot?

What on this earth could answer thy requiring,
   For earnest faith – for love, the deep and true,
The beautiful, which was thy soul's desiring,
   But only from thyself its being drew.
How is the warm and loving heart requited
   In this harsh world, where it awhile must dwell!
Its best affections wrong'd, betray'd, and slighted –
   Such is the doom of those who love too well.
Better the weary dove should close its pinion.
   Fold up its golden wings and be at peace,
Enter, O ladye, that serene dominion,
   Where earthly cares and earthly sorrows cease.
Fame's troubled hour has clear'd, and now replying,
   A thousand hearts their music ask of thine.
Sleep with a light the lovely and undying
   Around thy grave – a grave which is a shrine.

WALTER SAVAGE LANDOR
(1775–1834)

Rose Aylmer

Ah, what avails the sceptred race!
   Ah, what the form divine!
What every virtue, every grace!
   Rose Aylmer, all were thine.

Rose Aylmer, whom these wakeful eyes
   May weep, but never see,
A night of memories and sighs
   I consecrate to thee.

PHILIP LARKIN

(1922–1985)

The Explosion

On the day of the explosion
Shadows pointed towards the pithead:
In the sun the slagheap slept.

Down the lane came men in pitboots
Coughing oath-edged talk and pipe-smoke,
Shouldering off the freshened silence.

One chased after rabbits; lost them;
Came back with a nest of lark's eggs;
Showed them; lodged them in the grasses.

So they passed in beards and moleskins,
Fathers, brothers, nicknames, laughter,
Through the tall gates standing open.

At noon, there came a tremor; cows
Stopped chewing for a second; sun,
Scarfed as in a heat-haze, dimmed.

The dead go on before us, they
Are sitting in God's house in comfort,
We shall see them face to face –

Plain as lettering in the chapels
It was said, and for a second
Wives saw men of the explosion

Larger than in life they managed –
Gold as on a coin, or walking
Somehow from the sun towards them,

One showing the eggs unbroken.

FRANCIS LEDWIDGE
(1887–1917)

Thomas MacDonagh

He shall not hear the bittern cry
In the wild sky, where he is lain,
Nor voices of the sweeter birds
Above the wailing of the rain.

Nor shall he know when loud March blows
Through slanting snows her fanfare shrill,
Blowing to flame the golden cup
Of many an upset daffodil.

But when the Dark Cow leaves the moor,
And pastures poor with greedy weeds,
Perhaps he'll hear her low at morn
Lifting her horn in pleasant meads.

AMY LEVY

(1861–1889)

Epitaph

On a Commonplace Person Who Died in Bed

This is the end of him, here he lies:
The dust in his throat, the worm in his eyes,
The mould in his mouth, the turf on his breast;
This is the end of him, this is best.
He will never lie on his couch awake,
Wide-eyed, tearless, till dim daybreak.
Never again will he smile and smile
When his heart is breaking all the while.
He will never stretch out his hands in vain
Groping and groping – never again.
Never ask for bread, get a stone instead.
Never pretend that the stone is bread.
Never sway and sway 'twixt the false and true,
Weighing and noting the long hours through.
Never ache and ache with the chok'd-up sighs;
This is the end of him, here he lies.

HENRY WADSWORTH LONGFELLOW
(1807–1882)

The Cross of Snow

In the long, sleepless watches of the night,
    A gentle face – the face of one long dead –
    Looks at me from the wall, where round its head
    The night-lamp casts a halo of pale light.
Here in this room she died; and soul more white
    Never through martyrdom of fire was led
    To its repose; nor can in books be read
    The legend of a life more benedight.
There is a mountain in the distant West
    That, sun-defying, in its deep ravines
    Displays a cross of snow upon its side.
Such is the cross I wear upon my breast
    These eighteen years, through all the changing scenes
    And seasons, changeless since the day she died.

MICHAEL LONGLEY

(1939–)

Wounds

Here are two pictures from my father's head –
I have kept them like secrets until now:
First, the Ulster Division at the Somme
Going over the top with 'Fuck the Pope!'
'No Surrender!': a boy about to die,
Screaming 'Give 'em one for the Shankill!'
'Wilder than Gurkhas' were my father's words
Of admiration and bewilderment.
Next comes the London-Scottish padre
Resettling kilts with his swagger-stick,
With a stylish backhand and a prayer.
Over a landscape of dead buttocks
My father followed him for fifty years.
At last, a belated casualty,
He said – lead traces flaring till they hurt –
'I am dying for King and Country, slowly.'
I touched his hand, his thin head I touched.

Now, with military honours of a kind,
With his badges, his medals like rainbows,
His spinning compass, I bury beside him
Three teenage soldiers, bellies full of
Bullets and Irish beer, their flies undone.
A packet of Woodbines I throw in,
A lucifer, the Sacred Heart of Jesus
Paralysed as heavy guns put out
The night-light in a nursery for ever;
Also a bus-conductor's uniform –
He collapsed beside his carpet-slippers
Without a murmur, shot through the head
By a shivering boy who wandered in

Before they could turn the television down
Or tidy away the supper dishes.
To the children, to a bewildered wife,
I think 'Sorry Missus' was what he said.

ROBERT LOWELL

(1917–1977)

Sailing Home from Rapallo

February 1954

Your nurse could only speak Italian,
but after twenty minutes I could imagine your final week,
and tears ran down my cheeks . . .

When I embarked from Italy with my Mother's body,
the whole shoreline of the *Golfo di Genova*
was breaking into fiery flower.
The crazy yellow and azure sea-sleds
blasting like jack-hammers across
the *spumante*-bubbling wake of our liner,
recalled the clashing colours of my Ford.
Mother travelled first-class in the hold,
her *Risorgimento* black and gold casket
was like Napoleon's at the *Invalides* . . .

While the passengers were tanning
on the Mediterranean in deck chairs,
our family cemetery in Dunbarton
lay under the White Mountains
in the sub-zero weather.
The graveyard's soil was changing to stone –
so many of its deaths had been midwinter.
Dour and dark against the blinding snowdrifts,
its black brook and fir trunks were as smooth as masts.
A fence of iron spear-hafts
black-bordered its mostly Colonial grave-slates.
The only 'unhistoric' soul to come here
was Father, now buried beneath his recent
unweathered pink-veined slice of marble.

Even the Latin of his Lowell motto:
Occasionem cognosce,
seemed too businesslike and pushing here,
where the burning cold illuminated
the hewn inscriptions of Mother's relatives:
twenty or thirty Winslows and Starks.
Frost had given their names a diamond edge . . .

In the grandiloquent lettering on Mother's coffin,
Lowell had been misspelled *LOVEL.*
The corpse
was wrapped like *panetone* in Italian tinfoil.

LUCRETIUS

(c. 99–55 BCE)

from *On the Nature of Things*

What has this bugbear, death, to frighten man,
If souls can die, as well as bodies can?
For, as before our birth we felt no pain,
When Punic arms infested land and main,
When heaven and earth were in confusion hurled,
For the debated empire of the world,
Which awed with dreadful expectation lay,
Sure to be slaves, uncertain who should sway:
So, when our mortal frame shall be disjoined,
The lifeless lump uncoupled from the mind,
From sense of grief and pain we shall be free;
We shall not feel, because we shall not be.
Though earth in seas, and seas in heaven were lost,
We should not move, we only should be tossed.
Nay, e'en suppose when we have suffered fate,
The soul could feel in her divided state,
What's that to us? for we are only we,
While souls and bodies in one frame agree.
Nay, though our atoms should revolve by chance,
And matter leap into the former dance;
Though time our life and motion could restore,
And make our bodies what they were before;
What gain to us would all this bustle bring?
The new-made man would be another thing.
When once an interrupting pause is made,
That individual being is decayed.
We, who are dead and gone, shall bear no part
In all the pleasures, nor shall feel the smart,
Which to that other mortal shall accrue,
Whom of our matter time shall mould anew.
For backward if you look on that long space

Of ages past, and view the changing face
Of matter, tossed, and variously combined
In sundry shapes, 'tis easy for the mind
From thence to infer, that seeds of things have been
In the same order as they now are seen;
Which yet our dark remembrance cannot trace,
Because a pause of life, a gaping space,
Has come betwixt, where memory lies dead,
And all the wandering motions from the sense are fled.
For, whosoe'er shall in misfortunes live,
Must *be*, when those misfortunes shall arrive;
And since the man who *is* not, feels not woe,
(For death exempts him, and wards off the blow,
Which we, the living, only feel and bear,)
What is there left for us in death to fear?
When once that pause of life has come between,
'Tis just the same as we had never been.
    And therefore if a man bemoan his lot,
That after death his mouldering limbs shall rot,
Or flames, or jaws of beasts devour his mass,
Know, he's an unsincere, unthinking ass.
A secret sting remains within his mind;
The fool is to his own cast offals kind.
He boasts no sense can after death remain,
Yet makes himself a part of life again,
As if some other he could feel the pain.
If, while he live, this thought molest his head,
What wolf or vulture shall devour me dead?
He wastes his days in idle grief, nor can
Distinguish 'twixt the body and the man;
But thinks himself can still himself survive,
And what when dead he feels not, feels alive.
Then he repines that he was born to die,
Nor knows in death there is no other he,
No living he remains his grief to vent,
And o'er his senseless carcase to lament.
If, after death, 'tis painful to be torn
By birds and beasts, then why not so to burn,
Or drenched in floods of honey to be soaked,

Embalmed to be at once preserved and choked;
Or on an airy mountain's top to lie,
Exposed to cold and heaven's inclemency;
Or crowded in a tomb, to be oppressed
With monumental marble on thy breast?
But to be snatched from all thy household joys,
From thy chaste wife, and thy dear prattling boys,
Whose little arms about thy legs are cast,
And climbing for a kiss prevent their mother's haste,
Inspiring secret pleasure through thy breast;
All these shall be no more; thy friends oppressed,
Thy care and courage now no more shall free;
'Ah! wretch,' thou criest, 'ah! miserable me!
One woeful day sweeps children, friends, and wife,
And all the brittle blessings of my life!'
Add one thing more, and all thou say'st is true;
Thy want and wish of them is vanished too;
Which well considered were a quick relief
To all thy vain imaginary grief.
For thou shalt sleep, and never wake again,
And, quitting life, shalt quit thy living pain.
But we, thy friends, shall all those sorrows find,
Which in forgetful death thou leav'st behind;
No time shall dry our tears, nor drive thee from our mind.
The worst that can befall thee, measured right,
Is a sound slumber, and a long goodnight.
Yet thus the fools, that would be thought the wits,
Disturb their mirth with melancholy fits;
When healths go round, and kindly brimmers flow,
Till the fresh garlands on their foreheads glow,
They whine, and cry: 'Let us make haste to live,
Short are the joys that human life can give.'
Eternal preachers, that corrupt the draught,
And pall the god that never thinks with thought;
Idiots with all that thought, to whom the worst
Of death, is want of drink, and endless thirst,
Or any fond desire as vain as these.
For, e'en in sleep, the body, wrapped in ease,
Supinely lies, as in the peaceful grave;

And wanting nothing, nothing can it crave.
Were that sound sleep eternal, it were death;
Yet the first atoms then, the seeds of breath,
Are moving near to sense; we do but shake
And rouse that sense, and straight we are awake.
Then death to us, and death's anxiety,
Is less than nothing, if a less could be;
For then our atoms, which in order lay,
Are scattered from their heap, and puffed away,
And never can return into their place,
When once the pause of life has left an empty space.
   And, last, suppose great nature's voice should call
To thee, or me, or any of us all,
'What dost thou mean, ungrateful wretch, thou vain,
Thou mortal thing, thus idly to complain,
And sigh and sob, that thou shalt be no more?
For if thy life were pleasant heretofore,
If all the bounteous blessings I could give
Thou hast enjoyed, if thou hast known to live,
And pleasure not leaked through thee like a sieve,
Why dost thou not give thanks as at a plenteous feast,
Crammed to the throat with life, and rise and take thy rest?
But if my blessings thou hast thrown away,
If undigested joys passed through, and would not stay,
Why dost thou wish for more to squander still?
If life be grown a load, a real ill,
And I would all thy cares and labours end,
Lay down thy burden, fool, and know thy friend.
To please thee, I have emptied all my store;
I can invent, and can supply no more,
But run the round again, the round I ran before.
Suppose thou art not broken yet with years,
Yet still the selfsame scene of things appears,
And would be ever, couldst thou ever live;
For life is still but life, there's nothing new to give.'
What can we plead against so just a bill?
We stand convicted, and our cause goes ill.
But if a wretch, a man oppressed by fate,
Should beg of nature to prolong his date,

She speaks aloud to him with more disdain,
'Be still, thou martyr fool, thou covetous of pain.'
But if an old decrepit sot lament,
'What, thou,' she cries, 'who hast outlived content!
Dost thou complain, who hast enjoyed my store?
But this is still the effect of wishing more.
Unsatisfied with all that nature brings;
Loathing the present, liking absent things;
From hence it comes, thy vain desires, at strife
Within themselves, have tantalised thy life,
And ghastly death appeared before thy sight,
Ere thou hadst gorged thy soul and senses with delight.
Now leave those joys unsuiting to thy age
To a fresh comer, and resign the stage.'
   Is nature to be blamed if thus she chide?
No, sure; for 'tis her business to provide
Against this ever-changing frame's decay,
New things to come, and old to pass away.
One being, worn, another being makes;
Changed, but not lost; for nature gives and takes:
New matter must be found for things to come,
And these must waste like those, and follow nature's doom.
All things, like thee, have time to rise and rot,
And from each other's ruin are begot:
For life is not confined to him or thee;
'Tis given to all for use, to none for property.
Consider former ages past and gone,
Whose circles ended long ere thine begun,
Then tell me, fool, what part in them thou hast?
Thus mayst thou judge the future by the past.
What horror seest thou in that quiet state,
What bugbear dreams to fright thee after fate?
No ghost, no goblins, that still passage keep;
But all is there serene, in that eternal sleep.
For all the dismal tales that poets tell
Are verified on earth, and not in hell.
No Tantalus looks up with fearful eye,
Or dreads the impending rock to crush him from on high;
But fear of chance on earth disturbs our easy hours,

Or vain imagined wrath of vain imagined powers.
No Tityus torn by vultures lies in hell;
Nor could the lobes of his rank liver swell
To that prodigious mass for their eternal meal;
Not though his monstrous bulk had covered o'er
Nine spreading acres, or nine thousand more;
Not though the globe of earth had been the giant's floor;
Nor in eternal torments could he lie,
Nor could his corpse sufficient food supply.
But he's the Tityus, who, by love oppressed,
Or tyrant passion preying on his breast,
And ever anxious thoughts, is robbed of rest.
The Sisyphus is he, whom noise and strife
Seduce from all the soft retreats of life,
To vex the government, disturb the laws;
Drunk with the fumes of popular applause,
He courts the giddy crowd to make him great,
And sweats and toils in vain, to mount the sovereign seat.
For still to aim at power, and still to fail,
Ever to strive, and never to prevail,
What is it but in reason's true account,
To heave the stone against the rising mount?
Which urged, and laboured, and forced up with pain,
Recoils, and rolls impetuous down, and smokes along the plain.
Then still to treat thy ever-craving mind
With every blessing, and of every kind,
Yet never fill thy ravening appetite,
Though years and seasons vary thy delight,
Yet nothing to be seen of all the store,
But still the wolf within thee barks for more;
This is the fable's moral, which they tell
Of fifty foolish virgins damned in hell
To leaky vessels, which the liquor spill;
To vessels of their sex, which none could ever fill.
As for the dog, the furies, and their snakes,
The gloomy caverns, and the burning lakes,
And all the vain infernal trumpery,
They neither are, nor were, nor e'er can be.
But here on earth the guilty have in view

The mighty pains to mighty mischiefs due:
Racks, prisons, poisons, the Tarpeian rock,
Stripes, hangmen, pitch, and suffocating smoke;
And last, and most, if these were cast behind,
The avenging horror of a conscious mind,
Whose deadly fear anticipates the blow,
And sees no end of punishment and woe,
But looks for more, at the last gasp of breath:
This makes a hell on earth, and life a death.
    Meantime, when thoughts of death disturb thy head,
Consider, Ancus, great and good, is dead;
Ancus, thy better far, was born to die,
And thou, dost thou bewail mortality?
So many monarchs with their mighty state,
Who ruled the world, were overruled by fate.
That haughty king, who lorded o'er the main,
And whose stupendous bridge did the wild waves restrain,
(In vain they foamed, in vain they threatened wreck,
While his proud legions marched upon their back):
Him death, a greater monarch, overcame;
Nor spared his guards the more, for their immortal name.
The Roman chief, the Carthaginian dread,
Scipio, the thunderbolt of war, is dead,
And like a common slave, by fate in triumph led.
The founders of invented arts are lost,
And wits who made eternity their boast.
Where now is Homer, who possessed the throne?
The immortal work remains, the mortal author's gone.
Democritus, perceiving age invade,
His body weakened, and his mind decayed,
Obeyed the summons with a cheerful face;
Made haste to welcome death, and met him half the race.
That stroke e'en Epicurus could not bar,
Though he in wit surpassed mankind, as far
As does the midday sun the midnight star.
And thou, dost thou disdain to yield thy breath,
Whose very life is little more than death?
More than one half by lazy sleep possessed;
And when awake, thy soul but nods at best,

Day-dreams and sickly thoughts revolving in thy breast,
Eternal troubles haunt thy anxious mind,
Whose cause and cure thou never hop'st to find;
But still uncertain, with thyself at strife,
Thou wanderest in the labyrinth of life.
   Oh, if the foolish race of man, who find
A weight of cares still pressing on their mind,
Could find as well the cause of this unrest,
And all this burden lodged within the breast;
Sure they would change their course, nor live as now,
Uncertain what to wish or what to vow.
Uneasy both in country and in town,
They search a place to lay their burden down.
One, restless in his palace, walks abroad,
And vainly thinks to leave behind the load,
But straight returns; for he's as restless there,
And finds there's no relief in open air.
Another to his villa would retire,
And spurs as hard as if it were on fire;
No sooner entered at his country door,
But he begins to stretch, and yawn, and snore,
Or seeks the city, which he left before.
Thus every man o'erworks his weary will,
To shun himself, and to shake off his ill;
The shaking fit returns, and hangs upon him still.
No prospect of repose, nor hope of ease,
The wretch is ignorant of his disease;
Which known, would all his fruitless trouble spare,
For he would know the world not worth his care:
Then would he search more deeply for the cause,
And study nature well, and nature's laws:
For in this moment lies not the debate,
But on our future, fixed, eternal state;
That never-changing state, which all must keep,
Whom death has doomed to everlasting sleep.
   Why are we then so fond of mortal life,
Beset with dangers, and maintained with strife?
A life, which all our care can never save;
One fate attends us, and one common grave.

Besides we tread but a perpetual round;
We ne'er strike out, but beat the former ground,
And the same mawkish joys in the same track are found.
For still we think an absent blessing best,
Which cloys, and is no blessing when possessed;
A new arising wish expels it from the breast.
The feverish thirst of life increases still;
We call for more and more, and never have our fill;
Yet know not what tomorrow we shall try,
What dregs of life in the last draught may lie.
Nor, by the longest life we can attain,
One moment from the length of death we gain;
For all behind belongs to his eternal reign.
When once the fates have cut the mortal thread,
The man as much to all intents is dead,
Who dies today, and will as long be so,
As he who died a thousand years ago.

Translated by John Dryden

LOUIS MACNEICE
(1907–1963)

The Suicide

And this, ladies and gentlemen, whom I am not in fact
Conducting, was his office all those minutes ago,
This man you never heard of. There are the bills
In the intray, the ash in the ashtray, the grey memoranda stacked
Against him, the serried ranks of the box-files, the packed
Jury of his unanswered correspondence
Nodding under the paperweight in the breeze
From the window by which he left; and here is the cracked
Receiver that never got mended and here is the jotter
With his last doodle which might be his own digestive tract
Ulcer and all or might be the flowery maze
Through which he had wandered deliciously till he stumbled
Suddenly finally conscious of all he lacked
On a manhole under the hollyhocks. The pencil
Point had obviously broken, yet, when he left this room
By catdrop sleight-of-foot or simple vanishing act,
To those who knew him for all that mess in the street
This man with the shy smile has left behind
Something that was intact.

DEREK MAHON

(1941–2020)

A Disused Shed in Co. Wexford

'Let them not forget us, the weak souls among the asphodels.'
Seferis, Mythistorema

For J. G. Farrell

Even now there are places where a thought might grow –
Peruvian mines, worked out and abandoned
to a slow clock of condensation,
an echo trapped for ever, and a flutter
of wildflowers in the lift-shaft,
Indian compounds where the winds dance
and a door bangs with diminished confidence,
lime crevices behind rippling rain barrels,
dog corners for bone burials;
and in a disused shed in Co. Wexford,

deep in the grounds of a burnt-out hotel,
among the bathtubs and the washbasins
a thousand mushrooms crowd to a keyhole.
This is the one star in their firmament
or frames a star within a star.
What should they do there but desire?
So many days beyond the rhododendrons
with the world revolving in its bowl of cloud,
they have learnt patience and silence
listening to the rooks querulous in the high wood.

They have been waiting for us in a foetor
of vegetable sweat since civil war days,
since the gravel-crunching, interminable departure
of the expropriated mycologist.

He never came back, and light since then
is a keyhole rusting gently after rain.
Spiders have spun, flies dusted to mildew
and once a day, perhaps, they have heard something –
a trickle of masonry, a shout from the blue
or a lorry changing gear at the end of the lane.

There have been deaths, the pale flesh flaking
into the earth that nourished it;
and nightmares, born of these and the grim
dominion of stale air and rank moisture.
Those nearest the door grow strong –
'Elbow room! Elbow room!'
The rest, dim in a twilight of crumbling
utensils and broken pitchers, groaning
for their deliverance, have been so long
expectant that there is left only the posture.

A half century, without visitors, in the dark –
poor preparation for the cracking lock
and creak of hinges; magi, moonmen,
powdery prisoners of the old regime,
web-throated, stalked like triffids, racked by drought
and insomnia, only the ghost of a scream
at the flash-bulb firing-squad we wake them with
shows there is life yet in their feverish forms.
Grown beyond nature now, soft food for worms,
they lift frail heads in gravity and good faith.

They are begging us, you see, in their wordless way,
to do something, to speak on their behalf
or at least not to close the door again.
Lost people of Treblinka and Pompeii!
'Save us, save us,' they seem to say,
'let the god not abandon us
who have come so far in darkness and in pain.
We too had our lives to live.
You with your light meter and relaxed itinerary,
let not our naive labours have been in vain!'

ANDREW MARVELL

(1621–1678)

from A Poem upon the Death of His Late Highness the Lord Protector

I saw him dead. A leaden slumber lies
And mortal sleep over those wakeful eyes:
Those gentle rays under the lids were fled,
Which through his looks that piercing sweetness shed;
That port which so majestic was and strong,
Loose and deprived of vigour, stretched along:
All withered, all discoloured, pale and wan –
How much another thing, nor more that man?
Oh human glory vain, oh death, oh wings,
Oh worthless world, oh transitory things!
　　Yet dwelt that greatness in his shape decayed,
That still though dead, greater than death he laid;
And in his altered face you something feign
That threatens death he yet will live again.
　　Not much unlike the sacred oak which shoots
To heaven its branches and through earth its roots,
Whose spacious boughs are hung with trophies round,
And honoured wreaths have oft the victor crowned.
When angry Jove darts lightning through the air,
At mortals' sins, nor his own plant will spare,
(It groans, and bruises all below, that stood
So many years the shelter of the wood.)
The tree erewhile foreshortened to our view,
When fall'n shows taller yet than as it grew:
　　So shall his praise to after times increase,
When truth shall be allowed, and faction cease,
And his own shadows with him fall. The eye
Detracts from objects than itself more high:
But when death takes them from that envied seat,
Seeing how little, we confess how great.

PAULA MEEHAN

(1955–)

Child Burial

I chose your grave clothes with care,
your favourite stripey shirt,

your blue cotton trousers.
They smelt of woodsmoke, of October,

your own smell there too.
I chose a gansy of handspun wool,

warm and fleecy for you. It is
so cold down in the dark.

No light can reach you and teach you
the paths of wild birds,

the names of the flowers,
the fishes, the creatures.

Ignorant you must remain
of the sun and its work,

my lamb, my calf, my eaglet,
my cub, my kid, my nestling,

my suckling, my colt. I would spin
time back, take you again

within my womb, your amniotic lair,
and further spin you back

through nine waxing months
to the split seeding moment

you chose to be made flesh,
word within me.

I'd cancel the love feast
the hot night of your making.

I would travel alone
to a quiet mossy place,

you would spill from me into the earth
drop by bright red drop.

HERMAN MELVILLE
(1819–1891)

Monody

To have known him, to have loved him
   After loneness long;
And then to be estranged in life,
   And neither in the wrong;
And now for death to set his seal –
   Ease me, a little ease, my song!

By wintry hills his hermit-mound
   The sheeted snow-drifts drape,
And houseless there the snow-bird flits
   Beneath the fir-trees' crape:
Glazed now with ice the cloistral vine
   That hid the shyest grape.

CHARLOTTE MEW

(1896–1928)

The Farmer's Bride

Three summers since I chose a maid,
Too young maybe – but more's to do
At harvest-time than bide and woo.
    When us was wed she turned afraid
Of love and me and all things human;
Like the shut of a winter's day
Her smile went out, and 'twadn't a woman –
    More like a little frightened fay.
        One night, in the Fall, she runned away.

'Out 'mong the sheep, her be,' they said,
'Should properly have been abed;
But sure enough she wadn't there
Lying awake with her wide brown stare.
So over seven-acre field and up-along across the down
  We chased her, flying like a hare
  Before out lanterns. To Church-Town
    All in a shiver and a scare
  We caught her, fetched her home at last
    And turned the key upon her, fast.

She does the work about the house
As well as most, but like a mouse:
    Happy enough to chat and play
    With birds and rabbits and such as they,
    So long as men-folk keep away.
'Not near, not near!' her eyes beseech
When one of us comes within reach.
    The women say that beasts in stall
    Look round like children at her call.
    I've hardly heard her speak at all.

Shy as a leveret, swift as he,
Straight and slight as a young larch tree,
Sweet as the first wild violets, she,
To her wild self. But what to me?
The short days shorten and the oaks are brown,
    The blue smoke rises to the low grey sky,
One leaf in the still air falls slowly down,
    A magpie's spotted feathers lie
On the black earth spread white with rime,
The berries redden up to Christmas-time.
    What's Christmas-time without there be
    Some other in the house than we!

    She sleeps up in the attic there
    Alone, poor maid. 'Tis but a stair
Betwixt us. Oh! my God! the down,
The soft young down of her, the brown,
The brown of her – her eyes, her hair, her hair!

EDNA ST VINCENT MILLAY

(1892–1950)

Burial

Mine is a body that should die at sea!
And have for a grave, instead of a grave
Six feet deep and the length of me,
All the water that is under the wave!
And terrible fishes to seize my flesh,
Such as a living man might fear,
And eat me while I am firm and fresh, –
Not wait till I've been dead for a year!

JOHN MILTON
(1608–1674)

Lycidas

Yet once more, O ye laurels, and once more
Ye myrtles brown, with ivy never sere,
I come to pluck your berries harsh and crude,
And with forced fingers rude,
Shatter your leaves before the mellowing year.
Bitter constraint, and sad occasion dear,
Compels me to disturb your season due;
For Lycidas is dead, dead ere his prime,
Young Lycidas, and hath not left his peer.
Who would not sing for Lycidas? He knew
Himself to sing, and build the lofty rhyme.
He must not float upon his watery bier
Unwept, and welter to the parching wind,
Without the meed of some melodious tear.
  Begin then, sisters of the sacred well
That from beneath the seat of Jove doth spring,
Begin, and somewhat loudly sweep the string.
Hence with denial vain, and coy excuse;
So may some gentle Muse
With lucky words favor my destined urn,
And as he passes turn,
And bid fair peace be to my sable shroud.
For we were nursed upon the selfsame hill,
Fed the same flock, by fountain, shade, and rill.
  Together both, ere the high lawns appeared
Under the opening eyelids of the morn,
We drove afield, and both together heard
What time the grayfly winds her sultry horn,
Battening our flocks with the fresh dews of night,
Oft till the star that rose at evening bright

Toward heaven's descent had sloped his westering wheel.
Meanwhile the rural ditties were not mute,
Tempered to th' oaten flute,
Rough satyrs danced, and fauns with cloven heel
From the glad sound would not be absent long,
And old Damoetas loved to hear our song.
    But O the heavy change, now thou art gone,
Now thou art gone, and never must return!
Thee, shepherd, thee the woods and desert caves,
With wild thyme and the gadding vine o'ergrown,
And all their echoes mourn.
The willows and the hazel copses green
Shall now no more be seen,
Fanning their joyous leaves to thy soft lays.
As killing as the canker to the rose,
Or taint-worm to the weanling herds that graze,
Or frost to flowers that their gay wardrobe wear
When first the white-thorn blows;
Such, Lycidas, thy loss to shepherd's ear.
    Where were ye, nymphs, when the remorseless deep
Closed o'er the head of your loved Lycidas?
For neither were ye playing on the steep
Where your old bards, the famous Druids, lie,
Nor on the shaggy top of Mona high,
Nor yet where Deva spreads her wizard stream:
Ay me! I fondly dream –
Had ye been there – for what could that have done?
What could the Muse herself that Orpheus bore,
The Muse herself, for her inchanting son
Whom universal Nature did lament,
When by the rout that made the hideous roar
His gory visage down the stream was sent,
Down the swift Hebrus to the Lesbian shore?
    Alas! What boots it with incessant care
To tend the homely slighted shepherd's trade,
And strictly meditate the thankless Muse?
Were it not better done as others use,
To sport with Amaryllis in the shade,
Or with the tangles of Neaera's hair?

Fame is the spur that the clear spirit doth raise
(That last infirmity of noble mind)
To scorn delights, and live laborious days;
But the fair guerdon when we hope to find,
And think to burst out into sudden blaze,
Comes the blind Fury with th' abhorrèd shears,
And slits the thin-spun life. 'But not the praise,'
Phoebus replied, and touched my trembling ears;
'Fame is no plant that grows on mortal soil,
Nor in the glistering foil
Set off to th' world, nor in broad rumor lies,
But lives and spreads aloft by those pure eyes,
And perfect witness of all-judging Jove;
As he pronounces lastly on each deed,
Of so much fame in heaven expect thy meed.'
    O fountain Arethuse, and thou honored flood,
Smooth-sliding Mincius, crowned with vocal reeds,
That strain I heard was of a higher mood.
But now my oat proceeds,
And listens to the herald of the sea
That came in Neptune's plea.
He asked the waves, and asked the felon winds,
'What hard mishap hath doomed this gentle swain?'
And questioned every gust of rugged wings
That blows from off each beakèd promontory;
They knew not of his story,
And sage Hippotades their answer brings,
That not a blast was from his dungeon strayed;
The air was calm, and on the level brine,
Sleek Panope with all her sisters played.
It was that fatal and perfidious bark,
Built in th' eclipse, and rigged with curses dark,
That sunk so low that sacred head of thine.
    Next Camus, reverend sire, went footing slow,
His mantle hairy, and his bonnet sedge,
Inwrought with figures dim, and on the edge
Like to that sanguine flower inscribed with woe.
'Ah! who hath reft,' quoth he, 'my dearest pledge?'
Last came and last did go

The pilot of the Galilean lake;
Two massy keys he bore of metals twain
(The golden opes, the iron shuts amain).
He shook his mitered locks, and stern bespake:
'How well could I have spared for thee, young swain,
Enow of such as for their bellies' sake
Creep and intrude and climb into the fold!
Of other care they little reckoning make,
Than how to scramble at the shearers' feast,
And shove away the worthy bidden guest.
Blind mouths! that scarce themselves know how to hold
A sheep-hook, or have learned aught else the least
That to the faithful herdsman's art belongs!
What recks it them? What need they? They are sped;
And when they list, their lean and flashy songs
Grate on their scrannel pipes of wretched straw.
The hungry sheep look up, and are not fed,
But swoln with wind, and the rank mist they draw,
Rot inwardly, and foul contagion spread,
Besides what the grim wolf with privy paw
Daily devours apace, and nothing said.
But that two-handed engine at the door
Stands ready to smite once, and smite no more.'
    Return, Alpheus, the dread voice is past,
That shrunk thy streams; return, Sicilian muse,
And call the vales, and bid them hither cast
Their bells and flowerets of a thousand hues.
Ye valleys low where the mild whispers use,
Of shades and wanton winds, and gushing brooks,
On whose fresh lap the swart star sparely looks,
Throw hither all your quaint enameled eyes,
That on the green turf suck the honeyed showers,
And purple all the ground with vernal flowers.
Bring the rathe primrose that forsaken dies,
The tufted crow-toe, and pale jessamine,
The white pink, and the pansy freaked with jet,
The glowing violet,
The musk-rose, and the well-attired woodbine,

With cowslips wan that hang the pensive head,
And every flower that sad embroidery wears:
Bid amaranthus all his beauty shed,
And daffadillies fill their cups with tears,
To strew the laureate hearse where Lycid lies.
For so to interpose a little ease,
Let our frail thoughts dally with false surmise.
Ay me! whilst thee the shores and sounding seas
Wash far away, where'er thy bones are hurled,
Whether beyond the stormy Hebrides,
Where thou perhaps under the whelming tide
Visit'st the bottom of the monstrous world;
Or whether thou, to our moist vows denied,
Sleep'st by the fable of Bellerus old,
Where the great vision of the guarded mount
Looks toward Namancos and Bayona's hold;
Look homeward angel now, and melt with ruth:
And, O ye dolphins, waft the hapless youth.
  Weep no more, woeful shepherds, weep no more,
For Lycidas your sorrow is not dead.
Sunk though he be beneath the wat'ry floor;
So sinks the day-star in the ocean bed,
And yet anon repairs his drooping head,
And tricks his beams, and with new-spangled ore
Flames in the forehead of the morning sky:
So Lycidas sunk low, but mounted high,
Through the dear might of him that walked the waves,
Where, other groves and other streams along,
With nectar pure his oozy locks he laves,
And hears the unexpressive nuptial song,
In the blest kingdoms meek of joy and love.
There entertain him all the saints above,
In solemn troops and sweet societies
That sing, and singing in their glory move,
And wipe the tears forever from his eyes.
Now, Lycidas, the shepherds weep no more;
Henceforth thou art the genius of the shore,
In thy large recompense, and shalt be good

To all that wander in that perilous flood.
  Thus sang the uncouth swain to th' oaks and rills,
While the still morn went out with sandals gray;
He touched the tender stops of various quills,
With eager thought warbling his Doric lay:
And now the sun had stretched out all the hills,
And now was dropped into the western bay;
At last he rose, and twitched his mantle blue:
Tomorrow to fresh woods, and pastures new.

'When I consider how my light is spent'

When I consider how my light is spent,
    Ere half my days, in this dark world and wide,
    And that one Talent which is death to hide
    Lodged with me useless, though my Soul more bent
To serve therewith my Maker, and present
    My true account, lest he returning chide;
    'Doth God exact day-labour, light denied?'
    I fondly ask. But patience, to prevent
That murmur, soon replies, 'God doth not need
    Either man's work or his own gifts; who best
    Bear his mild yoke, they serve him best. His state
Is Kingly. Thousands at his bidding speed
    And post o'er Land and Ocean without rest:
    They also serve who only stand and wait.'

'Methought I saw my late espousèd saint'

Methought I saw my late espousèd saint
    Brought to me, like Alcestis, from the grave,
    Whom Jove's great son to her glad husband gave,
    Rescued from death by force though pale and faint.

Mine, as whom washed from spot of child-bed taint
    Purification in the old Law did save,
    And such, as yet once more I trust to have
    Full sight of her in Heaven without restraint,
Came vested all in white, pure as her mind:
    Her face was veiled, yet to my fancied sight,
    Love, sweetness, goodness, in her person shined
So clear, as in no face with more delight.
    But O as to embrace me she inclined,
    I waked, she fled, and day brought back my night.

MARIANNE MOORE
(1887–1972)

W. S. Landor

There
is someone I can bear –
  'a master of indignation . . .
meant for a soldier
  converted to letters,' who could

throw
a man through the window,
  yet, 'tender toward plants,' say, 'Good God,
the violets!' (below).
  'Accomplished in every

style
and tint' – considering meanwhile
  infinity and eternity,
he could only say, 'I'll
  talk about them when I understand them.'

MOSCHUS

(*fl.* 150 BCE)

Lament for Bion

Join, glades, my hymn of mourning;
Dorian waters, lament with me;
weep, rivers, weep for Bion, for his beauty.
Now orchards, sorrow with me; sigh, groves;
flowers, breathe grief from your tight clusters;
now roses, deepen your red in mourning; and yours,
anemones; now hyacinth, let your lettering speak,
your leaves chatter their grief.
The beautiful flute-player is dead.

Sing, Sicilian Muses, raise your song of grief.

Nightingales, as you sing, deep among thick leaves,
tell Arethusa, Sicily's stream, that Bion
is dead, Bion the shepherd; that, with him,
music has died, and all Dorian song has perished.

Sing, Sicilian Muses, raise your song of grief.

Swans of Strymon, lament; raise your song
at the water's edge, your song of sorrow;
sing as you would at death's approach. Tell
the Oeagrian maidens, tell all the Bistonian Nymphs:
the Doric Orpheus is dead.

Sing, Sicilian Muses, raise your song of grief.

Now he will be heard no more
he that tenderly cared for his stock;
no longer will he sit and sing
alone among the oaks; but in the house of Hades

now must raise the song of Lethe.
And so the hills are silent; the cows,
wandering among the bulls, low mournfully,
and will no longer graze.

Sing, Sicilian Muses, raise your song of grief.

Bion, your sudden death brought tears
even to Apollo; the satyrs wept, and every Priapus
dressed in black; each Pan mourned your music;
all the springs bewailed it in the woods;
the waters changed to tears, Echo, too, is weeping
in the rocks, for she is silent, she may imitate
your voice no more. At your death
trees threw down their fruit, flowers
all wasted away. Now flocks no longer yield
rich milk, nor hives sweet honey.
In the honeycomb it dies of grief, and may no more
be gathered, since the day your honey perished.

Sing, Sicilian Muses, raise your song of grief.

Never before was the Siren's song so sad
along the beach, the nightingale's among the rocks,
the swallow's around the long hills;
never so sad was Ceyx' lament
for poor Halcyon, never the seabird's call
across the grey waves, the bird of Memnon's,
hovering in the vales over the son of Dawn's tomb:
never so sad as when mourning Bion's death.

Sing, Sicilian Muses, raise your song of grief.

The nightingales and all the swallows,
to whom he would give joy, and whom
he taught to sing, now sit among the branches
and sing alternately. The second choir replies:
'Birds, raise your mourning-hymn
and we will join it.'

Sing, Sicilian Muses, raise your song of grief.

Thrice-beloved, who now will play your pipe?
Who will put your flute to his mouth?
What man would dare? For your lips and your breath
live on; the sound of your music still echoes
in those reeds. Shall I carry your pipe to Pan?
Yet even he, perhaps, would fear
to play, lest he prove second to you.

Sing, Sicilian Muses, raise your song of grief.

And Galatea: she too sighs for your music,
she who would love to sit beside you
at the water's edge. The Cyclops' song
could not compare; from him she turned away,
lovely Galatea, but on you she looked
more happily than on the sea. And now,
its waves forgotten, she sits alone
upon the sand; but still she tends your herds.

Sing, Sicilian Muses, raise your song of grief.

All the Muses' gifts have died with you,
my herdsman; the sweet kisses of young girls,
the lips of boys. Around your corpse
the Loves weep pitifully; and Cypris longs for you
much more than for that kiss
she gave Adonis as he, that day, lay dying.

This, most tuneful of rivers, is for you
a second grief; this for you, Meles, another pain.
Homer, that first rich voice of Calliope,
has long been dead; men say that your great streams
were tears for your sweet son,
and that your grief quite filled the sea.
Now Bion: now you mourn another child,
and grief again dissolves you.
Both were cherished by fountains: for one drank

at Pegasus' spring, the other at Arethusa's.
One sang of Tyndareus' lovely daughter,
of Thetis' great son, and of Atreus' Menelaus;
the other sang neither of war nor tears,
but of Pan. His was a herdsman's voice;
he sang as he tended his cattle;
he would carve his pipes, and milk
his gentle heifers; he taught the young to kiss;
he nurtured Love as his own child
and roused the passions of Aphrodite.

Sing, Sicilian Muses, raise your song of grief.

Every glorious city, Bion, mourns you,
every town: Ascra weeps for you
more than for Hesiod; Boeotia yearns for you
more than for Pindar; lovely Lesbos
grieved less for Alcaeus, Teos less for Anacreon;
Paros misses you more than Archilochus;
and Mitylene, who sorrowed for Sappho,
now grieves for your song. To Syracuse
you are a Theocritus; and Ausonia's lament
is this hymn of mine. For I am no stranger
to pastoral song, but a pupil of yours,
an heir to your Dorian style,
honoured, when others inherited
your wealth, to be left your music.

Sing, Sicilian Muses, raise your song of grief.

Ah, when the mallows perish in the orchard,
or the green parsley, or the thickly blossoming dill,
they grow again, and live another year;
but we who are so great and strong, we men
who are so wise, as soon as we are dead,
at once we sleep, in a hole beneath the earth,
a sleep so deep, so long, with no end,
no reawakening. And so it is for you:
in the earth you shall lie, shrouded in silence;

whilst, if it pleases the Nymphs, a frog
may sing forever. I do not envy them
his music: there is no beauty in it.

Sing, Sicilian Muses, raise your song of grief.

Poison, Bion, poison came to your lips,
and you took it. How could it touch
such lips without becoming nectar?
And what man on earth could be so vicious
as to mix poison and give it you
when you asked? He has poisoned music.

Sing, Sicilian Muses, raise your song of grief.

But justice comes to all. For me, this song
shall be my mournful elegy upon your death.
Had I been able to descend to Tartarus,
as Orpheus did, Odysseus, and once Alcides,
then perhaps I would have come
to Hades' throne, and, if you sing for him,
listened to you, and to what it is you sing.
Let it be some song of Sicily,
for Persephone, some sweet country song,
for she too is Sicilian, she once played
on Etna's shores; she knows Dorian music;
your singing would not go unrewarded.
As once she granted Orpheus, for the rhythms
of his harp, the return of his Eurydice,
so shall she return you, Bion, to the hills.
Could my pipe ever match the magic of his harp,
I would myself have sung for you to Hades.

Translated by Anthony Holden

Serenade

There were the two ponies
and there was Serenade,
which belonged to my mother.

Though 'who belonged' would be better,
in view of the girlish head-lift she had,
and her flounce to and fro in the lumpy field,
and that big womanish rump I always gave a wide berth to.

When the blacksmith came to shoe her,
which was seldom in summer
but otherwise often,
she would let him hoist and stretch out first one hind leg,
then the other
with a definitely melancholy, embarrassed restraint.

The blacksmith was ferret-faced and rat-bodied,
hardly man enough to keep aloft the great weight
of one-foot-at-a-time,
although he did keep it sort of aloft,
crouched over double and bent at the knees,
to make a peculiar angle which held each hoof still
on his battle-scarred apron.

He would set up shop
under the covered entrance-way
between our house and the stable block:
a ramshackle clapboard affair,
black (or black weathering to green),
with swallows' mud villages proliferating in the rafters.

I liked it there in the drive-through,
which was also where we parked the car
(but not on his days) –
for the oil maps on the dusty cement
brilliant as the wet skin of a trout,
and for the puzzling swallow-shit patterns,
and most of all for that place by the corner drain
where a grass-snake had appeared once,
an electric-green, sleepy-looking marvel
which, when it disappeared, left a print of itself.
that stayed in the mind for ever.

The blacksmith always did cold shoeing,
prising off each thin moon-crescent
then carving the hoof with a bone-handled,
long-bladed knife.

The miracle of no pain!

Serenade gone loose in her skin,
her strength out of her,
so she seemed suspended in water,
her hypnotised breathing steady,
the smell of piss
and musty hay
and ammonia sweat coming off her,
her head dropping down,
eyes half closed now,
and me a boy
watching the earth-stained sole of her hoof
turning pure white as the blacksmith pared and trimmed,
leaving the nervous diamond of the frog well alone
but showing me,
just by looking,
how even to touch that,
much worse cut it,
would wake her
and break the spell
and our two heads with it.

Our collie dog sat near where the snake had been,
ravenous black and white,
all ears,
sometimes fidgeting her two slim front feet,
glancing away as if about to dash off,
then twisting back,
licking her lips and swallowing with a half-whine.

She knew better than to get under anyone's feet,
but when the blacksmith had done with his cutting,
and offered a new shoe,
and fiddled it downwards or sideways,
and hammered it with quick hits
which drove the nail-points clean through
(but these could be filed off later, and were) –
when this was all done,
he kicked the clippings across the cement
and now it was the collie's turn to show a sad restraint,
taking one delicate piece between her pink lips,
ashamed to be a slave of appetite,
and curving away into the yard
to eat it in private.

The blacksmith straightened himself,
one hand smoothing the small of his back,
the other picking a few remaining nails
from between his own darker lips,
then slapped Serenade on the flank with his red palm,
rousing her from her trance,
running his fingers up her mane and over her ears,
giving each a soft tug
and saying 'She'll do',
or 'Good lady',
or 'There's a girl.'

Whereupon my mother herself appeared to pay him –
their hands met, and touched, and parted,
and something passed between them –

and the blacksmith took off his apron
with its colours of a battered tin bowl,
folded it,
and carried it before him in a lordly fashion,
using it as a cushion for his collapsed bag
of hammers, clippers, knives, files, pliers and nails
to the van
which he had parked in the lane some distance from us,
while my mother untied the halter
and led her horse away.

There was a crisp clip-clop over the stable yard,
and a train of hoof-prints
with the neat shoes obvious to me,
who had stayed behind
with nothing better to do than look.

This was Serenade,
who would later throw my mother
as they jumped out of a wood into sunlight,
and who, taking all possible pains not to trample her down
or even touch her,
was nevertheless the means to an end,
which was death.

Now I am as old as my mother was then,
at the time of her fall,
and I can see Serenade clearly in her own later life,
poor dumb creature nobody blamed,
or could easily like any more either,
which meant nobody came to talk to her much
in the spot she eventually found
under the spiky may tree in the field,
and still less came to shoe her,
so her hooves grew long and crinkled round the edges
like wet cardboard (except they were hard)

while she just stood there,
not knowing what she had done,
or went off with her girlish flounce and conker-coloured arse,
waiting for something important to happen,
only nothing ever did,
beyond the next day and the next,
and one thing leading to another.

PAUL MULDOON
(1951–)

Incantata

In Memory of Mary Farl Powers

I thought of you tonight, *a leanbh*, lying there in your long barrow
colder and dumber than a fish by Francisco de Herrera,
as I X-Actoed from a spud the Inca
glyph for a mouth: thought of that first time I saw your pink
spotted torso, distant-near as a nautilus,
when you undid your portfolio, yes indeedy,
and held the print of what looked like a cankered potato
at arm's length – your arms being longer, it seemed, than Lugh's.

Even Lugh of the Long (sometimes the Silver) Arm
would have wanted some distance between himself and the
    army-worms
that so clouded the sky over St Cloud you'd have to seal
the doors and windows and steel
yourself against their nightmarish *déjeuner sur l'herbe*:
try as you might to run a foil
across their tracks, it was to no avail;
the army-worms shinnied down the stove-pipe on an army-worm
    rope.

I can hardly believe that, when we met, my idea of 'R and R'
was to get smashed, almost every night, on sickly-sweet Demarara
rum and Coke: as well as leaving you a grass widow
(remember how Krapp looks up 'viduity'?),
after eight or ten or twelve of those dark rums
it might be eight or ten or twelve o'clock before I'd land
back home in Landseer Street, deaf and blind
to the fact that not only was I all at sea, but in the doldrums.

Again and again you'd hold forth on your own version of
    Thomism,
your own *Summa*
Theologiae that in everything there is an order,
that the things of the world sing out in a great oratorio:
it was Thomism, though, tempered by *La Nausée,*
by His Nibs Sam Bethicket,
and by that Dublin thing, that an artist must walk down Baggott
Street wearing a hair-shirt under the shirt of Nessus.

'*D'éirigh me ar maidin,*' I sang, '*a tharraingt chun aoinigh mhóir*':
our first night, you just had to let slip that your secret amour
for a friend of mine was such
that you'd ended up lying with him in a ditch
under a bit of whin, or gorse, or furze,
somewhere on the border of Leitrim, perhaps, or Roscommon:
'gamine,' I wanted to say, 'kimono';
even then it was clear I'd never be at the centre of your universe.

Nor should I have been, since you were there already, your own
    Ding
an sich, no less likely to take wing
than the Christ you drew for a Christmas card as a pupa
in swaddling clothes: and how resolutely you would pooh-pooh
the idea I shared with Vladimir and Estragon,
with whom I'd been having a couple of jars,
that this image of the Christ-child swaddled and laid in the
    manger
could be traced directly to those army-worm dragoons.

I thought of the night Vladimir was explaining to all and sundry
the difference between *geantrai* and *suantrai*
and you remarked on how you used to have a crush
on Burt Lancaster as Elmer Gantry, and Vladimir went to brush
the ash off his sleeve with a legerdemain
that meant only one thing – 'Why does he put up with this crap?' –
and you weighed in with 'To live in a dustbin, eating scrap,
seemed to Nagg and Nell a most eminent domain.'

How little you were exercised by those tiresome literary intrigues,
how you urged me to have no more truck
than the Thane of Calder
with a fourth estate that professes itself to be '*égalitaire*'
but wants only blood on the sand: yet, irony of ironies,
you were the one who, in the end,
got yourself up as a *retiarius* and, armed with net and trident,
marched from Mount Street to the Merrion Square arena.

In the end, you were the one who went forth to beard the lion,
you who took the DART line
every day from Jane's flat in Dun Laoghaire, or Dalkey,
dreaming your dream that the subterranean Dodder and Tolka
might again be heard above the *hoi polloi*
for whom Irish 'art' means a High Cross at Carndonagh or Corofin
and *The Book of Kells*: not until the lion cried craven
would the poor Tolka and the poor Dodder again sing out for joy.

I saw you again tonight, in your jump-suit, thin as a rake,
your hand moving in such a deliberate arc
as you ground a lithographic stone
that your hand and the stone blurred to one
and your face blurred into the face of your mother, Betty Wahl,
who took your failing, ink-stained hand
in her failing, ink-stained hand
and together you ground down that stone by sheer force of will.

I remember your pooh-poohing, as we sat there on the
    Enterprise,
my theory that if your name is Powers
you grow into it or, at least,
are less inclined to tremble before the likes of this bomb-blast
further up the track: I myself was shaking like a leaf
as we wondered whether the I.R.A. or the Red
Hand Commandos or even the Red
Brigades had brought us to a standstill worthy of Hamm and Clov.

Hamm and Clov; Nagg and Nell; Watt and Knott;
the fact is that we'd been at a standstill long before the night

things came to a head,
long before we'd sat for half the day in the sweltering heat
somewhere just south of Killnasaggart
and I let slip a name – her name – off my tongue
and you turned away (I see it now) the better to deliver the sting
in your own tail, to let slip your own little secret.

I thought of you again tonight, thin as a rake, as you bent
over the copper plate of 'Emblements',
its tidal wave of army-worms into which you all but disappeared:
I wanted to catch something of its spirit
and yours, to body out your disembodied *vox*
clamantis in deserto, to let this all-too-cumbersome device
of a potato-mouth in a potato-face
speak out, unencumbered, from its long, low, mould-filled box.

I wanted it to speak to what seems always true of the truly great,
that you had a winningly inaccurate
sense of your own worth, that you would second-guess
yourself too readily by far, that you would rally to any cause
before your own, mine even,
though you detected in me a tendency to put
on too much artificiality, both as man and poet,
which is why you called me 'Polyester' or 'Polyurethane'.

That last time in Dublin, I copied with a quill dipped in oak-gall
onto a sheet of vellum, or maybe a human caul,
a poem for *The Great Book of Ireland*: as I watched the low
swoop over the lawn today of a swallow
I thought of your animated talk of Camille Pissarro
and André Derain's *The Turning Road, L'Estaque*:
when I saw in that swallow's nest a face in a mud-pack
from that muddy road I was filled again with a profound sorrow.

You must have known already, as we moved from the 'Hurly Burly'
to McDaid's or Riley's,
that something was amiss: I think you even mentioned a
    homeopath
as you showed off the great new acid-bath

in the Graphic Studio, and again undid your portfolio
to lay out your latest works; I try to imagine the strain
you must have been under, pretending to be as right as rain
while hearing the bells of a church from some long-flooded valley.

From the Quabbin reservoir, maybe, where the banks and bakeries
of a dozen little submerged Pompeii reliquaries
still do a roaring trade: as clearly as I saw your death-mask
in that swallow's nest, you must have heard the music
rise from the muddy ground between
your breasts as a nocturne, maybe, by John Field;
to think that you thought yourself so invulnerable, so inviolate,
that a little cancer could be beaten.

You must have known, as we walked through the ankle-deep
    clabber
with Katherine and Jean and the long-winded Quintus Calaber,
that cancer had already made such a breach
that you would almost surely perish:
you must have thought, as we walked through the woods
along the edge of the Quabbin,
that rather than let some doctor cut you open
you'd rely on infusions of hardock, hemlock, all the idle weeds.

I thought again of how art may be made, as it was by André
    Derain,
of nothing more than a turn
in the road where a swallow dips into the mire
or plucks a strand of bloody wool from a strand of barbed wire
in the aftermath of Chickamauga or Culloden
and builds from pain, from misery, from a deep-seated hurt,
a monument to the human heart
that shines like a golden dome among roofs rain-glazed and leaden.

I wanted the mouth in this potato-cut
to be heard far beyond the leaden, rain-glazed roofs of Quito,
to be heard all the way from the southern hemisphere
to Clontarf or Clondalkin, to wherever your sweet-severe
spirit might still find a toe-hold

in this world: it struck me then how you would be aghast
at the thought of my thinking you were some kind of ghost
who might still roam the earth in search of an earthly delight.

You'd be aghast at the idea of your spirit hanging over this vale
of tears like a jump-suited jump-jet whose vapour-trail
unravels a sky: for there's nothing, you'd say, nothing over
and above the sky itself, nothing but cloud-cover
reflected in a thousand lakes; it seems that Minne-
sota itself means 'sky-tinted water', that the sky is a great slab
of granite or iron ore that might at any moment slip
back into the worked-out sky-quarry, into the worked-out
    sky-mines.

To use the word 'might' is to betray you once too often, to betray
your notion that nothing's random, nothing arbitrary:
the gelignite weeps, the hands fly by on the alarm clock,
the '*Enterprise*' goes clackety-clack
as they all must; even the car hijacked that morning in the Cross,
that was preordained, its owner spread on the bonnet
before being gagged and bound or bound
and gagged, that was fixed like the stars in the Southern Cross.

The fact that you were determined to cut yourself off in your
    prime
because it was *pre*-determined has my eyes abrim:
I crouch with Belacqua
and Lucky and Pozzo in the Acacacac-
ademy of Anthropopopometry, trying to make sense of the
    '*quaquaqua*'
of that potato-mouth; that mouth as prim
and proper as it's full of self-opprobrium,
with its '*quaquaqua*', with its 'Quoiquoiquoiquoiquoiquoiquoiq'.

That's all that's left of the voice of Enrico Caruso
from all that's left of an opera-house somewhere in Matto Grosso,
all that's left of the hogweed and horehound and cuckoo-pint,
of the eighteen soldiers dead at Warrenpoint,
of the Black Church clique and the Graphic Studio claque,

of the many moons of glasses on a tray,
of the brewery-carts drawn by moon-booted drays,
of those jump-suits worn under your bottle-green worsted cloak.

Of the great big dishes of chicken lo mein and beef chow mein,
of what's mine is yours and what's yours mine,
of the oxlips and cowslips
on the banks of the Liffey at Leixlip
where the salmon breaks through the either/or neither/nor nether
reaches despite the temple-veil
of itself being rent and the penny left out overnight on the rail
is a sheet of copper when the mail-train has passed over.

Of the bride carried over the threshold, hey, only to alight
on the limestone slab of another threshold,
of the swarm, the cast,
the colt, the spew of bees hanging like a bottle of Lucozade
from a branch the groom must sever,
of Emily Post's ruling, in *Etiquette*,
on how best to deal with the butler being in cahoots
with the cook when they're both in cahoots with the chauffeur.

Of that poplar-flanked stretch of road between Leiden
and The Hague, of the road between Rathmullen and Ramelton,
where we looked so long and hard
for some trace of Spinoza or Amelia Earhart,
both of them going down with their engines on fire:
of the stretch of road somewhere near Urney
where Orpheus was again overwhelmed by that urge to turn
back and lost not only Eurydice but his steel-strung lyre.

Of the sparrows and finches in their bell of suet,
of the bitter-sweet
bottle of Calvados we felt obliged to open
somewhere near Falaise, so as to toast our new-found *copains*,
of the priest of the parish
who came enquiring about our 'status', of the hedge-clippers
I somehow had to hand, of him running like the clappers
up Landseer Street, of my subsequent self-reproach.

Of the remnants of Airey Neave, of the remnants of Mountbatten,
of the famous *andouilles*, of the famous *boudins
noirs et blancs*, of the barrel-vault
of the Cathedral at Rouen, of the flashlight, fat and roll of felt
on each of their sledges, of the music
of Joseph Beuys's pack of huskies, of that baldy little bugger
mushing them all the way from Berncastel through Bacarrat
to Belfast, his head stuck with honey and gold-leaf like a mosque.

Of Benjamin Britten's *Lachrymae*, with its gut-wrenching viola,
of Vivaldi's *Four Seasons*, of Frankie Valli's,
of Braque's great painting *The Shower of Rain,*
of the fizzy, lemon or sherbet-green *Rana
temporaria* plonked down in Trinity like a little Naugahyde
     pouffe,
of eighteen soldiers dead in Oriel,
of the weakness for a little fol-de-rol-de-rolly
suggested by the gap between the front teeth of the Wife of Bath.

Of *A Sunday Afternoon on the Island of La Grande Jatte*, of Seurat's
piling of tesserae upon tesserae
to give us a monkey arching its back
and the smoke arching out from a smoke-stack,
of Sunday afternoons in the Botanic Gardens, going with the flow
of the burghers of Sandy Row and Donegal
Pass and Andersonstown and Rathcoole,
of the army Landrover flaunt-flouncing by with its heavy
     furbelow.

Of Marlborough Park, of Notting Hill, of the Fitzroy Avenue
immortalized by Van 'His real name's Ivan'
Morrison, 'and him the dead spit
of Padraic Fiacc', of John Hewitt, the famous expat,
in whose memory they offer every year six of their best milch
     cows,
of the Bard of Ballymacarrett,
of every ungodly poet in his or her godly garret,
of Medhbh and Michael and Frank and Ciaran and 'wee' John
     Qughes.

Of the Belfast school, so called, of the school of hard knocks,
of your fervent eschewal of stockings and socks
as you set out to hunt down your foes
as implacably as the *tóraidheacht* through the Fews
of Redmond O'Hanlon, of how that 'd' and that 'c' aspirate
in *tóraidheacht* make it sound like a last gasp in an oxygen-tent,
of your refusal to open a vent
but to breathe in spirit of salt, the mordant salt-spirit.

Of how mordantly hydrochloric acid must have scored and
    scarred,
of the claim that boiled skirrets
can cure the spitting of blood, of that dank
flat somewhere off Morehampton Road, of the unbelievable
    stink
of valerian or feverfew simmering over a low heat,
of your sitting there, pale and gaunt,
with that great prescriber of boiled skirrets, Dr John Arbuthnot,
your face in a bowl of feverfew, a towel over your head.

Of the great roll of paper like a bolt of cloth
running out again and again like a road at the edge of a cliff,
of how you called a Red Admiral a Red
Admirable, of how you were never in the red
on either the first or the last
of the month, of your habit of loosing the drawstring of your
    purse
and finding one scrunched-up, obstreperous
note and smoothing it out and holding it up, pristine and
    pellucid.

Of how you spent your whole life with your back to the wall,
of your generosity when all the while
you yourself lived from hand
to mouth, of Joseph Beuys's pack of hounds
crying out from their felt and fat 'Atone, atone, atone',
of Watt remembering the '*Krak! Krek! Krik!*'
of those three frogs' karaoke
like the still, sad *basso continuo* of the great quotidian.

Of a ground bass of sadness, yes, but also a sennet of hautboys
as the fat and felt hounds of Beuys O'Beuys
bayed at the moon over a caravan
in Dunmore East, I'm pretty sure it was, or Dungarvan:
of my guest appearance in your self-portrait not as a hidalgo
from a long line
of hidalgos but a hound-dog, a *leanbh*,
a dog that skulks in the background, a dog that skulks and stalks.

Of that self-portrait, of the self-portraits by Rembrandt van Rijn,
of all that's revelation, all that's rune,
of all that's composed, all composed of odds and ends,
of that daft urge to make amends
when it's far too late, too late even to make sense of the clutter
of false trails and reversed horseshoe tracks
and the aniseed we took it in turn to drag
across each other's scents, when only a fish is dumber and colder.

Of your avoidance of canned goods, in the main,
on account of the exceeeeeeeeeeeeeeeedingly high risk of
    ptomaine,
of corned beef in particular being full of crap,
of your delight, so, in eating a banana as ceremoniously as
    Krapp
but flinging the skin over your shoulder like a thrush
flinging off a shell from which it's only just managed to disinter
a snail, like a stone-faced, twelfth-century
FitzKrapp eating his banana by the mellow yellow light of a
    rush.

Of the 'Yes, let's go' spoken by Monsieur Tarragon,
of the early-ripening jargonelle, the tumorous jardon, the jargon
of jays, the jars
of tomato relish and the jars
of Victoria plums, absolutely *de rigueur* for a passable plum
    baba,
of the drawers full of balls of twine and butcher's string,
of Dire Straits playing 'The Sultans of Swing',
of the horse's hock suddenly erupting in those boils and buboes.

Of the Greek figurine of a pig, of the pig on a terracotta frieze,
of the sow dropping dead from some mysterious virus,
of your predilection for gammon
served with a sauce of coriander or cumin,
of the slippery elm, of the hornbeam or witch-, or even wych-,
hazel that's good for stopping a haemor-
rhage in mid-flow, of the merest of mere
hints of elderberry curing everything from sciatica to a stitch.

Of the decree *condemnator,* the decree *absolvitor,* the decree *nisi,*
of *Aosdána,* of an *chraobh cnuais,*
of the fields of buckwheat
taken over by garget, inkberry, scoke – all names for pokeweed –
of *Mother Courage,* of *Arturo Ui,*
of those Sunday mornings spent picking at sesame
noodles and all sorts and conditions of dim sum,
of tea and ham sandwiches in the Nesbitt Arms Hotel in
        Ardara.

Of the day your father came to call, of your leaving your
        sick-room
in what can only have been a state of delirium,
of how you simply wouldn't relent
from your vision of a blind
watch-maker, of your fatal belief that fate
governs everything from the honey-rust of your father's terrier's
eyebrows to the horse that rusts and rears
in the furrow, of the furrows from which we can no more
        deviate

than they can from themselves, no more than the map of Europe
can be redrawn, than that Hermes might make a harp from his
        harpe,
than that we must live in a vale
of tears on the banks of the Lagan or the Foyle,
than that what we have is a done deal,
than that the Irish Hermes,
Lugh, might have leafed through his vast herbarium
for the leaf that had it within it, Mary, to anoint and anneal,

than that Lugh of the Long Arm might have found in the
    midst of *lus*
na leac or *lus na treatha* or *Frannc-lus,*
in the midst of eyebright, or speedwell, or tansy, an antidote,
than that this *Incantata*
might have you look up from your plate of copper or zinc
on which you've etched the row upon row
of army-worms, than that you might reach out, arrah,
and take in your ink-stained hands my own hands stained with ink.

LES MURRAY

(1938–2019)

Midsummer Ice

Remember how I used
to carry ice in from the road
for the ice chest, half running,
the white rectangle clamped in bare hands
the only utter cold
in all those summer paddocks?

How, swaying, I'd hurry it inside
en bloc and watering, with the butter
and the wrapped bread precarious on top of it?
'Poor Leslie,' you would say,
'your hands are cold as charity–'
You made me take the barrow
but uphill it was heavy.

We'd no tongs, and a bag
would have soaked and bumped, off balance.
I loved to eat the ice,
chip it out with the butcher knife's grey steel.
It stopped good things rotting
and it had a strange comb at its heart,
a splintered horizon rife with zero pearls.

But you don't remember.
A doorstep of numbed creek water the colour of tears
but you don't remember.
I will have to die before you remember.

THOMAS NASHE

(c. 1567–1601)

Adieu, Farewell, Earth's Bliss

Adieu, farewell, earth's bliss;
This world uncertain is;
Fond are life's lustful joys;
Death proves them all but toys;
None from his darts can fly;
I am sick, I must die.
   Lord, have mercy on us!

Rich men, trust not in wealth,
Gold cannot buy you health;
Physic himself must fade.
All things to end are made,
The plague full swift goes by;
I am sick, I must die.
   Lord, have mercy on us!

Beauty is but a flower
Which wrinkles will devour;
Brightness falls from the air;
Queens have died young and fair;
Dust hath closed Helen's eye.
I am sick, I must die.
   Lord, have mercy on us!

Strength stoops unto the grave,
Worms feed on Hector's brave;
Swords may not fight with fate,
Earth still holds ope her gate.
'Come, come!' the bells do cry.
I am sick, I must die.
   Lord, have mercy on us.

Wit with his wantonness
Tasteth death's bitterness;
Hell's executioner
Hath no ears for to hear
What vain art can reply.
I am sick, I must die.
   Lord, have mercy on us.

Haste, therefore, each degree,
To welcome destiny;
Heaven is our heritage,
Earth but a player's stage;
Mount we unto the sky.
I am sick, I must die.
   Lord, have mercy on us.

BERNARD O'DONOGHUE
(1945–)

The Day I Outlived My Father

Yet no one sent me flowers, or even
asked me out for a drink. If anything
it makes it worse, your early death, that
having now at last outlived you, I too
have broken ranks, lacking maybe
the imagination to follow you
in investigating that other, older world.

So I am in new territory from here on:
must blaze my trail, read alone
the hooftracks in the summer-powdered dust
and set a good face to the future:
at liberty at last like mad Arnaut
to cultivate the wind, to hunt the bull
on hare-back, to swim against the tide.

FRANK O'HARA

(1926–1966)

The Day Lady Died

It is 12:20 in New York a Friday
three days after Bastille day, yes
it is 1959 and I go get a shoeshine
because I will get off the 4:19 in Easthampton
at 7:15 and then go straight to dinner
and I don't know the people who will feed me

I walk up the muggy street beginning to sun
and have a hamburger and a malted and buy
an ugly NEW WORLD WRITING to see what the poets
in Ghana are doing these days
$\qquad\qquad\qquad$ I go on to the bank
and Miss Stillwagon (first name Linda I once heard)
doesn't even look up my balance for once in her life
and in the GOLDEN GRIFFIN I get a little Verlaine
for Patsy with drawings by Bonnard although I do
think of Hesiod, trans. Richmond Lattimore or
Brendan Behan's new play or *Le Balcon* or *Les Nègres*
of Genet, but I don't, I stick with Verlaine
after practically going to sleep with quandariness

and for Mike I just stroll into the PARK LANE
Liquor Store and ask for a bottle of Strega and
then I go back where I came from to 6th Avenue
and the tobacconist in the Ziegfeld Theatre and
casually ask for a carton of Gauloises and a carton
of Picayunes, and a NEW YORK POST with her face on it

and I am sweating a lot by now and thinking of
leaning on the john door in the 5 SPOT
while she whispered a song along the keyboard
to Mal Waldron and everyone and I stopped breathing

SHARON OLDS

(1942–)

The Exact Moment of His Death

When he breathed his last breath, it was he,
my father, although he was so transformed
no one who had not been with him
for the last hour would know him – the skin
now physical as animal fat,
the eyes cast halfway back into his head,
the nose thinned, the mouth racked open,
with that tongue in it like the fact of the mortal,
a tongue so dried, scalloped, darkened
and material. We could see the fluid
risen into the back of his mouth
but it was he, the huge, slack arms,
the spots of blood under the skin
black and precise, we had come this far with him
step by step, it was he, his last
breath was his, not taken with desire
but his, light as a milkweed seed,
coming out of his mouth and floating across the room.
And when the nurse listened for his heart,
and his stomach was silvery, it was his stomach,
when she did not shake her head but stood and
nodded at me, for a moment it was fully
he, my father, dead but completely
himself, a man with an open mouth and
black spots on his arms. He looked like
someone killed in a bloodless struggle –
the strain in his neck and the base of his head,
as if he were violently pulling back.
He seemed to be holding still, then the skin
tightened slightly around his whole body
as if the purely physical were claiming him,

and then it was not my father,
it was not a man, it was not an animal,
I ran my hand slowly through the hair,
lifted my fingers up through the grey
waves of it, the unliving glistening
matter of this world.

ALICE OSWALD

(1966–)

from *Memorial*

And Hector died like everyone else
He was in charge of the Trojans
But a spear found out the little patch of white
Between his collarbone and his throat
Just exactly where a man's soul sits
Waiting for the mouth to open
He always knew it would happen
He who was so boastful and anxious
And used to nip home deafened by weapons
To stand in full armour in the doorway
Like a man rushing in leaving his motorbike running
All women loved him
His wife was Andromache
One day he looked at her quietly
He said I know what will happen
And an image stared at him of himself dead
And her in Argos weaving for some foreign woman
He blinked and went back to his work
Hector loved Andromache
But in the end he let her face slide from his mind
He came back to her sightless
Strengthless expressionless
Asking only to be washed and burned
And his bones wrapped in soft cloths
And returned to the ground

OVID

(*c.* 43 BCE–18 CE)

Tristia 3.3

To his wife at Rome, when he was sick

Dearest! if you those fair eyes (wondering) stick
On this strange character, know, *I am sick.*
Sick in the *skirts* of the lost world, where I
Breathe hopeless of all comforts, but to die.
What heart (think'st thou?) have I in this sad seat
Tormented 'twixt the *Sauromate* and *Gete?*
Nor *air* nor *water* please; their very *sky*
Looks strange and unaccustomed to my eye,
I scarce dare breathe it, and I know not how
The earth that bears me shows unpleasant now.
Nor *diet* here's, nor *lodging* for my ease,
Nor any one that *studies* a disease;
No friend to comfort me, none to defray
With smooth discourse the charges of the day.
All tired alone I lie, and (thus) what e'er
Is absent, and at *Rome* I fancy here,
But when thou com'st, I blot the *airy scroll*,
And give thee full possession of my soul,
Thee (absent) I embrace, thee only *voice,*
And night and day *belie* a husband's joys;
Nay, of thy name so oft I mention make
That I am thought distracted for thy sake;
When my tired spirits fail, and my sick heart
Draws in that *fire* which actuates each part,
If any say, th'art come! I force my pain,
And hope to see thee, gives me life again.
Thus I for thee, whilst thou (perhaps) more blest
Careless of me dost breathe all peace and rest,
Which yet I think not, for (*dear soul!*) too well

Know I thy grief, since my first woes befell.
But if strict heaven my stock of days hath spun
And with my life my error will be gone,
How easy then (*O Caesar!*) wer't for thee
To pardon one, that now doth cease to be?
That I might yield my native air this breath,
And banish not my ashes after death;
Would thou hadst either spared me until dead,
Or with my blood redeemed my absent head,
Thou shouldst have had both freely, but O! thou
Wouldst have me live to die an *exile* now.
And must I then from *Rome* so far meet death,
And double by the place my loss of breath?
Nor in my last of hours on my own bed
(In the sad conflict) rest my dying head?
Nor my soul's *whispers* (the last pledge of life,)
Mix with the tears and kisses of a wife?
My last words none must treasure, none will rise
And (with a tear) seal up my vanquished eyes,
Without these *rites* I die, distressed in all
The *splendid sorrows* of a funeral,
Unpitied, and unmourned for, my sad head
In a strange land goes friendless to the dead.
When thou hear'st this, O how thy faithful soul
Will sink, whilst grief doth every part control!
How often wilt thou look this way, and cry,
O where is't yonder that my love doth lie!
Yet spare these tears, and mourn not now for me,
Long since (*dear heart!*) have I been dead to thee,
Think then I died, when *thee* and *Rome* I lost
That death to me more grief than this hath cost;
Now, if thou canst (but thou canst not) *best wife*
Rejoice, my cares are ended with my life,
At least, yield not to sorrows, frequent use
Should make these miseries to thee no news.
And here I wish my soul died with my breath
And that no part of me were free from death,
For, if it be immortal, and outlives

The body, as *Pythagoras* believes,
Betwixt these *Sarmates' ghosts*, a *Roman* I
Shall wander, vexed to all eternity.
    But thou (for after death I shall be free,)
Fetch home these bones, and what is left of me,
A few *flowers* give them, with some *balm*, and lay
Them in some *suburb-grave* hard by the way,
And to inform posterity, who's there,
This sad inscription let my marble wear,
    Here lies the soft-souled lecturer of love,
    Whose envied wit did his own ruin prove.
But thou, (who e'er thou beest, that passing by
Lend'st to this *sudden stone* a *hasty* eye,)
If e'er thou knew'st of *love* the sweet disease,
Grudge not to say, *May* Ovid *rest in peace!*
This for my tomb; but in my books they'll see
More strong and lasting monuments of me,
Which I believe (though fatal) will afford
An endless name unto their ruined lord.
    And now thus gone, it rests for love of me
Thou show'st some sorrow to my memory;
Thy funeral offerings to my ashes bear
With wreaths of *cypress* bathed in many a tear,
Though nothing there but dust of me remain,
Yet shall that *dust* perceive thy pious pain.
But I have done, and my tired sickly head
Though I would fain write more, desires the bed;
Take then this word (perhaps my last to tell)
Which though I want, I wish it thee, *Fare-well.*

                    Translated by Henry Vaughan

WILFRED OWEN
(1893–1918)

Anthem for Doomed Youth

What passing-bells for these who die as cattle?
  – Only the monstrous anger of the guns.
  Only the stuttering rifles' rapid rattle
Can patter out their hasty orisons.
No mockeries now for them; no prayers nor bells;
  Nor any voice of mourning save the choirs, –
The shrill, demented choirs of wailing shells;
  And bugles calling for them from sad shires.

What candles may be held to speed them all?
  Not in the hands of boys, but in their eyes
Shall shine the holy glimmers of goodbyes.
  The pallor of girls' brows shall be their pall;
Their flowers the tenderness of patient minds,
And each slow dusk a drawing-down of blinds.

'I saw his round mouth's crimson'

I saw his round mouth's crimson deepen as it fell,
  Like a Sun, in his last deep hour;
Watched the magnificent recession of farewell,
  Clouding, half gleam, half glower,
And a last splendour burn the heavens of his cheek,
  And in his eyes
The cold stars lighting, very old and bleak,
  In different skies.

Futility

Move him into the sun –
Gently its touch awoke him once,
At home, whispering of fields unsown.
Always it woke him, even in France,
Until this morning and this snow.
If anything might rouse him now
The kind old sun will know.

Think how it wakes the seeds, –
Woke, once, the clays of a cold star.
Are limbs, so dear-achieved, are sides,
Full-nerved – still warm – too hard to stir?
Was it for this the clay grew tall?
– O what made fatuous sunbeams toil
To break earth's sleep at all?

KATHERINE PHILIPS

(1632–1664)

On the Death of My First and Dearest Child, Hector Philips

Twice forty months in wedlock I did stay.
  Then had my vows crowned with a lovely boy.
And yet in forty days he dropped away:
  O! swift vicissitude of human joy!

I did but see him, and he disappeared.
  I did but touch the rosebud, and it fell;
A sorrow unforeseen and scarcely feared.
  So ill can mortals their afflictions spell.

And now (sweet babe) what can my trembling heart
  Suggest to right my doleful fate or thee?
Tears are my muse, and sorrow all my art.
  So piercing groans must be thy elegy.

Thus whilst no eye is witness of my moan,
  I grieve thy loss (Ah, boy too dear to live!)
And let the unconcernèd world alone.
  Who neither will, nor can, refreshment give.

An offering too for thy sad tomb I have,
  Too just a tribute to thy early hearse;
Receive these gasping numbers to thy grave.
  The last of thy unhappy mother's verse.

'Tis True, Our Life is But a Long Disease

'Tis true, our life is but a long disease,
Made up of real pain and seeming ease;
You stars, who these entangled fortunes give,

    O tell me why
    It is so hard to dy,
      Yet such a task to live?
If with some pleasure we our griefs betray,
It costs us dearer than it can repay:
For time or fortune all things so devours;
    Our hopes are cross'd,
    Or els the object lost,
      Ere we can call it ours.

TOM PICKARD

(1946–)

Spring Tide

For Basil Bunting, Spring 1900 to Spring 1985

1

A filthy winter to have lived through.
Dragged by the hair kicked and kicking into Spring.

A year-long miners' strike,
broken.

Police road blocks blocked the motorways
and all roads leading to the north.

More reactionary than the thirties
the old fascist-fighting conchie told me.

2

While you lay dying in Hexham General Hospital,
we climbed Parliament Hill with our word learner son
to see the city from the lip of the basin
and to see the kites.

The little Geordie-Polak cried *keats*
when he saw the rainbow-winged mosquitoes
stringed against the cockney clouds.

You wanted sleep; a blood-clot
rushed to your brain. We pushed our faces into May:
snowflower our blossom told us,
thanking frothing hawthorn for the gift.

3

We stood by the North Sea,
a wash swirled around our feet.
Furthest from the shore
you stared towards a squall
on the dark horizon.

I warned against a threatening wave; swelling
it would overwhelm us.

Leaping to safety I glanced back and saw you,
steady, silent, still,
tracing the trajectory
of the wave's engulfing curve.

My son's warm hand on my leg
woke me drowning
in a cold sweat.

You, the dark spring tide,
and the spring
were gone.

SYLVIA PLATH

(1932–1963)

Electra on Azalea Path

The day you died I went into the dirt,
Into the lightless hibernaculum
Where bees, striped black and gold, sleep out the blizzard
Like hieratic stones, and the ground is hard.
It was good for twenty years, that wintering –
As if you had never existed, as if I came
God-fathered into the world from my mother's belly:
Her wide bed wore the stain of divinity.
I had nothing to do with guilt or anything
When I wormed back under my mother's heart.

Small as a doll in my dress of innocence
I lay dreaming your epic, image by image.
Nobody died or withered on that stage.
Everything took place in a durable whiteness.
The day I woke, I woke on Churchyard Hill.
I found your name, I found your bones and all
Enlisted in a cramped necropolis,
Your speckled stone askew by an iron fence.

In this charity ward, this poorhouse, where the dead
Crowd foot to foot, head to head, no flower
Breaks the soil. This is Azalea Path.
A field of burdock opens to the south.
Six feet of yellow gravel cover you.
The artificial red sage does not stir
In the basket of plastic evergreens they put
At the headstone next to yours, nor does it rot,
Although the rains dissolve a bloody dye:
The ersatz petals drip, and they drip red.

Another kind of redness bothers me:
The day your slack sail drank my sister's breath
The flat sea purpled like that evil cloth
My mother unrolled at your last homecoming.
I borrow the stilts of an old tragedy.
The truth is, one late October, at my birth-cry
A scorpion stung its head, an ill-starred thing;
My mother dreamed you face down in the sea.

The stony actors poise and pause for breath.
I brought my love to bear, and then you died.
It was the gangrene ate you to the bone
My mother said; you died like any man.
How shall I age into that state of mind?
I am the ghost of an infamous suicide,
My own blue razor rusting in my throat.
O pardon the one who knocks for pardon at
Your gate, father – your hound-bitch, daughter, friend.
It was my love that did us both to death.

ALEXANDER POPE
(1688–1744)

Elegy to the Memory of an Unfortunate Lady

What beckoning ghost along the moonlight shade
Invites my steps, and points to yonder glade?
'Tis she! but why that bleeding bosom gored,
Why dimly gleams the visionary sword?
Oh ever beauteous, ever friendly! tell,
Is it, in heaven, a crime to love too well?
To bear too tender, or too firm a heart,
To act a lover's or a Roman's part?
Is there no bright reversion in the sky,
For those who greatly think, or bravely die?

   Why bade ye else, ye powers! her soul aspire
Above the vulgar flight of low desire?
Ambition first sprung from your blest abodes;
The glorious fault of angels and of gods;
Thence to their images on earth it flows,
And in the breasts of kings and heroes glows.
Most souls, 'tis true, but peep out once an age,
Dull sullen pris'ners in the body's cage:
Dim lights of life, that burn a length of years
Useless, unseen, as lamps in sepulchres;
Like Eastern kings a lazy state they keep,
And close confined to their own palace, sleep.

   From these perhaps (ere nature bade her die)
Fate snatched her early to the pitying sky.
As into air the purer spirits flow,
And separate from their kindred dregs below;
So flew the soul to its congenial place,
Nor left one virtue to redeem her race.

   But thou, false guardian of a charge too good,
Thou, mean deserter of thy brother's blood!
See on these ruby lips the trembling breath,

These cheeks now fading at the blast of death:
Cold is that breast which warm'd the world before,
And those love-darting eyes must roll no more.
Thus, if eternal justice rules the ball,
Thus shall your wives, and thus your children fall;
On all the line a sudden vengeance waits,
And frequent hearses shall besiege your gates.
There passengers shall stand, and pointing say,
(While the long funerals blacken all the way)
'Lo these were they, whose souls the furies steel'd,
And cursed with hearts unknowing how to yield.
Thus unlamented pass the proud away,
The gaze of fools, and pageant of a day!
So perish all, whose breast ne'er learned to glow
For others' good, or melt at others' woe.'
   What can atone (oh ever-injured shade!)
Thy fate unpitied, and thy rites unpaid?
No friend's complaint, no kind domestic tear
Pleased thy pale ghost, or graced thy mournful bier.
By foreign hands thy dying eyes were closed,
By foreign hands thy decent limbs composed,
By foreign hands thy humble grave adorned,
By strangers honoured, and by strangers mourned!
What though no friends in sable weeds appear,
Grieve for an hour, perhaps, then mourn a year,
And bear about the mockery of woe
To midnight dances, and the public show?
What though no weeping loves thy ashes grace,
Nor polished marble emulate thy face?
What though no sacred earth allow thee room,
Nor hallowed dirge be muttered o'er thy tomb?
Yet shall thy grave with rising flowers be drest,
And the green turf lie lightly on thy breast:
There shall the morn her earliest tears bestow,
There the first roses of the year shall blow;
While angels with their silver wings o'ershade
The ground, now sacred by thy reliques made.
   So peaceful rests, without a stone, a name,

What once had beauty, titles, wealth, and fame.
How loved, how honoured once, avails thee not,
To whom related, or by whom begot;
A heap of dust alone remains of thee,
'Tis all thou art, and all the proud shall be!
   Poets themselves must fall, like those they sung,
Deaf the praised ear, and mute the tuneful tongue.
Even he, whose soul now melts in mournful lays,
Shall shortly want the generous tear he pays;
Then from his closing eyes thy form shall part,
And the last pang shall tear thee from his heart,
Life's idle business at one gasp be o'er,
The Muse forgot, and thou beloved no more!

Three Epitaphs on John Hewet and Sarah Drew

I

When Eastern lovers feed the funeral fire,
On the same pile the faithful fair expire;
Here pitying heaven that virtue mutual found,
And blasted both, that it might neither wound.
Hearts so sincere th' Almighty saw well pleas'd,
Sent his own lightning, and the victims seiz'd.

2

Think not by rigorous judgment seiz'd,
   A pair so faithful could expire;
Victims so pure Heav'n saw well pleas'd
   And snatch'd them in celestial fire.

Live well and fear no sudden fate;
   When God calls virtue to the grave,

Alike tis Justice, soon or late,
   Mercy alike to kill or save.

Virtue unmov'd can hear the Call,
And face the Flash that melts the Ball.

3

Here lye two poor Lovers, who had the mishap
Tho very chaste people, to die of a Clap.

Epitaph on Sir Isaac Newton, in Westminster Abbey

Nature and Nature's Laws lay hid in Night:
God said, 'Let Newton be!' and all was light.

PETER PORTER

(1929–2010)

An Exequy

In wet May, in the months of change,
In a country you wouldn't visit, strange
Dreams pursue me in my sleep,
Black creatures of the upper deep –
Though you are five months dead, I see
You in guilt's iconography,
Dear Wife, lost beast, beleaguered child,
The stranded monster with the mild
Appearance, whom small waves tease,
(Andromeda upon her knees
In orthodox deliverance)
And you alone of pure substance,
The unformed form of life, the earth
Which Piero's brushes brought to birth
For all to greet as myth, a thing
Out of the box of imagining.

This introduction serves to sing
Your mortal death as Bishop King
Once hymned in tetrametric rhyme
His young wife, lost before her time;
Though he lived on for many years
His poem each day fed new tears
To that unreaching spot, her grave,
His lines a baroque architrave
The Sunday poor with bottled flowers
Would by-pass in their mourning hours,
Esteeming ragged natural life
('Most dearly loved, most gentle wife'),
Yet, looking back when at the gate
And seeing grief in formal state

Upon a sculpted angel group,
Were glad that men of god could stoop
To give the dead a public stance
And freeze them in their mortal dance.
The words and faces proper to
My misery are private – you
Would never share your heart with those
Whose only talent's to suppose,
Nor from your final childish bed
Raise a remote confessing head –
The channels of our lives are blocked,
The hand is stopped upon the clock,
No one can say why hearts will break
And marriages are all opaque:
A map of loss, some posted cards,
The living house reduced to shards,
The abstract hell of memory,
The pointlessness of poetry –
These are the instances which tell
Of something which I know full well,
I owe a death to you – one day
The time will come for me to pay
When your slim shape from photographs
Stands at my door and gently asks
If I have any work to do
Or will I come to bed with you.
O *scala enigmatica,*
I'll climb up to that attic where
The curtain of your life was drawn
Some time between despair and dawn –
I'll never know with what halt steps
You mounted to this plain eclipse
But each stair now will station me
A black responsibility
And point me to that shut-down room,
'This be your due appointed tomb.'

I think of us in Italy:
Gin-and-chianti-fuelled, we
Move in a trance through Paradise,
Feeding at last our starving eyes,
Two people of the English blindness
Doing each masterpiece the kindness
Of discovering it – from Baldovinetti
To Venice's most obscure jetty.
A true unfortunate traveller, I
Depend upon your nurse's eye
To pick the altars where no Grinner
Puts us off our tourists' dinner
And in hotels to bandy words
With Genevan girls and talking birds,
To wear your feet out following me
To night's end and true amity,
And call my rational fear of flying
A paradigm of Holy Dying –
And, oh my love, I wish you were
Once more with me, at night somewhere
In narrow streets applauding wines,
The moon above the Apennines
As large as logic and the stars,
Most middle-aged of avatars,
As bright as when they shone for truth
Upon untried and avid youth.

The rooms and days we wandered through
Shrink in my mind to one – there you
Lie quite absorbed by peace – the calm
Which life could not provide is balm
In death. Unseen by me, you look
Past bed and stairs and half-read book
Eternally upon your home,
The end of pain, the left alone.
I have no friend, no intercessor,
No psychopomp or true confessor
But only you who know my heart
In every cramped and devious part –

Then take my hand and lead me out,
The sky is overcast by doubt,
The time has come, I listen for
Your words of comfort at the door,
O guide me through the shoals of fear –
'Fürchte dich nicht, ich bin bei dir.'

EZRA POUND

(1885–1972)

from *Hugh Selwyn Mauberley*

4

These fought in any case,
and some believing,

 pro domo, in any case . . .

Some quick to arm,
some for adventure,
some from fear or weakness,
some from fear or censure,
some for love of slaughter, in imagination,
learning later . . .
some in fear, learning love of slaughter;

Died some, pro patria,

 non 'dulce' non 'et decor' . . .
walked eye-deep in hell
believing in old men's lies, then unbelieving
came home, home to a lie,
home to many deceits,
home to old lies and new infamy;
usury age-old and age-thick
and liars in public places.

Daring as never before, wastage as never before.
Young blood and high blood,
fair cheeks, and fine bodies;

fortitude as never before
frankness as never before,
disillusions as never told in the old days,
hysterias, trench confessions,
laughter out of dead bellies.

5

There died a myriad,
And of the best, among them,
For an old bitch gone in the teeth,
For a botched civilization,

Charm, smiling at the good mouth,
Quick eyes gone under earth's lid,

For two gross of broken statues,
For a few thousand battered books.

PROPERTIUS

(c. 50–15 BCE)

from *The Elegies* (2.28)

My sweetheart's sick: Jupiter, show some pity!
Keep her death off your hands – she's far too pretty!
Now summer's here, the Dog hangs high and dry,
boiling the earth, and sweltering in the sky.
But weather's not to blame, nor the sky baking:
it's her slights to the gods, and her oath-breaking.
It leads girls – always has – into despair
when wind and water scatter what they swear.

    Was Venus mad you were compared with her?
She's jealous of any girl thought lovelier.
Did you make light of Argive Juno's shrine,
or say Minerva's eyes are sub-divine?
You lookers don't know how to stop your nagging:
your beauty's guilty, and your sharp tongue wagging.
But at the last, after so many trials,
a day will come when sweeter weather smiles.

    Io spent *her* youth mooing like a cow;
that cow who drank the Nile's a goddess now.
Ino, who wandered, young, through earth and sea,
wrecked sailors pray to as Leucothoe.
Andromeda, vowed to Leviathan,
was saved by Perseus, and wed the man.
Callisto, in bear form, roamed Greece's vales;
at night her stars conduct benighted sails.

    But if you're destined for untimely rest,
even your destined burial will be blest:
you'll speak of beauty's risks with Semele;
she'll understand, taught by catastrophe.
And Homer's heroines will all defer
to you and own you their superior.
Now, if you can, endure, although you burn:

the god and the god's destiny may turn.
    The spells have failed, the whirligig's not working;
on the cold hearth, the laurel lies unsmoking;
the moon will not descend, unfazed, inhuman;
the horned owl blackly hoots its dire omen.
The same ghost ship will take us both as one,
hoisting its midnight sails on Acheron.
Let two lives move you, Jove, if one won't do:
I live if she lives; if she dies, I die too.
    Help her, I'll write a hymn in gratitude:
'This girl was saved by Jove the great and good.'
She'll sit before your feet, and worship you,
and tell the long tale of her torments through.
Juno will pardon your benevolence;
when a girl's dying, even she relents.
I pray, Persephone, stay merciful,
and you, her husband – don't become more cruel!
    Beauties unnumbered dwell in endless night;
let one, just one, still drink the earthly light!
Fair Tyro's there, and there, Antiope,
Europa, and perverse Pasiphae;
and all whom ancient Crete and Hellas bore,
and Thebes, and Priam's kingdom, now no more,
and Roman beauties immemorial
are there; the gluttonous pyre has them all.
No wealth or beauty is immortal here;
late or soon, our day of death draws near.
    But you, my darling, rescued from death's door,
offer Diana the dances that you swore;
thank Isis, now divine, bovine back then,
and pay the nights you owe me – that makes ten!

Translated by Christopher Childers

SIR WALTER RALEIGH
(c. 1554–1618)

'Even such is time'

Even such is time, that takes in trust
Our youth, our joys, our all we have,
And pays us but with earth and dust;
Who, in the dark and silent grave,
When we have wandered all our ways,
Shuts up the story of our days;
But from this earth, this grave, this dust,
My God shall raise me up, I trust!

HENRIETTA CORDELIA RAY
(1852–1916)

Toussaint L'Ouverture

To those fair isles where crimson sunsets burn,
We send a backward glance to gaze on thee,
Brave Toussaint! thou wast surely born to be
A hero; thy proud spirit could but spurn
Each outrage on thy race. Couldst thou unlearn
The lessons taught by instinct? Nay! and we
Who share the zeal that would make all men free,
Must e'en with pride unto thy life-work turn.
Soul-dignity was thine and purest aim;
And ah! how sad that thou wast left to mourn
In chains 'neath alien skies. On him, shame! shame!
That mighty conqueror who dared to claim
The right to bind thee. Him we heap with scorn,
And noble patriot! guard with love thy name.

GARETH REEVES

(1947–)

The Great Fire

'Help fire fire' flapping across the lawn
and down the street in pyjamas. What are they doing
leaving the poor old man in the house
all on his own like that? You ask him.

He woke in the early dawn to a smell,
thought the house was ablaze, and beat it.
He'd gone to bed two hours before.

Smouldering . . . Rooms with doors ajar
got soot-stained; the rest were untouched.
At the centre, his arm-chair,
the winged family heirloom, tasselled in gold:

he was nodding late at night to Schubert
when the stub in his right hand
declined in a twitching arc.

The chair was replaced with a fireproof
imitation leather thing, bolt upright.
Above it clacked an extractor fan
but he drew the line at smoke-detectors –

they'd be detecting him all the time.
The plastic lampshades, which he myopically
thought were attractive, had melted.

Sitting beneath bare bulbs he said
he looked like an ad for Shelter –
a study in black and white.

Half my things are his. Peninsulas of soot
have crept over matt boards. It won't come off the books,
and even today I find mono LPs
with WARPED across the sleeve in felt-tip:

the stylus rises and sinks,
the music lurches and there he is
squiffily leaving a half-full whisky
and swaying up to bed in the small hours.

CHRISTOPHER REID
(1949–)

A Scattering

I expect you've seen the footage: elephants,
finding the bones of one of their own kind
dropped by the wayside, picked clean by scavengers
and the sun, then untidily left there,
     decide to do something about it.

But what, exactly? They can't, of course,
reassemble the old elephant magnificence;
they can't even make a tidier heap. But they can
hook up bones with their trunks and chuck them
     this way and that way. So they do.

And their scattering has an air
of deliberate ritual, ancient and necessary.
Their great size, too, makes them the very
embodiment of grief, while the play of their trunks
     lends sprezzatura.

Elephants puzzling out
the anagram of their own anatomy,
elephants at their abstracted lamentations –
may their spirit guide me as I place
     my own sad thoughts in new, hopeful arrangements.

DENISE RILEY

(1948–)

A Part Song

i

You principle of song, what are you *for* now
Perking up under any spasmodic light
To trot out your shadowed warblings?
Mince, slight pillar. And sleek down
Your furriness. Slim as a whippy wire
Shall be your hope, and ultraflexible.
Flap thinly, sheet of beaten tin
That won't affectionately plump up
More cushioned and receptive lays.
But little song, don't so instruct yourself
For none are hanging around to hear you.
They have gone bustling or stumbling well away.

ii

What is the first duty of a mother to a child?
At least to keep the wretched thing alive – Band
Of fierce cicadas, stop this shrilling.
My daughter lightly leaves our house.
The thought rears up: *fix in your mind this*
Maybe final glimpse of her. Yes, lightning could.
I make this note of dread, I register it.
Neither my note nor my critique of it
Will save us one iota. I know it. And.

iii

Maybe a retouched photograph or memory,
This beaming one with his striped snake-belt
And eczema scabs, but either way it's framed
Glassed in, breathed hard on, and curated.
It's odd how boys live so much in their knees.
Then both of us had nothing. You lacked guile
And were transparent, easy, which felt natural.

iv

Each child gets cannibalised by its years.
It was a man who died, and in him died
The large-eyed boy, then the teen peacock
In the unremarked placid self-devouring
That makes up being alive. But all at once
Those natural overlaps got cut, then shuffled
Tight in a block, their layers patted square.

v

It's late. And it always will be late.
Your small monument's atop its hillock
Set with pennants that slap, slap, over the soil.
Here's a denatured thing, whose one eye rummages
Into the mound, her other eye swivelled straight up:
A short while only, then I come, she carols – but is only
A fat-lot-of-good mother with a pointless alibi: 'I didn't
Know.' Yet might there still be some part for me
To play upon this lovely earth? Say. Or
Say *No*, earth at my inner ear.

vi

A wardrobe gapes, a mourner tries
Her several styles of howling-guise:
You'd rather not, yet you must go
Briskly around on beaming show.
A soft black gown with pearl corsage
Won't assuage your smashed ménage.
It suits you as you are so pale.
Still, do not get that saffron veil.
Your dead don't want you lying flat.
There'll soon be time enough for that.

vii

Oh my dead son you daft bugger
This is one glum mum. Come home I tell you
And end this tasteless melodrama – quit
Playing dead at all, by now it's well beyond
A joke, but your humour never got cruel
Like this. Give over, you indifferent lad,
Take pity on your two bruised sisters. For
Didn't we love you. As we do. But by now
We're bored with our unproductive love,
And infinitely more bored by your staying dead
Which can hardly interest you much, either.

viii

Here I sit poleaxed, stunned by your vanishing
As you practise your charm in the underworld
Airily flirting with Persephone. Not *so hard*
To imagine what her mother *had gone through*
To be ferreting around those dark sweet halls.

ix

They'd sworn to stay for ever but they went
Or else I went – then concentrated hard
On the puzzle of what it ever truly *meant*
For someone to be here then, just like that
To not. Training in mild loss was useless
Given the final thing. And me lamentably
Slow to 'take it in' – far better toss it out,
How should I take in such a bad idea. No,
I'll stick it out instead for presence. If my
Exquisite hope can wrench you right back
Here, resigned boy, do let it as I'm waiting.

x

I can't get sold on reincarnating you
As those bloody 'gentle showers of rain'
Or in 'fields of ripening grain' – oooh
Anodyne – nor yet on shadowing you
In the hope of eventually pinpointing
You bemused among the *flocking souls*
Clustered like bats, as all thronged gibbering
Dusk-veiled – nor in modern creepiness.
Lighthearted presence, be bodied forth
Straightforwardly. Lounge again under
The sturdy sun you'd loved to bake in.
Even ten seconds' worth of a sighting
Of you would help me get through
This better. With a camera running.

xi

Ardent bee, still you go blundering
With downy saddlebags stuffed tight
All over the fuchsia's drop earrings.
I'll cry 'Oh bee!' to you, instead –
Since my own dead, apostrophised,
Keep mute as this clear garnet glaze
You're bumping into. Blind diligence,
Bee, or idiocy – this banging on and on
Against such shiny crimson unresponse.

xii

Outgoing soul, I try to catch
You calling over the distances
Though your voice is echoey,
Maybe tuned out by the noise
Rolling through me – or is it
You orchestrating that now,
Who'd laugh at the thought
Of me being sung in by you
And being kindly dictated to.
It's not like hearing you live was.
It is what you're saying in me
Of what is left, gaily affirming.

xiii

Flat on a cliff I inch toward its edge
Then scrutinise the chopped-up sea
Where gannets' ivory helmet skulls
Crash down in tiny plumes of white
To vivify the languid afternoon –
Pressed round my fingertips are spikes
And papery calyx frills of fading thrift
That men call sea pinks – so I can take

A studied joy in natural separateness.
And I shan't fabricate some nodding:
'She's off again somewhere, a good sign
By now, she must have got over it.'

xiv

Dun blur of this evening's lurch to
Eventual navy night. Yet another
Night, day, night over and over.
I so want to join you.

xv

The flaws in suicide are clear
Apart from causing bother
To those alive who hold us dear
We could miss one another
We might be trapped eternally
Oblivious to each other
One crying *Where are you, my child*
The other calling *Mother.*

xvi

Dead, keep me company
That sears like titanium
Compacted in the pale
Blaze of living on alone.

xvii

Suspended in unsparing light
The sloping gull arrests its curl
The glassy sea is hardened waves
Its waters lean through shining air
Yet never crash but hold their arc
Hung rigidly in glaucous ropes
Muscled and gleaming. All that
Should flow is sealed, is poised
In implacable stillness. Joined in
Non-time and halted in free fall.

xviii

It's all a resurrection song.
Would it ever be got right
The dead could rush home
Keen to press their chinos.

xix

She do the bereaved in different voices
For the point of this address is to prod
And shepherd you back within range
Of my strained ears; extort your reply
By finding any device to hack through
The thickening shades to you, you now
Strangely unresponsive son, who were
Such reliably kind and easy company,
Won't you be summoned up once more
By my prancing and writhing in a dozen
Mawkish modes of reedy piping to you
– Still no? Then let me rest, my dear.

XX

My sisters and my mother
Weep dark tears for me
I drift as lightest ashes
Under a southern sea
O let me be, my mother
In no unquiet grave
My bone-dust is faint coral
Under the fretful wave

RAINER MARIA RILKE

(1875–1926)

The Ninth Elegy

Why, when this span of life might be fleeted away
as laurel, a little darker than all
the surrounding green, with tiny waves on the border
of every leaf (like the smile of a wind): – oh, why
have to be human, and, shunning Destiny,
long for Destiny? . . .
                              Not because happiness really
exists, that premature profit of imminent loss.
Not out of curiosity, not just to practise the heart,
that could still be there in laurel . . .
But because being here amounts to so much, because all
this Here and Now, so fleeting, seems to require us and strangely
concern us. Us the most fleeting of all. Just once,
everything, only for once. Once and no more. And we, too,
once. And never again. But this
having been once, though only once,
having been once on earth – can it ever be cancelled?

And so we keep pressing on and trying to perform it,
trying to contain it within our simple hands,
in the more and more crowded gaze, in the speechless heart.
Trying to become it. To give it to whom? We'd rather
hold on to it all for ever . . . Alas, but the other relation, –
what can be taken across? Not the art of seeing, learnt here
so slowly, and nothing that's happened here. Nothing at all.
Sufferings, then. Above all, the hardness of life,
the long experience of love; in fact,
purely untellable things. But later,
under the stars, what then? the more deeply untellable stars?
For the wanderer doesn't bring from the mountain slope
a handful of earth to the valley, untellable earth, but only

some word he has won, a pure word, the yellow and blue
gentian. Are we, perhaps, here just for saying: House,
Bridge, Fountain, Gate, Jug, Olive tree, Window, –
possibly: Pillar, Tower? . . . but for saying, remember,
oh, for such saying as never the things themselves
hoped so intensely to be. Is not the secret purpose
of this sly earth, in urging a pair of lovers,
just to make everything leap with ecstasy in them?
Threshold: how much it can mean
to two lovers, that they should be wearing their own
worn threshold a little, they too, after the many before,
before the many to come, . . . as a matter of course!

Here is the time for the Tellable, *here* is its home.
Speak and proclaim. More than ever
the things we can live with are falling away, and their place
being oustingly taken up by an imageless act.
Act under crusts, that will readily split as soon
as the doing within outgrows them and takes a new outline.
Between the hammers lives on
our heart, as between the teeth
the tongue, which, nevertheless,
remains the bestower of praise.

Praise the world to the Angel, not the untellable: you
can't impress him with the splendour you've felt; in the cosmos
where he more feelingly feels you're only a tyro. So show him
some simple thing, remoulded by age after age,
till it lives in your hands and eyes as a part of ourselves.
Tell him *things*. He'll stand more astonished; as you did
beside the roper in Rome or the potter in Egypt.
Show him how happy a thing can be, how guileless and ours;
how even the moaning of grief purely determines on form,
serves as a thing, or dies into a thing, – to escape
to a bliss beyond the fiddle. These things that live on departure
understand when you praise them: fleeting, they look for
rescue through something in us, the most fleeting of all.
Want us to change them entirely, within our invisible hearts,
into – oh, endlessly – into ourselves! Whosoever we are.

Earth, isn't this what you want: an invisible
re-arising in us? Is it not your dream
to be one day invisible? Earth! invisible!
What is your urgent command, if not transformation?
Earth, you darling, I will! Oh, believe me, you need
your Springs no longer to win me: a single one,
just one, is already more than my blood can endure.
I've now been unspeakably yours for ages and ages.
You were always right, and your holiest inspiration's
Death, that friendly Death.

Look, I am living. On what? Neither childhood nor future
are growing less . . . Supernumerous existence
wells up in my heart.

Translated by J. B. Leishman and Stephen Spender

EDWIN ARLINGTON ROBINSON
(1869–1935)

Reuben Bright

Because he was a butcher and thereby
Did earn an honest living (and did right),
I would not have you think that Reuben Bright
Was any more a brute than you or I;
For when they told him that his wife must die,
He stared at them, and shook with grief and fright,
And cried like a great baby half that night,
And made the women cry to see him cry.

And after she was dead, and he had paid
The singers and the sexton and the rest,
He packed a lot of things that she had made
Most mournfully away in an old chest
Of hers, and put some chopped-up cedar boughs
In with them, and tore down the slaughter house.

CHRISTINA ROSSETTI

(1830–1894)

Song

When I am dead, my dearest,
  Sing no sad songs for me;
Plant thou no roses at my head,
  Nor shady cypress tree:
Be the green grass above me
  With showers and dewdrops wet;
And if thou wilt, remember,
  And if thou wilt, forget.

I shall not see the shadows,
  I shall not feel the rain;
I shall not hear the nightingale
  Sing on, as if in pain;
And dreaming through the twilight
  That doth not rise nor set,
Haply I may remember,
  And haply may forget.

Remember

Remember me when I am gone away,
  Gone far away into the silent land;
  When you can no more hold me by the hand,
Nor I half turn to go yet turning stay.
Remember me when no more day by day
  You tell me of our future that you planned:
  Only remember me; you understand
It will be late to counsel then or pray.
Yet if you should forget me for a while

And afterwards remember, do not grieve:
For if the darkness and corruption leave
   A vestige of the thoughts that once I had,
Better by far you should forget and smile
   Than that you should remember and be sad.

Rest

O Earth, lie heavily upon her eyes;
Seal her sweet eyes weary of watching, Earth;
   Lie close around her; leave no room for mirth
With its harsh laughter, nor for sound of sighs.
She hath no questions, she hath no replies,
   Hushed in and curtained with a blessed dearth
   Of all that irked her from the hour of birth;
With stillness that is almost Paradise.
Darkness more clear than noonday holdeth her,
   Silence more musical than any song;
Even her very heart has ceased to stir:
Until the morning of Eternity
Her rest shall not begin nor end, but be;
   And when she wakes she will not think it long.

ELIZABETH ROWE

(1674–1737)

Upon the Death of Her Husband

In what soft language shall my thoughts get free,
My dear Alexis, when I talk of thee?
Ye muses, graces, all ye gentle train
Of weeping loves, assist the pensive strain!
But why should I implore your moving art?
'Tis but to speak the dictates of my heart.
And all that knew the charming youth will join
Their friendly sighs, and pious tears to mine:
For all that knew his merit must confess.
In grief for him there can be no excess.

  His soul was form'd to act each Glorious part
Of life, unstain'd with vanity, or art.
No thought within his gen'rous mind had birth,
But what he might have own'd to heav'n and earth.
Practis'd by him, each virtue grew more bright,
And shone with more than its own native light.
Whatever noble warmth could recommend
The just, the active, and the constant friend
Was all his own – but oh! a dearer name,
And softer ties my endless sorrow claim;
Lost in despair, distracted, and forlorn,
The lover I, and tender husband mourn.
Whate'er to such superior worth was due,
Whate'er excess the fondest passion knew,
I felt for thee, dear youth; my joy, my care;
My prayers themselves were thine, and only where
Thou wast concern'd, my virtue was sincere.
Whene'er I begg'd for blessings on thy head,

Nothing was cold, or formal, that I said;
My warmest vows to Heav'n were made for thee,
And love still mingled with my piety.

O Thou wast all my glory, all my pride!
Thro' life's uncertain paths, my constant guide:
Regardless of the world, to gain thy praise.
Was all that could my just ambition raise.

Why has my heart this fond engagement known?
Or why has Heav'n dissolv'd the tie so soon?
Why was the charming youth so form'd to move?
Or why was all my soul so turn'd for love?
But virtue here a vain defence had made,
Where so much worth and eloquence could plead.
For he could talk – 'twas extasy to hear,
'Twas joy, 'twas harmony to ev'ry ear!
Eternal music dwelt upon his tongue,
Soft and transporting as the muse's song:
List'ning to him, my cares were charm'd to rest,
And love, and silent rapture fill'd my breast;
Unheeded the gay moments took their flight,
And time was only measur'd by delight,
I hear the lov'd, the melting accents still,
And still the kind, the tender transport feel:
Again I see the sprightly passions rise,
And life and pleasure sparkle in his eyes.
My fancy paints him now with ev'ry grace,
But, ah! the dear delusion mocks my fond embrace:
The smiling vision takes its hasty flight,
And scenes of horror swim before my sight,
Grief and despair in all their terrors rise,
A dying lover pale and gasping lies;
Each dismal circumstance appears in view,
The fatal object is for ever new:
His anguish, with the quickest sense I feel,
And hear this sad, this moving language still.

My dearest wife! my last, my fondest care!
Sure Heav'n for thee will hear a dying pray'r:
Be thou the charge of sacred Providence,
When I am gone, be that thy kind defence;
Ten thousand smiling blessings crown thy head,
When I am cold, and number'd with the dead.
Think on thy vows, be to my mem'ry just,

My future fame and honour are thy trust.
From all engagements here I now am free,
But that which keeps my ling'ring soul with thee.
How much I love, thy bleeding heart can tell,
Which does, like mine, the pangs of parting feel:
But haste to meet me on those happy plains,
Where mighty love in endless triumph reigns.

He ceas'd; then gently yielded up his breath,
And fell a blooming sacrifice to death:
But, oh! what words, what numbers can express,
What thought conceive the height of my distress?
Why did they tear me from thy breathless clay?
I should have staid, and wept my life away.
Yet, gentle shade, whether thou now dost rove,
Thro' some blest vale, or ever-verdant grove;
One moment listen to my grief, and take
The softest vows that constant love can make.

For thee all thoughts of pleasure I forego,
For thee my tears shall never cease to flow;
For thee at once I from the world retire,
To feed, in silent shades, a hopeless fire.
My bosom all thy image shall retain,
The full impression there shall still remain.
As thou hast taught my constant heart to prove
The noblest height and elegance of love;
That sacred passion I to thee confine,
My spotless faith shall be for ever thine.

TADEUSZ RÓŻEWICZ
(1921–2014)

The Survivor

I am twenty-four
led to slaughter
I survived.

The following are empty synonyms:
man and beast
love and hate
friend and foe
darkness and light.

The way of killing men and beasts is the same
I've seen it:
truckfuls of chopped-up men
who will not be saved.

Ideas are mere words:
virtue and crime
truth and lies
beauty and ugliness
courage and cowardice.

Virtue and crime weigh the same
I've seen it:
in a man who was both
criminal and virtuous.

I seek a teacher and a master
may he restore my sight hearing and speech
may he again name objects and ideas
may he separate darkness from light.

I am twenty-four
led to slaughter
I survived.

Translated by Adam Czerniawski

SONIA SANCHEZ
(1934–)

for our lady

yeh.
      billie.   if someone
had loved u like u
shud have been loved
ain't no tellen what
kinds of songs
                u wud have swung
gainst this country's wite mind.
or what kinds of lyrics
                  wud have pushed us from
our blue / nites.
            yeh.   billie.
if some blk / man
            had reallee
made u feel
        permanentlee warm.
ain't no tellen
            where the jazz of yo/songs
              wud have led us.

SIEGFRIED SASSOON
(1886–1967)

Suicide in the Trenches

I knew a simple soldier boy
Who grinned at life in empty joy,
Slept soundly through the lonesome dark,
And whistled early with the lark.

In winter trenches, cowed and glum,
With crumps and lice and lack of rum,
He put a bullet through his brain.
No one spoke of him again.

• • • •

You smug-faced crowds with kindling eye
Who cheer when soldier lads march by,
Sneak home and pray you'll never know
The hell where youth and laughter go.

ANNA SEWARD

(1742–1809)

An Old Cat's Dying Soliloquy

Years saw me still Acasto's mansion grace,
The gentlest, fondest of the tabby race;
Before him frisking through the garden glade,
Or at his feet in quiet slumber laid;
Praised for my glossy back of zebra streak,
And wreaths of jet encircling round my neck;
Soft paws that ne'er extend the clawing nail,
The snowy whisker and the sinuous tail;
Now feeble age each glazing eyeball dims,
And pain has stiffened these once supple limbs;
Fate of eight lives the forfeit gasp obtains,
And e'en the ninth creeps languid through my veins.
    Much sure of good the future has in store,
When on my master's hearth I bask no more,
In those blest climes, where fishes oft forsake
The winding river and the glassy lake;
There, as our silent-footed race behold
The crimson spots and fins of lucid gold,
Venturing without the shielding waves to play,
They gasp on shelving banks, our easy prey:
While birds unwinged hop careless o'er the ground,
And the plump mouse incessant trots around,
Near wells of cream that mortals never skim,
Warm marum creeping round their shallow brim;
Where green valerian tufts, luxuriant spread,
Cleanse the sleek hide and form the fragrant bed.
    Yet, stern dispenser of the final blow,
Before thou lay'st an aged grimalkin low,
Bend to her last request a gracious ear,
Some days, some few short days, to linger here:
So to the guardian of his tabby's weal

Shall softest purrs these tender truths reveal:
  'Ne'er shall thy now expiring puss forget
To thy kind care her long-enduring debt,
Nor shall the joys that painless realms decree
Efface the comforts once bestowed by thee;
To countless mice thy chicken-bones preferred,
Thy toast to golden fish and wingless bird;
O'er marum borders and valerian bed
Thy Selima shall bend her moping head,
Sigh that no more she climbs, with grateful glee,
Thy downy sofa and thy cradling knee;
Nay, e'en at founts of cream shall sullen swear,
Since thou, her more loved master, art not there.'

ANNE SEXTON
(1928–1974)

The Truth the Dead Know

For my mother, born March 1902, died March 1959
and my father, born February 1900, died June 1959

Gone, I say and walk from church,
refusing the stiff procession to the grave,
letting the dead ride alone in the hearse.
It is June. I am tired of being brave.

We drive to the Cape. I cultivate
myself where the sun gutters from the sky,
where the sea swings in like an iron gate
and we touch. In another country people die.

My darling, the wind falls in like stones
from the whitehearted water and when we touch
we enter touch entirely. No one's alone.
Men kill for this, or for as much.

And what of the dead? They lie without shoes
in their stone boats. They are more like stone
than the sea would be if it stopped. They refuse
to be blessed, throat, eye and knucklebone.

WILLIAM SHAKESPEARE
(1564–1616)

Sonnet 71

No longer mourn for me when I am dead
Than you shall hear the surly sullen bell
Give warning to the world that I am fled
From this vile world with vilest worms to dwell:
Nay, if you read this line, remember not
The hand that writ it, for I love you so
That I in your sweet thoughts would be forgot,
If thinking on me then should make you woe.
O, if (I say) you look upon this verse
When I (perhaps) compounded am with clay,
Do not so much as my poor name rehearse;
But let your love even with my life decay,
    Lest the wise world should look into your moan
    And mock you with me after I am gone.

Sonnet 73

That time of year thou mayst in me behold
When yellow leaves, or none, or few, do hang
Upon those boughs which shake against the cold,
Bare ruined choirs, where late the sweet birds sang.
In me thou seest the twilight of such day
As after sunset fadeth in the west,
Which by and by black night doth take away,
Death's second self, that seals up all in rest.
In me thou seest the glowing of such fire
That on the ashes of his youth doth lie,
As the death-bed whereon it must expire,
Consumed with that which it was nourished by.

This thou perceiv'st, which makes thy love more strong,
To love that well, which thou must leave ere long.

'When that I was and a little tiny boy
(With hey, ho, the wind and the rain)'

When that I was and a little tiny boy,
  With hey, ho, the wind and the rain,
A foolish thing was but a toy,
  For the rain it raineth every day.

But when I came to man's estate,
  With hey, ho, the wind and the rain,
'Gainst knaves and thieves men shut their gate,
  For the rain it raineth every day.

But when I came, alas! to wive,
  With hey, ho, the wind and the rain,
By swaggering could I never thrive,
  For the rain it raineth every day.

But when I came unto my beds,
  With hey, ho, the wind and the rain,
With toss-pots still had drunken heads,
  For the rain it raineth every day.

A great while ago the world begun,
  With hey, ho, the wind and the rain,
But that's all one, our play is done,
  And we'll strive to please you every day.

'Fear no more the heat o' the sun'

Fear no more the heat o' the sun,
Nor the furious winter's rages;
Thou thy worldly task hast done,
Home art gone, and ta'en thy wages:
Golden lads and girls all must,
As chimney-sweepers, come to dust.

Fear no more the frown o' the great;
Thou art past the tyrant's stroke;
Care no more to clothe and eat;
To thee the reed is as the oak:
The scepter, learning, physic, must
All follow this, and come to dust.

Fear no more the lightning flash,
Nor the all-dreaded thunder stone;
Fear not slander, censure rash;
Thou hast finished joy and moan:
All lovers young, all lovers must
Consign to thee, and come to dust.

No exorciser harm thee!
Nor no witchcraft charm thee!
Ghost unlaid forbear thee!
Nothing ill come near thee!
Quiet consummation have;
And renownèd be thy grave!

'Full fathom five thy father lies'

Full fathom five thy father lies;
Of his bones are coral made;
Those are pearls that were his eyes:
Nothing of him that doth fade,
But doth suffer a sea-change
Into something rich and strange.
Sea-nymphs hourly ring his knell:
                              Ding-dong.
Hark! now I hear them, – ding-dong, bell.

PERCY BYSSHE SHELLEY
(1792–1822)

To Wordsworth

Poet of Nature, thou hast wept to know
  That things depart which never may return;
  Childhood and youth, friendship and love's first glow,
  Have fled like sweet dreams, leaving thee to mourn.
These common woes I feel. One loss is mine,
  Which thou too feel'st, yet I alone deplore;
  Thou wert as a lone star whose light did shine
  On some frail bark in winter's midnight roar;
Thou hast like to a rock-built refuge stood
  Above the blind and battling multitude;
  In honored poverty thy voice did weave
Songs consecrate to truth and liberty; –
  Deserting these, thou leavest me to grieve,
  Thus having been, that thou shouldst cease to be.

from *Adonais*

An Elegy on the Death of John Keats,
Author of Endymion, Hyperion, etc.

'Thou wert the morning star among the living.
Ere thy fair light had fled –
Now, having died, thou art as Hesperus, giving
New splendour to the dead.'

Plato, translated by Shelley

I

I weep for Adonais – he is dead!
O, weep for Adonais! though our tears
Thaw not the frost which binds so dear a head!
And thou, sad Hour, selected from all years
To mourn our loss, rouse thy obscure compeers,
And teach them thine own sorrow, say: with me
Died Adonais; till the Future dares
Forget the Past, his fate and fame shall be
An echo and a light unto eternity!

2

Where wert thou mighty Mother when he lay,
When thy Son lay, pierced by the shaft which flies
In darkness? where was lorn Urania
When Adonais died? With veiled eyes,
'Mid listening Echoes, in her Paradise
She sate, while one, with soft enamoured breath,
Rekindled all the fading melodies,
With which, like flowers that mock the corse beneath,
He had adorned and hid the coming bulk of death.

3

O, weep for Adonais – he is dead!
Wake, melancholy Mother, wake and weep!
Yet wherefore? Quench within their burning bed
Thy fiery tears, and let thy loud heart keep
Like his, a mute and uncomplaining sleep;
For he is gone, where all things wise and fair
Descend; – oh, dream not that the amorous Deep
Will yet restore him to the vital air;
Death feeds on his mute voice, and laughs at our despair.

4

Most musical of mourners, weep again!
Lament anew, Urania! – He died,
Who was the Sire of an immortal strain,
Blind, old, and lonely, when his country's pride,
The priest, the slave, and the liberticide,
Trampled and mocked with many a loathed rite
Of lust and blood; he went, unterrified,
Into the gulph of death; but his clear Sprite
Yet reigns o'er earth; the third among the sons of light.

5

Most musical of mourners, weep anew!
Not all to that bright station dared to climb;
And happier they their happiness who knew,
Whose tapers yet burn through that night of time
In which suns perished; others more sublime,
Struck by the envious wrath of man or God,
Have sunk, extinct in their refulgent prime;
And some yet live, treading the thorny road,
Which leads, through toil and hate, to Fame's serene abode.

6

But now, thy youngest, dearest one, has perished –
The nursling of thy widowhood, who grew,
Like a pale flower by some sad maiden cherished,
And fed with true love tears, instead of dew;
Most musical of mourners, weep anew!
Thy extreme hope, the loveliest and the last,
The bloom, whose petals nipt before they blew
Died on the promise of the fruit, is waste;
The broken lily lies – the storm is overpast.

7

To that high Capital, where kingly Death
Keeps his pale court in beauty and decay,
He came; and bought, with price of purest breath,
A grave among the eternal. – Come away!
Haste, while the vault of blue Italian day
Is yet his fitting charnel-roof! while still
He lies, as if in dewy sleep he lay;
Awake him not! surely he takes his fill
Of deep and liquid rest, forgetful of all ill.

8

He will awake no more, oh, never more! –
Within the twilight chamber spreads apace,
The shadow of white Death, and at the door
Invisible Corruption waits to trace
His extreme way to her dim dwelling-place;
The eternal Hunger sits, but pity and awe
Soothe her pale rage, nor dares she to deface
So fair a prey, till darkness, and the law
Of change, shall o'er his sleep the mortal curtain draw.

9

O, weep for Adonais! – The quick Dreams,
The passion-winged Ministers of thought,
Who were his flocks, whom near the living streams
Of his young spirit he fed, and whom he taught
The love which was its music, wander not, –
Wander no more, from kindling brain to brain,
But droop there, whence they sprung; and mourn their lot
Round the cold heart, where, after their sweet pain,
They ne'er will gather strength, or find a home again.

10

And one with trembling hands clasps his cold head,
And fans him with her moonlight wings, and cries;
'Our love, our hope, our sorrow, is not dead;
See, on the silken fringe of his faint eyes,
Like dew upon a sleeping flower, there lies
A tear some Dream has loosened from his brain.'
Lost Angel of a ruined Paradise!
She knew not 'twas her own; as with no stain
She faded, like a cloud which had outwept its rain.

45

The inheritors of unfulfilled renown
Rose from their thrones, built beyond mortal thought,
Far in the Unapparent, Chatterton
Rose pale, his solemn agony had not
Yet faded from him; Sidney, as he fought
And as he fell and as he lived and loved
Sublimely mild, a Spirit without spot,
Arose; and Lucan, by his death approved:
Oblivion as they rose shrank like a thing reproved.

46

And many more, whose names on Earth are dark
But whose transmitted effluence cannot die
So long as fire outlives the parent spark,
Rose, robed in dazzling immortality.
'Thou art become as one of us,' they cry,
'It was for thee yon kingless sphere has long
Swung blind in unascended majesty,
Silent alone amid an Heaven of song.
Assume thy winged throne, thou Vesper of our throng!'

47

Who mourns for Adonais? oh come forth
Fond wretch! and know thyself and him aright.
Clasp with thy panting soul the pendulous Earth;
As from a centre, dart thy spirit's light
Beyond all worlds, until its spacious might
Satiate the void circumference: then shrink
Even to a point within our day and night;
And keep thy heart light lest it make thee sink
When hope has kindled hope, and lured thee to the brink.

48

Or go to Rome, which is the sepulchre
O, not of him, but of our joy: 'tis nought
That ages, empires, and religions there
Lie buried in the ravage they have wrought;
For such as he can lend, – they borrow not
Glory from those who made the world their prey;
And he is gathered to the kings of thought
Who waged contention with their time's decay,
And of the past are all that cannot pass away.

49

Go thou to Rome, – at once the Paradise,
The grave, the city, and the wilderness;
And where its wrecks like shattered mountains rise,
And flowering weeds, and fragrant copses dress
The bones of Desolation's nakedness
Pass, till the Spirit of the spot shall lead
Thy footsteps to a slope of green access
Where, like an infant's smile, over the dead,
A light of laughing flowers along the grass is spread.

50

And grey walls moulder round, on which dull Time
Feeds, like slow fire upon a hoary brand;
And one keen pyramid with wedge sublime,
Pavilioning the dust of him who planned
This refuge for his memory, doth stand
Like flame transformed to marble; and beneath,
A field is spread, on which a newer band
Have pitched in Heaven's smile their camp of death
Welcoming him we lose with scarce extinguished breath.

51

Here pause: these graves are all too young as yet
To have outgrown the sorrow which consigned
Its charge to each; and if the seal is set,
Here, on one fountain of a mourning mind,
Break it not thou! too surely shalt thou find
Thine own well full, if thou returnest home,
Of tears and gall. From the world's bitter wind
Seek shelter in the shadow of the tomb.
What Adonais is, why fear we to become?

52

The One remains, the many change and pass;
Heaven's light forever shines, Earth's shadows fly;
Life, like a dome of many-coloured glass,
Stains the white radiance of Eternity.
Until Death tramples it to fragments. – Die,
If thou wouldst be with that which thou dost seek!
Follow where all is fled! – Rome's azure sky,
Flowers, ruins, statues, music, words, are weak
The glory they transfuse with fitting truth to speak.

53

Why linger, why turn back, why shrink, my Heart?
Thy hopes are gone before; from all things here
They have departed; thou shouldst now depart!
A light is past from the revolving year,
And man, and woman; and what still is dear
Attracts to crush, repels to make thee wither.
The soft sky smiles, – the low wind whispers near:
'Tis Adonais calls! oh, hasten thither,
No more let Life divide what Death can join together.

54

That Light whose smile kindles the Universe,
That Beauty in which all things work and move,
That Benediction which the eclipsing Curse
Of birth can quench not, that sustaining Love
Which through the web of being blindly wove
By man and beast and earth and air and sea,
Burns bright or dim, as each are mirrors of
The fire for which all thirst; now beams on me,
Consuming the last clouds of cold mortality.

55

The breath whose might I have invoked in song
Descends on me; my spirit's bark is driven,
Far from the shore, far from the trembling throng
Whose sails were never to the tempest given;
The massy earth and sphered skies are riven!
I am borne darkly, fearfully, afar;
Whilst burning through the inmost veil of Heaven,
The soul of Adonais, like a star,
Beacons from the abode where the Eternal are.

JAMES SHIRLEY

(1596–1666)

Epitaph on the Duke of Buckingham

Here lies the best and worst of Fate,
Two Kings delight, the peoples hate,
The Courtiers star, the Kingdoms eye,
A man to draw an Angel by,
   Fears despiser, *Villiers* glory,
   The Great mans volume, all times story.

JOHN SKELTON
(1463–1529)

from Phillip Sparrow

Pla ce bo,
Who is there, who?
Di le xi,
Dame Margery;
Fa, re, my, my,
Wherfore and why, why?
For the sowle of Philip Sparowe,
That was late slayn at Carowe,
Among the Nones Blake,
For that swete soules sake,
And for all sparowes soules,
Set in our bede rolles,
Pater noster qui,
With an *Ave Mari,*
And with the corner of a Crede,
The more shal be your mede.

Whan I remembre agayn
How mi Philyp was slayn,
Never halfe the payne
Was betwene you twayne,
Pyramus and Thesbe,
As than befell to me:
I wept and I wayled,
The tearys downe hayled;
But nothinge it avayled
To call Phylyp agayne,
Whom Gyb our cat hath slayne.

Gyb, I saye, our cat,
Worrowyd her on that
Which I loved best:
It can not be exprest
My sorowfull hevynesse,
But all without redresse;
For within that stounde,
Halfe slumbrynge, in a sounde
I fell downe to the grounde.
    Unneth I kest myne eyes
Towarde the cloudy skyes:
But whan I dyd beholde
My sparow dead and colde,
No creatuer but that wolde
Have rewed upon me,
To behold and se
What hevynesse dyd me pange;
Wherewith my handes I wrange,
That my senaws cracked,
As though I had ben racked,
So payned and so strayned,
That no lyfe well nye remayned.
    I syghed and I sobbed,
For that I was robbed
Of my sparowes lyfe.
O mayden, wydow, and wyfe,
Of what estate ye be,
Of hye or lowe degre,
Great sorowe than ye myght se,
And lerne to wepe at me!
Such paynes dyd me frete,
That myne hert dyd bete,
My vysage pale and dead,
Wanne, and blewe as lead;
The panges of hatefull death
Wellnye had stopped my breath.

Heu, heu, me,
That I am wo for the!

Ad Dominum, cum tribularer, clamavi:
Of God nothynge els crave I
But Phyllypes soule to kepe
From the marees deepe
Of Acherontes well,
That is a flode of hell;
And from the great Pluto,
The prynce of endles wo;
And from foule Alecto,
With vysage blacke and blo;
And from Medusa, that mare,
That lyke a fende doth stare;
And from Megeras edders,
For rufflynge of Phillips fethers,
And from her fyry sparklynges,
For burnynge of his wynges;
And from the smokes sowre
Of Proserpinas bowre;
And from the dennes darke,
Wher Cerberus doth barke,
Whom Theseus dyd afraye,
Whom Hercules dyd outraye,
As famous poetes say;
From that hell-hounde,
That lyeth in cheynes bounde,
With gastly hedes thre,
To Jupyter pray we
That Phyllyp preserved may be!
Amen, say ye with me!

Do mi nus,
Helpe nowe, swete Jesus!
Levavi oculos meos in montes:
    Wolde God I had Zenophontes,
Or Socrates the wyse
To shew me their devyse,
Moderatly to take
This sorrow that I make
For Phylyp Sparowes sake!

So fervently I shake,
I fele my body quake;
So urgently I am brought
Into carefull thought.
   Like Andromach, Hectors wyfe,
Was wery of her lyfe,
Whan she had lost her joye,
Noble Hector of Troye;
In lyke maner also
Encreaseth my dedly wo,
For my sparowe is go.
It was so prety a fole,
It wold syt on a stole,
And lerned after my scole
For to kepe his cut,
With, 'Phyllyp, kepe your cut!'
   It had a velvet cap,
And wold syt upon my lap,
And seke after small wormes,
And somtyme white bred crommes;
And many tymes and ofte
Betwene my brestes softe
It wolde lye and rest;
It was propre and prest.
   Somtyme he wolde gaspe
Whan he sawe a waspe;
A fly or a gnat,
He wolde flye at that;
And prytely he wold pant
Whan he saw an ant;
Lord, how he wolde pry
After the butterfly!
Lorde, how he wolde hop
After the gressop!
And whan I sayd, 'Phyp! Phyp!'
Than he wold lepe and skyp,
And take me by the lyp.
Alas, it wyll me slo,
That Phillyp is gone me fro!

STEVIE SMITH

(1902–1971)

Scorpion

'This night shall thy soul be required of thee'
My soul is never required of *me*
It always has to be somebody else of course
Will my soul be required of me tonight perhaps?

(I often wonder what it will be like
To have one's soul required of one
But all I can think of is the Out-Patients' Department –
'Are you Mrs Briggs, dear?'
No, I am Scorpion.)

I should like my soul to be required of me, so as
To waft over grass till it comes to the blue sea
I am very fond of grass, I always have been, but there must
Be no cow, person or house to be seen.

Sea and *grass* must be quite empty
Other souls can find somewhere *else*.

O Lord God please come
And require the soul of thy Scorpion

Scorpion so wishes to be gone.

TRACY K. SMITH

1972–

Wade in the Water

For the Geechee Gullah Ring Shouters

One of the women greeted me.
I love you, she said. She didn't
Know me, but I believed her,
And a terrible new ache
Rolled over in my chest,
Like in a room where the drapes
Have been swept back. I love you,
I love you, as she continued
Down the hall past other strangers,
Each feeling pierced suddenly
By pillars of heavy light.
I love you, throughout
The performance, in every
Handclap, every stomp.
I love you in the rusted iron
Chains someone was made
To drag until love let them be
Unclasped and left empty
In the center of the ring.
I love you in the water
Where they pretended to wade,
Singing that old blood-deep song
That dragged us to those banks
And cast us in. I love you,
The angles of it scraping at
Each throat, shouldering past
The swirling dust motes
In those beams of light
That whatever we now knew
We could let ourselves feel, knew

To climb. O Woods – O Dogs –
O Tree – O Gun – O *Girl, run* –
O Miraculous Many Gone –
O Lord – O Lord – O Lord –
Is this love the trouble you promised?

LAYLI LONG SOLDIER

(1976–)

38

Here, the sentence will be respected.

I will compose each sentence with care by minding what the rules of writing dictate.

For example, all sentences will begin with capital letters.

Likewise, the history of the sentence will be honored by ending each one with appropriate punctuation such as a period or question mark, thus bringing the idea to (momentary) completion.

You may like to know, I do not consider this a 'creative piece.'

I do not regard this as a poem of great imagination or a work of fiction.

Also, historical events will not be dramatized for an 'interesting' read.

Therefore, I feel most responsible to the orderly sentence; conveyor of thought.

That said, I will begin:

You may or may not have heard about the Dakota 38.

If this is the first time you've heard of it, you might wonder, 'What is the Dakota 38?'

The Dakota 38 refers to thirty-eight Dakota men who were executed by hanging, under orders from President Abraham Lincoln.

To date, this is the largest 'legal' mass execution in U.S. history.

The hanging took place on December 26, 1862 – the day after Christmas.

This was the *same week* that President Lincoln signed The Emancipation Proclamation.

In the preceding sentence, I italicize 'same week' for emphasis.

There was a movie titled *Lincoln* about the presidency of Abraham Lincoln.

The signing of The Emancipation Proclamation was included in the film Lincoln; the hanging of the Dakota 38 was not.

In any case, you might be asking, 'Why were thirty-eight Dakota men hung?'

As a side note, the past tense of hang is *hung*, but when referring to the capital punishment of hanging, the correct tense is *hanged*.

So it's possible that you're asking, 'Why were thirty-eight Dakota men hanged?'

They were hanged for The Sioux Uprising.

I want to tell you about The Sioux Uprising, but I don't know where to begin.

I may jump around and details will not unfold in chronological order.

Keep in mind, I am not a historian.

So I will recount facts as best as I can, given limited resources and understanding.

Before Minnesota was a state, the Minnesota region, generally speaking, was the traditional homeland for Dakota, Anishnaabeg and Ho-Chunk people.

During the 1800s, when the U.S. expanded territory, they 'purchased' land from the Dakota people as well as the other tribes.

But another way to understand that sort of 'purchase' is: Dakota leaders ceded land to the U. S. Government in exchange for money and goods, but most importantly, the safety of their people.

Some say that Dakota leaders did not understand the terms they were entering, or they never would have agreed.

Even others call the entire negotiation 'trickery.'

But to make whatever-it-was official and binding, the U. S. Government drew up an initial treaty.

This treaty was later replaced by another (more convenient) treaty, and then another.

I've had difficulty unraveling the terms of these treaties, given the legal speak and congressional language.

As treaties were abrogated (broken) and new treaties were drafted, one after another, the new treaties often referenced old defunct treaties and it is a muddy, switchback trail to follow.

Although I often feel lost on this trail, I know I am not alone.

However, as best as I can put the facts together, in 1851, Dakota territory was contained to a 12-mile by 150-mile long strip along the Minnesota river.

But just seven years later, in 1858, the northern portion was ceded (taken) and the southern portion was (conveniently) allotted, which reduced Dakota land to a stark 10-mile tract.

These amended and broken treaties are often referred to as The Minnesota Treaties.

The word *Minnesota* comes from *mni* which means water; *sota* which means turbid.

Synonyms for turbid include muddy, unclear, cloudy, confused and smoky.

Everything is in the language we use.

For example, a treaty is, essentially, a contract between two sovereign nations.

The U.S. treaties with the Dakota Nation were legal contracts that promised money.

It could be said, this money was payment for the land the Dakota ceded; for living within assigned boundaries (a reservation); and for relinquishing rights to their vast hunting territory which, in turn, made Dakota people dependent on other means to survive: money.

The previous sentence is circular, which is akin to so many aspects of history.

As you may have guessed by now, the money promised in the turbid treaties did not make it into the hands of Dakota people.

In addition, local government traders would not offer credit to 'Indians' to purchase food or goods.

Without money, store credit or rights to hunt beyond their 10-mile tract of land, Dakota people began to starve.

The Dakota people were starving.

The Dakota people starved.

In the preceding sentence, the word 'starved' does not need italics for emphasis.

One should read, 'The Dakota people starved,' as a straightforward and plainly stated fact.

As a result – and without other options but to continue to starve – Dakota people retaliated.

Dakota warriors organized, struck out and killed settlers and traders.

This revolt is called The Sioux Uprising.

Eventually, the U.S. Cavalry came to Mnisota to confront the Uprising.

More than one thousand Dakota people were sent to prison.

As already mentioned, thirty-eight Dakota men were subsequently hanged.

After the hanging, those one thousand Dakota prisoners were released.

However, as further consequence, what remained of Dakota territory in Mnisota was dissolved (stolen). The Dakota people had no land to return to.

This means they were exiled.

Homeless, the Dakota people of Mnisota were relocated (forced) onto reservations in South Dakota and Nebraska.

Now, every year, a group called the The Dakota 38 + 2 Riders conduct a memorial horse ride from Lower Brule, South Dakota to Mankato, Mnisota.

The Memorial Riders travel 325 miles on horseback for eighteen days, sometimes through sub-zero blizzards.

They conclude their journey on December 26, the day of the hanging. Memorials help focus our memory on particular people or events.

Often, memorials come in the forms of plaques, statues or gravestones.

The memorial for the Dakota 38 is not an object inscribed with words, but an *act*.

Yet, I started this piece because I was interested in writing about grasses.

So, there is one other event to include, although it's not in chronological order and we must backtrack a little.

When the Dakota people were starving, as you may remember, government traders would not extend store credit to 'Indians.'

One trader named Andrew Myrick is famous for his refusal to provide credit to Dakotas by saying, 'If they are hungry, let them eat grass.'

There are variations of Myrick's words, but they are all something to that effect.

When settlers and traders were killed during the Sioux Uprising, one of the first to be executed by the Dakota was Andrew Myrick.

When Myrick's body was found,

his mouth was stuffed with grass.

I am inclined to call this act by the Dakota warriors a poem.

There's irony in their poem.

There was no text.

'Real' poems do not 'really' require words.

I have italicized the previous sentence to indicate inner dialogue; a revealing moment.

But, on second thought, the words 'Let them eat grass,' click the gears of the poem into place.

So, we could also say, language and word choice are crucial to the poem's work.

Things are circling back again.

Sometimes, when in a circle, if I wish to exit, I must leap.

And let the body   swing.

From the platform.

                              Out

                                        to the grasses.

CHARLES HAMILTON SORLEY
(1895–1915)

'When you see millions of the mouthless dead'

When you see millions of the mouthless dead
Across your dreams in pale battalions go,
Say not soft things as other men have said,
That you'll remember. For you need not so.
Give them not praise. For, deaf, how should they know
It is not curses heaped on each gashed head?
Nor tears. Their blind eyes see not your tears flow.
Nor honour. It is easy to be dead.
Say only this, 'They are dead.' Then add thereto,
'Yet many a better one has died before.'
Then, scanning all the o'ercrowded mass, should you
Perceive one face that you loved heretofore,
It is a spook. None wears the face you knew.
Great death has made all his for evermore.

EDMUND SPENSER

(1552–1599)

Astrophel

*A Pastorall Elegie vpon the death of the most Noble
and valorous Knight, Sir Philip Sidney.*

*Dedicated to the most beautifull and vertuous Ladie,
the Countesse of Essex.*

Shepheards that wont on pipes of oaten reed,
Oft times to plaint your loues concealed smart:
And with your piteous layes haue learnd to breed
Compassion in a countrey lasses hart.
Hearken ye gentle shepheards to my song,
And place my dolefull plaint your plaints emong.

To you alone I sing this mournfull verse,
The mournfulst verse that euer man heard tell:
To you whose softened hearts it may empierse,
With dolours dart for death of Astrophel.
To you I sing and to none other wight,
For well I wot my rymes bene rudely dight.

Yet as they been, if any nycer wit
Shall hap to heare, or couet them to read:
Thinke he, that such are for such ones most fit,
Made not to please the liuing but the dead.
And if in him found pity euer place,
Let him be moou'd to pity such a case.

A Gentle Shepheard borne in Arcady,
Of gentlest race that euer shepheard bore:
About the grassie bancks of Hæmony,

Did keepe his sheep, his litle stock and store.
Full carefully he kept them day and night,
In fairest fields, and Astrophel he hight.

Young Astrophel the pride of shepheards praise,
Young Astrophel the rusticke lasses loue:
Far passing all the pastors of his daies,
In all that seemly shepheard might behoue.
In one thing onely fayling of the best,
That he was not so happie as the rest.

For from the time that first the Nymph his mother
Him forth did bring, and taught her lambs to feed:
A sclender swaine excelling far each other,
In comely shape, like her that did him breed.
He grew vp fast in goodnesse and in grace,
And doubly faire wox both in mynd and face.

Which daily more and more he did augment,
With gentle vsage and demeanure myld:
That all mens hearts with secret rauishment
He stole away, and weetingly beguyld.
Ne spight it selfe that all good things doth spill,
Found ought in him, that she could say was ill.

His sports were faire, his ioyance innocent,
Sweet without sowre, and honny without gall:
And he himselfe seemd made for meriment,
Merily masking both in bowre and hall.
There was no pleasure nor delightfull play,
When Astrophel so euer was away.

For he could pipe and daunce, and caroll sweet,
Emongst the shepheards in their shearing feast:
As Somers larke that with her song doth greet,
The dawning day forth comming from the East.
And layes of loue he also could compose,
Thrise happie she, whom he to praise did chose.

Full many Maydens often did him woo,
Them to vouchsafe emongst his rimes to name,
Or make for them as he was wont to doo,
For her that did his heart with loue inflame.
For which they promised to dight for him,
Gay chapelets of flowers and gyrlonds trim.

And many a Nymph both of the wood and brooke,
Soone as his oaten pipe began to shrill:
Both christall wells and shadie groues forsooke,
To heare the charmes of his enchanting skill.
And brought him presents, flowers if it were prime,
Or mellow fruit if it were haruest time.

But he for none of them did care a whit,
Yet wood Gods for them often sighed sore:
Ne for their gifts vnworthie of his wit,
Yet not vnworthie of the countries store.
For one alone he cared, for one he sight,
His lifes desire, and his deare loues delight.

Stella the faire, the fairest star in skie,
As faire as Venus or the fairest faire:
A fairer star saw neuer liuing eie,
[S]hot her sharp pointed beames through purest aire.
Her he did loue, her he alone did honor,
His thoughts, his rimes, his songs were all upon her.

To her he vowd the seruice of his daies,
On her he spent the riches of his wit:
For her he made hymnes of immortall praise,
Of onely her he sung, he thought, he writ.
Her, and but her of loue he deemed,
For all the rest but little he esteemed.

Ne her with ydle words alone he wowed,
And verses vaine (yet verses are not vaine)
But with braue deeds to her sole seruice vowed,
And bold achieuements her did entertaine.
For both in deeds and words he nourtred was,
Both wise and hardie (too hardie alas).

In wrestling nimble, and in renning swift,
In shooting steddie, and in swimming strong:
Well made to strike, to throw, to leape, to lift,
And all the sports that shepheards are emong.
In euery one he vanquisht euery one,
He vanquist all, and vanquisht was of none.

Besides, in hunting such felicitie,
Or rather infelicitie he found:
That euery field and forest far away,
He sought, where saluage beasts do most abound.
No beast so saluage but he could it kill,
No chace so hard, but he therein had skill.

Such skill matcht with such courage as he had,
Did prick him foorth with proud desire of praise:
To seek abroad, of daunger nought y'drad,
His mistresse name, and his owne fame to raise.
What needeth perill to be sought abroad,
Since round about vs, it doth make aboad?

It fortuned as he, that perlous game
In forreine soyle pursued far away:
Into a forest wide, and waste he came
Where store he heard to be of saluage pray.
So wide a forest and so waste as this,
Nor famous Ardeyn, nor fowle Arlo is.

There his welwouen toyles and subtil traines,
He laid the brutish nation to enwrap:
So well he wrought with practise and with paines,
That he of them great troups did soone entrap.
Full happie man (misweening much) was hee,
So rich a spoile within his power to see.

Eftsoones all heedlesse of his dearest hale,
Full greedily into the heard he thrust:
To slaughter them, and work their finall bale,
Least that his tolye should of their troups be brust.
Wide wounds emongst them many a one he made,
Now with his sharp borespeare, now with his blade.

His care was all how he them all might kill,
That none might scape (so partiall vnto none)
Ill mynd so much to mynd anothers ill,
As to become vnmyndfull of his owne.
But pardon that vnto the cruell skies,
That from himselfe to them withdrew his eies.

So as he rag'd emongst that beastly rout,
A cruell beast of most accursed brood:
Vpon him turnd (despeyre makes cowards stout)
And with fell tooth accustomed to blood,
Launched his thigh with so mischieuous might,
That it both bone and muscles ryued quight.

So deadly was the dint and deep the wound,
And so huge streames of blood thereout did flow:
That he endured not the direfull stound,
But on the cold deare earth himselfe did throw.
The whiles the captiue heard his nets did rend,
And hauing none to let, to wood did wend.

Ah where were ye this while his shepheard peares,
To whom aliue was nought so deare as hee:
And ye faire Mayds the matches of his yeares,
Which in his grace did boast you most to bee?
Ah where were ye, when he of you had need,
To stop his wound that wondrously did bleed?

Ah wretched boy the shape of dreryhead,
And sad ensample of mans suddein end:
Full litle faileth but thou shalt be dead,
Vnpitied, vnplaynd, of foe or frend.
Whilest none is nigh, thine eylids vp to close,
And kisse thy lips like faded leaues of rose.

A sort of shepheards sewing of the chace,
As they the forest raunged on a day:
By fate or fortune came vnto the place,
Where as the lucklesse boy yet bleeding lay.
Yet bleeding lay, and yet would still haue bled,
Had not good hap those shepheards thether led.

They stopt his wound (too late to stop it was)
And in their armes they softly did him reare:
Tho (as he wild) vnto his loued lasse,
His dearest loue him dolefully did beare.
The dolefulst beare that euer man did see,
Was Astrophel, but dearest vnto mee.

She when she saw her loue in such a plight,
With crudled blood and filthie gore deformed:
That wont to be with flowers and gyrlonds dight,
And her deare fauours dearly well adorned
Her face, the fairest face that eye mote see,
She likewise did deforme like him to bee.

Her yellow locks that shone so bright and long,
As Sunny beames in fairest somers day:
She fiersly tore, and with outragious wrong
From her red cheeks the roses rent away.
And her faire brest the threasury of ioy,
She spoyld therof, and filled with annoy.

His palled face impictured with death,
She bathed oft with teares and dried oft:
And with sweet kisses suckt the wasting breath,
Out of his lips like lillies pale and soft.
And oft she cald to him, who answerd nought,
But onely by his lookes did tell his thought.

The rest of her impatient regret,
And piteous mone the which she for him made:
No toong can tell, nor any forth can set,
But he whose heart like sorrow did inuade.
At last when paine his vitall powres had spent,
His wasted life her weary lodge forwent.

Which when she saw, she staied not a whit,
But after him did make vntimely haste:
Forth with her ghost out of her corpse did flit,
And followed her make like Turtle chaste.
To proue that death their hearts cannot diuide,
Which liuing were in loue so firmly tide.

The Gods which all things see, this same beheld,
And pittying this paire of louers trew:
Transformed them there lying on the field,
Into one flowre that is both red and blew.
It first growes red, and then to blew doth fade,
Like Astrophel, which thereinto was made.

And in the midst thereof a star appeares,
As fairly formd as any star in skyes:
Resembling Stella in her freshest yeares,
Forth darting beames of beautie from her eyes,
And all the day it standeth full of deow,
Which is the teares, that from her eyes did flow.

That hearbe of some, Starlight is cald by name,
Of others Penthia, though not so well:
But thou where euer thou dost finde the same,
From this day forth do call it Astrophel.
And when so euer thou it vp doest take,
Do pluck it softly for that shepheards sake.

Hereof when tydings far abroad did passe,
The shepheards all which loued him full deare:
And sure full deare of all he loued was,
Did thether flock to see what they did heare.
And when that pitteous spectacle they vewed,
The same with bitter teares they all bedewed.

And euery one did make exceeding mone,
With inward anguish and great griefe opprest:
And euery one did weep and waile and mone,
And meanes deuiz'd to shew his sorrow best.
That from that houre since first on grassie greene,
Shepheards kept sheep, was not like mourning seen.

WALLACE STEVENS

(1879–1955)

The Emperor of Ice-Cream

Call the roller of big cigars,
The muscular one, and bid him whip
In kitchen cups concupiscent curds.
Let the wenches dawdle in such dress
As they are used to wear, and let the boys
Bring flowers in last month's newspapers.
Let be be finale of seem.
The only emperor is the emperor of ice-cream.

Take from the dresser of deal,
Lacking the three glass knobs, that sheet
On which she embroidered fantails once
And spread it so as to cover her face.
If her horny feet protrude, they come
To show how cold she is, and dumb.
Let the lamp affix its beam.
The only emperor is the emperor of ice-cream.

ANNE STEVENSON

(1933–2020)

Orcop

In Memoriam: Frances Horovitz, 1938–1983

Driving south from Hereford one day in March
memorable for trickling piles of snow, with sideshows,
drift upon drift of snowdrops lapping the hedgerows,
we sighted the signpost and, on impulse, turned up
the winding, vertical road to Orcop. The church,
further away from the village than I remembered,
was no less an image of you than I remembered,
with its high-pitched, peasant roof and wooden steeple
on a slope with yew trees and a painter's view –
ploughed red soil, a pasture, a working barn –
that set it apart from the ordinary, just as your field stone,
when we found it, set you apart from the good people
labelled in polished marble, buried around you.
As in your life, though never aloof, you were alone.
I remembered how, when quietly you entered a room
in one of those woven dresses you used to wear,
heather or lavender, all senseless chattering would cease,
shamed by your dignity. I remembered your beautiful things:
your pots, your books, your cat, silver as your cross,
your delicate drawings. Yes, I remembered you exactly.
And there you were, still – beautiful, exceptional, subtle –
in a landscape of lichen I had to read like Braille
to find your name. I heard the first blackbird, then a thrush.
Later, as we left, the children we'd seen playing
among the graves when we arrived resumed their game,
using your stone, a hump from another century,
to hide behind, while one, the smallest, counted slowly.

ROBERT LOUIS STEVENSON
(1850–1894)

A Martial Elegy for Some Lead Soldiers

For certain soldiers lately dead
Our reverent dirge shall here be said.
Them, when their martial leader called,
No dread preparative appalled;
But leaden hearted, leaden heeled,
I marked them steadfast in the field.
Death grimly sided with the foe,
And smote each leaden hero low.
Proudly they perished one by one:
The dread Pea-cannon's work was done!
O not for them the tears we shed,
Consigned to their congenial lead;
But while unmoved their sleep they take,
We mourn for their dear Captain's sake,
For their dear Captain, who shall smart
Both in his pocket and his heart,
Who saw his heroes shed their gore
And lacked a shilling to buy more!

Requiem

Under the wide and starry sky,
Dig the grave and let me lie.
Glad did I live and gladly die,
  And I laid me down with a will.

This be the verse you grave for me:
Here he lies where he longed to be;
Home is the sailor, home from sea,
  And the hunter home from the hill.

HANNAH SULLIVAN

(1979–)

from *The Sandpit After Rain*

Forget the transplant your father waited for,
The middle-of-the-night phone call that never came.
Forget the parched brain fizzing with morphine,
The body turning away in the bed, bored.
Forget the negligence of nurses.

Start with a daughter looking for her father,
Waking in shuttered rooms, in vandalised suites.
Start with your father listening for his mother,
Waking in the Acton orphanage, in wet sheets.

Forget the children's sandpit after rain.
Forget the pitch contour of rain . . .
It flaps like leather soles on last year's slippers,
Muffles the sound of binmen lobbing rubbish.

Start anywhere, everything dissipates.
Wet brains batter the limousine at noon.
End as a girl again, even Isolde,
Stranded in front of the fallen curtain,
Starting to sing.
End with a happy birthday, last but one.

You started dying on the morning you were made
While your father soaped himself in the sink
And your mother worked a porcelain-handled knife
Into a Simnel cake, sucking a marzipan ball.
Crumbs flew like chaff behind the harvester.
The letters of the code flipped in their pairs,
AATCCGCT: the odd proliferated error.

Because this is what death is:
Grant me the patience.
Start with a woman watching a man
Catching his daughter. End with a photo.
End as a woman older than either,
Feeling her own child sag in her arms,
Seeing it all, now for the first time,
After the ending:

The sideboard with the touched-up teak veneer,
Your mother's watchful shrug of hair,
And your own mouth slewed with laughter,
Feet tilted like a landing goose,
Falling, and your father's slender hands
Stretched out in the wind,
Henna-stained, praying.
Northolt, the old front room,
The photo with its reddish colour cast.
The faded figure in the catacomb,
Scouring the ceiling.

Watch contre-jour, a shadow
In the shade of the capiz-shell lamp,
A mother and the child you were.
You have been among the living twice,
And loved both times.
You have fallen in the lurid air.

JONATHAN SWIFT

(1667–1745)

A Satirical Elegy on the Death of a Late Famous General

His Grace! impossible! what, dead!
Of old age too, and in his bed!
And could that Mighty Warrior fall?
And so inglorious, after all!
Well, since he's gone, no matter how,
The last loud trump must wake him now:
And, trust me, as the noise grows stronger,
He'd wish to sleep a little longer.
And could he be indeed so old
As by the newspapers we're told?
Threescore, I think, is pretty high;
'Twas time in conscience he should die.
This world he cumbered long enough;
He burnt his candle to the snuff;
And that's the reason, some folks think,
He left behind *so great a stink*.
Behold his funeral appears,
Nor widow's sighs, nor orphan's tears,
Wont at such times each heart to pierce,
Attend the progress of his hearse.
But what of that, his friends may say,
He had those honours in his day.
True to his profit and his pride,
He made them weep before he died.

Come hither, all ye empty things,
Ye bubbles raised by breath of kings;
Who float upon the tide of state,
Come hither, and behold your fate.

Let pride be taught by this rebuke,
How very mean a thing's a Duke;
From all his ill-got honours flung,
Turned to that dirt from whence he sprung.

from *Verses on the Death of Doctor Swift*

The time is not remote when I
Must by the course of nature die:
When I foresee my special friends
Will try to find their private ends:
Though it is hardly understood
Which way my death can do them good;
Yet, thus methinks I hear 'em speak:
'See how the Dean begins to break,
Poor gentleman, he droops apace,
You plainly find it in his face;
That old vertigo in his head
Will never leave him till he's dead:
Besides, his memory decays,
He recollects not what he says,
He cannot call his friends to mind,
Forgets the place where last he dined,
Plies you with stories o'er and o'er –
He told them fifty times before.
How does he fancy we can sit
To hear his out-of-fashioned wit?
But he takes up with younger folks,
Who for his wine will bear his jokes,
Faith, he must make his stories shorter,
Or change his comrades once a quarter;
In half the time he talks them round,
There must another set be found.

For poetry, he's past his prime,
He takes an hour to find a rhyme;
His fire is out, his wit decayed,
His fancy sunk, his muse a jade.
I'd have him throw away his pen,
But there's no talking to some men.'

And then their tenderness appears,
By adding largely to my years:
'He's older than he would be reckoned,
And well remembers Charles the Second.'

'He hardly drinks a pint of wine,
And that, I doubt, is no good sign.
His stomach too begins to fail:
Last year we thought him strong and hale,
But now he's quite another thing;
I wish he may hold out till spring.'

Then hug themselves, and reason thus;
'It is not yet so bad with us.'

Suppose me dead; and then suppose
A club assembled at the Rose,
Where from discourse of this and that
I grow the subject of their chat;
And, while they toss my name about,
With favour some, and some without,
One quite indifferent in the cause
My character impartial draws:

'The Dean, if we believe report,
Was never ill-received at Court;
As for his works in verse and prose,
I own myself no judge of those;
Nor can I tell what critics thought 'em,
But this I know, all people bought 'em;
As with a moral view designed
To cure the vices of mankind;

His vein, ironically grave,
Exposed the fool, and lashed the knave;
To steal a hint was never known,
But what he writ was all his own.

He never thought an honour done him
Because a Duke was proud to own him;
Would rather slip aside, and choose
To talk with wits in dirty shoes;
Despised the fools with Stars and Garters,
So often seen caressing Chartres;
He never courted men in station
Nor persons had in admiration;
Of no man's greatness was afraid,
Because he sought for no man's aid.
Though trusted long in great affairs
He gave himself no haughty airs;
Without regarding private ends
Spent all his credit for his friends;
And only chose the wise and good,
No flatterers, no allies in blood;
But succoured virtue in distress,
And seldom failed of good success,
As numbers in their hearts must own,
Who, but for him, had been unknown.

With Princes kept a due decorum,
But never stood in awe before 'em;
And to her Majesty, God bless her,
Would speak as free as to her dresser;
She thought it his peculiar whim,
Nor took it ill as come from him.
He followed David's lesson just,
'In Princes never put thy trust.'
And would you make him truly sour,
Provoke him with 'a slave in power';
The Irish senate, if you named,
With what impatience he declaimed!
Fair Liberty was all his cry;

For her he stood prepared to die;
For her he boldly stood alone;
For her he oft exposed his own.
Two kingdoms, just as faction led,
Had set a price upon his head,
But not a traitor could be found
To sell him for six hundred pound.

Had he but spared his tongue and pen
He might have rose like other men;
But power was never in his thought,
And wealth he valued not a groat;
Ingratitude he often found,
And pitied those who meant the wound;
But kept the tenor of his mind
To merit well of human kind;
Nor made a sacrifice of those
Who still were true, to please his foes.
He laboured many a fruitless hour
To reconcile his friends in power;
Saw mischief by a faction brewing,
While they pursued each other's ruin.
But, finding vain was all his care,
He left the Court in mere despair.'

'Perhaps I may allow, the Dean
Had too much satire in his vein,
And seemed determined not to starve it
Because no age could more deserve it.
Yet malice never was his aim:
He lashed the vice, but spared the name.
No individual could resent
Where thousands equally were meant.
His satire points at no defect
But what all mortals may correct;
For he abhorred that senseless tribe,
Who call it humour when they jibe;
He spared a hump or crooked nose
Whose owners set not up for beaux.

True genuine dullness moved his pity,
Unless it offered to be witty.
Those who their ignorance confessed
He ne'er offended with a jest,
But laughed to hear an idiot quote
A verse from Horace, learned by rote.

He knew an hundred pleasant stories,
With all the turns of Whigs and Tories:
Was cheerful to his dying day,
And friends would let him have his way.

He gave the little wealth he had
To build a house for fools and mad:
And shewed by one satiric touch
No nation wanted it so much;
That kingdom he hath left his debtor,
I wish it soon may have a better.'

ALGERNON CHARLES SWINBURNE

(1837–1909)

from *Ave atque Vale*

In Memory of Charles Baudelaire

Shall I strew on thee rose or rue or laurel,
    Brother, on this that was the veil of thee?
    Or quiet sea-flower moulded by the sea,
Or simplest growth of meadow-sweet or sorrel,
    Such as the summer-sleepy Dryads weave,
    Waked up by snow-soft sudden rains at eve?
Or wilt thou rather, as on earth before,
    Half-faded fiery blossoms, pale with heat
    And full of bitter summer, but more sweet
To thee than gleanings of a northern shore
    Trod by no tropic feet?

For always thee the fervid languid glories
    Allured of heavier suns in mightier skies;
    Thine ears knew all the wandering watery sighs
Where the sea sobs round Lesbian promontories,
    The barren kiss of piteous wave to wave
    That knows not where is that Leucadian grave
Which hides too deep the supreme head of song.
    Ah, salt and sterile as her kisses were,
    The wild sea winds her and the green gulfs bear
Hither and thither, and vex and work her wrong,
    Blind gods that cannot spare.

Thou sawest, in thine old singing season, brother,
   Secrets and sorrows unbeheld of us:
   Fierce loves, and lovely leaf-buds poisonous,
Bare to thy subtler eye, but for none other
   Blowing by night in some unbreathed-in clime;
   The hidden harvest of luxurious time,
Sin without shape, and pleasure without speech;
   And where strange dreams in a tumultuous sleep
   Make the shut eyes of stricken spirits weep;
And with each face thou saw'st the shadow on each,
   Seeing as men sow men reap.

O sleepless heart and sombre soul unsleeping,
   That were athirst for sleep and no more life
   And no more love, for peace and no more strife!
Now the dim gods of death have in their keeping
   Spirit and body and all the springs of song,
   Is it well now where love can do no wrong,
Where stingless pleasure has no foam or fang
   Behind the unopening closure of her lips?
   Is it not well where soul from body slips
And flesh from bone divides without a pang
   As dew from flower-bell drips?

It is enough; the end and the beginning
   Are one thing to thee, who art past the end.
   O hand unclasped of unbeholden friend,
For thee no fruits to pluck, no palms for winning,
   No triumph and no labour and no lust,
   Only dead yew-leaves and a little dust.
O quiet eyes wherein the light saith nought,
   Whereto the day is dumb, nor any night
   With obscure finger silences your sight,
Nor in your speech the sudden soul speaks thought,
   Sleep, and have sleep for light.

Now all strange hours and all strange loves are over,
  Dreams and desires and sombre songs and sweet,
  Hast thou found place at the great knees and feet
Of some pale Titan-woman like a lover,
  Such as thy vision here solicited,
  Under the shadow of her fair vast head,
The deep division of prodigious breasts,
  The solemn slope of mighty limbs asleep,
  The weight of awful tresses that still keep
The savour and shade of old-world pine-forests
  Where the wet hill-winds weep?

Hast thou found any likeness for thy vision?
  O gardener of strange flowers, what bud, what bloom,
  Hast thou found sown, what gathered in the gloom?
What of despair, of rapture, of derision,
  What of life is there, what of ill or good?
  Are the fruits grey like dust or bright like blood?
Does the dim ground grow any seed of ours,
  The faint fields quicken any terrene root,
  In low lands where the sun and moon are mute
And all the stars keep silence? Are there flowers
  At all, or any fruit?

Alas, but though my flying song flies after,
  O sweet strange elder singer, thy more fleet
  Singing, and footprints of thy fleeter feet,
Some dim derision of mysterious laughter
  From the blind tongueless warders of the dead,
  Some gainless glimpse of Proserpine's veiled head,
Some little sound of unregarded tears
  Wept by effaced unprofitable eyes,
  And from pale mouths some cadence of dead sighs
These only, these the hearkening spirit hears,
  Sees only such things rise.

Thou art far too far for wings of words to follow,
　Far too far off for thought or any prayer.
　What ails us with thee, who art wind and air?
What ails us gazing where all seen is hollow?
　Yet with some fancy, yet with some desire,
　Dreams pursue death as winds a flying fire,
Our dreams pursue our dead and do not find.
　Still, and more swift than they, the thin flame flies,
　The low light fails us in elusive skies,
Still the foiled earnest ear is deaf, and blind
　Are still the eluded eyes.

Not thee, O never thee, in all time's changes,
　Not thee, but this the sound of thy sad soul,
　The shadow of thy swift spirit, this shut scroll
I lay my hand on, and not death estranges
　My spirit from communion of thy song –
　These memories and these melodies that throng
Veiled porches of a Muse funereal –
　These I salute, these touch, these clasp and fold
　As though a hand were in my hand to hold,
Or through mine ears a mourning musical
　Of many mourners rolled.

A Forsaken Garden

In a coign of the cliff between lowland and highland,
　At the sea-down's edge between windward and lee,
Walled round with rocks as an inland island,
　The ghost of a garden fronts the sea.
A girdle of brushwood and thorn encloses
　The steep square slope of the blossomless bed
Where the weeds that grew green from the graves of its roses
　　　Now lie dead.

The fields fall southward, abrupt and broken,
  To the low last edge of the long lone land.
If a step should sound or a word be spoken,
  Would a ghost not rise at the strange guest's hand?
So long have the grey bare walks lain guestless,
  Through branches and briars if a man make way,
He shall find no life but the sea-wind's, restless
            Night and day.

The dense hard passage is blind and stifled
  That crawls by a track none turn to climb
To the strait waste place that the years have rifled
  Of all but the thorns that are touched not of time.
The thorns he spares when the rose is taken;
  The rocks are left when he wastes the plain.
The wind that wanders, the weeds wind-shaken,
            These remain.

Not a flower to be pressed of the foot that falls not;
  As the heart of a dead man the seed-plots are dry;
From the thicket of thorns whence the nightingale calls not,
  Could she call, there were never a rose to reply.
Over the meadows that blossom and wither
  Rings but the note of a sea-bird's song;
Only the sun and the rain come hither
            All year long.

The sun burns sere and the rain dishevels
  One gaunt bleak blossom of scentless breath.
Only the wind here hovers and revels
  In a round where life seems barren as death.
Here there was laughing of old, there was weeping,
  Haply, of lovers none ever will know,
Whose eyes went seaward a hundred sleeping
            Years ago.

Heart handfast in heart as they stood, 'Look thither,'
  Did he whisper? 'look forth from the flowers to the sea;
For the foam-flowers endure when the rose-blossoms wither,
  And men that love lightly may die – but we?'
And the same wind sang and the same waves whitened,
  And or ever the garden's last petals were shed,
In the lips that had whispered, the eyes that had lightened,
      Love was dead.

Or they loved their life through, and then went whither?
  And were one to the end – but what end who knows?
Love deep as the sea as a rose must wither,
  As the rose-red seaweed that mocks the rose.
Shall the dead take thought for the dead to love them?
  What love was ever as deep as a grave?
They are loveless now as the grass above them
      Or the wave.

All are at one now, roses and lovers,
  Not known of the cliffs and the fields and the sea.
Not a breath of the time that has been hovers
  In the air now soft with a summer to be.
Not a breath shall there sweeten the seasons hereafter
  Of the flowers or the lovers that laugh now or weep,
When as they that are free now of weeping and laughter
      We shall sleep.

Here death may deal not again for ever;
  Here change may come not till all change end.
From the graves they have made they shall rise up never,
  Who have left nought living to ravage and rend.
Earth, stones, and thorns of the wild ground growing,
  While the sun and the rain live, these shall be;
Till a last wind's breath upon all these blowing
      Roll the sea.

Till the slow sea rise and the sheer cliff crumble,
    Till terrace and meadow the deep gulfs drink,
Till the strength of the waves of the high tides humble
    The fields that lessen, the rocks that shrink,
Here now in his triumph where all things falter,
    Stretched out on the spoils that his own hand spread,
As a god self-slain on his own strange altar,
        Death lies dead.

ALFRED, LORD TENNYSON
(1809–1892)

from *In Memoriam*

5

I sometimes hold it half a sin
   To put in words the grief I feel;
   For words, like Nature, half reveal
And half conceal the Soul within.

But, for the unquiet heart and brain,
   A use in measured language lies;
   The sad mechanic exercise,
Like dull narcotics, numbing pain.

In words, like weeds, I'll wrap me o'er,
   Like coarsest clothes against the cold:
   But that large grief which these enfold
Is given in outline and no more.

7

Dark house, by which once more I stand
   Here in the long unlovely street,
   Doors, where my heart was used to beat
So quickly, waiting for a hand,

A hand that can be clasp'd no more –
   Behold me, for I cannot sleep,
   And like a guilty thing I creep
At earliest morning to the door.

He is not here; but far away
  The noise of life begins again,
  And ghastly thro' the drizzling rain
On the bald street breaks the blank day.

I I

Calm is the morn without a sound,
  Calm as to suit a calmer grief,
  And only thro' the faded leaf
The chestnut pattering to the ground:

Calm and deep peace on this high wold,
  And on these dews that drench the furze,
  And all the silvery gossamers
That twinkle into green and gold:

Calm and still light on yon great plain
  That sweeps with all its autumn bowers,
  And crowded farms and lessening towers,
To mingle with the bounding main:

Calm and deep peace in this wide air,
  These leaves that redden to the fall;
  And in my heart, if calm at all,
If any calm, a calm despair:

Calm on the seas, and silver sleep,
  And waves that sway themselves in rest,
  And dead calm in that noble breast
Which heaves but with the heaving deep.

19

The Danube to the Severn gave
   The darken'd heart that beat no more;
   They laid him by the pleasant shore,
And in the hearing of the wave.

There twice a day the Severn fills;
   The salt sea-water passes by,
   And hushes half the babbling Wye,
And makes a silence in the hills.

The Wye is hush'd nor moved along,
   And hush'd my deepest grief of all,
   When fill'd with tears that cannot fall,
I brim with sorrow drowning song.

The tide flows down, the wave again
   Is vocal in its wooded walls;
   My deeper anguish also falls,
And I can speak a little then.

50

Be near me when my light is low,
   When the blood creeps, and the nerves prick
   And tingle; and the heart is sick,
And all the wheels of Being slow.

Be near me when the sensuous frame
   Is rack'd with pangs that conquer trust;
   And Time, a maniac scattering dust,
And Life, a Fury slinging flame.

Be near me when my faith is dry,
   And men the flies of latter spring
   That lay their eggs, and sting and sing
And weave their petty cells and die.

Be near me when I fade away,
　　To point the term of human strife,
　　And on the low dark verge of life
The twilight of eternal day.

70

I cannot see the features right,
　　When on the gloom I strive to paint
　　The face I know; the hues are faint
And mix with hollow masks of night;

Cloud-towers by ghostly masons wrought,
　　A gulf that ever shuts and gapes,
　　A hand that points, and palled shapes
In shadowy thoroughfares of thought;

And crowds that stream from yawning doors,
　　And shoals of pucker'd faces drive;
　　Dark bulks that tumble half alive,
And lazy lengths on boundless shores;

Till all at once beyond the will
　　I hear a wizard music roll,
　　And thro' a lattice on the soul
Looks thy fair face and makes it still

91

When rosy plumelets tuft the larch,
　　And rarely pipes the mounted thrush;
　　Or underneath the barren bush
Flits by the sea-blue bird of March;

Come, wear the form by which I know
  Thy spirit in time among thy peers;
  The hope of unaccomplish'd years
Be large and lucid round thy brow.

When summer's hourly-mellowing change
  May breathe, with many roses sweet,
  Upon the thousand waves of wheat,
That ripple round the lonely grange;

Come: not in watches of the night,
  But where the sunbeam broodeth warm,
  Come, beauteous in thine after form,
And like a finer light in light.

100

I climb the hill: from end to end
  Of all the landscape underneath,
  I find no place that does not breathe
Some gracious memory of my friend;

No gray old grange, or lonely fold,
  Or low morass and whispering reed,
  Or simple stile from mead to mead,
Or sheepwalk up the windy wold;

Nor hoary knoll of ash and haw
  That hears the latest linnet trill,
  Nor quarry trench'd along the hill
And haunted by the wrangling daw;

Nor runlet tinkling from the rock;
  Nor pastoral rivulet that swerves
  To left and right thro' meadowy curves,
That feed the mothers of the flock;

But each has pleased a kindred eye,
  And each reflects a kindlier day;
  And, leaving these, to pass away,
I think once more he seems to die.

115

Now fades the last long streak of snow,
  Now burgeons every maze of quick
  About the flowering squares, and thick
By ashen roots the violets blow.

Now rings the woodland loud and long,
  The distance takes a lovelier hue,
  And drown'd in yonder living blue
The lark becomes a sightless song.

Now dance the lights on lawn and lea,
  The flocks are whiter down the vale,
  And milkier every milky sail
On winding stream or distant sea;

Where now the seamew pipes, or dives
  In yonder greening gleam, and fly
  The happy birds, that change their sky
To build and brood; that live their lives

From land to land; and in my breast
  Spring wakens too; and my regret
  Becomes an April violet,
And buds and blossoms like the rest.

Crossing the Bar

Sunset and evening star,
  And one clear call for me!
And may there be no moaning of the bar,
  When I put out to sea,

But such a tide as moving seems asleep,
  Too full for sound and foam,
When that which drew from out the boundless deep
  Turns again home.

Twilight and evening bell,
  And after that the dark!
And may there be no sadness of farewell,
  When I embark;

For though from out our bourne of Time and Place
  The flood may bear me far,
I hope to see my Pilot face to face
  When I have crost the bar.

WILLIAM MAKEPEACE THACKERAY
(1811–1863)

The Sorrows of Werther

Werther had a love for Charlotte
Such as words could never utter;
Would you know how first he met her?
She was cutting bread and butter.

Charlotte was a married lady,
And a moral man was Werther,
And for all the wealth of Indies
Would do nothing for to hurt her.

So he sigh'd and pined and ogled,
And his passion boil'd and bubbled,
Till he blew his silly brains out,
And no more was by it troubled.

Charlotte, having seen his body
Borne before her on a shutter,
Like a well-conducted person,
Went on cutting bread and butter.

THEOCRITUS

(c. 310–250 BCE)

Idyll 1
Lament for Daphnis

THYRSIS

There's subtle music in the whispers of that pine
down by the spring; yet your piping, goatherd,
rivals it. You shall have second prize
to Pan. Should he select as his reward
the he-goat's horns, the she-goat shall be yours;
if he take her, then you shall have her kid.
Kidflesh is good until they come to milking.

GOATHERD

Sweeter, shepherd, and more subtle is your song
than the tuneful splashing of that waterfall
among the rocks. If the Muses pick the ewe
as their reward, you'll win the hand-reared lamb;
if they prefer the lamb, the ewe is yours.

THYRSIS

Come, goatherd, by the Nymphs: please, come sit down
here on this hill, among the tamarisks,
and play for me. I'll watch your goats.

GOATHERD

No, shepherd, no, not I. Not at midday;
I'm afraid of Pan. It's the time he rests,
weary from the hunt. His temper is quick;
fierce anger is always on his breath.
But you, Thyrsis, you used to sing of Daphnis
and his death. In the art of country song
you have no equal. Come then: you sit with me,
here beneath this elm, facing Priapus' stream,

where the shepherds have their seat among the oaks.
And if you sing as you sang that day,
in your contest with Chromis of Libya,
I shall give you a goat to milk three times,
which though it has twins will yield three pails.
And I shall give you a cup, deep, two-handled,
new made, highly polished with perfumed wax,
yet smelling still of the engraver's knife.
Along the lip wind shoots of ivy, rich ivy
with golden leaves, spiralling around itself,
exulting in its yellow fruit. Inside a woman,
a woman worthy of a god, is carved:
she wears a cloak and headdress. On each side
stand two young men who both have fine long hair,
each quarrelling with the other, turn by turn.
But these things do not touch her heart.
For now she turns to him and smiles, and now
to him, while they, both hollow-eyed with love,
still waste themselves away in vain.
Beside them an old fisherman is carved
standing on a jagged rock, gathering his net
for a mighty cast: he struggles hard.
That old man, you'd say, puts all his strength
into his fishing. His hair is grey,
his sinews heave and swell around his neck;
yet his is the strength of a youth in his prime.
Close by that old and weather-beaten man
there is a vineyard, rich, well-stocked
with ripening, reddening bunches: a young boy,
lolling on the wall, keeps watch. On either side
a fox: one ranges up and down among the vines,
rifling the ripest; the other eyes the boy's wallet,
setting his villainous heart upon it,
determined not to let the child alone
until it has deprived him of his breakfast.
This guard, meanwhile, is busy weaving,
threading reeds and rushes, fashioning a trap
for insects. His mind is on his work;

he has no thought of vineyards or of wallets.
And, last, around the cup at every turn
supple acanthus winds. It is a sight to see,
to wonder at, to dazzle country eyes.
I paid Calydna's ferryman a goat for it,
and I gave him a giant milk-white cheese,
but never has it come near my lips, never yet:
it lies untouched, immaculate. My friend,
if you will sing that song, it's yours:
and gladly, too. Such beauty would deserve it.
No, no mockery. I mean it. Come, man
surely you don't mean to take your song
to Hades? All is forgotten there.

THYRSIS
Sing, beloved Muses, sing my country song.

I am Thyrsis of Etna, blessed with a tuneful voice.

Where were you, Nymphs, where were you,
where when Daphnis died?
In the valleys of Peneius?
In Pindus' pretty glades?
You were nowhere near Anapus,
nowhere near that mighty tide,
you were not on Etna's summit
nor by Acis' spring.

Sing, beloved Muses, sing my country song.

For him the wolves were howling,
for him the jackals bayed.
When Daphnis died, the lions
of the forest wept.

Sing, beloved Muses, sing my country song.

Great herds of bulls and cattle
were gathered round his feet
with crowds of lowing heifers
and their moaning calves.

Sing, beloved Muses, sing my country song.

The first to come was Hermes,
Hermes from the hills,
saying, 'Daphnis, who torments you?
Who is it you love?'

Sing, beloved Muses, sing my country song.

Then neatherds, shepherds, goatherds,
came to ask him what was wrong.
And Priapus said, 'Poor Daphnis,
why waste yourself away
when by every glade and fountain
that girl looks for you?'

Sing, beloved Muses, sing my country song.

'Your love is cursed, you're helpless.
You're no herdsman now.
More like a common goatherd
who looks with jealous eyes
and who weeps that he is human
when his goats make love.'

Sing, beloved Muses, sing my country song.

'You see the young girls laughing
and you weep more tears
that you can't join their dances . . .'
But answer came there none.
Though the herdsman's love was cruel
it was bravely borne.

Sing, Muses, sing again my country song.

Then Cypris came and smiled
though she raged within.
'So mastering love is easy?'
she said. 'Not so it seems.
Have you not yourself been mastered
by that same cruel love?'

Sing, Muses, sing again my country song.

'Jealous Cypris,' Daphnis answered,
'hated by mankind,
so you think my sun is setting,
that my light is nearly spent?
Daphnis even down in Hades
will make war on love.'

Sing, Muses, sing again my country song.

'Do men not talk of Cypris
and the herdsman still?
Go, take yourself to Ida,
go see Anchises there.
You'll find oaks, and sedge, and honey-bees
buzzing round their hives.'

Sing, Muses, sing again my country song.

'Is not Adonis in his heyday?
Does not he too tend sheep?
He shoots, kills hares, goes hunting
for all kinds of beast.'

Sing, Muses, sing again my country song.

'Go, look for Diomedes;
tell him, "I have won.
I've outdone Daphnis the herdsman.
Now come, fight with me."'

Sing, Muses, sing again my country song.

'Farewell now, wolves and jackals,
now farewell, mountain bears.
You'll see no more of Daphnis
in your forests or your groves.
Farewell to Arethusa,
and fair Thybris' streams.'

Sing, Muses, sing again my country song.

'I am Daphnis, I'm the herdsman,
I drove cattle here;
here I brought my bulls and heifers
and I watered them.'

Sing, Muses, sing again my country song.

'O Pan, O Pan, where are you?
On Lycaeus' slopes?
On Maenalus? On Helice?
O come to Sicily!
Leave the sacred tomb of Arcas
to the gods' great love.'

Cease, Muses, come cease my country song.

'Come, Pan, my pipe awaits you,
its breath still honey-sweet;
its wax is firm, its binding
still tight around the lip.
Now I am bound for Hades:
Eros calls me there.'

Cease, Muses, come cease my country song.

'May violets grow on thistles,
may they grow on thorns!
May narcissus grow on juniper!
The world must change.
Daphnis dies! Pears grow on pine trees!
Now the deer must chase the hounds,
and the screech-owl's song sound sweeter
than the nightingale's!'

Cease, Muses, come cease my country song.

And with these words, he finished.
He would rise again
if Aphrodite's wish were granted.
But his thread was spun.
Fate took Daphnis to the river;
the waters closed above his head,
took the man the Nymphs had cherished
and the Muses loved.

Cease, Muses, come cease my country song.

Let me have the goat, the pail;
I would milk her now,
make my libation to the Muses,
bid them many times farewell.
In time, I trust, I'll sing you
a less mournful song.

GOATHERD

Sweeten your sweet mouth with honey,
Thyrsis, and with honeycomb. Eat your fill
of Aegilus' finest figs, for your voice
outsings the cricket's. Here is the cup:
smell, friend, its sharp freshness –
you would think it had been dipped
and bathed in the holy well of Hours.
Here, Cissaetha; she is yours to milk.
You others, stop that frisking,
or you'll get the ram worked up.

Translated by Anthony Holden

DYLAN THOMAS

(1914–1953)

A Refusal to Mourn the Death, by Fire, of a Child in London

Never until the mankind making
Bird beast and flower
Fathering and all humbling darkness
Tells with silence the last light breaking
And the still hour
Is come of the sea tumbling in harness

And I must enter again the round
Zion of the water bead
And the synagogue of the ear of corn
Shall I let pray the shadow of a sound
Or sow my salt seed
In the least valley of sackcloth to mourn

The majesty and burning of the child's death.
I shall not murder
The mankind of her going with a grave truth
Nor blaspheme down the stations of the breath
With any further
Elegy of innocence and youth.

Deep with the first dead lies London's daughter,
Robed in the long friends,
The grains beyond age, the dark veins of her mother,
Secret by the unmourning water
Of the riding Thames.
After the first death, there is no other.

'Do not go gentle into that good night'

Do not go gentle into that good night,
Old age should burn and rave at close of day;
Rage, rage against the dying of the light.

Though wise men at their end know dark is right,
Because their words had forked no lightning they
Do not go gentle into that good night.

Good men, the last wave by, crying how bright
Their frail deeds might have danced in a green bay,
Rage, rage against the dying of the light.

Wild men who caught and sang the sun in flight,
And learn, too late, they grieved it on its way,
Do not go gentle into that good night.

Grave men, near death, who see with blinding sight
Blind eyes could blaze like meteors and be gay,
Rage, rage against the dying of the light.

And you, my father, there on the sad height,
Curse, bless, me now with your fierce tears, I pray.
Do not go gentle into that good night.
Rage, rage against the dying of the light.

EDWARD THOMAS
(1878–1917)

Tears

It seems I have no tears left. They should have fallen –
Their ghosts, if tears have ghosts, did fall – that day
When twenty hounds streamed by me, not yet combed out
But still all equals in their rage of gladness
Upon the scent, made one, like a great dragon
In Blooming Meadow that bends towards the sun
And once bore hops: and on that other day
When I stepped out from the double-shadowed Tower
Into an April morning, stirring and sweet
And warm. Strange solitude was there and silence.
A mightier charm than any in the Tower
Possessed the courtyard. They were changing guard,
Soldiers in line, young English countrymen,
Fair-haired and ruddy, in white tunics. Drums
And fifes were playing 'The British Grenadiers'.
The men, the music piercing that solitude
And silence, told me truths I had not dreamed,
And have forgotten since their beauty passed.

In Memoriam (Easter, 1915)

The flowers left thick at nightfall in the wood
This Eastertide call into mind the men,
Now far from home, who, with their sweethearts, should
Have gathered them and will do never again.

Rain

Rain, midnight rain, nothing but the wild rain
On this bleak hut, and solitude, and me
Remembering again that I shall die
And neither hear the rain nor give it thanks
For washing me cleaner than I have been
Since I was born into this solitude.
Blessed are the dead that the rain rains upon:
But here I pray that none whom once I loved
Is dying to-night, or lying still awake
Solitary, listening to the rain,
Either in pain or thus in sympathy
Helpless among the living and the dead,
Like a cold water among broken reeds,
Myriads of broken reeds all still and stiff,
Like me who have no love which this wild rain
Has not dissolved except the love of death,
If love it be for what is perfect and
Cannot, the tempest tells me, disappoint.

As the Team's Head-Brass

As the team's head-brass flashed out on the turn
The lovers disappeared into the wood.
I sat among the boughs of the fallen elm
That strewed the angle of the fallow, and
Watched the plough narrowing a yellow square
Of charlock. Every time the horses turned
Instead of treading me down, the ploughman leaned
Upon the handles to say or ask a word,
About the weather, next about the war.
Scraping the share he faced towards the wood,
And screwed along the furrow till the brass flashed
Once more.

The blizzard felled the elm whose crest
I sat in, by a woodpecker's round hole,
The ploughman said. 'When will they take it away?'
'When the war's over.' So the talk began –
One minute and an interval of ten,
A minute more and the same interval.
'Have you been out?' 'No.' 'And don't want to, perhaps?'
'If I could only come back again, I should.
I could spare an arm. I shouldn't want to lose
A leg. If I should lose my head, why, so,
I should want nothing more . . . Have many gone
From here?' 'Yes.' 'Many lost?' 'Yes, a good few.
Only two teams work on the farm this year.
One of my mates is dead. The second day
In France they killed him. It was back in March,
The very night of the blizzard, too. Now if
He had stayed here we should have moved the tree.'
'And I should not have sat here. Everything
Would have been different. For it would have been
Another world.' 'Ay, and a better, though
If we could see all all might seem good.' Then
The lovers came out of the wood again:
The horses started and for the last time
I watched the clods crumble and topple over
After the ploughshare and the stumbling team.

CHIDIOCK TICHBORNE
(1562–1586)

Elegy For Himself

Written in the Tower before His Execution, 1586

My prime of youth is but a frost of cares;
   My feast of joy is but a dish of pain;
My crop of corn is but a field of tares;
   And all my good is but vain hope of gain:
The day is past, and yet I saw no sun;
And now I live, and now my life is done.

My tale was heard, and yet it was not told;
   My fruit is fall'n, and yet my leaves are green;
My youth is spent, and yet I am not old;
   I saw the world, and yet I was not seen:
My thread is cut, and yet it is not spun;
And now I live, and now my life is done.

I sought my death, and found it in my womb;
   I looked for life, and saw it was a shade;
I trod the earth, and knew it was my tomb;
   And now I die, and now I was but made;
My glass is full, and now my glass is run;
And now I live, and now my life is done.

TOMAS TRANSTRÖMER
(1931–2015)

After Someone's Death

Once there was a shock
which left behind a long pale glimmering comet's tail.
It contains us. It makes TV pictures blurred.
It deposits itself as cold drops on the aerials.

You can still shuffle along on skis in the winter sun
among groves where last year's leaves still hang.
They are like pages torn from old telephone directories –
the subscribers' names are eaten up by the cold.

It is still beautiful to feel your heart throbbing.
But often the shadow feels more real than the body.
The samurai looks insignificant
beside his armour of black dragon-scales.

Translated by Robin Fulton

FREDERICK GODDARD TUCKERMAN
(1821–1873)

'An upper chamber in a darkened house'

An upper chamber in a darkened house
Where, ere his footsteps reached ripe manhood's brink,
Terror and anguish were his lot to drink;
I cannot rid the thought nor hold it close
But dimly dream upon that man alone:
Now though the autumn clouds most softly pass,
The cricket chides beneath the doorstep stone
And greener than the season grows the grass.
Nor can I drop my lids nor shade my brows,
But there he stands beside the lifted sash;
And with a swooning of the heart, I think
Where the black shingles slope to meet the boughs
And, shattered on the roof like smallest snows,
The tiny petals of the mountain ash.

HENRY VAUGHAN

(1621–1695)

They Are All Gone into the World of Light!

They are all gone into the world of light!
   And I alone sit ling'ring here;
Their very memory is fair and bright,
   And my sad thoughts doth clear.

It glows and glitters in my cloudy breast
   Like stars upon some gloomy grove,
Or those faint beams in which this hill is dressed
   After the sun's remove.

I see them walking in an air of glory,
   Whose light doth trample on my days;
My days, which are at best but dull and hoary,
   Mere glimmering and decays.

O holy hope, and high humility,
   High as the heavens above!
These are your walks, and you have showed them me
   To kindle my cold love.

Dear, beauteous death! the jewel of the just,
   Shining nowhere but in the dark;
What mysteries do lie beyond thy dust,
   Could man outlook that mark!

He that hath found some fledged bird's nest may know
   At first sight if the bird be flown;
But what fair well or grove he sings in now,
   That is to him unknown.

And yet, as angels in some brighter dreams
   Call to the soul when man doth sleep,
So some strange thoughts transcend our wonted themes,
   And into glory peep.

If a star were confined into a tomb,
   Her captive flames must needs burn there;
But when the hand that locked her up gives room,
   She'll shine through all the sphere.

O Father of eternal life, and all
   Created glories under thee!
Resume thy spirit from this world of thrall
   Into true liberty!

Either disperse these mists, which blot and fill
   My perspective still as they pass;
Or else remove me hence unto that hill
   Where I shall need no glass.

VIRGIL

(70–19 BCE)

from *Eclogue 5*

The Death of Daphnis

MENALCAS
Daphnis now wondering at the glorious show,
Through heaven's bright pavement does triumphant go,
And sees the moving clouds, and the fixt stars below.
Therefore new joys make glad the woods, the plains,
Pan and the Dryads, and the cheerful swains.
The wolf no ambush for the flock does lay,
No cheating nets the harmless deer betray,
Daphnis a general peace commands, and nature does obey.
Hark! the glad mountains raise to heaven their voice!
Hark! the hard rocks in mystic tunes rejoice!
Hark! through the thickets wondrous songs resound,
A god! a god! Menalcas, he is crown'd!
O be propitious! O be good to thine!
See! here four hallowed altars we design,
To Daphnis two, to Phoebus two we raise,
To pay the yearly tribute of our praise.
Sacred to thee they each returning year
Two bowls of milk and two of oil shall bear:
Feasts I'll ordain, and to thy deathless praise
Thy votaries exalted thoughts to raise,
Rich Chian wines shall in full goblets flow,
And give a taste of nectar here below.
Dametas shall with Lictian Argon join,
To celebrate with songs the rites divine.
Alphesiboeus with a reeling gait
Shall the wild satyrs dancing imitate.
When to the nymphs we vows and offerings pay,
When we with solemn rites our fields survey,

These honours ever shall be thine; the boar
Shall in the fields and hills delight no more,
No more in streams the fish, in flowers the bee,
E'er, Daphnis, we forget our songs to thee.
Offerings to thee the shepherds every year
Shall, as to Bacchus and to Ceres, bear.
To thee as to those gods shall vows be made,
And vengeance wait on those, by whom they are not paid.

MOPSUS

What present worth thy verse can Mopsus find?
Not the soft whispers of the southern wind
So much delight my ear, or charm my mind,
Not sounding shores beat by the murmuring tide,
Nor rivers that through stony valleys glide.

MENALCAS

First you this pipe shall take: and 'tis the same
That played poor Corydon's unhappy flame:
The same that taught me Meliboeus' sheep.

MOPSUS

You then shall for my sake this sheephook keep,
Adorned with brass, which I have oft denied
To young Antigenes in his beauty's pride.
And who could think he then in vain could sue?
Yet him I would deny, and freely give it you.

Translated by Richard Duke

from *Georgics*, Book 4

Orpheus and Eurydice

He, lonely, on his harp, 'mid wilds unknown,
Sooth'd his sad love with melancholy tone:
On thee, sweet bride! still dwelt th' undying lay,
Thee first at dawn deplor'd, thee last at close of day,
For thee he dar'd to pass the jaws of hell,
And gates where death and darkness ever dwell,
Trod with firm foot in horror's gloomy grove,
Approach'd the throne of subterraneous Jove,
Nor fear'd the maenads and stem host below,
And hearts that never felt for human woe.
Drawn by his song from Erebus profound
Shades and unbodied phantoms flock around,
Countless as birds that fill the leafy bower
Beneath pale eve, or winter's driving shower.
Matrons and sires, and unaffianc'd maids,
Forms of bold warriors and heroic shades,
Youths and pale infants laid upon the pyre,
While their fond parents saw th' ascending fire:
All whom the squalid reeds and sable mud
Of slow Cocytus' unrejoicing flood,
All whom the Stygian lake's dark confine bounds,
And with nine circles maze in maze surrounds.
On him, astonish'd Death and Tartarus gaz'd,
Their viper hair the wondering Furies rais'd :
Grim Cerberus stood, his triple jaws half clos'd,
And fix'd in air Ixion's wheel repos'd.
Now every peril o'er, when Orpheus led
His rescu'd prize in triumph from the dead,
And the fair bride, so Proserpine enjoin'd,
Press'd on his path, and followed close behind,
In sweet oblivious trance of amorous thought
The lover err'd, to sudden frenzy wrought:
Ah! venial fault! if hell had ever known
Mercy, or sense of suffering not its own.

He stopp'd, and, ah! forgetful, weak of mind,
Cast, as she reach'd the light, one look behind.
There died his hopes, by love alone betray'd,
He broke the law that hell's stern tyrant made;
Thrice o'er the Stygian lake a hollow sound
Portentous murmur'd from its depth profound.
'Alas! what fates our hapless love divide,
What frenzy, Orpheus, tears thee from thy bride!
Again I sink; a voice resistless calls,
Lo! on my swimming eye cold slumber falls.
Now, now farewell! involv'd in thickest night,
Borne far away, I vanish from thy sight,
And stretch tow'rds thee, all hope for ever o'er,
These unavailing arms, ah! thine no more.' –
She spoke, and from his gaze for ever fled,
Swift as dissolving smoke through aether spread,
Nor more beheld him, while he fondly strove
To catch her shade, and pour the plaints of love.
Deaf to his prayer no more stern Charon gave
To cross the Stygian lake's forbidden wave.
What shall he do? where, dead to hope, reside?
'Reft of all joy, and doubly lost his bride;
What tears shall sooth th' inexorable God?
Pale swam her spirit to its last abode.

Translated by William Sotheby

from *Aeneid,* Book 2

The Death of Priam

Perhaps you may of Priam's fate enquire.
He, when he saw his regal town on fire,
His ruin'd palace, and his ent'ring foes,
On ev'ry side inevitable woes,
In arms, disus'd, invests his limbs, decay'd,

Like them, with age; a late and useless aid.
His feeble shoulders scarce the weight sustain;
Loaded, not arm'd, he creeps along with pain,
Despairing of success, ambitious to be slain!
Uncover'd but by heav'n, there stood in view
An altar; near the hearth a laurel grew,
Dodder'd with age, whose boughs encompass round
The household gods, and shade the holy ground.
Here Hecuba, with all her helpless train
Of dames, for shelter sought, but sought in vain.
Driv'n like a flock of doves along the sky,
Their images they hug, and to their altars fly.
The Queen, when she beheld her trembling lord, And
hanging by his side a heavy sword,
'What rage,' she cried, 'has seiz'd my husband's mind?
What arms are these, and to what use design'd?
These times want other aids! Were Hector here,
Ev'n Hector now in vain, like Priam, would appear.
With us, one common shelter thou shalt find,
Or in one common fate with us be join'd.'
She said, and with a last salute embrac'd
The poor old man, and by the laurel plac'd.
Behold! Polites, one of Priam's sons,
Pursued by Pyrrhus, there for safety runs.
Thro' swords and foes, amaz'd and hurt, he flies
Thro' empty courts and open galleries.
Him Pyrrhus, urging with his lance, pursues,
And often reaches, and his thrusts renews.
The youth, transfix'd, with lamentable cries,
Expires before his wretched parent's eyes:
Whom gasping at his feet when Priam saw,
The fear of death gave place to nature's law;
And, shaking more with anger than with age,
'The gods,' said he, 'requite thy brutal rage!
As sure they will, barbarian, sure they must,
If there be gods in heav'n, and gods be just –
Who tak'st in wrongs an insolent delight;
With a son's death t' infect a father's sight.
Not he, whom thou and lying fame conspire

To call thee his – not he, thy vaunted sire,
Thus us'd my wretched age: the gods he fear'd,
The laws of nature and of nations heard.
He cheer'd my sorrows, and, for sums of gold,
The bloodless carcass of my Hector sold;
Pitied the woes a parent underwent,
And sent me back in safety from his tent.'
This said, his feeble hand a javelin threw,
Which, flutt'ring, seem'd to loiter as it flew:
Just, and but barely, to the mark it held,
And faintly tinkled on the brazen shield.
Then Pyrrhus thus: 'Go thou from me to fate,
And to my father my foul deeds relate.
Now die!' With that he dragg'd the trembling sire,
Slidd'ring thro' clotter'd blood and holy mire,
(The mingled paste his murder'd son had made,)
Haul'd from beneath the violated shade,
And on the sacred pile the royal victim laid.
His right hand held his bloody falchion bare,
His left he twisted in his hoary hair;
Then, with a speeding thrust, his heart he found:
The lukewarm blood came rushing thro' the wound,
And sanguine streams distain'd the sacred ground.
Thus Priam fell, and shar'd one common fate
With Troy in ashes, and his ruin'd state:
He, who the scepter of all Asia sway'd,
Whom monarchs like domestic slaves obey'd.
On the bleak shore now lies th' abandon'd king,
A headless carcass, and a nameless thing.

Translated by John Dryden

DEREK WALCOTT

(1930–2017)

Sea Canes

Half my friends are dead.
I will make you new ones, said earth.
No, give me them back, as they were, instead,
with faults and all, I cried.

Tonight I can snatch their talk
from the faint surf's drone
through the canes, but I cannot walk

on the moonlit leaves of ocean
down that white road alone,
or float with the dreaming motion

of owls leaving earth's load.
O earth, the number of friends you keep
exceeds those left to be loved.

The sea canes by the cliff flash green and silver;
they were the seraph lances of my faith,
but out of what is lost grows something stronger

that has the rational radiance of stone,
enduring moonlight, further than despair,
strong as the wind, that through dividing canes

brings those we love before us, as they were,
with faults and all, not nobler, just there.

For Malcolm X

All you violated ones with gentle hearts;
You violent dreamers whose cries shout heartbreak;
Whose voices echo clamors of our cool capers,
And whose black faces have hollowed pits for eyes.
All you gambling sons and hooked children and bowery bums
Hating white devils and black bourgeoisie,
Thumbing your noses at your burning red suns,
Gather round this coffin and mourn your dying swan.

Snow-white moslem head-dress around a dead black face!
Beautiful were your sand-papering words against our skins!
Our blood and water pour from your flowing wounds.
You have cut open our breasts and dug scalpels in our brains.
When and Where will another come to take your holy place?
Old man mumbling in his dotage, crying child, unborn?

PHILLIS WHEATLEY

(1753–1784)

On the Death of the Rev. Mr George Whitefield

Hail, happy saint! on thine immortal throne,
Possest of glory, life, and bliss unknown:
We hear no more the music of thy tongue;
Thy wonted auditories cease to throng.
Thy sermons in unequalled accents flowed,
And ev'ry bosom with devotion glowed;
Thou didst, in strains of eloquence refined,
Inflame the heart, and captivate the mind.
Unhappy, we the setting sun deplore,
So glorious once, but ah! it shines no more.

Behold the prophet in his towering flight!
He leaves the earth for heaven's unmeasured height,
And worlds unknown receive him from our sight.
There Whitefield wings with rapid course his way,
And sails to Zion through vast seas of day.
Thy prayers, great saint, and thine incessant cries,
Have pierced the bosom of thy native skies.
Thou, moon, hast seen, and all the stars of light,
How he has wrestled with his God by night.
He prayed that grace in ev'ry heart might dwell;
He longed to see America excel;
He charged its youth that ev'ry grace divine
Should with full lustre in their conduct shine.
That Saviour, which his soul did first receive,
The greatest gift that ev'n a God can give,
He freely offered to the numerous throng,
That on his lips with list'ning pleasure hung.

'Take him, ye wretched, for your only good,
'Take him ye starving sinners, for your food;
'Ye thirsty, come to this life-giving stream,
'Ye preachers, take him for your joyful theme;
'Take him my dear Americans,' he said,
'Be your complaints on his kind bosom laid:
'Take him, ye Africans, he longs for you;
'Impartial Saviour is his title due:
'Washed in the fountain of redeeming blood,
'You shall be sons, and kings, and priests to God.'

Great Countess, we Americans revere
Thy name, and mingle in thy grief sincere;
New England deeply feels, the orphans mourn,
Their more than father will no more return.
But though arrested by the hand of death,
Whitefield no more exerts his lab'ring breath,
Yet let us view him in th' eternal skies,
Let ev'ry heart to this bright vision rise;
While the tomb, safe, retains its sacred trust,
Till life divine reanimates his dust.

JAMES MONROE WHITFIELD
(1822–1871)

Lines on the Death of John Quincy Adams

The great, the good, the just, the true,
   Has yielded up his latest breath;
The noblest man our country knew,
   Bows to the ghastly monster, Death;
The son of one whose deathless name
   Stands first on history's brightest page;
The highest on the list of fame
   As statesman, patriot, and sage.

In early youth he learned to prize
   The freedom which his father won;
The mantle of the patriot sire
   Descended on his mightier son.
Science her deepest hidden lore
   Beneath his potent touch revealed;
Philosophy's abundant store,
   Alike his mighty mind could wield.

The brilliant page of poetry
   Received additions from his pen,
Of holy truth and purity,
   And thoughts which rouse the souls of men,
Eloquence did his heart inspire,
   And from his lips in glory blazed,
Till nations caught the glowing fire,
   And senates trembled as they praised.

While all the recreant of the land
   To slavery's idol bowed the knee –
A fawning, sycophantic band,
   Fit tools of petty tyranny –

He stood amid the recreant throng,
   The chosen champion of the free,
And battled fearlessly and long
   For justice, right, and liberty.

What though grim Death has sealed his doom
   Who faithful proved to God and us;
And slavery, o'er the patriot's tomb
   Exulting pours its deadliest curse?
Among the virtuous and free
   His memory will ever live;
Champion of right and liberty,
   The blessings, truth and virtue give.

WALT WHITMAN

(1819–1892)

O Captain! My Captain!

O Captain! my Captain! our fearful trip is done,
The ship has weather'd every rack, the prize we sought is won,
The port is near, the bells I hear, the people all exulting,
While follow eyes the steady keel, the vessel grim and daring;
       But O heart! heart! heart!
         O the bleeding drops of red,
           Where on the deck my Captain lies,
           Fallen cold and dead.

O Captain! my Captain! rise up and hear the bells;
Rise up – for you the flag is flung – for you the bugle trills,
For you bouquets and ribbon'd wreaths – for you the shores
    a-crowding,
For you they call, the swaying mass, their eager faces turning;
       Here Captain! dear father!
         This arm beneath your head!
           It is some dream that on the deck,
           You've fallen cold and dead.

My Captain does not answer, his lips are pale and still,
My father does not feel my arm, he has no pulse nor will,
The ship is anchor'd safe and sound, its voyage closed and done,
From fearful trip the victor ship comes in with object won;
       Exult, O shores, and ring, O bells!
         But I with mournful tread,
           Walk the deck my Captain lies,
           Fallen cold and dead.

Vigil Strange I Kept on the Field One Night

Vigil strange I kept on the field one night;

When you, my son and my comrade, dropt at my side that day,

One look I but gave which your dear eyes return'd with a look I
shall never forget,

One touch of your hand to mine, O boy, reach'd up as you lay on
the ground,

Then onward I sped in the battle, the even-contested battle,

Till late in the night reliev'd to the place at last again I made
my way,

Found you in death so cold, dear comrade, found your body, son
of responding kisses (never again on earth responding),

Bared your face in the starlight, curious the scene, cool blew the
moderate night-wind,

Long there and then in vigil I stood, dimly around me the battle-
field spreading,

Vigil wondrous and vigil sweet there in the fragrant silent night,

But not a tear fell, not even a long-drawn sigh, long, long I gazed,

Then on the earth partially reclining sat by your side leaning my
chin in my hands,

Passing sweet hours, immortal and mystic hours with you,
dearest comrade – not a tear, not a word,

Vigil of silence, love and death, vigil for you, my son and my
soldier,

As onward silently stars aloft, eastward new ones upward stole,

Vigil final for you, brave boy (I could not save you, swift was
your death,

I faithfully loved you and cared for you living, I think we shall
surely meet again),

Till at latest lingering of the night, indeed just as the dawn
appear'd,

My comrade I wrapt in his blanket, envelop'd well his form,

Folded the blanket well, tucking it carefully over head and
carefully under feet,

And there and then and bathed by the rising run, my son in his
grave, in his rude-dug grave I deposited,

Ending my vigil strange with that, vigil of night and battle-
field dim,
Vigil for boy of responding kisses (never again on earth
responding),
Vigil for comrade swiftly slain, vigil I never forget, how as day
brighten'd,
I rose from the chill ground and folded my soldier well in his
blanket,
And buried him where he fell.

When Lilacs Last in the Dooryard Bloom'd

I

When lilacs last in the dooryard bloom'd,
And the great star early droop'd in the western sky in the night,
I mourn'd, and yet shall mourn with ever-returning spring.

Ever-returning spring, trinity sure to me you bring,
Lilac blooming perennial and drooping star in the west,
And thought of him I love.

2

O powerful western fallen star!
O shades of night – O moody, tearful night!
O great star disappear'd – O the black murk that hides the star!
O cruel hands that hold me powerless – O helpless soul of me!
O harsh surrounding cloud that will not free my soul.

3

In the dooryard fronting an old farm-house near the white-
wash'd palings,
Stands the lilac-bush tall-growing with heart-shaped leaves of
    rich green,
With many a pointed blossom rising delicate, with the perfume
    strong I love,
With every leaf a miracle – and from this bush in the dooryard,
With delicate-color'd blossoms and heart-shaped leaves of rich
    green,
A sprig with its flower I break.

4

In the swamp in secluded recesses,
A shy and hidden bird is warbling a song.
Solitary the thrush,
The hermit withdrawn to himself, avoiding the settlements,
Sings by himself a song.

Song of the bleeding throat,
Death's outlet song of life, (for well dear brother I know,
If thou wast not granted to sing thou would'st surely die.)

5

Over the breast of the spring, the land, amid cities,
Amid lanes and through old woods, where lately the violets
peep'd from the ground, spotting the gray debris,
Amid the grass in the fields each side of the lanes, passing the
    endless grass,
Passing the yellow-spear'd wheat, every grain from its shroud in
    the dark-brown fields uprisen,
Passing the apple-tree blows of white and pink in the orchards,
Carrying a corpse to where it shall rest in the grave,
Night and day journeys a coffin.

6

Coffin that passes through lanes and streets,
Through day and night with the great cloud darkening the land,
With the pomp of the inloop'd flags with the cities draped in
    black,
With the show of the States themselves as of crape-veil'd women
    standing,
With processions long and winding and the flambeaus of the
    night,
With the countless torches lit, with the silent sea of faces and the
    unbared heads,
With the waiting depot, the arriving coffin, and the sombre faces,
With dirges through the night, with the thousand voices rising
    strong and solemn,
With all the mournful voices of the dirges pour'd around the
    coffin,
The dim-lit churches and the shuddering organs – where amid
    these you journey,
With the tolling tolling bells' perpetual clang,
Here, coffin that slowly passes,
I give you my sprig of lilac.

7

(Nor for you, for one alone,
Blossoms and branches green to coffins all I bring,
For fresh as the morning, thus would I chant a song for you O
    sane and sacred death.

All over bouquets of roses,
O death, I cover you over with roses and early lilies,
But mostly and now the lilac that blooms the first,
Copious I break, I break the sprigs from the bushes,
With loaded arms I come, pouring for you,
For you and the coffins all of you O death.)

8

O western orb sailing the heaven,
Now I know what you must have meant as a month since I
    walk'd,
As I walk'd in silence the transparent shadowy night,
As I saw you had something to tell as you bent to me night after
    night,
As you droop'd from the sky low down as if to my side, (while
    the other stars all look'd on,)
As we wander'd together the solemn night, (for something I
    know not what kept me from sleep,)
As the night advanced, and I saw on the rim of the west how full
    you were of woe,
As I stood on the rising ground in the breeze in the cool
    transparent night,
As I watch'd where you pass'd and was lost in the netherward
    black of the night,
As my soul in its trouble dissatisfied sank, as where you sad orb,
Concluded, dropt in the night, and was gone.

9

Sing on there in the swamp,
O singer bashful and tender, I hear your notes, I hear your call,
I hear, I come presently, I understand you,
But a moment I linger, for the lustrous star has detain'd me,
The star my departing comrade holds and detains me.

10

O how shall I warble myself for the dead one there I loved?
And how shall I deck my song for the large sweet soul that has
    gone?
And what shall my perfume be for the grave of him I love?

Sea-winds blown from east and west,
Blown from the Eastern sea and blown from the Western sea, till
there on the prairies meeting,
These and with these and the breath of my chant,
I'll perfume the grave of him I love.

11

O what shall I hang on the chamber walls?
And what shall the pictures be that I hang on the walls,
To adorn the burial-house of him I love?

Pictures of growing spring and farms and homes,
With the Fourth-month eve at sundown, and the gray smoke
lucid and bright,
With floods of the yellow gold of the gorgeous, indolent, sinking
sun, burning, expanding the air,
With the fresh sweet herbage under foot, and the pale green
leaves of the trees prolific,
In the distance the flowing glaze, the breast of the river, with a
wind-dapple here and there,
With ranging hills on the banks, with many a line against the sky,
and shadows,
And the city at hand with dwellings so dense, and stacks of
chimneys,
And all the scenes of life and the workshops, and the workmen
homeward returning.

12

Lo, body and soul – this land,
My own Manhattan with spires, and the sparkling and hurrying
tides, and the ships,
The varied and ample land, the South and the North in the light,
Ohio's shores and flashing Missouri,
And ever the far-spreading prairies cover'd with grass and corn.

Lo, the most excellent sun so calm and haughty,
The violet and purple morn with just-felt breezes,
The gentle soft-born measureless light,
The miracle spreading bathing all, the fulfill'd noon,
The coming eve delicious, the welcome night and the stars,
Over my cities shining all, enveloping man and land.

13

Sing on, sing on you gray-brown bird,
Sing from the swamps, the recesses, pour your chant from the
    bushes,
Limitless out of the dusk, out of the cedars and pines.

Sing on dearest brother, warble your reedy song,
Loud human song, with voice of uttermost woe.

O liquid and free and tender!
O wild and loose to my soul! – O wondrous singer!
You only I hear – yet the star holds me, (but will soon depart,)
Yet the lilac with mastering odor holds me.

14

Now while I sat in the day and look'd forth,
In the close of the day with its light and the fields of spring, and
    the farmers preparing their crops,
In the large unconscious scenery of my land with its lakes and
    forests,
In the heavenly aerial beauty, (after the perturb'd winds and the
    storms,)
Under the arching heavens of the afternoon swift passing, and the
    voices of children and women,
The many-moving sea-tides, and I saw the ships how they sail'd,
And the summer approaching with richness, and the fields all
    busy with labor,

And the infinite separate houses, how they all went on, each with
    its meals and minutia of daily usages,
And the streets how their throbbings throbb'd, and the cities
    pent – lo, then and there,
Falling upon them all and among them all, enveloping me with
    the rest,
Appear'd the cloud, appear'd the long black trail,
And I knew death, its thought, and the sacred knowledge of death.

Then with the knowledge of death as walking one side of me,
And the thought of death close-walking the other side of me,
And I in the middle as with companions, and as holding the
    hands of companions,
I fled forth to the hiding receiving night that talks not,
Down to the shores of the water, the path by the swamp in the
    dimness,
To the solemn shadowy cedars and ghostly pines so still.

And the singer so shy to the rest receiv'd me,
The gray-brown bird I know receiv'd us comrades three,
And he sang the carol of death, and a verse for him I love.

From deep secluded recesses,
From the fragrant cedars and the ghostly pines so still,
Came the carol of the bird.
And the charm of the carol rapt me,
As I held as if by their hands my comrades in the night,
And the voice of my spirit tallied the song of the bird.

Come lovely and soothing death,
Undulate round the world, serenely arriving, arriving,
In the day, in the night, to all, to each,
Sooner or later delicate death.

Prais'd be the fathomless universe,
For life and joy, and for objects and knowledge curious,
And for love, sweet love – but praise! praise! praise!
For the sure-enwinding arms of cool-enfolding death.

Dark mother always gliding near with soft feet,
Have none chanted for thee a chant of fullest welcome?
Then I chant it for thee, I glorify thee above all,
I bring thee a song that when thou must indeed come, come
    unfalteringly.

Approach strong deliveress,
When it is so, when thou hast taken them I joyously sing the
    dead,
Lost in the loving floating ocean of thee,
Laved in the flood of thy bliss O death.

From me to thee glad serenades,
Dances for thee I propose saluting thee, adornments and
    feastings for thee,
And the sights of the open landscape and the high-spread sky are
    fitting,
And life and the fields, and the huge and thoughtful night.

The night in silence under many a star,
The ocean shore and the husky whispering wave whose voice
    I know,
And the soul turning to thee O vast and well-veil'd death,
And the body gratefully nestling close to thee.

Over the tree-tops I float thee a song,
Over the rising and sinking waves, over the myriad fields and the
    prairies wide,
Over the dense-pack'd cities all and the teeming wharves and
    ways,
I float this carol with joy, with joy to thee O death.

15

To the tally of my soul,
Loud and strong kept up the gray-brown bird,
With pure deliberate notes spreading filling the night.

Loud in the pines and cedars dim,
Clear in the freshness moist and the swamp-perfume,
And I with my comrades there in the night.

While my sight that was bound in my eyes unclosed,
As to long panoramas of visions.

And I saw askant the armies,
I saw as in noiseless dreams hundreds of battle-flags,
Borne through the smoke of the battles and pierc'd with missiles
    I saw them,
And carried hither and yon through the smoke, and torn and
    bloody,
And at last but a few shreds left on the staffs, (and all in silence,)
And the staffs all splinter'd and broken.

I saw battle-corpses, myriads of them,
And the white skeletons of young men, I saw them,
I saw the debris and debris of all the slain soldiers of the war,
But I saw they were not as was thought,
They themselves were fully at rest, they suffer'd not,
The living remain'd and suffer'd, the mother suffer'd,
And the wife and the child and the musing comrade suffer'd,
And the armies that remain'd suffer'd.

16

Passing the visions, passing the night,
Passing, unloosing the hold of my comrades' hands,
Passing the song of the hermit bird and the tallying song of
    my soul,
Victorious song, death's outlet song, yet varying ever-altering
    song,
As low and wailing, yet clear the notes, rising and falling,
    flooding the night,
Sadly sinking and fainting, as warning and warning, and yet
    again bursting with joy,
Covering the earth and filling the spread of the heaven,

As that powerful psalm in the night I heard from recesses,
Passing, I leave thee lilac with heart-shaped leaves,
I leave thee there in the door-yard, blooming, returning with spring.

I cease from my song for thee,
From my gaze on thee in the west, fronting the west, communing
    with thee,
O comrade lustrous with silver face in the night.

Yet each to keep and all, retrievements out of the night,
The song, the wondrous chant of the gray-brown bird,
And the tallying chant, the echo arous'd in my soul,
With the lustrous and drooping star with the countenance full
    of woe,
With the holders holding my hand nearing the call of the bird,
Comrades mine and I in the midst, and their memory ever to
    keep, for the dead I loved so well,
For the sweetest, wisest soul of all my days and lands – and this
    for his dear sake,
Lilac and star and bird twined with the chant of my soul,
There in the fragrant pines and the cedars dusk and dim.

OSCAR WILDE

(1854–1900)

Requiescat

Tread lightly, she is near
   Under the snow,
Speak gently, she can hear
   The daisies grow.

All her bright golden hair
   Tarnished with rust,
She that was young and fair
   Fallen to dust.

Lily-like, white as snow,
   She hardly knew
She was a woman, so
   Sweetly she grew.

Coffin-board, heavy stone,
   Lie on her breast,
I vex my heart alone,
   She is at rest.

Peace, Peace, she cannot hear
   Lyre or sonnet,
All my life's buried here,
   Heap earth upon it.

HELEN MARIA WILLIAMS

(1761–1827)

Elegy on a Young Thrush, Which Escaped from the Writer's Hand, and Falling Down the Area of a House, Could Not Be Found

Mistaken Bird, ah whither hast thou stray'd?
  My friendly grasp why eager to elude?
This hand was on thy pinion lightly laid,
  And fear'd to hurt thee by a touch too rude.

Is there no foresight in a Thrush's breast,
  That thou down yonder gulph from me wouldst go?
That gloomy area lurking cats infest.
  And there the dog may rove, alike thy toe.

I would with lavish crumbs my bird have fed,
  And brought a crystal cup to wet thy bill;
I would have made of down and moss thy bed.
  Soft, though not fashion'd with a Thrush's skill.

Soon as thy strengthen'd wing could mount the sky,
  My willing hand had set my captive free;
Ah, not for her who loves the Muse, to buy
  A selfish pleasure, bought with pain to thee!

The vital air, and liberty, and light
  Had all been thine; and love, and rapt'rous song,
And sweet parental joys, in rapid flight,
  Had led the circle of thy life along.

Securely to my window hadst thou flown,
    And ever thy accustom'd morsel found;
Nor should thy trusting breast the wants have known
    Which other Thrushes knew when winter frown'd.

Fram'd with the wisdom nature lent to thee,
    Thy house of straw had brav'd the tempest's rage,
And thou through many a Spring hadst liv'd to see
    The utmost limit of a Thrush's age.

Ill-fated bird! – and does the Thrush's race,
    Like Man's, mistake the path that leads to bliss?
Or, when his eye that tranquil path can trace,
    The good he well discerns through folly miss?

WILLIAM CARLOS WILLIAMS
(1883–1963)

The Last Words of My English Grandmother

There were some dirty plates
and a glass of milk
beside her on a small table
near the rank, disheveled bed –

Wrinkled and nearly blind
she lay and snored
rousing with anger in her tones
to cry for food,

Gimme something to eat –
They're starving me –
I'm all right I won't go
to the hospital. No, no, no

Give me something to eat
Let me take you
to the hospital, I said
and after you are well

you can do as you please.
She smiled, Yes
you do what you please first
then I can do what I please –

Oh, oh, oh! she cried
as the ambulance men lifted
her to the stretcher –
Is this what you call

making me comfortable?
By now her mind was clear –
Oh you think you're smart
you young people,

she said, but I'll tell you
you don't know anything.
Then we started.
On the way

we passed a long row
of elms. She looked at them
awhile out of
the ambulance window and said,

What are all those
fuzzy-looking things out there?
Trees? Well, I'm tired
of them and rolled her head away.

CHARLES WOLFE
(1791–1823)

The Burial of Sir John Moore after Corunna

Not a drum was heard, not a funeral note,
  As his corse to the rampart we hurried;
Not a soldier discharged his farewell shot
  O'er the grave where our hero we buried.

We buried him darkly at dead of night,
  The sods with our bayonets turning,
By the struggling moonbeam's misty light
  And the lanthorn dimly burning.

No useless coffin enclosed his breast,
  Not in sheet or in shroud we wound him;
But he lay like a warrior taking his rest
  With his martial cloak around him.

Few and short were the prayers we said,
  And we spoke not a word of sorrow;
But we steadfastly gazed on the face that was dead,
  And we bitterly thought of the morrow.

We thought, as we hollowed his narrow bed
  And smoothed down his lonely pillow,
That the foe and the stranger would tread o'er his head,
  And we far away on the billow!

Lightly they'll talk of the spirit that's gone,
  And o'er his cold ashes upbraid him –
But little he'll reck, if they let him sleep on
  In the grave where a Briton has laid him.

But half of our heavy task was done
   When the clock struck the hour for retiring;
And we heard the distant and random gun
   That the foe was sullenly firing.

Slowly and sadly we laid him down,
   From the field of his fame fresh and gory;
We carved not a line, and we raised not a stone,
   But we left him alone with his glory.

WILLIAM WORDSWORTH

(1770–1850)

Remembrance of Collins

Composed upon the Thames near Richmond

Glide gently, thus for ever glide,
O Thames! that other bards may see
As lovely visions by thy side
As now, fair river! come to me.
O glide, fair stream! for ever so,
Thy quiet soul on all bestowing,
Till all our minds for ever flow
As thy deep waters now are flowing.

Vain thought! – Yet be as now thou art,
That in thy waters may be seen
The image of a poet's heart,
How bright, how solemn, how serene!
Such as did once the Poet bless,
Who murmuring here a later ditty,
Could find no refuge from distress
But in the milder grief of pity.

Now let us, as we float along,
For *him* suspend the dashing oar;
And pray that never child of song
May know that Poet's sorrows more.
How calm! how still! the only sound,
The dripping of the oar suspended!
– The evening darkness gathers round
By virtue's holiest Powers attended.

Old Man Travelling

The little hedge-row birds,
That peck along the road, regard him not.
He travels on, and in his face, his step,
His gait, is one expression; every limb,
His look and bending figure, all bespeak
A man who does not move with pain, but moves
With thought – He is insensibly subdued
To settled quiet: he is one by whom
All effort seems forgotten, one to whom
Long patience has such mild composure given,
That patience now doth seem a thing, of which
He hath no need. He is by nature led
To peace so perfect, that the young behold
With envy, what the old man hardly feels.
– I asked him whither he was bound, and what
The object of his journey; he replied
'Sir! I am going many miles to take
A last leave of my son, a mariner,
Who from a sea-fight has been brought to Falmouth,
And there is dying in an hospital.'

We Are Seven

A simple child, dear brother Jim,
That lightly draws its breath,
And feels its life in every limb,
What should it know of death?

I met a little cottage girl,
She was eight years old, she said;
Her hair was thick with many a curl
That clustered round her head.

She had a rustic, woodland air,
And she was wildly clad;
Her eyes were fair, and very fair,
– Her beauty made me glad.

'Sisters and brothers, little maid,
How many may you be?'
'How many? seven in all,' she said,
And wondering looked at me.

'And where are they, I pray you tell?'
She answered, 'Seven are we,
And two of us at Conway dwell,
And two are gone to sea.

Two of us in the church-yard lie,
My sister and my brother,
And in the church-yard cottage, I
Dwell near them with my mother.'

'You say that two at Conway dwell,
And two are gone to sea,
Yet you are seven; I pray you tell
Sweet Maid, how this may be?'

Then did the little Maid reply,
'Seven boys and girls are we;
Two of us in the church-yard lie,
Beneath the church-yard tree.'

'You run about, my little maid,
Your limbs they are alive;
If two are in the church-yard laid,
Then ye are only five.'

'Their graves are green, they may be seen,'
The little Maid replied,
'Twelve steps or more from my mother's door,
And they are side by side.

My stockings there I often knit,
My 'kerchief there I hem;
And there upon the ground I sit –
I sit and sing to them.

And often after sunset, Sir,
When it is light and fair,
I take my little porringer,
And eat my supper there.

The first that died was little Jane;
In bed she moaning lay,
Till God released her of her pain,
And then she went away.

So in the church-yard she was laid,
And all the summer dry,
Together round her grave we played,
My brother John and I.

And when the ground was white with snow,
And I could run and slide,
My brother John was forced to go,
And he lies by her side.'

'How many are you then,' said I,
'If they two are in Heaven?'
The little Maiden did reply,
'O Master! we are seven.'

'But they are dead; those two are dead!
Their spirits are in heaven!'
'Twas throwing words away; for still
The little Maid would have her will,
And said, 'Nay, we are seven!'

There was a Boy

There was a Boy; ye knew him well, ye cliffs
And islands of Winander! many a time,
At evening, when the earliest stars began
To move along the edges of the hills,
Rising or setting, would he stand alone,
Beneath the trees, or by the glimmering lake;
And there, with fingers interwoven, both hands
Pressed closely palm to palm and to his mouth
Uplifted, he, as through an instrument,
Blew mimic hootings to the silent owls
That they might answer him. – And they would shout
Across the watery vale, and shout again,
Responsive to his call, – with quivering peals,
And long halloos, and screams, and echoes loud
Redoubled and redoubled; concourse wild
Of jocund din! And, when there came a pause
Of silence such as baffled his best skill:
Then, sometimes, in that silence, while he hung
Listening, a gentle shock of mild surprise
Has carried far into his heart the voice
Of mountain-torrents; or the visible scene
Would enter unawares into his mind
With all its solemn imagery, its rocks,
Its woods, and that uncertain heaven received
Into the bosom of the steady lake.

This boy was taken from his mates, and died
In childhood, ere he was full twelve years old.
Pre-eminent in beauty is the vale
Where he was born and bred: the churchyard hangs
Upon a slope above the village-school;
And through that churchyard when my way has led
On summer-evenings, I believe that there
A long half-hour together I have stood
Mute – looking at the grave in which he lies!

The Two April Mornings

We walked along, while bright and red
Uprose the morning sun,
And Matthew stopped, he looked, and said,
'The will of God be done!'

A village schoolmaster was he,
With hair of glittering grey;
As blithe a man as you could see
On a spring holiday.

And on that morning, through the grass,
And by the steaming rills,
We travelled merrily to pass
A day among the hills.

'Our work,' said I, 'was well begun;
Then, from thy breast what thought,
Beneath so beautiful a sun,
So sad a sigh has brought?'

A second time did Matthew stop;
And fixing still his eye
Upon the eastern mountain-top
To me he made reply.

'Yon cloud with that long purple cleft
Brings fresh into my mind
A day like this which I have left
Full thirty years behind.

And on that slope of springing corn
The self-same crimson hue
Fell from the sky that April morn,
The same which now I view.

With rod and line my silent sport
I plied by Derwent's wave,
And, coming to the church, stopped short
Beside my daughter's grave.

Nine summers had she scarcely seen,
The pride of all the vale;
And then she sang! – she would have been
A very nightingale.

Six feet in earth my Emma lay,
And yet I loved her more,
For so it seemed, than till that day
I e'er had loved before.

And, turning from her grave, I met,
Beside the churchyard yew
A blooming girl, whose hair was wet
With points of morning dew.

A basket on her head she bare,
Her brow was smooth and white,
To see a child so very fair,
It was a pure delight!

No fountain from its rocky cave
E'er tripped with foot so free,
She seemed as happy as a wave
That dances on the sea.

There came from me a sigh of pain,
Which I could ill confine;
I looked at her and looked again;
– And did not wish her mine!'

Matthew is in his grave, yet now
Methinks I see him stand
As at that moment, with his bough
Of wilding in his hand.

'A slumber did my spirit seal'

A slumber did my spirit seal;
  I had no human fears:
She seemed a thing that could not feel
  The touch of earthly years.

No motion has she now, no force;
  She neither hears nor sees,
Rolled round in earth's diurnal course
  With rocks and stones and trees.

'She dwelt among the untrodden ways'

She dwelt among the untrodden ways
  Beside the springs of Dove,
A maid whom there were none to praise
  And very few to love.

A violet by a mossy stone
  Half-hidden from the eye!
– Fair as a star, when only one
  Is shining in the sky!

She lived unknown, and few could know
  When Lucy ceased to be;
But she is in her grave, and, oh,
  The difference to me!

'I travelled among unknown men'

I travelled among unknown men,
  In lands beyond the sea;
Nor England! did I know till then
  What love I bore to thee.

'Tis past, that melancholy dream!
  Nor will I quit thy shore
A second time; for still I seem
  To love thee more and more.

Among thy mountains did I feel
  The joy of my desire;
And she I cherished turned her wheel
  Beside an English fire.

Thy mornings showed, thy nights concealed,
  The bowers where Lucy played;
And thine too is the last green field
  That Lucy's eyes surveyed.

Elegiac Stanzas

Suggested by a picture of Peele Castle, in a storm, painted by Sir George Beaumont

I was thy Neighbour once, thou rugged Pile!
Four summer weeks I dwelt in sight of thee:
I saw thee every day; and all the while
Thy Form was sleeping on a glassy sea.

So pure the sky, so quiet was the air!
So like, so very like, was day to day!
Whene'er I looked, thy Image still was there;
It trembled, but it never passed away.

How perfect was the calm! it seemed no sleep;
No mood, which season takes away, or brings:
I could have fancied that the mighty Deep
Was even the gentlest of all gentle Things.

Ah! then, if mine had been the Painter's hand,
To express what then I saw; and add the gleam,
The light that never was, on sea or land,
The consecration, and the Poet's dream;

I would have planted thee, thou hoary Pile!
Amid a world how different from this!
Beside a sea that could not cease to smile;
On tranquil land, beneath a sky of bliss:

Thou shouldst have seemed a treasure-house, a mine
Of peaceful years; a chronicle of heaven: –
Of all the sunbeams that did ever shine
The very sweetest had to thee been given.

A Picture had it been of lasting ease,
Elysian quiet, without toil or strife;
No motion but the moving tide, a breeze,
Or merely silent Nature's breathing life.

Such, in the fond delusion of my heart,
Such Picture would I at that time have made:
And seen the soul of truth in every part;
A faith, a trust, that could not be betrayed.

So once it would have been, – 'tis so no more;
I have submitted to a new control:
A power is gone, which nothing can restore;
A deep distress hath humanized my Soul.

Not for a moment could I now behold
A smiling sea and be what I have been:
The feeling of my loss will ne'er be old;
This, which I know, I speak with mind serene.

Then, Beaumont, Friend! who would have been the Friend,
If he had lived, of Him whom I deplore,
This Work of thine I blame not, but commend;
This sea in anger, and the dismal shore.

Oh 'tis a passionate Work! – yet wise and well;
Well chosen is the spirit that is here;
That Hulk which labours in the deadly swell,
This rueful sky, this pageantry of fear!

And this huge Castle, standing here sublime,
I love to see the look with which it braves,
Cased in the unfeeling armour of old time,
The lightning, the fierce wind, and trampling waves.

Farewell, farewell the Heart that lives alone,
Housed in a dream, at distance from the Kind!
Such happiness, wherever it be known,
Is to be pitied; for 'tis surely blind.

But welcome fortitude, and patient cheer,
And frequent sights of what is to be borne!
Such sights, or worse, as are before me here. –
Not without hope we suffer and we mourn.

Elegiac Verses in Memory of My Brother, John Wordsworth

I

The Sheep-boy whistled loud, and lo!
That instant, startled by the shock,
The Buzzard mounted from the rock
Deliberate and slow:
Lord of the air, he took his flight;

Oh! could he on that woeful night
Have lent his wing, my Brother dear,
For one poor moment's space to Thee,
And all who struggled with the Sea,
When safety was so near.

2

Thus in the weakness of my heart
I spoke (but let that pang be still)
When rising from the rock at will,
I saw the Bird depart.
And let me calmly bless the Power
That meets me in this unknown Flower,
Affecting type of him I mourn!
With calmness suffer and believe,
And grieve, and known that I must grieve,
Not cheerless, though forlorn.

3

Here did we stop; and here looked round
While each into himself descends,
For that last thought of parting Friends
That is not to be found.
Hidden was Grasmere Vale from sight,
Our home and his, his heart's delight,
His quiet heart's selected home.
But time before him melts away,
And he hath feeling of a day
Of blessedness to come.

4

Full soon in sorrow did I weep,
Taught that the mutual hope was dust,
In sorrow, but for higher trust,
How miserably deep!
All vanished in a single word,
A breath, a sound, and scarcely heard.
Sea – Ship – drowned – Shipwreck – so it came,
The meek, the brave, the good, was gone;
He who had been our living John
Was nothing but a name.

5

That was indeed a parting! oh,
Glad am I, glad that it is past;
For there were some on whom it cast
Unutterable woe.
But they as well as I have gains; –
From many a humble source, to pains
Like these, there comes a mild release;
Even here I feel it, even this Plant
Is in its beauty ministrant
To comfort and to peace.

SIR HENRY WOTTON

(1568–1639)

Upon the Death of Sir Albert Morton's Wife

He first deceased; she for a little tried
To live without him, liked it not, and died.

KIT WRIGHT

(1944–)

The Boys Bump-starting the Hearse

The hearse has stalled in the lane overlooking the river
Where willows are plunging their heads in the bottle-green water
   And bills of green baize drakes kazoo.
   The hearse has stalled and what shall we do?

The old don comes on, a string bag his strongbox.
He knows what is known about Horace but carries no tool-box.
   Small boys shout in the Cambridge sun.
   The hearse has stalled and what's to be done?

Lime flowers drift in the lane to the baskets of bicycles,
Sticker the wall with yellow and powdery particles.
   Monosyllabic, the driver's curse.
   Everything fires. Except the hearse

Whose gastric and gastric whinnies shoot neutered tom cats
In through the kitchen flaps of back gardens where tomtits
   Wizen away from the dangling crust.
   Who shall restart the returned-to-dust?

Shrill and sudden as birds the boys have planted
Their excellent little shoulders against the lamented
   Who bumps in second. A fart of exhaust.
   On goes the don and the holocaust.

W. B. YEATS

(1865–1939)

September 1913

What need you, being come to sense,
But fumble in a greasy till
And add the halfpence to the pence
And prayer to shivering prayer, until
You have dried the marrow from the bone?
For men were born to pray and save:
Romantic Ireland's dead and gone,
It's with O'Leary in the grave.

Yet they were of a different kind,
The names that stilled your childish play,
They have gone about the world like wind,
But little time had they to pray
For whom the hangman's rope was spun,
And what, God help us, could they save?
Romantic Ireland's dead and gone,
It's with O'Leary in the grave.

Was it for this the wild geese spread
The grey wing upon every tide;
For this that all that blood was shed,
For this Edward Fitzgerald died,
And Robert Emmet and Wolfe Tone,
All that delirium of the brave?
Romantic Ireland's dead and gone,
It's with O'Leary in the grave.

Yet could we turn the years again,
And call those exiles as they were
In all their loneliness and pain,
You'd cry, 'Some woman's yellow hair
Has maddened every mother's son':
They weighed so lightly what they gave.
But let them be, they're dead and gone,
They're with O'Leary in the grave.

To a Shade

If you have revisited the town, thin Shade,
Whether to look upon your monument
(I wonder if the builder has been paid)
Or happier-thoughted when the day is spent
To drink of that salt breath out of the sea
When grey gulls flit about instead of men,
And the gaunt houses put on majesty:
Let these content you and be gone again;
For they are at their old tricks yet.
                                        A man
Of your own passionate serving kind who had brought
In his full hands what, had they only known,
Had given their children's children loftier thought,
Sweeter emotion, working in their veins
Like gentle blood, has been driven from the place,
And insult heaped upon him for his pains,
And for his open-handedness, disgrace;
Your enemy, an old foul mouth, had set
The pack upon him.

                    Go, unquiet wanderer,
And gather the Glasnevin coverlet
About your head till the dust stops your ear,
The time for you to taste of that salt breath
And listen at the corners has not come:
You had enough of sorrow before death –
Away, away! You are safer in the tomb.

                                        September 29, 1913

The Wild Swans at Coole

The trees are in their autumn beauty,
The woodland paths are dry,
Under the October twilight the water
Mirrors a still sky;
Upon the brimming water among the stones
Are nine-and-fifty swans.

The nineteenth autumn has come upon me
Since I first made my count;
I saw, before I had well finished,
All suddenly mount
And scatter wheeling in great broken rings
Upon their clamorous wings.

I have looked upon those brilliant creatures,
And now my heart is sore.
All's changed since I, hearing at twilight,
The first time on this shore,
The bell-beat of their wings above my head,
Trod with a lighter tread.

Unwearied still, lover by lover,
They paddle in the cold
Companionable streams or climb the air;

Their hearts have not grown old;
Passion or conquest, wander where they will,
Attend upon them still.

But now they drift on the still water,
Mysterious, beautiful;
Among what rushes will they build,
By what lake's edge or pool
Delight men's eyes when I awake some day
To find they have flown away?

In Memory of Major Robert Gregory

I

Now that we're almost settled in our house
I'll name the friends that cannot sup with us
Beside a fire of turf in th' ancient tower,
And having talked to some late hour
Climb up the narrow winding stair to bed:
Discoverers of forgotten truth
Or mere companions of my youth,
All, all are in my thoughts to-night being dead.

2

Always we'd have the new friend meet the old
And we are hurt if either friend seem cold,
And there is salt to lengthen out the smart
In the affections of our heart,
And quarrels are blown up upon that head;
But not a friend that I would bring
This night can set us quarrelling,
For all that come into my mind are dead.

3

Lionel Johnson comes the first to mind,
That loved his learning better than mankind,
Though courteous to the worst; much falling he
Brooded upon sanctity
Till all his Greek and Latin learning seemed
A long blast upon the horn that brought
A little nearer to his thought
A measureless consummation that he dreamed.

4

And that enquiring man John Synge comes next,
That dying chose the living world for text
And never could have rested in the tomb
But that, long travelling, he had come
Towards nightfall upon certain set apart
In a most desolate stony place,
Towards nightfall upon a race
Passionate and simple like his heart.

5

And then I think of old George Pollexfen,
In muscular youth well known to Mayo men
For horsemanship at meets or at racecourses,
That could have shown how pure-bred horses
And solid men, for all their passion, live
But as the outrageous stars incline
By opposition, square and trine;
Having grown sluggish and contemplative.

6

They were my close companions many a year,
A portion of my mind and life, as it were,
And now their breathless faces seem to look
Out of some old picture-book;
I am accustomed to their lack of breath,
But not that my dear friend's dear son,
Our Sidney and our perfect man,
Could share in that discourtesy of death.

7

For all things the delighted eye now sees
Were loved by him: the old storm-broken trees
That cast their shadows upon road and bridge;
The tower set on the stream's edge;
The ford where drinking cattle make a stir
Nightly, and startled by that sound
The water-hen must change her ground;
He might have been your heartiest welcomer.

8

When with the Galway foxhounds he would ride
From Castle Taylor to the Roxborough side
Or Esserkelly plain, few kept his pace;
At Mooneen he had leaped a place
So perilous that half the astonished meet
Had shut their eyes; and where was it
He rode a race without a bit?
And yet his mind outran the horses' feet.

9

We dreamed that a great painter had been born
To cold Clare rock and Galway rock and thorn,
To that stern colour and that delicate line
That are our secret discipline
Wherein the gazing heart doubles her might.
Soldier, scholar, horseman, he,
And yet he had the intensity
To have published all to be a world's delight.

10

What other could so well have counselled us
In all lovely intricacies of a house
As he that practised or that understood
All work in metal or in wood,
In moulded plaster or in carven stone?
Soldier, scholar, horseman, he,
And all he did done perfectly
As though he had but that one trade alone.

11

Some burn damp faggots, others may consume
The entire combustible world in one small room
As though dried straw, and if we turn about
The bare chimney is gone black out
Because the work had finished in that flare.
Soldier, scholar, horseman, he,
As 'twere all life's epitome.
What made us dream that he could comb grey hair?

12

I had thought, seeing how bitter is that wind
That shakes the shutter, to have brought to mind
All those that manhood tried, or childhood loved
Or boyish intellect approved,
With some appropriate commentary on each;
Until imagination brought
A fitter welcome; but a thought
Of that late death took all my heart for speech.

Easter 1916

I have met them at close of day
Coming with vivid faces
From counter or desk among grey
Eighteenth-century houses.
I have passed with a nod of the head
Or polite meaningless words,
Or have lingered awhile and said
Polite meaningless words,
And thought before I had done
Of a mocking tale or a gibe
To please a companion
Around the fire at the club,
Being certain that they and I
But lived where motley is worn:
All changed, changed utterly:
A terrible beauty is born.

That woman's days were spent
In ignorant good-will,
Her nights in argument
Until her voice grew shrill.
What voice more sweet than hers
When, young and beautiful,

She rode to harriers?
This man had kept a school
And rode our wingèd horse;
This other his helper and friend
Was coming into his force;
He might have won fame in the end,
So sensitive his nature seemed,
So daring and sweet his thought.
This other man I had dreamed
A drunken, vainglorious lout.
He had done most bitter wrong
To some who are near my heart,
Yet I number him in the song;
He, too, has resigned his part
In the casual comedy;
He, too, has been changed in his turn,
Transformed utterly:
A terrible beauty is born.

Hearts with one purpose alone
Through summer and winter seem
Enchanted to a stone
To trouble the living stream.
The horse that comes from the road,
The rider, the birds that range
From cloud to tumbling cloud,
Minute by minute they change;
A shadow of cloud on the stream
Changes minute by minute;
A horse-hoof slides on the brim,
And a horse plashes within it;
The long-legged moor-hens dive,
And hens to moor-cocks call;
Minute by minute they live:
The stone's in the midst of all.

Too long a sacrifice
Can make a stone of the heart.
O when may it suffice?

That is Heaven's part, our part
To murmur name upon name,
As a mother names her child
When sleep at last has come
On limbs that had run wild.
What is it but nightfall?
No, no, not night but death;
Was it needless death after all?
For England may keep faith
For all that is done and said.
We know their dream; enough
To know they dreamed and are dead;
And what if excess of love
Bewildered them till they died?
I write it out in a verse –
MacDonagh and MacBride
And Connolly and Pearse
Now and in time to be,
Wherever green is worn,
Are changed, changed utterly:
A terrible beauty is born.

September 25, 1916

In Memory of Eva Gore-Booth and Con Markiewicz

The light of evening, Lissadell,
Great windows open to the south,
Two girls in silk kimonos, both
Beautiful, one a gazelle.
But a raving autumn shears
Blossom from the summer's wreath;
The older is condemned to death,
Pardoned, drags out lonely years
Conspiring among the ignorant.

I know not what the younger dreams –
Some vague Utopia – and she seems,
When withered old and skeleton-gaunt,
An image of such politics.
Many a time I think to seek
One or the other out and speak
Of that old Georgian mansion, mix
Pictures of the mind, recall
That table and the talk of youth,
Two girls in silk kimonos, both
Beautiful, one a gazelle.

Dear shadows, now you know it all,
All the folly of a fight
With a common wrong or right.
The innocent and the beautiful
Have no enemy but time;
Arise and bid me strike a match
And strike another till time catch;
Should the conflagration climb,
Run till all the sages know.
We the great gazebo built,
They convicted us of guilt;
Bid me strike a match and blow.

Beautiful Lofty Things

Beautiful lofty things; O'Leary's noble head;
My father upon the Abbey stage, before him a raging crowd.
'This Land of Saints', and then as the applause died out,
'Of plaster Saints'; his beautiful mischievous head thrown back.
Standish O'Grady supporting himself between the tables
Speaking to a drunken audience high nonsensical words;
Augusta Gregory seated at her great ormolu table
Her eightieth winter approaching; 'Yesterday he threatened my life,

I told him that nightly from six to seven I sat at this table
The blinds drawn up'; Maud Gonne at Howth station waiting a
    train,
Pallas Athena in that straight back and arrogant head:
All the Olympians; a thing never known again.

ANDREW YOUNG

(1885–1971)

A Dead Mole

Strong-shouldered mole,
That so much lived below the ground,
Dug, fought and loved, hunted and fed,
For you to raise a mound
Was as for us to make a hole;
What wonder now that being dead
Your body lies here stout and square
Buried within the blue vault of the air?

Notes

Anonymous, 'Cock Robin'
The earliest known record of 'Cock Robin' is in *Tommy Thumb's Pretty Song Book*, thought to be the first collection of English nursery rhymes, published in London in 1744, although only the first four verses are included. The extended version was printed in 1770 and went through many later printings, due to its popularity in the nineteenth century. There have been many notable illustrations of the work, including those of the American artist, H. L. Stephens, in the New York edition of 1865.

Anonymous, 'The Corpus Christi Carol'
The title suggests both the sacrament of Holy Communion (the body of Christ) and the Feast of Corpus Christi honouring the Eucharist. The words written on the stone at the end of the carol have led some readers to see the wounded knight as the crucified Christ or as the wounded Fisher King in ancient fertility myths. It is thought that the lyrics were written in a commonplace book by an apprentice grocer, Richard Hill, in the early 1500s, although the author remains anonymous.

Anonymous, 'The Three Ravens'
First printed in a songbook in 1611. All stanzas follow the pattern established in the first, with the refrain in lines 2, 4 and 7 repeated throughout, and with the first line of each stanza being repeated in lines 3 and 5. The two lines given in verses 2–9 are thereby extended to seven.

fallow doe: female fallow deer.

earthen lake: a ditch.

the prime: the first hour of daylight.

leman: lover or sweetheart.

Anonymous, 'Sir Patrick Spens'
'Sir Patrick Spens' is a Scottish ballad, probably composed in the fifteenth century. It was first published in 1765 in Thomas Percy's *Reliques of Ancient English Poetry*.

Dunferline: Dunfermline in Fife, Scotland.

skeely: skilful.

a braid letter: a broad (long) letter.

gurly: stormy.

cork-heelt shuin: cork heeled shoes.

gowd kames: gold combs.

ane dear loes: own dear loves (though some versions of the ballad give 'own dear lords').

Anonymous, 'The Wife of Usher's Well'
A traditional ballad, first collected in Sir Walter Scott's *Minstrelsy of the Scottish Border* (1802–3).

ane: one

carline: old

fashes: troubles

Martinmas: the Feast of St Martin (11 November)

mirk: murky

o' the birk: made of birch

syke: trench

sheugh: furrow

mantle: cloak

channerin': fretting

Gin: if

sair: sore

maun: must

Anonymous, from *Pearl*
Pearl was written in the later fourteenth century by an unknown author, probably living in the English midlands. The poem is a dream vision

occasioned by the death of a child, possibly the poet's daughter. There are 101 stanzas, each of 12 lines. The translation used here is that of Sir Israel Gollancz (1863–1930), published in 1891 and revised in 1921.

14 *merry mere*: a beautiful stretch of water.

Anonymous, 'Dahn the Plug'ole'
This is a traditional song of uncertain origin, though it appears to have been a popular music hall song in the 1940s. The transcription provides an approximation of a cockney accent ('biby' for 'baby', etc.).

Raymond Antrobus, 'Sound Machine'
Raymond Antrobus was born in Hackney, East London, to an English mother and a Jamaican father. He draws on this heritage in his writing, as well as addressing questions to do with masculinity, deafness and bereavement. This poem was first published in the Spring 2017 issue of *Poetry Review* (107:1). It was later included in *The Perseverance* (2018).

Manor Park Cemetery: one of the largest cemeteries in East London.

Matthew Arnold, 'Memorial Verses'
Although this poem pays tribute to Goethe and Byron, its principal subject is Wordsworth, who died on 23 April 1850. It was first published in *Fraser's Magazine* in June 1850 and then in *Empedocles in Etna* (1852).

Goethe in Weimar: Johann Wolfgang von Goethe (1749–1832) died in Weimar, Germany, where he spent part of his early life and then eventually settled (1782–1832).

Byron's struggle: Byron participated in the Greek War of Independence, dying in Missolonghi on 19 April 1824.

Orpheus: Arnold is recalling the myth of Orpheus singing in the Underworld of Hades in search of his wife, Eurydice.

Rotha: the River Rothay in the English Lake District.

W. H. Auden, 'In Memory of W. B. Yeats'
W. B. Yeats (see pp. 520–31) died in Roquebrune, southern France, on 29 January 1939. W. H. Auden had arrived in New York just three days earlier, having emigrated from England to America with Christopher Isherwood. He quickly began work on a startlingly modern elegy in which poetic tribute for another's writer's craft is combined with affectionate criticism for his human failings. The poem has a complicated compositional history, with an early version of just two sections appearing in *The*

New Republic on 8 March 1939. It was first published in book form in *Another Time* (1940).

another kind of wood: a possible allusion to Dante's 'dark wood' at the beginning of the *Inferno*.

the floor of the Bourse: the French stock exchange.

All the dogs of Europe bark: a reference to the unsettling political conditions in Europe that would culminate in the outbreak of the Second World War in September 1939.

Still persuade us to rejoice: an echo of one of Yeats's late poems, 'The Gyres' (1938): 'Out of cavern comes a voice, / And all it knows is that one word, "Rejoice!"'

Make a vineyard of the curse: Section 3 of the poem is composed in trochaic tetrameter, a meter associated with curses and chants (examples can be found in the speech of the witches in Shakespeare's *Macbeth* and in William Blake's song 'The Tyger'). Yeats had written a poem containing his own epitaph, 'Under Ben Bulben', in this meter.

William Barnes, 'The Music o' the Dead'

William Barnes was born in the Blackmore Vale, Dorset, England, and much of his work was inspired by his love of rural Dorset and his enthusiastic interest in the Dorset dialect. This poem was published in *Poems of Rural Life in the Dorset Dialect* (1844).

wold: old.

with'rèn: withering.

tuèns: tunes.

lew: place of shelter.

drough: through.

gwaïn: going.

vo'k's zongs: folks' songs.

William Barnes, 'The Wife a-Lost'

Written after the death of Barnes's wife, Julia Miles (1805–1852), this poem was published in *Hwomely Rhymes: A Second Collection of Poems in the Dorset Dialect* (1859).

het: heat.

Drough: through.

dinner-bwoard: dinner-table.

A-vield: in a field.

woone: one.

William Barnes, 'Woak Hill'
From *Poems of Rural Life in the Dorset Dialect, Third Collection* (1862).

Woak: oak.

doust: dust.

a-sheenèn: shining.

vloorèn: flooring.

jaÿ: joy.

To hor vor: in anxious care for.

Zoo: so.

house-riddèn: moving house.

wi lippèns: with movements of the lips.

vo'k: folk.

Paul Batchelor, 'Pit Ponies'
Paul Batchelor was born in Northumberland, and his work draws on the history and culture of North East England, including its mining traditions. 'Pit Ponies' was first published in *Poetry Review*, Summer 2012 (102:2), and included in *The Love Darg* (2014).

Hilaire Belloc, 'Matilda'
'Matilda' was one of eleven tales included in *Cautionary Tales: Designed for the Admonition of Children between the ages of eight and fourteen years* (1907). Like the others, it was composed as a parody of the cautionary moralizing tales that were common in the nineteenth century. The book was illustrated by Basil Temple Blackwood and was hugely popular. Several tales, including 'Matilda', have been set to music or recorded as vocal performances since 1907.

The Second Mrs Tanqueray: a play by Arthur Wing Pinero (1855–1934), first performed in 1893.

Gwendolyn Bennett, 'Epitaph'

Gwendolyn Bennett was an American artist, poet and journalist, who worked to support the aims of the Harlem Renaissance and the advancement of African-American culture and cultural institutions. She was assistant editor of *Opportunity: A Journal of Negro Life*, in which this poem appeared in March 1934.

John Berryman, Dream Song 155

Dream Song 155 is one of a series of poems for the American poet and short storywriter, Delmore Schwartz (1913–1966). It was published in *His Toy, His Dream, His Rest* (1968) and then in *The Dream Songs* (1969).

Bellevue: America's oldest public hospital, specialising in the 1960s in the treatment of mental health disorders.

Providence: the capital city of the US state of Rhode Island, about 50 miles from Cambridge, Massachusetts.

The King James Bible

The texts of Samuel 2 and Ecclesiastes 3 are from the King James Bible, also known as the King James Version or the Authorised Version of the Bible. It was commissioned in 1604 and published in 1611 under the auspices of King James I of England.

Laurence Binyon, 'For the Fallen'

Written shortly after the outbreak of the First World War, this poem was printed in *The Times* on 21 September 1914. It was also published in *The Winnowing Fan: Poems of the Great War* (1914). Binyon himself was considered too old for active service in the war, though he joined the Volunteer Civil Force and worked as a nursing orderly in the Red Cross Hospital in France in 1915.

Bion, 'Lament for Adonis'

Bion was an Ancient Greek poet from Phlossa, near Smyrna, thought to have been active as a writer at the beginning of the first century BCE. He spent time in Sicily and is closely associated with the bucolic or pastoral poetry of Theocritus (see pp. 456–63). The text given here is from the translation of his work by Anthony Holden in *Greek Pastoral Poetry* (Penguin 1974).

Adonis: a Greek youth famed for his beauty and loved by Aphrodite. He was killed by a boar while out hunting and was thought thereafter to spend half of each year on earth with Aphrodite and half beneath it with Persephone. He was the son of Cinyras and his daughter, Myrrha.

Cypris: another name for Aphrodite, referring to her temple in Cyprus.

Aphrodite: the goddess of beauty and mother of Love.

Cytherea: also a name for Aphrodite, because of her association with the isle of Cythera.

Acheron's shore: the banks of the River Acheron, in Greek mythology often depicted as the entrance to the underworld and thus as the river of death.

Persephone: the daughter of Zeus and Demeter. She was abducted by Hades as she played in the fields in Sicily and taken to the underworld to be his wife.

Hymen: the son of Dionysus and Aphrodite. He was known as the god of marriage.

Cinyras: King of Cyprus, son of Paphos. He was tricked into sleeping with his daughter Myrrha, who gave birth to Adonis.

Elizabeth Bishop, 'North Haven'
This elegy for Robert Lowell (see pp. 281–2) first appeared in the *New Yorker* in December 1978 and was later included in Elizabeth Bishop's *Complete Poems 1929–1979*. The two poets had spent time, together and separately, at North Haven, an island off the coast of Maine, New England.

carded horse's tail: i.e., one backcombed to add volume.

William Blake, 'Nurse's Song' (*Songs of Innocence*) and 'Nurse's Song' (*Songs of Experience*)
William Blake wrote his Songs of Innocence in 1789, but published them together with the later Songs of Experience in 1794, hoping to show 'the Two Contrary States of the Human Soul'. The two poems printed here were included in *Songs of Innocence and of Experience* (1794).

William Blake, 'The Chimney Sweeper' (*Songs of Innocence*) and The Chimney Sweeper (*Songs of Experience*)
From *Songs of Innocence and of Experience* (1794).

Malika Booker, 'Death of an Overseer'
Melika Booker is a British poet with Guyanese and Grenadian roots, some of whose work explores the legacy of slavery in the Caribbean. This poem was published in *Pepper Seed* (2013).

jumbie: spirit or demon

Elizabeth Boyd, 'On the Death of an Infant of Five Days Old'
Elizabeth Boyd was an English writer who wrote fiction as well as poetry, and who experimented with several genres, including satire, romance and political commentary. This poem was included in *The Humorous Miscellany* (1733).

Anne Bradstreet, 'In Memory of My Dear Grandchild, Elizabeth Bradstreet'
Written in 1665, this poem was originally titled 'In memory of my dear grand-child Elizabeth Bradstreet, who deceased August, 1665, being a year and half old'. Elizabeth was the daughter of the poet's son, Samuel.

Kamau Brathwaite, 'Elegy for Rosita'
Kamau Brathwaite was a Barbadian poet and critic, with a strong interest in West African cultural traditions. He worked in Ghana (formerly the Gold Coast) between 1955 and 1962. This poem was published in *Elegguas* (2010), the title of which combines *elegy* and *Eleggua* (the Yoruba deity of thresholds and crossroads).

Robert Bridges, 'On a Dead Child'
From *The Shorter Poems of Robert Bridges* (1890). Bridges was an assistant physician at the Great Ormond Street Hospital for Children in London and the poem possibly derives from his experience there.

Charlotte Brontë, 'On the Death of Emily Jane Brontë'
Emily Brontë died at Haworth, West Yorkshire, on 19 December 1848. This poem was written soon after and the manuscript was dated 24 December 1848. It was first published in the Victorian journal *The Woman at Home* in December 1896.

Emily Brontë, 'Remembrance'
This poem was written in 1845 and included in a volume of poems by the three Brontë sisters, Charlotte, Emily and Anne, under the title *Poems by Currer, Ellis, and Acton Bell* (1846).

Rupert Brooke, 'The Soldier'
'The Soldier' was written as part of a sequence of five sonnets about the First World War, titled '1914'. It was first published in the fourth issue of the *New Numbers* quarterly journal (associated with the Dymock Poets in Gloucestershire) in December 1914, and reprinted in *1914 and Other Poems* in 1915.

Jericho Brown, 'The Tradition'
This is the title poem of *The Tradition* (2019). The book draws on a long tradition of pastoral and garden imagery in its response to the political urgencies of modern America.

John Crawford. Eric Garner. Mike Brown: Black men killed by police in the USA in 2014.

William Browne, 'On the Countess Dowager of Pembroke'
This poem is an epitaph for Mary Herbert, Countess of Pembroke (1561–1621), the sister of Sir Philip Sidney and mother of William Herbert, 3rd Earl of Pembroke. She was well known for her poetry and her literary patronage. The poem was included in the manuscript of the third book of Browne's *Britannia's Pastorals*, probably in the 1620s, although the book was not published until 1852.

Elizabeth Barrett Browning, 'Felicia Hemans'
Felicia Hemans died on 16 May 1835. First published in *The Seraphim and Other Poems* (1838) under the title 'Stanzas on the Death of Mrs Hemans', Elizabeth Barrett Browning's poem is addressed to Letitia Landon, who had written an elegy for Felicia Hemans (see pp. 267–70).

Elizabeth Barrett Browning, 'L. E. L.'s Last Question'
First published in *Poems* (1844). Letitia Landon died on 15 October 1838 in Cape Coast, Ghana.

Elizabeth Barrett Browning, 'Mother and Poet'
First published in *Last Poems* (1862). The figure of the mother who is also a poet is based on Olimpia Savio (1815–1889), a Turin poet and patriot, whose sons Alfredo and Emilio died at Gaeta and Ancona in the Risorgimento (the nineteenth-century movement for Italian unification). The Siege of Gaeta took place on 22 January 1861.

Basil Bunting, from *Briggflatts*
Published in 1966, *Briggflatts* takes its inspiration from a small Quaker hamlet (spelled Brigflatts) near Sedbergh in Cumbria, North West

England. Bunting described the poem both as an autobiography and as a hymn to death.

Brag, sweet tenor bull: the opening line calls on the bull, in the way that Classical poems summon the Muse, to sing its part in the music of the local river, the Rawthey.

descant: used here in the verbal sense, to sing or improvise a counter-melody above the established song (of the river).

madrigal: secular vocal music.

black against may: the black of the bull is contrasted with the pink and white flowers of the may or hawthorn tree.

the slowworm's way: the slowworm (sometimes called a deaf adder, though actually a legless lizard rather than a snake) is a symbol of death, along with the mason's mallet used to chisel the name on a gravestone.

felloe: the exterior rim of a cart wheel.

Garsdale: a dale in the south-east of Cumbria, also part of the Yorkshire Dales National Park.

Hawes: a small market town in the Yorkshire Dales.

Baltic plainsong speech: the vernacular idiom of the Viking settlers in the north of England; plainsong here implies chanting, as with the plainsong tradition associated with the liturgies of the Western Church.

Bloodaxe: Eric Bloodaxe, ruler of the Viking kingdom of Northumberland, killed in Stainmore in 954.

becks: agricultural tools (mattocks) used for breaking up soil.

peewit: northern lapwing, so called because of its piercing cry.

pricked rag mat: a rough mat made by sewing strips of cloth to sacking.

Orkney: the archipelago off the north-east coast of Scotland.

Robert Burns, 'Epitaph for James Smith'
James Smith (1765–1823) was a draper in Mauchline, East Ayrshire, Scotland, and a friend of Burns. This poem was written in 1785 and published in the Kilmarnock edition of *Poems, Chiefly in the Scottish Dialect* (1786).

Robert Burns, 'Lament for James, Earl of Glencairn'
James Cunningham, Burns's friend and patron, died on 30 January 1791. This poem was written in 1791 and published in the Edinburgh edition of *Poems, Chiefly in the Scottish Dialect* (1793).

Lugar: a river in East Ayrshire, Scotland.

meikle: much.

George Gordon, Lord Byron, 'Stanzas for Music'
This poem was first published in the *Examiner* (June 1815) and later included in *Hebrew Melodies* (1824), a collection of poems composed by Byron for musical settings by Isaac Nathan.

George Gordon, Lord Byron, 'Remember thee! Remember thee!'
This poem is thought to have been written in 1813, in the aftermath of a relationship with Lady Caroline Lamb. It was printed without the italicised words in Thomas Medwin's *Journal of the Conversations of Lord Byron* in 1824.

George Gordon, Lord Byron, 'On This Day I Complete My Thirty-Sixth Year'
Byron wrote these lines in his Cephalonia Journal just a few months before his death. They are thought to allude to his friendship with Loukas Chalandritsanos, who was with him in Greece during his support for the war of independence from Turkey.

The Spartan, borne upon his shield: in Ancient Greece, slain Spartan warriors were carried home on their shields.

George Gordon, Lord Byron, 'Elegy on Thyrza'
Written after the death of John Edleston, whom Byron had met at Trinity College, Cambridge, in 1805. Edleston died of consumption in 1811 and the poem was published in the second edition of *Childe Harold's Pilgrimage* the following year.

Christian Campbell, 'Rudical (Derek Bennett, killed by the police)'
Derek Bennett was a twenty-nine-year-old man, shot and killed by police in Brixton, South London on 16 July 2001. He was allegedly holding another man hostage and was thought to be in possession of a handgun (that was, in fact, a novelty lighter). This poem for Bennett was published in *Running the Dusk* (2010).

Windrush: the Empire Windrush was the ship that brought one of the first groups of Caribbean immigrants to London in the post-war period, arriving 22 June 1948.

New Cross . . . Brixton: all places in England.

Nassau . . . Kingston: all places in the Caribbean.

this England: subversion of John of Gaunt's patriotic speech in *Richard II* (2.1.40).

Thomas Campion, 'O Come Quickly!'
From *Two Bookes of Ayres* (1613). Campion was a prolific writer of lyrics to be accompanied by lute. The compositions in his *Two Bookes of Ayres* were explicitly written to be sung to the lute and viols. The first book contains 'divine and moral songs' (including this one) and the second contains 'light conceits of lovers'.

Thomas Carew, An Elegy upon the Death of the Dean of Paul's, Dr John Donne
John Donne died on 31 March 1631. This elegy was first published together with Donne's *Poems* (1633), and then in Carew's own *Poems* (1640).

Delphic choir: the voices of Ancient Greek song, inspired by the oracle of Apollo at Delphi.

Promethean breath: derived from Prometheus, who stole fire from the gods to give to humanity.

Anacreon's ecstasy: Anacreon, the Greek lyric poet, is famed for his songs of love and wine.

Pindar: the Ancient Greek lyric poet from Thebes.

Orpheus: a musician, poet and prophet in Greek mythology.

Metamorphoses: the Latin narrative poem by the Roman poet Ovid.

flamens: priests serving particular deities in Ancient Rome.

Apollo's first, at last the true God's priest: Donne is acknowledged as both poet (serving Apollo) and priest (in the Church of England).

Thomas Carew, 'Epitaph for Maria Wentworth'
Maria Wentworth died in 1632 at the age of eighteen. This poem was inscribed on her tomb in the Church of St George in Toddington in Bedfordshire in 1633. It was later published in Carew's *Poems* (1640).

Ciaran Carson, 'In Memory'
Carson's poem is an elegy for Seamus Heaney, who died in 2013. Alluded to is Heaney's early poem 'Personal Helicon' (*Death of a Naturalist*, 1966), which recalls the childhood act of staring into a well. This poem was published in Carson's 2014 volume, *From Elsewhere*.

Elizabeth Carter, 'On the Death of Mrs Rowe'

This is an elegy for the poet and prose writer Elizabeth Rowe (née Singer), who died in Frome, Somerset, on 20 February 1737. The poem was included in Rowe's posthumously published *Miscellaneous Works* (1739) along with other tributes.

Catullus, 'Elegy on the Sparrow'

This is one of two poems about a sparrow (*passer* in Latin) in the group of poems Catullus wrote for a woman called Lesbia, of uncertain identity. The version here was translated by Charles Abraham Elton (1778–1853) and included in his *Specimens of the Greek and Roman Classic Poets*, Volume 2 (1860).

Catullus, Two versions of Catullus 101

Catullus 101, also known as Carmen 101 (from *Carmina* or 'Songs'), is an elegy in which the poet addresses his dead brother, having travelled miles to attend his funeral rites. It has been translated many times. The closing words, *ave atque vale* (hail and farewell) are among the most famous in the works of Catullus.

The first version is a translation by Aubrey Beardsley, first published in *The Savoy* magazine in November 1896. The second version is by Anne Carson, from *Nox* (2010).

Charles Causley, 'Eden Rock'

Many of Causley's poems are set in Cornwall, where he grew up. However, Eden Rock is a fictitious placename, probably chosen for its biblical associations.

H. P. sauce: a popular British spiced brown sauce named after the Houses of Parliament in London.

C. P. Cavafy, 'For Ammonis, Who Died Aged 29 in 610'

Cavafy was born in Alexandria, Egypt, where his Greek parents had settled in the 1850s. The tension between his Greek ancestry and his adopted Egyptian culture is evident in this poem, which was written in 1916–18 and published in *Poiēmata* (Poems) in 1935.

Jane Cave, 'An Elegy on a Maiden Name'

Jane Cave was born in South Wales and returned there at the end of her life, having travelled around England with a husband who worked for the excise. She published her work under the name 'Mrs Rueful'. This poem is from *Poems on Various Subjects, Entertaining, Religious, and Elegiac* (1789).

Paul Celan, 'Deathfugue'

Celan's 'Deathfugue' ('Todesfuge' in German) was written in 1945. It appeared in a Romanian translation by Petre Solomon in the magazine *Contemporanul* in May 1947, under the title 'Tangoul Mortii' ('Tango of Death'). It was first published in book form in Celan's *Der Sand aus den Urnen* (*The Sand from the Urns*) in 1948, and then in a corrected version in *Mohn und Gedächtnis* (1952). Celan based the poem on accounts of concentration camp survivors returning to Romania in 1944–45. The poem's form, involving the repetition of a principal theme and a counterpoint, is based on the model of the baroque fugue. The translation here is by John Felstiner, from *Selected Poems and Prose of Paul Celan* (2001).

der Tod ist ein Meister aus Deutschland: Death is a master from Germany.

Amy Clampitt, 'A Procession at Candlemas'

An elegy for Amy Clampitt's mother, 'A Procession at Candlemas' was published in her fourth collection of poems, *The Kingfisher*, in 1983. The poem's extended meditation on birth and death draws on the images and rituals associated with Candlemas (2 February) and the Feast of the Purification of the Blessed Virgin Mary, as well as on Classical myths associated with Venus.

Route 80: a major east–west transcontinental highway from San Francisco to New Jersey.

transhumance: the seasonal movement of livestock from one grazing site to another, usually to lowlands in winter and highlands in summer.

Mosaic insult: a reference to the Law of Moses given by God to the Israelites through Moses, according to the Old Testament.

Arlington: Arlington National Cemetery in Virginia, USA. It houses the Tomb of the Unknown Soldier, a memorial for deceased US service members whose remains have not been identified.

the Potomac: the Potomac River, which flows through West Virginia, Maryland, Virginia, and Washington D.C.

gumball globes: chewing gum contained in a small plastic globe.

Life Savers: a popular American brand of ring-shaped sweets or candy.

Pennsylvania Avenue: a diagonal street in Washington D.C.

coracle: a small, rounded, one-person boat still popular in Wales and Ireland, though dating back to pre-Roman times.

Brauron, Argos, Samos: all places associated with Ancient Greek culture.

Athene: the patron of Athens and the virgin goddess of art and wisdom, as well as war.

peplos: a body-length garment worn by women in Ancient Greece.

Mississippi: the second-longest river in the United States, running through ten states.

John Clare, 'The Lament of Swordy Well'
Swordy Well was an area of open moorland close to Clare's home in Helpston, Northamptonshire. Under the Acts of Enclosure between 1750 and 1860, it ceased to be an area of common land for local people and was turned into a quarry. The poem is spoken in the imagined voice of Swordy Well and protests against the loss of common ownership.

The manuscript of the poem is dated 1832–7. It was not published in Clare's lifetime. The final volume of the Oxford edition of Clare's poetry provides a comprehensive record of the manuscript variants. See *John Clare: Poems of the Middle Period 1822–1837* (2003), pp. 105–14.

John Clare, 'I Am'
Written between 1844 and 1846 and first published in the *Bedford Times* in January 1848. It was printed in *The Life of John Clare* by Frederick Martin in 1865, and included in *Poems Chiefly from Manuscript by John Clare* (1893).

Lucille Clifton, 'the lost baby poem'
Lucille Clifton grew up in Buffalo, New York, and spent the later years of her life in Baltimore. Much of her work is concerned with women's history, especially the lives of African American women. This poem was first published in *Good News About the Earth: New Poems* (1972).

genesee hill: in Seattle, Washington, United States.

Samuel Taylor Coleridge, 'Epitaph'
This epitaph was written shortly before the poet's death and printed as the final poem in his *Poetical Works* of 1834.

Tony Connor, 'Elegy for Alfred Hubbard'
Tony Connor was born in Manchester, England, and draws on the local culture of the city in his work. This poem was included in Connor's first collection of poetry, *With Love Somehow* (1962). It was reprinted in *Things Unsaid: New and Selected Poems 1960–2005*.

ginnels: narrow passages between buildings.

Cheetham Hill: residential area of Manchester.

Abraham Cowley, 'On the Death of Mr William Hervey'
From *Poems Written by A. Cowley* (1656). William Hervey (1619–1642) was Cowley's close friend and fellow student at the University of Cambridge.

Ledaean stars: Gemini: the constellation also known as the Heavenly Twins and, in Greek mythology, taken to represent Castor and Pollux, the sons of Leda.

William Cowper, 'Epitaph on a Hare'
This poem was written in March 1783 and published in *The Gentleman's Magazine* in December 1784. It was later included in Cowper's *Poems* (1800).

jack-hare: the term 'jack rabbit' was sometimes used to distinguish a hare from a rabbit.

pippins' russet peel: the reddish peel of apples.

Puss: not a cat but the name of one of Cowper's three hares (Tiney, Puss and Bess).

William Cowper, 'The Poplar Field'
This poem was written in 1784 and published in *The Gentleman's Magazine* in January 1785. It was later included in Cowper's *Poems* (1800).

Ouse: the River Great Ouse (one of several British rivers named 'Ouse'), which flows through Norfolk.

Hart Crane, 'At Melville's Tomb'
This poem was published in Hart Crane's first volume of poems, *White Buildings*, in 1926. The tomb of the American poet and novelist Herman Melville (1819–1891) is in Woodlawn Cemetery, Bronx, New York.

The dice of drowned men's bones: small, broken pieces of bone (the image carries the usual associations of dice with chance and circumstance).

The calyx of death's bounty: calyx may mean the sepals, the outermost protective part of a flower, or any other similarly cuplike cavity or structure; the image ironically suggests both generative fecundity and the vortex created by a sinking ship.

Compass, quadrant and sextant: instruments of navigation for determining direction, angles and altitudes.

Monody: an elegiac song by a single voice. Milton uses the term to describe the form of 'Lycidas' (see pp. 302–7).

Richard Crashaw, 'A Hymn to the Name and Honour of the Admirable Saint Teresa'
Crashaw was deeply devoted to the Spanish mystic, St Teresa of Avila (1515–1582), who was canonised in 1622. The poem was first published in *Steps to the Temple: Sacred Poems, with Other Delights of the Muses* (1646).

Richard Crashaw, 'An Epitaph upon Husband and Wife'
From *Steps to the Temple: Sacred Poems, with Other Delights of the Muses* (1646).

Countee Cullen, 'Colored Blues Singer'
The work of Countee Cullen is closely associated with the intellectual and cultural movement known as the Harlem Renaissance in New York in the 1920s. He was active in promoting the work of African American writers and other artist through magazines such as *Opportunity*, of which he was the assistant editor. This poem was published in *Copper Sun* (1927).

keenings: cries or lamentations associated with death.

kraal: Dutch and Afrikaans word used in South Africa to describe an enclosure for livestock.

Jeritza: Maria Jeritza (1887–1982), Czech soprano singer. She gave notable performances in three of Verdi's operas: *Il Trovatore*, *Otello* and *Aida*.

Countee Cullen, 'Threnody for a Brown Girl'
This poem was first published in *Poetry: A Magazine of Verse* in May 1925 and included in *Copper Sun* (1927).

Threnody: a lament (from the Greek, 'to sing a dirge').

Solomon: biblical Israelite king renowned for his wisdom.

Walter de la Mare, 'Fare Well'
From *The Sunken Garden and Other Poems* (1917).

Traveller's Joy: a climbing plant (*Clematis vitalba*), also known as Old Man's Beard.

Toi Derricote, 'Elegy for My Husband'
The poem was written soon after the death of Bruce Derricote (1928–2011), to whom it is dedicated. It was published in *New and Selected Poems* (2019).

Emily Dickinson, 'Because I could not stop for Death'
American poet Emily Dickinson wrote extensively about death and the afterlife. Only ten of her almost 1,800 poems were published in her lifetime; this one was written in 1862 and published in *Poems of Emily Dickinson* in 1890.

Gossamer: very fine fabric.

Tippet: a shawl.

Tulle: silk netting.

Cornice: the decorative moulding that crowns some buildings.

Emily Dickinson, 'Safe in their Alabaster Chambers'
This is the revised version of 'Safe in their alabaster chambers' that Emily Dickinson sent in a letter to Thomas W. Higginson in 1862. It was published in *Poems of Emily Dickinson* in 1890.

Alabaster: a compact, fine-textured stone, usually white, and often used for carving sculptures.

Diadems: crowns.

Doges: elected dukes and highest officials in the Venetian Republic from the eighth to the eighteenth century.

Emily Dickinson, 'I felt a Funeral, in my Brain'
This poem was written in 1861–2 and published in *Poems of Emily Dickinson, Third Series* in 1896.

Maura Dooley, 'I've Been Thinking a Lot About Heaven'
Maura Dooley is a London-based writer of Irish descent. This elegy for her father was first published in *Five Fifty-Five* (2023).

blue-remembered: an echo of 'blue-remembered hills' in *A Shropshire Lad* (Poem XL) by A. E. Housman.

John Donne, 'A Funeral Elegy'
This poem was first published in *The Anniversaries* (1611), in which Donne meditates on the death in December 1610 of Elizabeth Drury, the

only surviving child of a wealthy landowning family. She was fourteen years old. It seems likely that the poem was commissioned by her father, Sir Robert Drury.

chrysolite: a green gemstone.

the two Indies: the West Indies (known for their gold) and the East Indies (known for their spices and scents).

Escurials: the Escorial, near Madrid, one of the most extensive and impressive religious establishments in the world, was built by Philip II between 1563 and 1584.

tabernacle: the ornamental locked box that holds the Blessed Sacrament – the sacramental bread and wine used in Holy Communion – in Christian services. Here the word is used metaphorically to suggest that the body is a temporary dwelling place for the soul and God.

divines: theologians.

spirits: i.e., those spirits that harmonise civil society ('This organ').

the Afric Niger: the opinion at the time was that the Niger flowed eastwards into the Nile, partly above ground and partly beneath ground.

An Angel made a Throne, or Cherubin: angels were considered to be the lowest of the nine celestial orders, with thrones and cherubins (cherubim) occupying a higher position.

We lose by't: i.e., because angels have care of human affairs, while thrones and cherubim serve God.

tasteless: with the senses dulled.

thin: as fine as glass or porcelain.

a through-light scarf: a fine scarf (through which the light can be seen).

enrol: register or record.

emulate: here, compete with each other.

when heaven looks on us with new eyes: when new stars appear.

artist: astronomer.

a lamp of balsamum: burning balsam, an aromatic mixture of oils and resins.

as served for opium: i.e., as much as would suffice to dull pain and to induce sleep.

ecstasy: the state in which the soul leaves the body and has a revelation of final truth.

play her: act her role.

Lord Alfred Douglas, 'The Dead Poet'
This elegiac sonnet was written for Oscar Wilde shortly after his death on 30 November 1900. It was published in *The Collected Poems of Lord Alfred Douglas* in 1919.

Keith Douglas, 'Simplify Me When I'm Dead'
Keith Douglas is best remembered for poems describing his experiences as a tank commander in North Africa during World War Two. This poem was probably written in May 1941. It was included in the 1943 volume by John Hall, Keith Douglas and Norman Nicholson, *Selected Poems*.

Keith Douglas, 'Vergissmeinnicht'
Probably written in Tunisia in May–June 1943, this poem was among the work included in *Selected Poems* (1943) by John Hall, Keith Douglas and Norman Nicholson.

Vergissmeinnicht: German for forget-me-not.

John Dryden, 'Upon the Death of the Lord Hastings'
Lord Hastings, the nineteen-year-old heir, and only surviving son, of the impoverished Earl of Huntingdon and his Countess, Lucy. Hastings died of smallpox on the evening before his wedding to Elizabeth Mayerne (daughter of the distinguished physician who attended to him in the weeks before his death on 24 June 1649). This, Dryden's earliest surviving poem, was included in *Lachrymae Musarum: Tears of the Muses*, a collection of elegies for Hastings, published in 1649.

Great Alexander: Alexander the Great, also known as Alexander III (356–323 BCE). King of Macedonia, he overthrew the Persian empire and created one of the greatest empires in history, stretching from Greece to India.

Archimedes' sphere: one of the most important mathematical discoveries was Archimedes' determination of the volume of a sphere.

Ptolemy: Claudius Ptolemy (*c.* 85–165 CE), born in Alexandria. One of the most influential astronomers and geographers of his time, his theories of the solar system remained dominant until the fifteenth century.

Tycho: Tycho Brahe (1546–1601), the Danish astronomer who conducted an extensive and influential exploration of the solar system thought to be the most precise before the invention of the telescope.

Ganymede: a satellite of Jupiter and the largest of the solar system's moons.

Pandora's box: in Hesiod's *Works and Days* (*c.* 700 BCE), Pandora had a jar containing evil, which, once opened, inflicted misery on the world. It became a box in sixteenth-century literary accounts of the Greek myth.

naeves: spots or blemishes.

Venus soil: a rough or pockmarked surface.

Seneca, Cato, Numa, Caesar: all notable statesmen of Ancient Rome.

metempsychosis: in Greek philososphy, the transmigration and reincarnation of the soul after death.

John Dryden, 'To the Memory of Mr Oldham'
First published in *The Remains of Mr John Oldham, 1684*. John Oldham (1653–1683) was a poet, satirist and schoolmaster.

Nisus: at the funeral of Anchises in Book 5 of Virgil's *Aeneid*, two friends, Nisus and Euryalus, take part in a race. Nisus slips but manages to trip the runner behind him, allowing Euryalus to win.

numbers: i.e., meter, versification.

Marcellus: the nephew of the emperor Augustus. His early death is recorded in the *Aeneid*, Book 6.

Paul Laurence Dunbar, 'A Death Song'
Dunbar was born in Ohio to parents who had been enslaved in Kentucky before the American Civil War. He became one of the most influential Black poets in American literature, well known for his handling of vernacular rhythms and expressions. This poem was published in *Lyrics of the Hearthside* (1899).

William Dunbar, 'Lament for the Makaris'
William Dunbar was a Scottish makar, or court poet, closely associated with the court of King James IV. 'Lament for the Makaris' (makers, poets), one of the earliest printed Scottish texts, was published in Edinburgh in 1508.

heill: health.

seikness: sickness.

Timor Mortis conturbat me: 'The fear of death dismays me' (from the liturgy for the Office of the Burial of the Dead in the Common Book of Prayer).

brukle: frail.

sle: sly.

blith: happy.

sary: sorry.

Now dansand mery, now like to dee: now dance and be merry, now likely to die.

erd: earth.

sickir: securely.

As with the wynd wavis the wikir: as the wind waves the willow.

all Estatis: those who rule, those who pray, and those who labour.

knychtis: knights.

anarmit: armed.

mellie: battles.

on the moderis breist sowkand: sucking on the mother's breast.

benignite: gentleness.

tour: tower.

bour: bower.

piscense: power.

clerk: scholar.

strak: stroke.

Rethoris: rhetoricians.

Leichis: doctors.

laif: remainder.

syne: then.

Sparit: spared.

Nocht: not.

Petuosly: piteously.

Chaucer: Geoffrey Chaucer (c. 1342–1400).

of makaris flour: the flower of poets.

The monk of Berry: John Lydgate of Berry (1370–1451), English monk and poet.

Gower: John Gower (c.1330–1408), English poet.

Syr Hew of Eglintoun . . . Walter Kennedy: a list of Scots poets.

supple: deliver.

eik: also.

infeck: infected.

Allace: alas.

le: lee or meadow.

Anteris: adventures.

schour: shower.

Quhilk: which.

He has reft Merseir his endite: Death has taken away from Mercer his style of writing.

hie: lively.

done roune: made a circuit.

Of quham all wichtis has pete: of whom all creatures have pity.

In poynt of dede lyis veraly: lies truly on the point of death.

suld: should.

On forse I-an his nyxt pray be: Of necessity, I must be his next prey.

dispone: prepare.

Douglas Dunn, 'The Kaleidoscope'
From *Elegies* (1985), this poem was written for Lesley Balfour Dunn, artist and curator, who died in 1981.

Lady Katherine Dyer, 'My dearest dust could not thy hasty day . . .'
This epitaph appears on the monument erected in 1641 by Lady Katherine Dyer to her husband Sir William Dyer in Colmworth Church, Bedfordshire. Katherine (sometimes printed Catherine) Doyley Dyer was born in Merton, Oxfordshire, and was one of the four daughters of John Doyley and Anne Barnard. She married Sir William Dyer in 1602.

T. S. Eliot, from *The Waste Land* ('Death by Water')
The Waste Land was first published in the UK in *The Criterion* (October 1922), then in the United States in *The Dial* (November 1922), then in book form in December 1922. 'Death by Water' is the fourth of the five sections in *The Waste Land*.

Phlebas the Phoenician: Eliot gives the name Phlebas to the figure of the drowned Phoenician sailor who appears on a tarot card in the opening section of *The Waste Land* ('The Burial of the Dead').

Ralph Waldo Emerson, from 'Threnody'
Emerson's 'Threnody' (lamentation) was written after the death by scarlet fever of his first child, Waldo, aged five, in January 1842. The poem was published in his *Poems* (1846).

Vicki Feaver, 'Gorilla'
Vicki Feaver was born in Nottingham, England, and spent much of her working life in Chichester. She has lived in Scotland since 2000. This poem is from *The Book of Blood* (2006).

Mendel: Gregor Mendel (1822–1884), who formulated the principles of inheritance governing the transmission of genetic traits.

Caleb Femi, 'The Story of Damilola Taylor'
Damilola Taylor was a ten-year-old boy who was stabbed to death near his home in the North Peckham Estate shortly after moving to London from Nigeria. This poem was published in Caleb Femi's collection *Poor* (2020).

James Fenton, 'At the Kerb'
Published in *Yellow Tulips: Poems 1968–2011* (2012), this poem is an elegy for poet and editor Mick Imlah (see pp. 238–242).

Sarah Louise Forten, 'At the Grave of the Slave'
This poem was published in the abolitionist magazine *The Liberator*, in January 1831.

Robert Frost, 'Nothing Gold Can Stay'
First published in the *Yale Review* in October 1923 and included in *New Hampshire* (1923).

Robert Garioch, 'Elegy'
Robert Garioch grew up in Edinburgh and studied English at Edinburgh University. He wrote almost exclusively in the Scots language. This elegy is from his *Selected Poems* (1966).

mowdert: mouldering.

agley: awry.

wycelike: sensible.

bienlie: pleasant.

taiglie: tangled.

weill-harnit: clever.

blate and fey: shy and fated.

new cleckit dominie: newly-hatched teacher.

kyte: paunch.

sneerit: sneered.

sniftert: scoffed.

gin: given that.

arena deid: aren't dead.

John Gay, 'My Own Epitaph'
John Gay is perhaps best remembered for *The Beggar's Opera* (1728). This epitaph was probably written in 1720. It was inscribed on Gay's monument in Westminster Abbey after his death in 1732.

Allen Ginsberg, from *Kaddish*
Ginsberg began writing this elegy for his mother Naomi in Paris in 1957 and completed it in New York in 1959. It was published in *Kaddish and Other Poems 1958–1960* (1961). The title refers to 'The Mourner's Kaddish', chanted as part of mourning rituals in Judaism. The closing section (5) is printed here.

Oliver Goldsmith, 'Retaliation'
Retaliation; a poem was published in 1774, just a few months after Goldsmith's death.

Lorna Goodison, 'For My Mother (May I Inherit Half Her Strength)'
Lorna Goodison is a Jamaican poet, essayist and memoirist. This poem was written for Doris Louise (Harvey) Goodison and appeared in *Tamarind Season* (1980).

Kingston and Harvey River, Hanover are in Jamaica.

Barnabe Googe, 'An Epytaphe of the Death of Nicolas Grimoald'
Nicholas Grimoald, variously spelled as Grimald, Grimalde and Grimaold (1519–1562), was one of the poets who contributed to the 1557 *Songs and Sonettes* anthology known as *Tottel's Miscellany*. As chaplain to Bishop Ridley, executed for his religious beliefs, he came under suspicion and was briefly imprisoned in 1555. This poem appeared in *Eclogs, Epytaphs, and Sonettes* (1563) under the title, 'Of Nicholas Grimaold'.

Minerva: the Roman goddess of arts and crafts, also associated with justice, wisdom, law and victory.

W. S. Graham, 'Lines on Roger Hilton's Watch'
This poem was written after the death of the artist Roger Hilton on 23 February 1975. It was included in Graham's *Collected Poems 1942–1977* (1979).

Botallack: the village in Cornwall, England, where Roger Hilton lived from 1965 onwards.

St Just: St Just in Penwith, where Hilton is buried, close to St Ives.

Teachers: Teacher's Blended Scotch Whisky.

Robert Graves, 'The Untidy Man'
Robert Graves was an English writer best known for his First World War memoir, *Good-bye to All That* (1929) and his study of poetic inspiration and myth-making, *The White Goddess* (1948). This poem appeared in *Less Familiar Nursery Rhymes* (1927).

Thomas Gray, 'On the Death of Richard West'
Sometimes printed as 'Sonnet [On the Death of Richard West]', this poem was composed in 1742 after the death of Gray's friend and fellow poet (1716–1742) and included in *The Poems of Mr Gray* (1775).

Thomas Gray, 'Elegy Written in a Country Churchyard'
This elegy, one of the best known in English, is thought to have been composed between 1742 and 1750. It was first printed in pamphlet form in 1751 and was originally titled 'Stanzas Wrote in a Country Church-Yard'. It was included in *Poems by Mr. T. Gray* (1756).

The curfew: the evening bell.

rude forefathers: rustic predecessors.

the echoing horn: a hunting horn.

glebe: land belonging to the clergy.

The boast of heraldry: the display of nobility through armorial bearings.

If Memory o'er their tomb no trophies raise: no memorial to record military or other heroic achievements.

the long-drawn aisle and fretted vault: respectively, the long passage between a church's seats or pews, and the carved arch of its high ceiling.

storied urn: a funeral urn telling a story in the form of an epitaph.

animated bust: a lifelike representation (of head and shoulders) in the form of a statue.

provoke the silent dust: call forth the dead.

Some village Hampden: John Hampden (1594–1643), English Parliamentary leader famous for his opposition to Charles I over ship money – a tax for the upkeep of the navy, and one of the grievances that led to the English Civil War. Hampden was killed in the Civil War.

Far from the madding crowd: well away from a crowd either maddening or acting madly.

some hoary-headed swain: a country worker or servant (swain is possibly derived from the Old English *swān* for swineherd) with white or greyish hair. Gray is recalling the 'uncouth swain' at the close of John Milton's 'Lycidas' (see pp. 302–7).

Fair Science: science in the older sense of learning, rather than the more specialised pursuit of knowledge via the experimental verification or falsification of hypotheses associated with modern science.

Thomas Gray, 'Ode on the Death of a Favourite Cat Drowned in a Tub of Goldfishes'
Composed in 1747 and included in *Poems by Mr. T. Gray* (1756).

Tyrian hue: reddish-purple; associated with Tyre, modern Lebanon, the purple dye is secreted by sea snails and was highly valued in ancient times, leading to its association with wealth and power.

Nereid: a sea nymph in Greek mythology.

Thom Gunn, 'Lament'
'Lament' was first published in the *London Review of Books*, with a dedication to Gunn's friend Alan Noseworthy, on 4 October 1984. It then appeared as a pamphlet poem illustrated by Bill Schuessler and published by Doe Press (Champaign, Illinois) in 1985. It was included in Gunn's book of poems written after the outbreak of the AIDS pandemic, *The Man with Night Sweats* (1992).

Ivor Gurney, 'To His Love'
Ivor Gurney was an English poet and composer of songs. He enlisted as a soldier in the First World War in February 1915 and started writing poetry seriously around that time. Although wounded in April 1917, he survived the war and carried on writing until the 1930s. This poem is from *War's Embers* (1919).

Cotswold: the Cotswolds rural area of south-west England, including parts of Gurney's Gloucestershire.

Severn river: the longest river in Great Britain. It flows through Gloucestershire.

Ivor Gurney, 'Song'
From *Severn and Somme* (1917).

Ivor Gurney, 'Cotswold Ways'
Written between 1920 and 1922. Included in *Collected Poems* (1982).

Birdlip: Birdlip, Portway and Crickley are all places in rural Gloucestershire.

goes: the word functions like a noun in the final line, suggesting 'ways'.

Ivor Gurney, 'Strange Hells'
Written between 1920 and 1922, and included in *Collected Poems* (1982).

'*Après la guerre fini*': 'After the War Is Over' (title of a popular soldiers' song).

Thomas Hardy, 'Drummer Hodge'
First published in the journal *Literature* on 23 November 1899 under the title of 'The Dead Drummer', this poem was prompted by the outbreak of the Second Boer War in South Africa (October 1899–May 1902). It was included (with the revised title) among Hardy's 'War Poems' in his *Poems of the Past and the Present* (1901).

kopje: a small hill.

veldt: open grassland.

Karoo: barren plateau.

Thomas Hardy, 'Thoughts of Phena'
This poem was written for Tryphena Sparks, Hardy's cousin, after her death in 1890. It was published in *Wessex Poems* (1898).

an aureate nimb: a gold cloud.

Thomas Hardy, 'A Singer Asleep'
Hardy's elegy for Algernon Charles Swinburne (1837–1909) was written after a visit he made with Florence Dugdale (Hardy's assistant and later his second wife) to the poet's grave at Bonchurch, Isle of Wight, in March 1910. It was published in *Satires of Circumstance: Lyrics and Reveries* (1914).

ness: a headland.

fulth: fullness, abundance.

freaked: elaborately decorated, as with flowers freaked with white.

His leaves of rhythm and rhyme: Swinburne's controversial volume, *Poems and Ballads,* published in 1866.

Glassing: reflecting.

Lesbian: Sappho, a Greek poet thought to have been born on the island of Lesbos. Lesbian later became a description of female homosexuality, as 'Sapphic' had earlier been. Swinburne celebrated unconventional sexual relationships in his poetry.

Leucadian steep: According to Greek legend, Sappho killed herself by leaping from the Leucadian cliffs in her hopeless love for the ferryman, Phaon.

orts: fragments, i.e., of Sappho's poems.

incarnadine: red, implying passion.

capes and chines: headlands and ridges (both common features of the Isle of Wight landscape).

Thomas Hardy, 'The Going'
This was the opening poem in Hardy's 'Poems of 1912–13', written after the death of his wife, Emma (Gifford), on 27 November 1912. The poems were published in *Satires of Circumstance: Lyrics and Reveries* (1914).

Beetling: overhanging.

Beeny Crest: Beeny Cliff in North Cornwall, England.

Thomas Hardy, 'The Voice'
From 'Poems of 1912–13', published in *Satires of Circumstance: Lyrics and Reveries* (1914).

Thomas Hardy, 'At Castle Boterel'
From 'Poems of 1912–13', published in *Satires of Circumstance: Lyrics and Reveries* (1914).

my sand is sinking: i.e., as in an hourglass.

Thomas Hardy, 'After a Journey'
From 'Poems of 1912–13', published in *Satires of Circumstance: Lyrics and Reveries* (1914).

Thomas Hardy, 'During Wind and Rain'
From *Moments of Vision* (1917).

Thomas Hardy, 'Lying Awake'
From *Winter Words in Various Moods and Metres* (1928).

Tony Harrison, 'Book Ends'
This poem is included among Harrison's elegies for his mother and father in the book titled *From the School of Eloquence* (1978).

Terrance Hayes, 'American Sonnet for My Past and Future Assassin'
This poem is from Terrance Hayes's *American Sonnets for My Past and Future Assassin* (2018), a collection of poems written after the American elections of 2016 in response to the growing fears generated by violence and racism.

James Baldwin: American writer and civil rights activist (1924–1987), renowned for *Notes of a Native Son* (1955) and other titles.

Seamus Heaney, 'The Strand at Lough Beg'
Seamus Heaney received the Nobel Prize in Literature in 1995. This poem was one of a number of elegies prompted by the political violence in Northern Ireland and published in Heaney's *Field Work* in 1979. Its subject is the death of the poet's second cousin, Colum McCartney, murdered by Loyalist paramilitaries in 1975. Heaney returns to the killing and his own memorialising of the event in *Station Island* (1984). Lough Beg is a small freshwater lake near Bellaghy, Co. Derry.

Newtonhamilton: a small town in County Armagh.

Sweeney: the legendary King Sweeney, subject of the medieval Irish romance, *Buile Suibhne*, which tells of how he was cursed and maddened in the Battle of Magh Rath (637 CE), turned into a bird, and made to live in exile in the trees of Ireland. Heaney was enchanted by the story and produced his own version under the title of *Sweeney Astray* in 1983.

scullions: domestic workers assigned to menial work in the kitchen.

To wash you, cousin: Heaney recalls how Virgil cleans the face of Dante with morning dew in Canto 1 of the *Purgatorio*.

Green scapulars: the vestments of a priest. Green, used in 'ordinary time' (outside the two great seasons of Christmas and Easter in the liturgy of the Catholic Church), signifies life, hope and anticipation. There is also an allusion here to 'The Wearing of the Green', an Irish nationalist song from the 1790s, as in W. B. Yeats's 'Easter 1916': 'Now and in time to be, / Wherever green is worn'.

Felicia Hemans, 'The Grave of a Poetess'
Felicia Hemans was born in Liverpool, England, but grew up in Wales. She spent her later years in Dublin. This poem is an elegy for the Irish poet Mary Tighe (1772–1810), buried in Inistioge, Co. Kilkenny. It was published in *Records of Woman: With Other Poems*, Second Edition, 1828.

Edward, Lord Herbert of Cherbury, 'Elegy Over a Tomb'
Edward Herbert, 1st Baron Herbert, was an English soldier, diplomat, historian and philosopher, as well as a writer associated with the metaphysical poets. He was the brother of the poet George Herbert. This elegy was written in 1617 and published in *Occasional Verses of Edward Lord Herbert* (1665).

George Herbert, 'Virtue'
George Herbert was an English poet, and also a priest in the Church of England. With John Donne, he is often considered to be one of the leading exponents of metaphysical poetry, as well as a devotional writer who influenced later poets such as Gerard Manley Hopkins. This poem appeared in *The Temple* (1633).

Mary Sidney Herbert, Countess of Pembroke, 'If Ever Hapless Woman Had a Cause'
The attribution of the poem to Mary Sidney Herbert is uncertain. It appears as a song in John Bartlett's *Booke of Ayres* (1606). However, the biographical link is strong. The Countess of Pembroke had lost her brother, Sir Philip Sidney, at the Battle of Zutphen in 1586.

Robert Herrick, 'Upon Himself'

Herrick was a seventeenth-century lyric poet and Anglican cleric, as well as one of the writers identified as a Cavalier poet (loyal to Charles I). This short poem is from *Hesperides: or, The Works Both Humane and Divine of Robert Herrick, Esq.* (1648).

Geoffrey Hill, 'September Song'

This poem was published in Hill's second volume of poetry, *King Log* (1968). The birthdate of the deported child is one day later than Hill's own birthday, 18 June 1932.

Zyklon: hydrocyanic acid, used in fumigation. Zyklon-B was used in the gas chambers of Nazi concentration camps.

Michael Hofmann, 'For Gert Hofmann, Died 1 July 1993'

From *Approximately Nowhere* (1999). Gert Hofmann, German writer and lecturer, was the poet's father.

Thomas Hood, 'I Remember, I Remember'

Thomas Hood was an English poet, journalist and humorist, as well as editor of several Victorian magazines. He wrote poems of social protest, such as 'Song of the Shirt', in addition to comic verse. This poem appeared in *The Plea of the Midsummer Fairies* (1827).

Gerard Manley Hopkins, 'Binsey Poplars'

This poem was written in 1879 after the felling of poplar trees in Binsey, on the banks of the River Thames near Oxford. It was published in *Poems of Gerard Manley Hopkins* (1918).

Gerard Manley Hopkins, 'Spring and Fall'

This poem was written in 1880 and published in *Poems of Gerard Manley Hopkins* (1918).

Gerard Manley Hopkins, 'Felix Randal'

Hopkins wrote this poem in 1880 to commemorate the death of Felix Spencer, a Liverpool farrier who died from pulmonary tuberculosis. Spencer died on 21 April 1880 and Hopkins dated the finished poem 28 April 1880. It was published in *Poems of Gerard Manley Hopkins* (1918).

Horace, *Odes* 3.30

Horace was a lyric poet at the time of Augustus (also known as Octavian). His first three books of *Odes* were written about 23 BCE, and the fourth book about 11 BCE.

A. E. Housman, 'To an Athlete Dying Young'
Housman was one of the leading scholars of Classical literature in his time, a Professor of Latin at University College London and then at the University of Cambridge, and an editor of Latin verse. Inspired by his love of Classical poetry, he composed *A Shropshire Lad*, a sequence of poems in which dying young is a prevalent theme. 'To an Athlete Dying Young' is poem 19 in *A Shropshire Lad*, published in 1896.

A. E. Housman, 'Is my team ploughing'
This poem is number 27 in *A Shropshire Lad* (1896).

A. E. Housman, 'Far in a western brookland'
This poem is number 52 in *A Shropshire Lad* (1896).

A. E. Housman, 'Epitaph on an Army of Mercenaries'
This poem is thought to have been written in 1914 after the First Battle of Ypres. It was published in *Last Poems* (1922).

A. E. Housman, 'Crossing alone the nighted ferry'
This poem was published in *More Poems* (1936).

With the one coin for fee: the coin paid to Charon, the ferryman, to cross the rivers of the underworld.

Henry Howard, Earl of Surrey, 'An Excellent Epitaph of Sir Thomas Wyatt'
Thomas Wyatt was an English ambassador, politician and lyric poet. He died at the beginning of October 1542. Along with Surrey, he is credited with having helped to establish the sonnet form in English poetry. This epitaph, the only poem published by Surrey in his lifetime, was printed as a separate work, *An excellent Epitaffe of syr Thomas Wyat. Imprynted for Robert Toye*, in 1542. Spelling in the version printed here has been modernised.

stith: also styth, an anvil.

unperfited: uncompleted.

Henry Howard, Earl of Surrey, 'Norfolk sprung thee, Lambeth holds thee dead'
This sonnet was written in memory of Thomas Clere, who died on 14 April 1545 after serving with Surrey at the siege of Montreuil in France the previous year. It was first published in *Remaines of a Greater Work concerning Britaine* by William Camden (1605).

Norfolk ... Lambeth: Clere was born at Ormesby in Norfolk and was buried in St Mary's Church, Lambeth, in London.

hight: named or called.

Ormondes: Clere was descended on his mother's side from Thomas Butler, Earl of Ormonde.

thy cosin: Anne Boleyn, who was crowned Queen on 1 June 1533.

Shelton: Mary Shelton, cousin to Surrey and engaged to Clere.

chase: chose.

Kelsall: the Scottish town of Kelsal was razed by the Duke of Norfolk's troops in October 1542.

Laundersey: Landrecy in France was set on fire by bombardment during the siege of October 1543, though not captured.

Bullen render: Boulogne in France surrendered to Henry VIII in September 1544.

At Muttrell gates: at the siege of Montreuil, France.

four times seaven: Clere was in his twenty-eighth year when he died.

if love had booted: if love had helped.

Langston Hughes, 'Silhouette'
'Silhouette' was published with 'Lynching Song' and 'Flight' under the title 'Three Songs about Lynching' in *Opportunity: A Journal of Negro Life* (June 1936). It was also included in *Seven Poets in Search of an Answer* (1944).

Ted Hughes, 'Sheep'
Ted Hughes's 'Sheep' is one of a number of poems that emerged from a journal that he kept between 1972 and 1976 at his Moortown Farm in Devon. The poems began life as journal notes set down soon after the event described, and took shape as improvised verses. They first appeared in a limited edition titled *Moortown Elegies* (1978) and were then included in *Moortown* (1979), later reissued as *Moortown Diary* (1989).

Leigh Hunt, 'On the Death of his Son Vincent'
The poet's youngest son, Vincent Leigh Hunt, died of tuberculosis in 1852. This poem appeared in *Poetical Works of Leigh Hunt* (1860).

Mick Imlah, 'Stephen Boyd (1957-95)'

Stephen Boyd died in 1995 at the age of 38. This poem was published in *The Lost Leader* (2008).

Saltire: St Andrew's cross (or the *crux decussata*), depicted on Scotland's national flag.

Magdalen MCR : Magdalen College, Oxford, Middle Common Room.

the Kirk: the Church of Scotland.

The Robe: Biblical epic film (1953).

Andy Irvine: Scottish international rugby player. The other surnames given in the poem (Deans, Rutherford *et al.*) are those of famous Scottish rugby players.

Giotto's Crucifixion: painting of the crucifixion (*c.* 1315) attributed to Giotto.

Balliol: Balliol College, Oxford.

Braveheart: historical film (1995) based on the life of the Scottish rebel, William Wallace.

Glasgow Kiss: a headbutt splitting open the victim's face.

Patras: the Greek city.

Crail: a fishing village in East Fife, Scotland.

Spey salmon: salmon from the River Spey in Scotland.

Major Jackson, 'Ferguson'

Published in the *Boston Review* in March 2016 and included in *Razzle Dazzle: New and Selected Poems* (2023). The title refers to the town in Missouri where a police officer shot dead an unarmed Black teenager, Michael Brown, on 9 August 2014.

Linton Kwesi Johnson, 'Reggae fi Dada'

'Reggae fi Dada' was written after Linton Kwesi Johnson's return to Jamaica to bury his father in August Town, Kingston, in 1982. It was included on his studio album of dub poems *Making History* in 1984, along with other spoken word performances with musical accompaniment. The poem is written in Jamaican patois (drawing on the varieties spoken in both Jamaica and England), and it blends the formal poetic expression of grief with the rhythms of reggae music, combining the imagery of natural decay with protests against the social and economic deprivation suffered by his father in Jamaica.

galang dada: the valedictory 'go along / so long' to his father is repeated towards the end of the poem.

galang gwaan yaw sah: go along, go on, you hear.

a deh soh mi bawn: ever since I was born.

ganja plane flyin high: a reference to the the illegal transport of marijuana.

Samuel Johnson, 'An Epitaph on Claudy Phillips, a Musician'
Charles Claudius Phillips was a Welsh violinist who, after successfully touring Europe, eventually died in poverty in 1732. This poem was first published in *The Gentleman's Magazine* in September 1740.

Samuel Johnson, 'On the Death of Dr Robert Levet'
Robert Levet (1705–1782) was a member of Johnson's household for many years. Although not formally educated, he studied medicine and set up a practice for the poor in London. He died unexpectedly of a heart attack in January 1782. This poem was first published in *The Gentleman's Magazine* in August 1783.

Ebenezer Jones, 'The Poet's Death'
Ebenezer Jones was a London poet of Welsh descent, with radical political sympathies. Although he had little success as a poet, he was befriended by Robert Browning and Dante Gabriel Rossetti. This poem was published in *Studies of Sensation and Event* (1843).

Ben Jonson, 'Epitaphs'
Jonson's daughter Mary died in 1593, aged six months, and his son Benjamin died in 1603 at the age of seven. Both poems were published in Jonson's *Epigrams* (1616).

Ben Jonson, 'To the Memory of My Beloved, the Author Mr William Shakespeare'
This poem was published in *Mr William Shakespeares Comedies, Histories & Tragedies* (The First Folio) in 1623.

Jackie Kay, 'Burying My African Father'
Jackie Kay was born in Edinburgh to a Scottish mother and a Nigerian father. She has written about the experience of adoption and the search

for her biological parents in *Red Dust Road* (2010) and elsewhere. This poem is from *Fiere* (2011).

Nzagha: small town in Gambon, Central Africa.

Odimma: (odi nma) Igbo for 'all right', 'good'.

Kedu: (kedu ka I mere) Igbo for 'how are you?'

Abuja: administrative capital of Nigeria.

John Keats, 'When I Have Fears That I May Cease to Be'
Keats wrote this self-elegy, adopting the Shakespearean sonnet form, in January 1818. It was published in *Life, Letters, and Literary Remains of John Keats* by Richard Monckton Milnes in 1848.

Henry King, 'Exequy on His Wife'
Henry King was an English poet, who was also Bishop of Chichester. 'The Exequy', as the poem is sometimes titled, was written in memory of his wife, Anne Berkeley, who died in 1624 at the age of twenty-four. The poem was published in *Poems, elegies, paradoxes, and sonnets* (1657).

Rudyard Kipling, 'The Appeal'
The appeal that Kipling makes in this poem is to rest in peace after death, though it has often been interpreted more specifically as an instruction not to be contacted by clairvoyants, and for critical attention to be given to his books rather than his life. It was first published in a copyright edition of his work (designed to protect copyright in the United States) titled *Doctors, The Waster, The Flight, Cain and Abel, The Appeal* (1939). It was collected in *Definitive Verse* (1940).

Yusef Komunyakaa, 'Elegy for Theolonious'
The elegy is for Thelonious Monk (1917–82), American jazz pianist and composer. It was published in *Copacetic* (1984).

Lenox Avenue: in Manhattan, New York.

Crepuscule with Nellie: music by Thelonious Monk for his wife, Nellie. Crepuscule is twilight.

Man Ray: American avant-garde artist (1890–1976).

Coming on the Hudson and *Monk's Dream*: jazz compositions by Monk.

Minton's: Minton's Playhouse, a jazz club in Harlem, New York.

modern malice: Louis Armstrong notoriously described bebop jazz as 'that modern malice'.

Charles Lamb, 'The Old Familiar Faces'

Charles Lamb was an English essayist, best known for his *Essays of Elia* (1823) and for *Tales from Shakespeare* (1803), which he wrote with his sister, Mary. This poem was published in *Blank Verse* (1798), which Lamb wrote in collaboration with Charles Lloyd.

Letitia Elizabeth Landon, 'Stanzas on the Death of Mrs Hemans'

Letitia Elizabeth Landon, also known by her initials L. E. L., was an English poet and novelist whose writings were popular and influential. Christina Rossetti and Elizabeth Barrett Browning both acknowledged her importance as a poetic predecessor. She was moved to write about her contemporary, Felicia Hemans (see pp. 211–12), who died on 16 May 1835. This poem was first published in the *New Monthly Magazine* (Volume 44) in July 1835 and reprinted in *The Poetical Works of Letitia Elizabeth Landon* (1873).

Letitia Elizabeth Landon, 'Felicia Hemans'

This elegy for Felicia Hemans was published in *Drawing-Room Scrap Book* in 1838 and included in *The Poetical Works of Miss Landon* (1839).

Castilian: Landon is here acknowledging how Hemans drew on the music of Spanish and Italian verse in her poetry.

Susquehanna: Landon's work was highly popular in America. Susquehanna was where Samuel Taylor Coleridge and Robert Southey had planned to establish their utopian community or 'Pantisocracy'.

Prometheus: in Greek mythology, one of the Titans who stole fire from Zeus to give to mortals. As punishment, he was bound to a rock and an eagle was sent to eat his liver, which renewed itself each day.

Walter Savage Landor, 'Rose Aylmer'

Rose Aylmer, whom Landor had known briefly in Wales in the late 1790s, died in India on 2 March 1800 at the age of twenty. This poem was published in *Simonidea* (1806).

Philip Larkin, 'The Explosion'

The explosion in question occurred at Trimdon Colliery, Durham, on 15 February 1882, killing seventy-four men and boys. Larkin's poem was inspired by a ballad, 'The Trimdon Grange Explosion' (performed by Thomas Armstrong), which he heard on a record: *The Collier's Rant: Mining Songs of the Northumberland–Durham Coalfield*. The poem was written in January 1970 and published in *High Windows* (1974).

Francis Ledwidge, 'Thomas MacDonagh'

Francis Ledwidge was an Irish poet who fought in the First World War in support of the Allied cause. He was killed in action at Ypres on 31 July 1917. This poem was written in 1916 after the execution of Thomas MacDonagh (3 May 1916) for his part in the Easter Rising of that year, and published in *Songs of Peace* (1917).

the bittern: a bird belonging to the heron family. There is an allusion here to Thomas MacDonagh's poem, 'The Yellow Bittern'.

Dark Cow: a personification of Ireland, sometimes given as 'dun cow', with which MacDonagh was familiar through his study of Irish poetry.

Amy Levy, 'Epitaph'

Amy Levy was an English poet, essayist and novelist, whose work attracted the interest of Oscar Wilde, Virginia Woolf and others. She was the first Jewish student to attend Newnham College, Cambridge. This poem is from *A Minor Poet and Other Verse* (1884).

Henry Wadsworth Longfellow, 'The Cross of Snow'

Longfellow gave the date of composition as 10 July 1879, eighteen years to the day since the death of his wife, Frances Appleton, after a fire in the family home in Cambridge, Massachusetts. The poem was published in *The Complete Poetical Works of Henry Wadsworth Longfellow* (1893).

Michael Longley, 'Wounds'

This poem is at once an elegy for the poet's father, who had fought in the First World War, and a poem of mourning for the casualties of political violence in Northern Ireland in the early 1970s. It was written in May 1972 and published in *An Exploded View* (1973).

Robert Lowell, 'Sailing Home from Rapallo'

Robert Lowell's mother, Charlotte, died in Rapallo in February 1954, and this elegy for her was included in *Life Studies* (1959). It was a review of *Life Studies* by M. L. Rosenthal that gave widespread currency to the term 'confessional poetry' in modern American culture.

her Risorgimento black and gold casket: the Risorgimento was the nineteenth-century movement in support of Italian unification, but Lowell associates it here with a baroque style (the line originally read 'In a baroque black and gold casket'). There is a grim pun in the line; Risorgimento translates as 'rising again'.

the Invalides: originally a home for retired soldiers in Paris, and later a museum of military history, housing the tomb of Napoleon.

Dunbarton: a town in New Hampshire, where members of the Lowell family (including Robert Lowell) are buried.

Occasionem cognosce: recognise your opportunity.

Lucretius, from *On the Nature of Things*

Titus Lucretius Carius was a Roman philosopher and poet, best known for his six volume Latin poem, *De rerum natura* (*On the Nature of Things*), which was composed around 54 BCE. The work explores the philosophical teachings of the Greek philosopher Epicurus (*c.* 341–270 BCE). The text given here is a section from Book 3, translated by the English poet John Dryden, and titled by him 'The latter part of the third book. Against the fear of Death'. It was first published in his *Sylvae* (1685).

When Punic arms: i.e., during the three wars between Rome and Carthage (264–146 BCE).

offals: carrion or waste.

brimmers: goblets.

the god that never thinks: Bacchus.

Tantalus: in Greek mythology, Tantalus stole ambrosia and nectar, the food of the Gods, to give to mortals.

Tityus: the giant who assaulted Leto (wife of Zeus and mother of Apollo) and was punished by vultures tearing at his liver.

Sisyphus: in Greek mythology, Sisyphus was punished by Hades for having twice cheated death. His punishment was to roll a stone uphill perpetually.

smokes: rushes.

fifty foolish virgins: the Danaides, daughters of Danaus. At their father's command, they killed their husbands on their wedding night, and were punished by having to carry water forever in leaking vessels.

the dog: Cerberus, guardian of the underworld.

the Tarpeian rock: the rock in Rome from which traitors and murderers were thrown.

Ancus: Ancus Marcius, regarded as the fourth king of Rome.

That haughty king: Xerxes, who bridged the Hellespont.

Democritus: the Ancient Greek philosopher (360–470 BCE), known for his development of the atomic theory of the universe.

Louis MacNeice, 'The Suicide'

MacNeice was closely associated with W. H. Auden and Stephen Spender, especially in the 1930s, sharing with them (as in this poem) strong powers of social observation and a sharply ironic perspective. This poem was written in 1961, in MacNeice's final year of employment with the BBC, and published in *The Burning Perch* (1963).

Derek Mahon, 'A Disused Shed in Co. Wexford'

Mahon's poem is dedicated to J. G. Farrell, the author of *Troubles* (1970), which records the final days of an Anglo-Irish hotel burned down in the summer of 1919 during the Anglo-Irish war. Although it is set in Co. Wexford in the south-east of Ireland, the poem has a wide-ranging geographical and historical vision. It was first published in *The Listener* in September 1973 and included in *The Snow Party* (1975).

Andrew Marvell, from 'A Poem upon the Death of His Late Highness the Lord Protector'

This poem is a long funeral elegy for Oliver Cromwell, who died on 3 September 1658. In all, it runs to 324 lines, of which ll. 247–76 are printed here. It was prepared for publication in Marvell's *Miscellaneous Poems* (1681) but then cancelled. It was later included in *The Works of Andrew Marvell* (1776).

feign: imagine.

honoured wreaths: oak garlands awarded for statesmanship.

Paula Meehan, 'Child Burial'

Paula Meehan is an Irish poet and playwright. She was appointed as Ireland Professor of Poetry from 2013 to 2016. 'Child Burial' was published in *The Man Who Was Marked by Winter* (1991). A slightly revised version, printed here, was included in *As If By Magic: Selected Poems* (2020).

Herman Melville, 'Monody'

Written in 1891, the final year of Melville's life, possibly for his estranged friend and fellow-writer, Nathaniel Hawthorne. Published in *Collected Poems of Herman Melville* (1947).

crape: a mourning band commonly worn at funerals in the nineteenth century.

Charlotte Mew, 'The Farmer's Bride'

Charlotte Mew was a British poet and short story writer who began her career publishing work in the *Yellow Book* and other magazines. 'The

Farmer's Bride' continues to be one of her best-known works. It was published in *The Nation* in 1912 and included in *The Farmer's Bride* (1916).

Edna St Vincent Millay, 'Burial'
Edna St Vincent Millay was an American poet and playwright, perhaps best known as a prolific writer of sonnets. This poem was published in *Second April* (1921).

John Milton, 'Lycidas'
Milton's elegy was written for Edward King, a young scholar, poet and clergyman who was a contemporary of his at Cambridge, and who was lost at sea when his ship sank on the way from Chester to Ireland in August 1637. It was first published in 1638 with a group of elegies by King's friends at Cambridge and was then included in Milton's *Poems* of 1645.

bier: the frame on which a coffin is placed before burial.

sweep the string: begin to play music.

sultry horn: the sound of an insect in the heat of day.

Battening our flocks: feeding (and fattening) sheep.

the star that rose at evening bright: Hesperus, the evening star.

Damoetas: like 'Lycidas' a shepherd name from Classical literature.

where Deva spreads her wizard stream: the geography here suggests North Wales, overlooking the Irish Sea where Edward King drowned. Mona is the Isle of Anglesey. Deva is the River Dee, known as a 'wizard stream' because its changes of course were thought to be prophetic of the country's fortunes.

Down the swift Hebrus to the Lesbian shore: the legendary Greek poet and musician, Orpheus, was said to have been torn apart by angry women; his severed head then floated downstream to Lesbos.

Amaryllis: a familiar name for a woman in Classical pastoral literature, as with Neaera in the line that follows.

guerdon: reward.

the blind Fury: Atropos, one of the three Classical goddesses known as the Fates, and the cutter of the thread of life.

Phoebus: also known as Apollo, Phoebus was the god of light and inspiration. There is an allusion here to Virgil's *Eclogues*, in which the poet's ears are tapped or tugged as an admonishment for excessive ambition.

the glistering foil: the setting for a gem.

Arethuse: a fountain in Sicily, mentioned in the pastoral poems of Theocritus.

Mincius: a river in Italy, mentioned in the pastoral poems of Virgil.

my oat: the pipe or flute of the poet/musician, traditionally made from the dried stalk of the oat.

the herald of the sea: presumably Triton, pleading that Neptune is innocent of Lycidas's death.

Hippotades: Aeolus, god of the winds in Greek mythology. The name means 'son of Hippotes'.

Panope: one of the Nereids, the daughters of Nereus (the Old Man of the Sea).

Camus: the god of the River Cam, representing Cambridge.

that sanguine flower inscribed with woe: the hyacinth, recalling the accidental killing of Hyacinthus by Apollo while throwing the discus.

The pilot of the Galilean lake: St Peter.

scrannel: thin and meagre.

that two-handed engine at the door: various interpretations exist: the two-handed sword of the archangel Michael, the two houses of Parliament, the forces of death and damnation.

Alpheus: the river god who fell in love with the nymph Arethusa.

the dread voice: presumably the voice is that of 'The pilot of the Galilean lake' (St Peter), though it has also been associated in readings of the poem with Moses and Christ.

the swart star: Sirius, the Dog Star, whose name means 'glowing'.

Hebrides: here, the geography associated with the death of Edward King extends as far as the islands to the west of Scotland.

Bellerus: adapted by Milton from Bellerium, the old Latin name for Land's End.

Namancos and Bayona's hold: the geography here extends from St Michael's Mount on the south-west tip of England to Namancos (Nemancos) and Bayona (Baiona) in Galicia, north-west Spain.

Look homeward angel now: the instruction to the archangel Michael anticipates the resurrection of Lycidas (Edward King).

And, O ye dolphins, waft the hapless youth: in Greek mythology, the body of the drowned boy Palaemon is carried to shore by a dolphin, but there are numerous references in both Christian and Classical art to dolphins transporting the souls of the dead.

the day-star: the sun.

the genius of the shore: i.e., the spirit of the place, acting in a protective way.

his Doric lay: a song or poem derived from the Greek of pastoral writers. Doric refers specifically to one of the four major ethnic groups in Classical Greece but came to be used more generally of the Ancient Greek people.

John Milton, 'When I consider how my light is spent'
This poem was written around 1652, when Milton became completely blind. It was published in *Poems* (1673).

that one talent: in the parable of the talents in St Matthew's Gospel (25. 14–30), a servant who buried the single talent (a measure of wealth) his lord had given to him (rather than investing it) is deprived of all he had and cast into darkness at the lord's return.

Doth God exact day-labour: in the parable of the vineyard (Matthew 20. 1–14), each labourer receives equal pay, regardless of the work completed. In St John's Gospel (9.4), Jesus gives sight to a blind man, saying, 'I must work the works of him that sent me, while it is day: the night cometh, when no man can work.'

John Milton, 'Methought I saw my late espousèd saint'
This poem was written around 1658 and published in *Poems* (1673).

my late espousèd saint: probably Milton's second wife, Katherine Woodcock, to whom he had been married less than two years when she died in 1658.

Alcestis: in *Alcestis* by Euripides, the heroine of the play is brought back from the dead to her husband, Admetus, by Hercules ('Jove's great son').

Purification in the Old Law: Hebrew law (Leviticus 12) prescribed certain sacrificial rituals for the purification of women after childbirth.

Marianne Moore, 'W. S. Landor'
Marianne Moore was an American modernist poet and critic, and also editor of the influential modernist magazine *The Dial* from 1925 to 1929.

Walter Savage Landor, the subject of this poem, was an influential English poet and essayist (see p.273). The poem was first published in *The New Yorker*, 14 February 1964, and included in *The Complete Poems of Marianne Moore* (1967).

Moschus, 'Lament for Bion'

Moscus was born in Syracuse, but little is known of his life, except that he was working around 150 BCE, some time after Theocritus and before Bion, the other Greek pastoral poets with whom he is associated. The translation provided here is by Anthony Holden, in *Greek Pastoral Poetry* (Penguin 1974).

Dorian: belonging to an area of Greece bounded by Phocis, Thessaly and Acarnania.

Arethusa: a fountain in Syracuse, the source of pastoral poetry, but originally a nymph magically changed into water.

Strymon: a river separating Thrace from Macedonia and flowing into the Aegean.

Oeagrian maidens: daughters of Oeagrus, King of Thrace.

Bistonian: Thracian.

Hades: the underworld, land of the dead; also the name of the god who ruled it.

Lethe: a river of the underworld, the waters of which induced forgetfulness of life.

Apollo: god of all the arts, son of Zeus.

Priapus: god of fertility, son of Aphrodite.

Pan: god of shepherds, flocks, and the countryside.

Echo: a nymph loved by Zeus. She was cursed by the goddess Hera, wife of Zeus, so that she could speak only the last words spoken to her.

Siren's song: the sirens lured passing sailors to their death by singing to them.

Ceyx: King of Trachis who drowned and turned into a bird (the halcyon).

Memnon: son of Tithonus and Aurora (Dawn). He was killed by Achilles and his ashes were turned into birds by Zeus.

Galatea: a sea nymph, daughter of Nereus and Doris.

Cyclops: a race of one-eyed giants who lived in Sicily.

Cypris: a name for Aphrodite, associated with her temple in Cyprus.

Meles: a river in Ionia near Smyrna. It was reputed to be the birthplace of both Homer and Bion.

Calliope: the Muse of poetry.

Pegasus' spring: Pegasus was the winged horse ridden by Bellerophon. The spring is the fountain of Hippocrene on the slopes of Mount Helicon, which he uncovered by striking his hoof.

Tyndareus' lovely daughter: Helen of Troy.

Thetis' great son: Achilles.

Atreus' Menelaus: Atreus was the father of Menelaus and Agamemnon.

Ascra: Boeotian town where the poet Hesiod was born.

Boeotia: a district of central Greece.

Pindar: lyric poet of Thebes (518–435 BCE).

Lesbos: a large island in the eastern Aegean.

Alcaeus: poet of Mitylene in Lesbos.

Teos: a coastal town of Ionia, birthplace of the poet Anacreon.

Paros: an island in the south Aegean, birthplace of the poet Archilochus.

Mitylene: the capital city of Lesbos and the birthplace of Sappho and Alcaeus.

Ausonia: southern Italy, but used as a name for all of Italy. Auson was the son of Odysseus.

Tartarus: a region of Hades.

Odysseus: King of Ithaca, and one of the Greek heroes at the siege of Troy. Homer relates his descent to the underworld in Book 9 of *The Odyssey*.

Alcides: Heracles, the son of Zeus.

Persephone: daughter of Zeus and Demeter, abducted by Hades as she was playing in the fields and taken back to the underworld to be his wife.

Etna: Mount Etna on the east coast of Sicily.

Eurydice: wife of Orpheus, the musician, who won her back from Hades by the beauty of his playing but lost her again by breaking his promise not to look back as they left the underworld.

Andrew Motion, 'Serenade'

'Serenade' is one of several elegies that Motion has written for his mother, who was hospitalised following a riding accident in 1969, and died in 1978. The poem, originally written in quatrains, was first published in *Public Property* (2002), then revised into its present form in *Coming in to Land* (2017).

Paul Muldoon, 'Incantata'

Paul Muldoon's elegy for the American artist and printmaker Mary Farl Powers (1948–1992) was published in an illustrated edition by the Graphic Studio in Dublin in 1994. It was included in *The Annals of Chile* (1994).

Incantata: enchanted or spellbound, but carrying suggestions of incantation.

a leanbh: Irish for my child, but used more generally as a term of endearment.

Francisco de Herrera: the Spanish painter, Francisco de Herrera the Younger (1576–1656), who painted *Still Life with Fish*.

X-Actoed: i.e., carved with a precision cutting knife of the kind sold under the American X-Acto brand.

Inca glyph: i.e., a graphic symbol based on Inca designs.

spotted torso: the title of a print by Marl Farl Powers, who produced numerous torso images.

Lugh: the Celtic god of sun and light.

St Cloud: St Cloud, Minnesota, where Mary Farl Powers was born.

Déjeuner sur l'herbe: the title of an Impressionist painting by Edouard Manet, completed in 1863.

Krapp: a reference to Samuel Beckett's play, *Krapp's Last Tape* (1958).

viduity: the state of being a widow; widowhood.

Landseer Street: in Belfast.

Thomism: the philosophical and theological legacy of Thomas Aquinas.

Summa Theologiae: the best-known work of Thomas Aquinas, published in 1485.

La Nausée: *Nausea*, the 1938 philosophical novel by Jean-Paul Sartre.

Sam Bethicket: wordplay on the name of Samuel Beckett.

Baggott Street: in Dublin.

shirt of Nessus: in Greek mythology, the shirt of Nessus was the poisoned shirt that killed Heracles.

D'éirigh me ar maidin: words of a popular Irish song ('I got up this morning . . .').

a tharraingt chun aoinigh mhóir: '. . . to be drawn to a great feast'.

gamine: (of a woman) elegantly boyish, often slender with short hair and a mischievous charm.

Ding an sich: In the philosophy of Immanuel Kant, a thing as it is in itself.

Vladimir and Estragon: characters in Samuel Beckett's *Waiting for Godot* (1952).

geantraí and suantraí: in Celtic mythology, two strains of harp music, one encouraging laugher and the other one sleep.

Burt Lancaster as Elmer Gantry: Burt Lancaster played the main role in the 1960 film of the novel by Sinclair Lewis.

Nagg and Nell: characters in Samuel Beckett's play, *Endgame* (1957).

eminent domain: a phrase made popular by the publication of Richard Ellmann's influential book, *Eminent Domain: Yeats Among Wilde, Pound, Joyce, Eliot and Auden* (1967).

Thane of Calder: the title given to Shakespeare's Macbeth before he becomes king is 'Thane of Cawdor'. There is a playful allusion to John Calder (1927–2018), opponent of censorship and publisher of Samuel Beckett, William Burroughs and others.

fourth estate: the press and news media in their capacity to influence public affairs. France, before the Revolution, divided society into three estates: clergy, nobility and commoners.

retiarius: Roman gladiator.

Mount Street . . . Merrion Square: in Dublin.

DART line: electric rail system (Dublin Area Rapid Transit), running along the coast of the Irish Sea.

Dun Laoghaire, or Dalkey: both places on the coast, near Dublin.

Dodder and Tolka: two of the three main rivers in Dublin (the other being the Liffey).

High Cross at Carndonagh or Corofin: St Patrick's High Cross in Carndonagh, Co. Donegal, and St Tola's High Cross in Corofin, Co. Clare. The high crosses were used as meeting points and also to mark boundaries.

The Book of Kells: an illuminated manuscript Gospel book in Latin; it takes its name from the Abbey of Kells, Co. Meath, in Ireland, where it was held for several centuries. It is now held in Trinity College Library, Dublin.

the Enterprise: the cross-border inter-city train service between Dublin and Belfast.

Hamm and Clov: characters in Samuel Beckett's play, *Endgame* (1957).

Killnasaggart: ancient inscribed stone at Jonesborough, South Armagh.

'Emblements': 1981 work (etchings) by Mary Farl Powers.

vox clamantis in deserto: the voice of one crying in the desert (St Mark's Gospel 1.1–3).

Camille Pissarro: French Impressionist painter (1830–1903).

André Derain's The Turning Road, L'Estaque: French painter and founder of Fauvism (1880–1954). *The Turning Road, L'Estaque* was painted in 1906.

Quabbin reservoir : the largest inland body of water in Massachusetts.

John Field: Irish composer (born in Dublin 1782, died in Moscow 1837), whose nocturnes provided the model for later composers, including Chopin.

Chickamauga or Culloden: famous battles. The Battle of Chickamauga was fought during the American Civil War (1863). The Battle of Culloden (1746) was fought between the Jacobite supporters of Bonnie Prince Charlie and the Royal Army of George II of Great Britain.

Quito: a city in Ecuador.

Clontarf . . . Clondalkin: both places close to Dublin.

Belacqua: Belacqua Shuah, a Dublin student in Samuel Becketts' collection of stories, *More Pricks Than Kicks* (1934). The name is derived from the figure of Belacqua in Dante's *Purgatorio* (Canto 4), who is saved from the punishment of Hell and remembered for his comic wit.

Lucky and Pozzo: characters in Samuel Beckett's *Waiting for Godot* (1952).

Enrico Caruso: Italian operatic singer (1873–1921).

Mato Grosso: one of the states of Brazil (the Portuguese name meaning 'thick bush').

Warrenpoint: small town in Co. Down, the site of an IRA (Irish Republican Army) ambush on a British Army convoy on 27 August 1979.

Leixlip: town overlooking the River Liffey in north-east Co. Kildare.

Emily Post: American author (1872–1960) famous for writing about etiquette.

Leiden ... The Hague: Leiden, a city in the Dutch province of southern Holland, and The Hague, a city on the north sea coast of the western Netherlands.

Rathmullen and Ramelton: both towns in Co. Donegal.

Spinoza: Baruch Spinoza (1632–1677), Dutch philosopher.

Amelia Earhart: American aviation pioneer (1897–1939).

Urney: townland in Co. Tyrone.

Orpheus: legendary musician who entered the underworld to bring back his beloved Eurydice.

Calvados: apple brandy from Normandy in France.

Falaise: commune in the Normandy region of north-west France.

copains: friends.

Airey Neave: British Shadow Secretary of State for Northern Ireland, assassinated on 30 March 1979 by the Irish National Liberation Army.

Mountbatten: Louis Mountbatten, 1st Earl Mountbatten of Burma, British statesman and close relative of the British Royal Family, assassinated on 27 August 1979 by the IRA (Irish Republican Army).

andouilles: smoked pork sausages.

boudins noirs et blancs: pig's blood sausages.

Joseph Beuys's pack of huskies: 'The Pack' by Joseph Beuys (1969) was a conceptual art work installation, featuring sledges that looked like huskies.

Berncastel ... Bacarrat ... Belfast: Beuys travelled from Germany to give two lectures in Belfast in 1974.

Benjamin Britten's Lachrymae: musical work composed by Britten in April 1950.

Vivaldi's Four Seasons: work composed by Vivaldi in 1718–20.

Frankie Valli: American singer (b. 1934), lead vocalist of The Four Seasons.

Braque ... Shower of Rain: painting by Georges Braques, *The Shower* (1952).

Oriel: Free State Intelligence Department (Oriel House) in Dublin in 1922–23.

Wife of Bath: Chaucer's Wife of Bath in *The Canterbury Tales* (c. 1387–1400).

La Grande Jatte: Georges Seurat's painting, *A Sunday Afternoon on the Island of La Grande Jatte* (1884–86).

Botanic Gardens: in Belfast.

Sandy Row: inner city estate in south Belfast.

Donegal Pass: place on the Ormeau Road in south Belfast.

Andersonstown: suburb in west Belfast.

Rathcoole: housing estate in Newtonabbey, Co. Antrim.

Van Morrison: Belfast R&B and soul singer (b. 1945).

Padraic Fiacc: Irish poet (1924–2019).

John Hewitt: Belfast poet and art historian (1907–1987).

Bard of Ballymacarrett: Julius Leckey M'Cullough Craig.

Medhbh and Michael and Frank and Ciaran: group of Belfast poets that included Medbh McGuckian, Michael Longley, Frank Ormsby and Ciaran Carson.

tóraidheacht: *Tóraidheacht an Ghiolla deacair agus a chapaill* (*The pursuit of the difficult Gill and his Horses*), an old Irish tale.

the Fews: Fews Forest in Co. Armagh.

Redmond O'Hanlon: Irish outlaw from Co. Armagh (1620–1681).

hydrochloric acid: strong acid used in etching and lithography (one of a number of allusions in the poem to the artistic work of Mary Farl Powers).

skirrets: perennial root vegetables.

Morehampton Road: in Dublin.

Dr John Arbuthnot: Scottish physician and satirist (1667–1735).

Red Admiral: *Vanessa atalanta*, butterfly common in Britain and Ireland. It was, in fact, originally known as 'the red admirable'.

Watt: titular protagonist of Samuel Beckett's 1953 novel.

sennet of hautboys: stage direction in Elizabethan drama, calling for a fanfare of hautboys (oboes) or other instruments.

Dunmore East: fishing village in Co. Waterford.

Dungarvan: also a coastal town in Co. Waterford.

hidalgo: Spanish hereditary noble.

Rembrandt van Rijn: Dutch painter (1606–1669).

ptomaine: organic substances produced by bacteria during putrefaction of animal or plant protein, and thought to be responsible for food poisoning.

Monsieur Tarragon: wordplay involving Monsieur Marcel Tarragon brand of mustards and vinegars and Estragon, who in *Waiting for Godot* utters the line, 'Yes, let's go.'

Dire Straits: Newcastle rock band led by Mark Knopfler, formed in 1977. 'Sultans of Swing', their first single, reached the top ten in the UK and US charts.

the decree condemnatory, *the decree* absolvitor, *the decree* nisi: orders by a court of law, in which, respectively, the pursuer's case is upheld, the defendant's case is upheld, or the court order comes into force at a future date unless a particular condition is met.

Aosdána: 'people of the arts', an Irish association of artists founded in 1981, honouring artists who have made a distinctive contribution to the creative arts in Ireland.

an chraobh cnuais: the pine tree.

Mother Courage . . . Arturo Ui: *Mother Courage* (1939) and *The Resistible Rise of Arturo Ui* (1941), plays by Bertolt Brecht.

Ardara: small town in Co. Donegal.

Hermes: messenger to the gods.

harpe: a type of sword or sickle mentioned in Greek and Roman mythology.

Lagan . . . Foyle: rivers in Belfast and Derry.

lus na leac: Irish name for rosewort.

lus na treatha: Irish name for speedwell.

arrah: Irish interjection, expressing deep feeling.

Les Murray, 'Midsummer Ice'

Les Murray was born in Nabiac, New South Wales, Australia. This poem is the second of 'Three Poems in Memory of My Mother, Miriam Murray, nee Arnall (Born 13.5.1915, Died 19.4.51)'. It was published in *Quadrant* (August 1981) and included in *The People's Otherworld: Poems* (1983).

Thomas Nashe, 'Adieu, Farewell, Earth's Bliss'

This poem was written in 1592 and performed as part of a play, *Summer's Last Will and Testament*. It was published in 1600. The title is sometimes given as 'A Litany in Time of Plague'.

Bernard O'Donoghue, 'The Day I Outlived My Father'

Bernard O'Donoghue was born in Cullen, Co. Cork, Ireland. His father died when he was sixteen years old, after which the family moved to Manchester, England. This poem was published in *Outliving* (2003).

mad Arnaut: the twelfth-century Provençal poet, Arnaut Daniel.

Frank O'Hara, 'The Day Lady Died'

The jazz singer Billie Holliday (Lady Day) died on 17 July 1959. This elegy for her was published in *Lunch Poems* (1964).

Bastille day: a national day in France, marking the anniversary of the fall of the Bastille (fortress and prison) in Paris on 14 July 1789 and the beginning of the French Revolution.

Golden Griffin: a bookstore that used to be on Madison Avenue, New York.

Verlaine: French symbolist poet, Paul Verlaine (1844–1896).

Bonnard: French modernist painter, Pierre Bonnard (1867–1947).

Hesiod: Ancient Greek poet and contemporary of Homer. Richard Lattimore's translation of his work appeared in 1959.

Brendan Behan's new play: *The Hostage* (1959).

Genet: Jean Genet (1910–1986), whose plays *Le Balcon* and *Les Nègres* were popular in the late 1950s.

Strega: Italian herbal liqueur.

Ziegfeld Theatre: a cinema in midtown Manhattan, New York.

Gauloises: cigarettes of French origin, using Turkish and Syrian tobacco.

Picayunes: cigarettes from New Orleans.

5 Spot: the Five Spot Jazz Café in the Bowery District of New York.

Mal Waldron: American jazz pianist and composer (1925–2002).

Sharon Olds, 'The Exact Moment of His Death'
Sharon Olds was born in San Francisco, but has spent much of her working life in New York. Her writing is often concerned with family life and parental relations. This poem is from *The Father* (1992).

Alice Oswald, from *Memorial*
Alice Oswald is a classicist who has found inspiration in revisiting the *Iliad* of Homer. Her *Memorial*, a version or 'excavation' of the *Iliad*, was published in 2011.

Ovid, from *Tristia* 3.3
Ovid (Latin full name Publius Ovidius Naso) was a Roman poet, well known for his vivid interpretations of Classical myth, especially in his Metamorphoses. His *Tristia* (*Sorrows*), composed *c.* 9–12 CE, is an autobiographical poem which tells of his banishment from Rome under the emperor Augustus and his life of exile in Tomis, on the Black Sea. The translation here, by the English poet Henry Vaughan, is of a section of *Tristia* in which Ovid prepares a death-bed letter for his wife in Rome, anticipating his own burial in exile. It was published in Vaughan's *Olor Iscanus* (1651).

Sauromate: the tribe of the Sarmate, who inhabited Sarmatia, the region to which Ovid was banished.

Gete: the Getae were members of a Thracian tribe occupying the lower Danube basin.

Pythagoras: the Ancient Greek philosopher, mathematician and scientist. He believed in metempsychosis, the transmigration (and reincarnation) of souls.

Sarmates' ghosts: the spirits of the Sarmatian dead.

balm: an aromatic resin secreted by certain trees and plants.

cypress: evergreen tree of the conifer family.

Wilfred Owen, 'Anthem for Doomed Youth'
Most of Wilfred Owen's poetry was written between August 1917 and September 1918, though only five of his poems were published in his lifetime. His instincts as a poet were sharpened by his meeting with Siegfried Sassoon (see p. 389) at Craiglockhart Hospital in Edinburgh in August 1917.

'Anthem for Doomed Youth' was written in 1917 at Craiglockhart Hospital and published posthumously in Owen's *Poems* in 1920.

Wilfred Owen, 'I saw his round mouth's crimson'
This poem, which was considered a 'fragment' by Owen's editors, was probably written in Scarborough in November and December 1917. It was published in *The Poems of Wilfred Owen* (1931).

Wilfred Owen, 'Futility'
This poem was written in May 1918 and published in *The Nation* on 15 June 1918. It was included in *Poems* (1920).

Katherine Philips, 'On the Death of My First and Dearest Child, Hector Philips'
Katherine Philips, who wrote under the *non de plume* of Orinda, was one of a small number of British women writers whose poems were widely circulated in the 1650s and 1660s. This poem was first published (with the variant title 'Orinda Upon Little Hector Philips') in *Poems By the Most Deservedly Admired Mrs Katherine Philips* (1667).

Katherine Philips, ''Tis True, Our Life is But a Long Disease'
This poem was published (under the title 'Song . . . to the tune of Adieu Phillis') in *Poems By the Most Deservedly Admired Mrs Katherine Philips* (1667).

Tom Pickard, 'Spring Tide'
Tom Pickard was born in Newcastle-upon-Tyne, England. He co-founded the Morden Tower poetry readings at which Basil Bunting gave the first public reading of *Briggflatts* (see pp. 67–71). Bunting died on 17 April 1985. This elegy for him was first published in the journal *Conjunctions* (No. 8) in 1985 and included in *Custom and Exile* (1985).

A year-long miners' strike: the miners' strike lasted from 6 March 1984 to 3 March 1985.

the old fascist-fighting conchie: Bunting fought in the Second World War in opposition to fascism, but was a conscientious objector ('conchie') in the First World War.

Hexham: a market town in Northumberland, on the south bank of the River Tyne, about 20 miles from Newcastle.

Parliament Hill: in London, where Tom Pickard was living at the time.

little Geordie-Polak: the son of Tom Pickard (Tyneside 'Geordie') and Joanna Voit (Polish).

keats: the child's word for 'kites' but also a reminder of 'cockney' John Keats.

Sylvia Plath, 'Electra on Azalea Path'
This poem is addressed to Plath's father, Otto Plath (1885–1940). It was written after she visited his grave for the first time at Winthrop Cemetery, Massachusetts, on 9 March 1959. Plath adopts the persona of Electra, who mourns her father Agamemnon in Greek tragedy. First published in the *Hudson Review* (Autumn 1960), the poem was included in *Sylvia Plath: Collected Poems* (1981).

Azalea Path: a cemetery path leading to Otto Plath's grave.

hibernaculum: a protective place or shelter for hibernation.

bees: Plath's father was a bee-keeper with a specialist knowledge of insects.

necropolis: city of the dead.

ersatz: not real or genuine.

Alexander Pope, 'Elegy to the Memory of an Unfortunate Lady'
There has been much speculation about the subject of Pope's elegy, without any conclusive evidence that it might be addressed to an actual person. It was written in 1717 and included in Pope's *Works* that same year.

to act a Roman's part: to take one's own life.

the ball: the orb, an emblem of the world, often held by statues of Justice personified.

Alexander Pope, 'Three Epitaphs on John Hewet and Sarah Drew'
John Hewet and Sarah Drew were farm workers engaged to be married the week after they were killed by lightning in the village of Stanton Harcourt, Oxfordshire, on 31 July 1718.

These poems were written in 1718 and included in *Works*, Volume II (1730).

Alexander Pope, 'Epitaph on Sir Isaac Newton, in Westminster Abbey'
Sir Isaac Newton, scientist, mathematician and astronomer, died on 21 March 1727 and was buried in Westminster Abbey on 28 March 1727. Pope's epitaph was written in 1727 and included in *Works*, Volume II (1730).

Peter Porter, 'An Exequy'

Peter Porter was born in Brisbane, Australia, but spent much of his life (from 1951 to 2010) in England. This poem was written after the death of the poet's wife, Jannice Henry, in 1974. It was published in *The Cost of Seriousness* (1978).

Andromeda: in Greek mythology, Andromeda is chained to a rock as a sacrifice to the sea monster Cetus and rescued by Perseus.

Piero: Piero della Francesca, Italian painter of the Renaissance.

Bishop King: the poet Henry King (1592–1669), author of 'The Exequy'.

scala enigmatica: the enigmatic scale used by Verdi in his 'Ave Maria'.

Baldovinetti: Alesso Baldovinetti, Italian painter of the Renaissance.

Fürchte dich nicht, ich bin bei dir: Be not afraid I am with you (Isaiah 41: 13–14). The German text recalls Bach's motet (BVW 228) for a funeral.

Ezra Pound, from *Hugh Selwyn Mauberley*

Ezra Pound was an expatriate American poet and critic who spent much of his working life in England, France and Italy. He was based in London during the First World War, but left in 1921. *Hugh Selwyn Mauberley*, first published in 1920, is an experimental modernist poem that reveals Pound's discontent with the London literary scene and with much of western civilisation at the time, though it does so often using satire and parody. The poem has eighteen sections, two of which (4 and 5) are printed here.

pro domo: for home (Latin).

pro patria, non 'dulce' non 'et decor': for one's native land, not sweetly, not gloriously (Latin). Adapted from Horace's *Odes* 3.2.13: 'dulce et decorum est pro patria mori' ('sweet and fitting it is to die for one's country').

Propertius, from *The Elegies* 2.28

The Roman poet Sextus Propertius was born in Assisi, Italy, some time between 50 and 43 BC. He died in Rome in 15 BCE. It is thought that the first book of *The Elegies* was published in 29 BCE and the second in 27 or 26 BCE. Often described as 'love elegies', the poems address the poet's mistress, Cynthia (her real name was probably Hostia), though the poems are wide ranging in their treatment of Roman mythology and politics. The text given here is from *The Penguin Book of Greek and Latin Lyric Verse* (2023), edited by Christopher Childers.

Jupiter: god of sky and thunder.

the Dog: the dog star, the brightest star in the constellation Canis Major.

Venus: goddess of love and beauty, closely associated with Rome's imperial power.

Argive Juno's shrine: a sanctuary to Juno, goddess of the state, purportedly built by a Greek sculptor (from the region of Argos).

Minerva: goddess of wisdom.

Io: In Roman mythology, Jupiter turns Io into a white cow to avoid being seen with her by Juno. In some versions of the story, it is Juno who turns her into a cow.

Ino: daughter of Cadmus and Harmonia. After her death she was known as Leucothia.

Andromeda: daughter of Cepheus and Cassiopeia. After Cassiopeia boasts that she is more beautiful than the Nereids (sea nymphs), Poseidon has the sea monster Cetus (conflated here with Leviathan) attack the coast of their home. Andromeda is chained to a rock to appease the monster but is rescued by Perseus.

Callisto: the daughter of King Lycaon. She was set among the stars (as Ursa Major) by Jupiter.

Semele: another daughter of Cadmus and Harmonia. She perished in a bolt of lightning.

Acheron: a river in the underworld.

Jove: another name for Jupiter.

Persephone: goddess of spring, grain and fertility; queen of the underworld and wife to Hades.

Tyro: daughter of Salmoneus and Alcidice, mother of the twins Pelias and Neleus by Poseidon.

Antiope: daughter of Nycteus and Polyxo, mother of the twins Amphion and Zethus by Jupiter.

Europa: Phoenician princess abducted by Jupiter.

Pasiphae: the wife of Minos and mother of the minotaur.

Priam's kingdom: Priam was King of Troy during the Trojan War.

Diana: goddess of the hunt, and strongly associated with the moon.

Isis: represented as a woman with a cow's head in Ancient Egyptian mythology and later absorbed (in the cult of Isis) into Roman religion.

Sir Walter Raleigh, 'Even such is time'

Sir Walter Raleigh was an English statesman, soldier, writer and explorer, imprisoned in 1603 for his involvement in a plot to dethrone King James I. He was released in 1616 to lead an expedition to El Dorado, the legendary city of gold, but the men under his command burned a Spanish settlement in violation of the 1604 Peace Treaty with Spain. He returned to England and was arrested for the offence. This poem is thought to have been written by Raleigh on the evening before his execution on 29 October 1618. It appeared in several collections of verse from 1619 onwards.

Henrietta Cordelia Ray, 'Toussaint L'Ouverture'

Toussaint L'Ouverture (1743–1803), also the subject of Wordsworth's sonnet 'To Toussaint L'Ouverture', was the son of a slave and leader of the insurrection against Napoleon's edict re-establishing slavery in Haiti. He died in prison in Paris. This elegy appeared in *Poems* (1910).

Gareth Reeves, 'The Great Fire'

Published in *Listening In* (1993), this poem is a paternal elegy for the writer James Reeves (1909–1978). It is part of a sequence titled 'Going Blind', describing the detrimental effects of the congenital eye disorder, duane syndrome.

Christopher Reid, 'A Scattering'

Christopher Reid's poem is taken from his sequence *A Scattering* (2009), which is dedicated to the memory of his wife, the actor Lucinda Gane (1949–2005).

Denise Riley, 'A Part Song'

An elegiac sequence in twenty parts for Denise Riley's son, Jacob, 'A Part Song' was first published in the *London Review of Books* on 9 February 2012. It was included in her 2016 volume of poems, *Say Something Back*.

viii: *Persephone*: in Greek mythology, Persephone was the daughter of Zeus and Demeter. She was abducted by Hades as she was playing in the fields, and taken back to the underworld to be his wife.

x: *gentle showers of rain . . . fields of ripening grain*: these lines are from a popular funeral poem, 'Do Not Stand at My Grave and Weep', originally titled 'Immortality' and published by Clare Harner in 1934. The opening line of Harner's poem is 'Do not stand by my grave and weep.'

x: *flocking souls . . . Dusk-veiled*: these lines are adapted from Homer, *The Odyssey*, Book 24.

xix: The opening line of this section, 'She do the bereaved in different voices', is an echo of the proposed subtitle of *The Waste Land* by T. S. Eliot: 'He Do the Police in Different Voices' (itself an allusion to *Our Mutual Friend* by Charles Dickens).

Rainer Maria Rilke, 'The Ninth Elegy'

Rainer Maria Rilke was born in Prague (then Austro-Hungary) and spent his later years in Montreux, Switzerland. He began writing his *Duino Elegies* (1923) after staying at Duino Castle in Trieste, on the Italian Adriatic Coast, in 1912. It took him ten years to complete the book. The text given here is from *Duino Elegies, The German Text*, with an English translation, introduction, and commentary by J. B. Leishman and Stephen Spender (1939).

Edward Arlington Robinson, 'Reuben Bright'

Edward Arlington Robinson was born in Head Tide, Maine, and many of his poems are set in small-town New England, charting the personal troubles and disappointments of those who live there. This poem is from *Children of the Night* (1897).

Christina Rossetti, 'Song'

Christina Rossetti was born in London, the youngest child in an artistically gifted Italian family. She was the sister of the painter and poet Dante Gabriel Rossetti. Her poems frequently combine the intense personal expression of love lyrics with the language and imagery of prayer. This poem was written in 1848 and published in *Goblin Market and Other Poems* (1862).

Christina Rossetti, 'Remember'

This poem was written in 1849 and published in *Goblin Market and Other Poems* (1862).

Christina Rossetti, 'Rest'

From *Goblin Market and Other Poems* (1862).

Elizabeth Rowe, 'Upon the Death of Her Husband'

This elegy for Thomas Rowe (1687–1715) was written between 1715 and 1717. It was first published in *Poems on Several Occasions by His Grace the Duke of Buckingham and Other Eminent Hands* (1717).

Alexis: Thomas Rowe is addressed with a poetic name from Ancient Greek literature.

Tadeusz Różewicz, 'The Survivor'

Tadeusz Różewicz was a Polish poet and playwright who started publishing his poetry in magazines in 1938. He served in the resistance movement in German-occupied Poland during the Second World War, an experience that was to inform much of his later work. This poem is from Różewicz's first full-length book of poems, *Niepokój* (Anxiety), published in 1947. A selection of his poems titled *The Survivor, and Other Poems*, translated into English by Magnus Krynski and Robert Maguire, was published in 1976.

Sonia Sanchez, 'for our lady'

Sonia Sanchez is an American poet and playwright. She was born in Birmingham, Alabama, but spent much of her childhood in Harlem, New York. She was active in the Black Arts Movement, promoting the work of African American writers and artists, especially in the 1960s and 1970s. This poem is from *We A BaddDDD People* (1970).

Billie: the jazz singer, Billie Holiday (1915–1959).

Siegfried Sassoon, 'Suicide in the Trenches'

Siegfried Sassoon first made his name as a fiercely satirical opponent of the First World War, despite being awarded the Military Cross for bravery in battle. In July 1917 he released his 'Soldier's Declaration', protesting against the continuation of the war. He was admitted to Craiglockhart Hospital in Edinburgh, where he met Wilfred Owen (see pp. 344–5). This poem was published in *Counter-Attack and Other Poems* (1918).

crumps: explosions.

Anna Seward, 'An Old Cat's Dying Soliloquy'

Anna Seward spent most of her life in Lichfield, Staffordshire, where her father was Canon of Lichfield Cathedral. This poem was published in *The Gentleman's Magazine* in April 1792 and included in *Poetical Works* (1810).

Anne Sexton, 'The Truth the Dead Know'

This double elegy for Anne Sexton's parents, Mary Gray Staples and Ralph Churchill Harvey, was first published in the *Hudson Review* (Spring 1961). It appeared as the opening poem in *All My Pretty Ones* (1962).

William Shakespeare, Sonnet 71

First published in Shakespeare's Sonnets (1609).

William Shakespeare, Sonnet 73

First published in Shakespeare's Sonnets (1609).

William Shakespeare, 'When that I was and a little tiny boy'
From *Twelfth Night*, written in 1601–2, and printed in the First Folio of 1623. Feste sings these lines at the end of the play (5.1.385)

William Shakespeare, 'Fear no more the heat o' the sun'
From *Cymbeline*, written in 1608–10 and printed in the First Folio of 1623. The lines are spoken or sung by Guiderius and Arviragus (4.2.259).

William Shakespeare, 'Full fathom five my father lies'
From *The Tempest*, written and performed in 1611 and printed in the First Folio of 1623. Ariel sings these lines to Ferdinand (1.2.399).

Percy Bysshe Shelley, 'To Wordsworth'
Although Shelley's poem ostensibly mourns the loss of one of the great poets of the Romantic movement, Wordsworth did not in fact die until 23 April 1850. What the poem sardonically mourns is the death of Wordsworth's radical political beliefs. It was published in *Alastor, or The Spirit of Solitude* (1816).

Percy Bysshe Shelley, from *Adonais*
Written and published in 1821, *Adonais* is an elegy for John Keats, who died in Rome on 23 February 1821. The full text has 55 stanzas, of which 1–10 and 45–55 are printed here.

Adonais: the name is derived from that of Adonis (in Greek mythology), a young hunter beloved of Aphrodite and killed by a wild boar. The root of the name, 'Adon', means 'lord'.

mighty Mother: Urania, one of the nine Muses, known as 'the heavenly one' for her association with astronomy.

the corse: the corpse.

He died ... Blind, old and lonely: i.e., John Milton did.

liberticide: the killer of liberty.

that high Capital: Rome.

Chatterton: Thomas Chatterton (1752–1770), a gifted poet who took his own life.

Sidney: Sir Philip Sidney (1554–1586), poet and courtier, fatally wounded in battle.

Lucan: a young Roman poet (39–65 CE) who took his own life rather than die under the sentence of the emperor, Nero.

copses: small woods.

one keen pyramid: the tomb of Gaius Cestius, an officer of Ancient Rome, close to where Keats is buried.

bark: a small boat.

James Shirley, 'Epitaph on the Duke of Buckingham'
George Villiers, First Duke of Buckingham (1592–1628), was an English courtier, statesman and patron of the arts. The poem was first published in *Poems* (1646).

Two Kings delight: Buckingham was the favourite of two kings: James I and Charles I.

John Skelton, from 'Phillip Sparrow'
This poem is a mock elegy for the death of a pet sparrow belonging to Jane Scrope, daughter of Sir Richard, 5th Baron Scrope of Bolton and Lady Eleanor Washbourne. It makes use of both Christian and Classical sources, including the liturgical Office for the Dead and the laments by Catullus for the death of a girl's sparrow. Written between 1502 and 1505, it was published in Skelton's *Works* (1568).

Pla ce bo: Latin *placebo*, meaning 'I please [the Lord]'. Vulgate Psalm (cxiv.9), the opening antiphon of the Vespers of the Office of the Dead. The spacing suggest a sung text.

Di le xi: Latin *dilexi*, meaning 'I delight [in the truth]'. Vulgate Psalm (cxiv.1), the opening psalm of the Vespers of the Office of the Dead.

Dame Margery: possibly the Mother Superior of St Mary's Convent at Carrow Abbey, where Jane Scrope and her sisters went to live with their mother after the death of their father, Sir Richard, and the execution of their step-father, Sir John Wyndham.

Nones Black: nuns black, a reference to the Benedictine order of nuns, who sometimes went under the name of the Black Ladies because of the colour of their habits.

Pater noster qui: Our Father who [art in heaven].

Ave Mari: Hail Mary.

Pyramus and Thesbe: Skelton compares the painful separation of girl and bird to the suffering of the two lovers, Pyramus and Thesbe, in Ovid's *Metamorphoses*.

mede: reward.

Phylyp: the name is variously given as Philip, Philyp and Phylyp. Philip (or Pip) was a popular name for a sparrow.

Gyb: a popular name for a cat (from Gylbert).

worrowyd: killed by seizing the throat.

stound: moment.

senaws: sinews.

Heu, heu, me: the second antiphon of the Vespers, Vulgate Psalm (cxix.5): 'Woe, woe is me'.

Ad Dominum . . .: the second psalm of the Vespers, Vulgate Psalm cxix.1: 'In my distress, I cried unto the Lord'.

marees depe: a deep marsh. Here, Skelton invokes numerous parallels with the descent into the underworld in Classical literature.

Acherontes: the region of the River Acheron in the underworld.

Pluto: ruler of the underworld (a later name for King Hades).

Alecto: Alecto and Megaera were two of the snake-headed Furies.

Medusa: one of the Gorgons. Her stare turned to stone those who looked at her.

Proserpina: the Latin name for Persephone, daughter of Zeus and Demeter, who was abducted by Hades and taken to the underworld to be his wife.

Cerberus: the three-headed dog guarding the entrance to the underworld.

Theseus: King of Athens and celebrated hero in Greek mythology.

afraye: disturb.

Hercules: Latin name for Heracles, son of Jupiter, famed for his strength.

Jupyeter: Jupiter, Roman god of the sky and thunder.

Do mi nus: the third antiphon of the Vespers, Vulgate Psalm cxx.5,7.

Levavi oculos . . .: the third Psalm of the Vespers, Vulgate Psalm cxx,1: 'I lifted up my eyes to the hills'.

Zenophontes: Xenophon (c. 428–354 BCE), Greek philosopher.

Andromach: Andromach(e) laments the death of her husband, Prince Hector, in the Ancient Greek accounts of the Trojan War.

Stevie Smith, 'Scorpion'

Stevie Smith was born Florence Margaret Smith in Hull, England, and spent most of her life in London. This poem is from *Scorpion and Other Poems* (1972).

Tracy K. Smith, 'Wade in the Water'

Tracy K. Smith was born in Massachusetts and raised in northern California. The title poem of her collection *Wade in the Water* recreates the psychic and emotional ordeal of escaping slavery. It is dedicated to the Geechee Gullah Ring Shouters, all descendants of African slaves, who continue to perform the dancing, singing and drumming rituals of their predecessors. *Wade in the Water: Poems* was published in 2018.

Layli Long Soldier, '38'

Layli Long Soldier is a Native American poet of the Oglala Lakota (Oglala Sioux tribe). This poem is a meditation on the Dakota 38, the 38 men executed by hanging under the orders of President Abraham Lincoln on 26 December 1862 for their part in the so-called Sioux Uprising. It was published in *Whereas* (2017).

Charles Hamilton Sorley, 'When you see millions of the mouthless dead'

Charles Hamilton Sorley was born in Aberdeen, Scotland. He served in the British Army in the First World War and was killed at the Battle of Loos in 1915 at the age of twenty. This poem, possibly a riposte to Rupert Brooke's sonnet 'The Soldier' (see p. 54), was written in 1915 and first published in *Marlborough and Other Poems* (1916).

Edmund Spenser, 'Astrophel'

First published in 1595, this poem mourns the death of Sir Philip Sidney (1544–1586), who had used the name Astrophel in his sequence of love sonnets, *Astrophel and Stella* (1591). The section given here closes with the penultimate stanza (the final stanza introduces the mourning song of Astrophel's sister, Clorinda).

Arcady: Arcadia, a region of the Peloponnese depicted in Virgil's *Eclogues* as a land of shepherds, and consequently a traditional setting for pastoral literature; in the Renaissance it came to be understood as an unspoiled paradise. Sidney was known as the author of the romance titled *Arcadia* (1590).

Haemony: pastoral name for the Greek Thessaly.

pastors: shepherds.

gentle vsage and demeanure mild: good conduct and mild demeanour (behaviour).

weetingly beguyld: skilfully charmed.

Ardeyn: the Forest of Ardennes.

fowle Arlo: the woods of Aherlow, near where Spenser was living in Ireland.

shape of dreryhead: image of sorrow.

sewing of the chace: pursuing the hunt.

Turtle chaste: turtle doves.

Penthia: the name Spenser gives to a plant ('hearbe') or flower associated with sorrow and lament.

Wallace Stevens, 'The Emperor of Ice-Cream'
Wallace Stevens was an American modernist poet who made a significant contribution to the development of American elegy through his exploration of 'the mythology of modern death' in his long poem, 'The Owl in the Sarcophagus'. 'The Emperor of Ice-Cream', depicting the preparations for a funeral or wake, was published in *Harmonium* (1923).

dresser of deal: dressing table made of pine or fir wood.

fantails: fantail pigeons.

Anne Stevenson, 'Orcop'
This poem is an elegy for the poet Frances Horovitz (1938–1983), who is buried in the grounds of St John the Baptist Church in Orcop, Herefordshire. It was published in *Stone Milk* (2007).

Robert Louis Stevenson, 'A Martial Elegy for Some Lead Soldiers'
Robert Louis Stevenson was born in Edinburgh, Scotland, and is best remembered for his novels, including *Treasure Island*, *Kidnapped*, and *The Strange Case of Dr Jekyll and Mr Hyde*. However, he was also a prolific poet, essayist and travel writer. This poem is from *A Child's Garden of Verses* (1885).

Robert Louis Stevenson, 'Requiem'
This poem was composed by Stevenson in 1880 as his own epitaph, and appears on his tombstone in Samoa. It was published posthumously in *Underwoods* (1898).

Hannah Sullivan, from 'The Sandpit After Rain'

Hannah Sullivan is an English poet and critic. 'The Sandpit After Rain', exploring at once the birth of her first child and her father's death, is the third of the poems in her collection *Three Poems* (2018). The extract printed here comes from the third section of the poem, 'The Year of Greeting Cards'.

Acton: large residential suburb in west London.

Isolde: the heroine in Richard Wagner's 1865 opera *Tristan und Isolde*.

Simnel cake: fruitcake made with layers of marzipan, associated with Easter in the UK and Ireland.

Northolt: town in west London.

Jonathan Swift, 'A Satirical Elegy on the Death of a Late Famous General'

Written in 1722 after the death of General John Churchill, 1st Duke of Marlborough, and published in Swift's *Works* (1765).

Jonathan Swift, from 'Verses on the Death of Dr Swift'

Written in 1731–32. Swift's initial expectation was that the verses would be published only after his death, but he shared the text with friends, one of whom (Dr William King) arranged for an amended version of the text to be printed in London in 1739. Dissatisfied with the censored version, Swift himself authorised a version to be printed in Dublin in 1741. The verses given here are a shortened version of the poem (ll. 73–116, 299–370, 455–484).

Charles the Second: the King of England, who died in 1685 when Swift was eighteen.

The Rose: a fashionable tavern in London, close to the Drury Lane Theatre.

Stars and Garters: honours and awards.

Chartres: Francis Charteris (1675–1732), a notorious 'rake' and gambler.

a house for fools and mad: Swift's will included a substantial sum for the building of a hospital for the insane, the first in Ireland, which opened in 1757 as St Patrick's Hospital, Dublin.

Algernon Charles Swinburne, from 'Ave atque Vale'

Swinburne began composing this elegy for Charles Baudelaire (1821–1867) in April 1867, mistakenly believing that Baudelaire had died that spring. In fact, Baudelaire lived until 31 August 1867. The elegy was published in the *Fortnightly Review* in January 1868 and reprinted in Swinburne's *Poems and Ballads, Second Series* in 1878. The first ten stanzas are printed here. The title is an allusion to the work of Catullus, Poem 101 (see pp. 90–91).

Dryads: tree nymphs or tree spirits in Greek mythology.

Leucadian grave: the poet Sappho, born on the Greek island of Lesbos, was thought to have killed herself by leaping from the Leucadian cliffs. Baudelaire's controversial volume *Les Fleurs du Mal* (1867) was condemned in part because of its depiction of same-sex love among women.

Titan-woman: belonging to the powerful deities who preceded the Olympians in Greek mythology.

Proserpine's veiled head: Proserpine or Proserpina is queen of the underworld in Roman mythology (Persephone in Greek mythology). She is the goddess of female and agricultural fertility and is associated with springtime growth.

Algernon Charles Swinburne, 'A Forsaken Garden'
One of Swinburne's most provocative responses to Christian ideals of resurrection and immortal love, 'A Forsaken Garden' was published in the *Athenaeum* in July 1876 and reprinted in *Poems and Ballads, Second Series* in 1878.

coign: projecting edge or angle.

Alfred, Lord Tennyson, from *In Memoriam*
Arthur Henry Hallam (1811–1833), Tennyson's close friend and fellow poet, died in Vienna on 15 September 1833. Tennyson started writing *In Memoriam* as a series of elegiac lyrics as early as October 1833, referring to these simply as his 'Elegies'. The finished poem, first published anonymously as *In Memoriam A. H. H.* in 1850, consists of a Prologue, 131 sections, and an Epilogue.

5: 'I sometimes hold it half a sin . . .'
weeds: mourning clothes (widows' weeds).

7: 'Dark house, by which once more I stand . . .'
like a guilty thing: an echo of Shakespeare's *Hamlet*: 'And then it started like a guilty thing' (Act 1, Scene 1, l.148).

19: 'The Danube to the Severn gave . . .'
Danube: Vienna, where Hallam died, is on the River Danube.

Severn: the River Severn empties into the Bristol Channel, near where Hallam was buried at Clevedon, Somerset.

Wye: the Wye is a tributary of the Severn, and was associated in Tennyson's mind with Tintern Abbey and Wordsworth's poem, 'Lines Composed a Few Miles above Tintern Abbey, On Revisiting the Banks of the Wye during a Tour. July 13, 1798'.

50: 'Be near me when my light is low . . .'
a Fury slinging flame: in Greek mythology the goddesses of vengeance brandished torches of flame.

70: 'I cannot see the features right . . .'
Dark bulks: as of beasts or monsters.

115: 'Now fades the last long streak of snow'
quick: quickset thorn (the English hawthorn).

'Crossing the Bar'
Written in October 1889 after Tennyson crossed the Solent (between the Isle of Wight and the southern English coast). It was published in *Demeter and Other Poems* (1889).

Bar: the bar is the area where the deep waters of the ocean meet the shallower waters near the mouth of a river. The image is used metaphorically to suggest the threshold between life and death.

William Makepeace Thackeray, 'The Sorrows of Werther'
This poem is a satirical response to the popular romantic novel by Johann Wolfgang von Goethe, *The Sorrows of Young Werther* (1774), in which the eponymous hero kills himself for love of Charlotte when she marries another man. It was published in Thackeray's *Miscellanies: Prose and Verse, Volume 1* (1855).

Theocritus, Idyll 1 (Lament for Daphnis)
Theocritus was a Sicilian, born in Syracuse around 308 BCE. His *Idylls* have come to be seen as the foundational texts of pastoral elegy, providing the shepherd figures and rural images adopted by later poets, including Virgil, Milton and Shelley. In Idyll 1, Thyrsis is encouraged to sing of how the legendary shepherd Daphnis died of unrequited love.

Pan: god of shepherds, flocks, and the countryside.

Priapus: son of Aphrodite, god of fertility.

Chromis: the name of a shepherd.

Calydna: an island in the Aegean.

Hades: the underworld, land of the dead; also the name of the king who rules it.

Peneius: a river in Thessaly, Greece.

Pindus: a mountain in Thessaly, sacred to the Muses and to Apollo.

Anapus: a river in Syracuse, Sicily.

Etna: Mount Etna in Sicily.

Acis' spring: a stream which rises on Etna. It takes its name from the legend of a shepherd boy who was turned into a stream for offending the gods.

Hermes: messenger of the gods and patron of shepherds

Cypris: another name for Aphrodite, referring to her temple in Cyprus.

Ida: a mountain in Troas, on the Aegean coast.

Anchises: a cowherd on Mount Ida who was loved by Aphrodite.

Adonis: a Greek youth famous for his beauty, also loved by Aphrodite. He was killed by a boar while out hunting and was thereafter believed to spend half of each year on earth with Aphrodite and half beneath it with Persephone.

Diomedes: King of Argos and one of the Greek heroes at the siege of Troy.

Arethusa: a fountain in Syracuse, thought to be the source of inspiration for pastoral poetry.

Thybris: a river in Sicily.

Lycaeus: a mountain in Arcadia, sacred to Pan and Zeus.

Maenalus: a mountain in Arcadia and a favourite haunt of shepherds.

Helice: the capital city of Achaea.

Arcas: son of Zeus and Callisto.

Eros: god of love.

Aegilus: a town in Attica, famous for its figs.

Cissaetha: a name given to a goat.

Dylan Thomas, 'A Refusal to Mourn the Death, by Fire, of a Child in London'
This poem was first published in *The New Republic* in May 1945 and included in *Deaths and Entrances* (1946). Its title alludes to the Blitz, the

intense bombing of London by the German Luftwaffe during the Second World War.

Zion: the biblical term for Jerusalem and an image of the City of God (heaven).

the long friends: worms.

Dylan Thomas, 'Do not go gentle into that good night'
This poem was written for the poet's father, David John Thomas, who died on 16 December 1952, though it is possible that Thomas started writing the poem as early as 1947. It was published in the Italian journal *Botteghe Oscure* (Vol. VIII) in 1951 and included in Thomas's *In Country Sleep and Other Poems* in 1952.

Edward Thomas, 'Tears'
Edward Thomas was an English writer of Welsh descent, who began writing poetry relatively late in life at the age of thirty-six. In 1915 he enlisted in the British Army to fight in the First World War. He was killed in action in the Battle of Arras in France on 9 April 1917. 'Tears' was written on 8 January 1915 and published in Edward Thomas's *Poems* (1917).

double-shadowed Tower: the Tower of London, shadowed both metaphorically (by its history of imprisonment and execution) and literally (by the effect of sunlight).

The British Grenadiers: a traditional marching song.

Edward Thomas, 'In Memoriam (Easter, 1915)'
'In Memoriam' was written on 6 April 1915 and published in *Poems* (1917).

Edward Thomas, 'Rain'
This poem was written in early 1916 at the Hare Hall training Camp in Romford, Essex, and published in *Poems* (1917). It is based on a description in Thomas's notebooks of a downpour on the Icknield Way in 1911.

Blessed are the dead: an echo of the Beatitudes, which open Christ's Sermon on the Mount as given in the Gospel of St Matthew (5:3–10).

Edward Thomas, 'As the Team's Head-Brass'
This poem was written in May 1916 and published in *Poems* (1917).

the team's head-brass: the metal part of the bridle worn by plough horses.

charlock: yellow mustard flower.

Chidiock Tichborne, 'Elegy for Himself'

Tichborne's self-elegy is thought to have been written in the Tower of London on 19 September 1586, the night before his execution. He was one of the Catholic conspirators involved in the Babington Plot to assassinate Queen Elizabeth I and replace her with Mary Queen of Scots. The poem was included in an anthology titled *Verses of Prayse and Joye* (1586).

Tomas Tranströmer, 'After Someone's Death'

First published in Swedish in *Klockor och Spår* (*Bells and Tracks*) in 1961, this poem was included in *Den stora gåtan* (2004), published in English translation as *The Great Enigma: New Collected Poems* (2006).

Frederick Goddard Tuckerman, 'An upper chamber in a darkened house'

Frederick Goddard Tuckerman was an American poet who was born in Boston and spent most of his life in relative seclusion in Greenfield, western Massachusetts. He was an avid writer of sonnets, distinguished by their sharply observed natural detail, by their strange and remote settings, and by their exploration of feelings of loneliness and melancholy. This is one of a series of sonnets published in *Poems by Frederick Goddard Tuckerman* (1864).

Henry Vaughan, 'They are All Gone into the World of Light!'

Henry Vaughan was a Welsh poet whose work is justifiably regarded as 'metaphysical', especially in the way that it uses elaborate conceits and a sensuous, physical imagery to explore philosophical and religious ideas to do with sin, death and resurrection. The devotional qualities of his poetry are reminiscent of those of George Herbert (see p. 215). This poem was included in the second edition of Vaughan's *Silex Scintillans* published in 1655.

that hill: Calvary, the site of Christ's crucifixion.

glass: telescope.

Virgil, from Eclogue 5 (The Death of Daphnis)

The Roman poet Virgil, best known for the *Aeneid*, lived between 70 BC and 19 BC. The *Eclogues*, a collection of 10 pastoral poems, was among his earliest work, probably written between 42 BC and 37 BC. In Eclogue 5, the shepherds Menalcas and Mopsus sing the praises of the deified shepherd hero, Daphnis, and lament his death by unrequited love. The translation given here is by Richard Duke (1659–1711).

Pan and the Dryads: Pan, the god of shepherds and the countryside, accompanied by tree spirits.

Phoebus: another name for Apollo, associated with light and the sun.

Chian wines: wine from the Greek island of Chios.

Dametas: a fictional person (Damoetas in the *Idylls* of Theocritus).

Lictian Argon: Lictian or Lyctian means Cretan (from the island of Crete). Argon is another fictional character.

Alphesiboeus: another imaginary person.

Bacchus: god of wine and celebration (also known as Dionysus).

Ceres: goddess of grain and the harvest.

Corydon: popular name for a shepherd.

Meliboeus' sheep: Meliboeus is another shepherd. When Menalcus claims that the pipe 'taught me Meliboeus' sheep' he means a song.

Antigenes: an imaginary character, with the name borrowed from Theocritus.

Virgil, from *Georgics*, Book 4 (Orpheus and Eurydice)
Virgil's *Georgics*, his series of poems on agricultural life, was composed between 37 and 30 BC, following a period of civil war and rural depopulation. Didactic in form, the poems are a celebration of traditional agricultural life in Italy and a plea for its restoration. In Book 4, Virgil recounts the story of how Orpheus, the legendary musician, goes in search of his beloved Eurydice in the underworld.

Jove: king of the gods and god of sky and thunder.

maenads: the female followers of Dionysus, god of fertility and of wine and pleasure.

Erebus: the personification of darkness.

Cocytus: the river of wailing which flows into the River Acheron in the underworld.

Stygian lake: a lake in the underworld, filled with water from the River Styx.

Tartarus: the infernal region, the deepest part of the underworld.

Cerberus: the three-headed hound of Hades that guards the entrance to the underworld.

Ixion's wheel: Zeus punished Ixion for murder by having him tied eternally to a fiery spinning wheel.

Proserpine: the Latin name for Persephone, wife of Hades, and goddess of spring was Proserpina.

Charon: the ferryman of Hades who transports the souls of the dead across the rivers of the underworld.

Virgil, from *The Aeneid*, Book 2 (The Death of Priam)
Virgil's epic Latin poem *The Aeneid* was written in twelve books between 29 and 19 BC. It tells the legendary story of Aeneas, a Trojan who fled the Trojan War and travelled to Italy. The section of Book 2 given here concerns the death of Priam, the King of Troy. It was translated by the English poet John Dryden, as part of his *Aeneis*, which was published in 1697.

Priam: King of Troy in Greek mythology.

Hecuba: wife of Priam and Queen of Troy.

Hector: Trojan prince, son of Priam and Hecuba.

Pyrrhus: King of Epirus, whose costly military campaigns against Macedonia and Rome gave rise to the term 'Pyrrhic victory'.

Derek Walcott, 'Sea Canes'
Derek Walcott was born in Castries, St Lucia, and much of his work draws on the landscapes and seascapes of the Caribbean. This poem is from *Sea Grapes* (1976).

Margaret Walker, 'For Malcolm X'
Malcolm X (1925–65) was an American Muslim minister and civil rights activist. He was assassinated on 21 February 1965. This poem was published in *Prophets for a New Day* (1970).

Phillis Wheatley, 'On the Death of the Rev. Mr George Whitefield'
George Whitefield (1714–70) was an English clergyman closely associated with the Methodist movement. A charismatic speaker, he visited America seven times between 1738 and his death in Massachusetts in 1770. He was one of the first clergymen to preach to slaves. Phillis Wheatley was brought from West Africa to Boston in 1861 (at around the age of seven), and there sold as a slave to the Boston tailor John Wheatley and his wife, Susanna. She learned to read and write in the Wheatley household, as well as acquiring Greek and Latin. This poem was published as a broadside on 11 October 1770 and reprinted many times (in

London as well as Boston). It was included in Wheatley's *Poems on Various Subjects, Religious and Moral* (1773).

Zion: the biblical name for Jerusalem, but also a term metaphorically associated with heaven and the afterlife.

Great Countess: Selina Hastings (1707–91), Countess of Huntingdon, to whom Whitefield was Chaplain. She was a benefactor of the Methodist movement and became Wheatley's patron.

the orphans mourn: Whitefield founded the Bethesda orphanage near Savannah, Georgia, in 1840.

James Monroe Whitfield, 'Lines on the Death of John Quincy Adams'
John Quincy Adams (1767–1848) was the sixth President of the United States (1825–29). He was a strong advocate for the abolition of slavery and mobilised support for the cause though his involvement in Congress in his post-presidential years. This poem was published in *America and other Poems* (1853).

Walt Whitman, 'O Captain! My Captain!'
This poem was first published in the *New York Saturday Press* on 4 November 1865 and included in 'Sequel to Drum-Taps' appended to the second issue of *Drum-Taps*, also November 1865, though Whitman attached the date 1865–66 to the book. Later, in 1871, it was part of a group of poems collected under the title 'President Lincoln's Burial Hymn' (amended in 1881 to 'Memories of President Lincoln').

Walt Whitman, 'Vigil Strange I Kept on the Field One Night'
This poem is from *Drum-Taps* (1865), in which Whitman records his experience as a volunteer army nurse in the American Civil War (1861–65).

Walt Whitman, 'When Lilacs Last in the Dooryard Bloom'd'
Written in the weeks immediately following the assassination of President Abraham Lincoln on 14 April 1865 and included in the 'Sequel to Drum-Taps' appended to the second issue of *Drum-Taps* (1865–66), this was the leading work in the group of poems collected in 1871 under the title 'President Lincoln's Burial Hymn' (amended in 1881 to 'Memories of President Lincoln').

Dooryard: North American: a yard or garden by the front door of a house

the great star: Venus.

the thrush: the North American hermit thrush.

Oscar Wilde, 'Requiescat'
The poem commemorates the death of Oscar Wilde's sister, Isola, on 23 February 1867 at the age of nine. It was published in Wilde's *Poems* (1881).

Helen Maria Williams, 'Elegy on a Young Thrush'
Helen Maria Williams, novelist, poet and translator, was born in London to a Scottish mother and a Welsh father. She was a religious dissenter who supported the abolition of slavery and sympathised with the ideals of the French Revolution. Admired by Wordsworth, she also demonstrated a sensitivity to nature that was fundamental to the Romantic movement in poetry. This poem was written in 1790 and published in *Poems on Various Subjects: With Introductory Remarks on the Present State of Science and Literature in France* (1823).

the Area of a House: the sunken courtyard that gives access to the basement in some houses, usually closed off from the street by railings and reached by steps from the pavement.

William Carlos Williams, 'The Last Words of My English Grandmother'
William Carlos Williams was an American modernist poet closely associated with the Imagist movement in poetry in the early years of the twentieth century. He also worked as a doctor for more than forty years. This elegy for his English grandmother demonstrates the characteristic honesty and directness of his poetry. It was published in *The Broken Span* (1941).

Charles Wolfe, 'The Burial of Sir John Moore after Corunna'
Thought to have been based on an account of Moore's death in the Edinburgh *Annual Register*, this poem was written in 1814 and published in the *Newry Telegraph* in 1817. It was later included in *The Burial of Sir John Moore, and Other Poems* (1909). Sir John Moore was the commander of a small army in Spain during the Peninsular War; he was forced to retreat to Corunna on the Spanish coast and was killed there in a battle with the French on 16 January 1809.

William Wordsworth, 'Remembrance of Collins'
William Collins (1721–59) was influential in changing the course of English poetry from the satirical mode of Alexander Pope and others towards a more reflective, descriptive style of writing. This poem was written in 1789 and published in *Lyrical Ballads* (1798) under the title 'Lines written near Richmond, upon the Thames, at Evening'. Its original had five stanzas, the first two of which were removed (at the suggestion of Samuel

Taylor Coleridge) to form a new poem titled 'Lines written when sailing in a Boat at Evening'. The two poems were published separately in the second edition of *Lyrical Ballads* in 1800. The poem appears in Wordsworth's *Poems* (1815) under the title 'Remembrance of Collins'.

a later ditty: Wordsworth alludes to Collins's 'Ode on the Death of Mr Thomson' (1749). James Thomson (1700–48) was the author of *The Seasons* (1730).

William Wordsworth, 'Old Man Travelling'
Written in 1796–97 and published in *Lyrical Ballads* (1798). In 1800 the title was changed to 'Animal Tranquillity and Decay, a Sketch'. The closing lines, 15–20, were removed after 1805.

Falmouth: a seaport in Cornwall.

William Wordsworth, 'We Are Seven'
Written in spring 1798 and published in *Lyrical Ballads* in 1798.

brother Jim: an imagined listener (based on a mutual friend of Wordsworth and Coleridge).

Conway: now Conwy, a market town in North Wales, though Wordsworth claimed elsewhere that he had met the child in the poem near Castle Goodrich, between Monmouth and Ross-on-Wye.

William Wordsworth, 'There was a Boy'
Written in November 1798 and published in *Lyrical Ballads* (1800).

Winander: Lake Windermere in the English Lake District, known as Winander Mere until the mid-nineteenth century.

William Wordsworth, 'The Two April Mornings'
Written in October–December 1798 and published in *Lyrical Ballads* (1800).

Derwent's wave: the River Derwent flows near to Wordsworth's birthplace in Cockermouth in the north of the English Lake District.

William Wordsworth, 'A slumber did my spirit seal'
Written in October–December 1798 and published in *Lyrical Ballads* (1800).

William Wordsworth, 'She dwelt among the untrodden ways'
Written in October–December 1798 and published in *Lyrical Ballads* (1800).

William Wordsworth, 'I travelled among unknown men'
Written in early 1801 and published in *Poems, in Two Volumes* (1807).

William Wordsworth, 'Elegiac Stanzas'

Wordsworth visited Peele Castle, near Barrow-in-Furness in Cumbria, when staying nearby in 1794. His memory of it was prompted by seeing Sir George Beaumont's painting *A Storm: Peele Castle* in 1806. This poem, written in May–June 1806 and published in *Poems, in Two Volumes* (1807), associates that memory with the 1805 death of Wordsworth's brother John in a storm at sea.

Him whom I deplore: John Wordsworth, drowned in February 1805 while captain of a merchant ship, *Earl of Abergavenny*. 'Deplore' in this instance means 'mourn'.

Not without hope: an echo of the liturgy for the 'Order for the Burial of the Dead' in the Book of Common Prayer: 'And now, Lord, what is my hope: truly my hope is even in thee.'

William Wordsworth, 'Elegiac Verses in memory of my brother, John Wordsworth'

These elegiac verses were written in memory of Wordsworth's brother John, who died in February 1805 (see note above). Composed in that year, they were not published until *Poems, Chiefly of Early and late Years* (1842).

even this Plant: the Moss Campion. Wordsworth's own note explained that 'this most beautiful plant is scarce in England, though it is found in great abundance upon the mountains of Scotland'.

Sir Henry Wotton, 'Upon the Death of Sir Albert Morton's Wife'

Elizabeth Apsley, Lady Morton, was an English courtier and companion to Elizabeth Stuart, Queen of Bohemia, with whom she travelled to Heidelberg in 1613. She returned to England in 1624 and married Sir Albert Morton. She died in 1626. Wotton's epitaph was published in *Reliquiae Wottonianae* (1672).

Kit Wright, 'The Boys Bump-starting the Hearse'

Kit Wright was born in Kent, England. He is an author of many children's books, as well as a poet who brings an unsettling combination of levity and seriousness to his writing, as demonstrated in the title poem of *Bump-starting the Hearse*, published in 1983.

W. B. Yeats, 'September 1913'

By 1913, the high hopes that Yeats had of inspiring a unified national culture in Ireland through the power of poetry and drama had diminished significantly, and he began to write bitterly of a modern Ireland more interested in commerce than art. One of his distinctions as an elegist is to write poems that mourn the loss of individuals such as John O'Leary while simultaneously grieving over the tragic history of Ireland itself. This elegy for both O'Leary and the Romantic Ireland he represented was published in *Responsibilities* (1914).

you: the people of Ireland.

O'Leary: John O' Leary (1830–1907). Irish nationalist and supporter of the Irish Republican Brotherhood. He greatly influenced Yeats, both politically and artistically.

the wild geese: Irish soldiers serving in Europe after the evacuation of the Irish Army to France under the terms of the Treaty of Limerick, 1691. The term was also applied to later recruits to Irish brigades in Continental and American armies.

Edward Fitzgerald: Lord Edward Fitzgerald (1763–98), one of the leaders of the 1798 rebellion, who died while resisting arrest.

Robert Emmett: Irish nationalist leader, remembered for his inspiring 'Speech from the Dock' after the failed uprising that he organised against British rule in 1803. He was hanged for treason on 20 September 1803.

Wolfe Tone: Irish revolutionary and one of the founding members of the United Irishmen, bringing together Irish people of all religious denominations in support of political independence. He was captured during the Irish Rebellion of 1798 and tried in Dublin in November of that year. He took his own life on the day that he was to be hanged.

Yet could we turn the years again: Yeats suggests that the modern age, no longer capable of comprehending the passionate commitment and sacrifice of the earlier generation, would instead attribute it to lovesickness.

W. B. Yeats, 'To a Shade'

'To a Shade' (published in Yeats's *Responsibilities* in 1914) was written in memory of Charles Stewart Parnell (1846–1891), who had been discredited as leader of the Irish Parliamentary Party after the exposure of his affair with a married woman, Katherine O'Shea.

A man: Sir Hugh Lane (1874–1915), who offered to donate his collection of French impressionist paintings to the Dublin Municipal Gallery on condition that the Dublin Corporation would build a new gallery.

Your enemy, an old foul mouth: probably William Martin Murphy (1844–1914), who owned two newspapers opposed to Parnell; he also objected to Hugh Lane's proposal.

the Glasnevin coverlet: Glasnevin Cemetery, Dublin, where Parnell is buried.

W. B. Yeats, 'The Wild Swans at Coole'

The title poem of Yeats's book of poems *The Wild Swans at Coole* (1919). Yeats first visited Coole Park, Co. Galway, the home of his friend, patron and collaborator, Lady Gregory, in 1897.

W. B. Yeats, 'In Memory of Major Robert Gregory'

Robert Gregory, the son of Lady Gregory, was killed in action on the Italian Front on 23 January 1918. He is the subject of another poem by Yeats, 'An Irish Airman Foresees His Death'. This elegy for Robert Gregory was written in 1918 and first published in the *English Review* in August of that year. It was included in *The Wild Swans at Coole* (1919).

our house: Thoor Ballylee, the Norman tower which Yeats acquired in 1917, and where he and his family spent most of their summers.

Lionel Johnson: poet and essayist (1867–1902), friend of Yeats and one of the Tragic Generation of poets that Yeats wrote about in his *Autobiographies*. He was a member of The Rhymers' Club, a group of poets who met at Ye Olde Cheshire Cheese Pub in London in the 1890s.

John Synge: John Millington Synge (1871–1909), Irish playwright, best known for *The Playboy of the Western World* (1907).

a most desolate stony place: the Aran Islands.

George Pollexfen: Yeats's maternal uncle, with whom he spent holidays in his early years.

Mayo: county in the west of Ireland.

Our Sidney: Robert Gregory is imagined as a versatile Renaissance man (*soldier, scholar, horseman*) like Sir Philip Sidney (1554–86).

Castle Taylor: a place in Co. Galway.

Roxborough: Lady Gregory's home as a child.

Esserkelly: a place in Co. Galway.

Mooneen: a place in Co. Galway.

Clare: Irish county, south of Co. Galway.

faggots: a bundle of sticks to light a fire.

W. B. Yeats, 'Easter 1916'

'Easter 1916' was inspired by the execution of 15 leaders of the Easter Rising of 24 April 1916, when Irish Republican forces occupied the centre of Dublin and came under fierce opposition from the British Army. Written by Yeats in 1916 and privately printed, it was published in the *New Statesman* on 23 October 1920. It did not appear in book form until the publication of *Michael Robartes and the Dancer* in 1921.

That woman: Constance Gore-Booth, who married Count Casimir Markiewicz (1847–1932). She took part in the Rising and was sentenced to death, but her sentence was commuted to life imprisonment. She was later released.

harriers: hunting dogs, originally bred for chasing rabbits.

This man: Patrick Pearse (1879–1916), poet, teacher and barrister. He was commander-in-chief of the Irish forces during the Rising, and president of the Irish provisional government established in Easter week.

wingèd horse: Pegasus, an emblem of poetic inspiration, and the insignia of St Enda's School, founded by Pearse in Rathfarnham, Dublin.

This other: Thomas MacDonagh (1878–1916), poet and scholar. His study of Irish poetry, *Literature in Ireland*, was published in the year of his execution (1916). He was one of the leaders of the Easter Rising and a signatory of the Proclamation of the Irish Republic.

This other man: Major John MacBride (1865–1916), estranged husband of Maud Gonne.

For England may keep faith: the Home Rule Bill, granting Ireland a measure of independence, had been passed in the British Parliament but then suspended for the duration of the First World War.

Connolly: James Connolly (1870–1916), socialist leader of the Irish Citizen Army during the Rising, and one of the signatories of the Proclamation of the Irish Republic.

W. B. Yeats, 'In Memory of Eva Gore-Booth and Con Markiewicz'

Yeats had met the sisters Constance (1868–1927) and Eva Gore-Booth (1870–1926) at Lissadell House in Sligo in the winter of 1894–95. Constance took part in the Easter Rising in 1916. Eva wrote poetry and worked for the women's suffrage movement. She had a deep interest in

Indian mysticism. This double elegy was written in 1927 and published in *The Winding Stair and Other Poems* (1933).

the great gazebo: an architectural construct or 'folly' for gazing on the landscape. Yeats uses it here to refer to the hopes and ideals (the vision) of the Anglo-Irish class of which he was part.

W. B. Yeats, 'Beautiful Lofty Things'
From *New Poems* (1938).

O'Leary's noble head: John O'Leary (see note above on 'September 1913').

My father: John Butler Yeats (1839–1922), painter and writer. He spoke at the debate in the Abbey Theatre against the public opposition to Synge's play, *The Playboy of the Western World* (1907).

Standish O'Grady: Irish historian and novelist (1846–1928).

Augusta Gregory: Lady Gregory, Yeats's friend, patron and collaborator (1852–1932).

Maud Gonne: English-born Irish republican and revolutionary, and the inspiration for much of Yeats's poetry (although this is the only poem in which she is named). Yeats is recalling their walks together at Howth on the coast north of Dublin, where he proposed to her unsuccessfully in August 1891.

Pallas Athena: the Greek goddess of wisdom, war and art.

Andrew Young, 'A Dead Mole'
Andrew Young was born in Elgin, Scotland. He was a minister in the Presbyterian Church and, from 1940 onwards, a minister in the Church of England. In addition to writing religious poems, he wrote poems inspired by his love of the natural landscape and wildlife. This poem was published in *Collected Poems of Andrew Young* (1950).

Acknowledgements

We wish to thank Laura McKenzie for her work as editorial assistant in the early stages of the project. We also greatly appreciate the advice and encouragement that we have received from friends and colleagues while preparing the book for publication, especially Ted Chamberlin, Rachel Falconer, Brendan Gleeson, Jahan Ramazani, Ronald Schleifer, and Helen Vendler.

The editors and publisher gratefully acknowledge the following for permission to reproduce copyright material:

RAYMOND ANTROBUS: 'Sound Machine' from *The Perseverance*, Penned in the Margins, 2018, copyright © Raymond Antrobus, 2018. Reprinted by permission of the publisher. W. H. AUDEN: 'In Memory of W. B. Yeats' from *Collected Poems* by W. H. Auden, edited by Edward Mendelson, copyright © W. H. Auden, 1940. Renewed 1968. Reprinted by permission of Random House, an imprint and division of Penguin Random House LLC; and Curtis Brown, Ltd. All rights reserved. PAUL BATCHELOR: 'Pit Ponies', published in *The Love Darg*, Clutag Press, 2014. Reprinted by permission of the publisher. HILAIRE BELLOC: 'Matilda' from *Cautionary Tales for Children*, copyright © Hilaire Belloc, 1907. Reprinted by permission of Peters Fraser & Dunlop on behalf of the Estate of Hilaire Belloc. GWENDOLYN BENNETT: 'Epitaph' from *Opportunity*, Vol 76, March 1934, copyright © NYPL. Reprinted by permission of The New York Public Library. JOHN BERRYMAN: 'Dream Song #155: I can't get him out of my mind' from *The Dream Songs* by John Berryman, Farrar, Straus & Giroux, 2014, copyright © John Berryman, 1969. Renewed Kate Donahue Berryman, 1997. Reprinted by permission of Farrar, Straus and Giroux. All Rights Reserved. BION: 'Lament for Adonis' translated by Anthony Holden in *Greek Pastoral Poetry* by Anthony Holden, Penguin, 1973, copyright © Anthony Holden. Reprinted by permission of the author c/o Rogers, Coleridge & White Ltd., 20 Powis Mews, London W11 1JN. ELIZABETH BISHOP: 'North Haven' from *Complete Poems* by Elizabeth Bishop, Jonathan Cape, copyright © Alice Helen

Methfessel, 1983; and *Poems* by Elizabeth Bishop, Farrar, Straus & Giroux, copyright © The Alice H. Methfessel Trust, 2011. Publisher's Note and compilation copyright © Farrar, Straus and Giroux, 2011. Reprinted by permission of The Random House Group Limited; and Farrar, Straus and Giroux. All Rights Reserved. MALIKA BOOKER: 'Death of an Overseer' from *Pepper Seed* by Malika Booker, Peepal Tree Press, 2013. Reprinted by permission of the publisher. KAMAU BRATHWAITE: 'Elegy for Rosita' from *Elegguas*, Wesleyan University Press, 2010, copyright © Kamau Brathwaite, 2010. Reprinted by permission of the publisher. JERICHO BROWN: 'The Tradition' from *The Tradition*, Picador, 2019, copyright © Jericho Brown, 2019. Reprinted by permission of Picador through PLSClear; and The Permissions Company, LLC on behalf of Copper Canyon Press, coppercanyonpress.org. BASIL BUNTING: Excerpt from 'Briggflatts' from *Complete Poems*, ed. Richard Caddel, Bloodaxe Books, 2000. Reprinted by permission of Bloodaxe Books, www.bloodaxebooks.com. CHRISTIAN CAMPBELL: 'Rudical' from *Running the Dusk*, Peepal Tree Press, 2010. Reprinted by permission of the publisher. CIARAN CARSON: 'In Memory' from *From Elsewhere,* The Gallery Press, 2014; and Wake Forest University Press, 2015. Reprinted by kind permission of the author's Estate, c/o The Gallery Press, Loughcrew, Oldcastle, County Meath, Ireland; and Wake Forest University Press. CATULLUS: 'Catullus 101' translated by Anne Carson in *Nox*, New Directions, 2010, copyright © Anne Carson, 2010. Reprinted by permission of New Directions Publishing Corp.. CHARLES CAUSLEY: 'Eden Rock' from *Collected Poems 1951-2000*, Macmillan, 2000. Reprinted by permission of David Higham Associates. PAUL CELAN: 'Deathfugue' translated by John Felstiner in *Selected Poems and Prose of Paul Celan*, Norton, 2001, copyright © John Felstiner, 2001. Originally published as 'Mohn und Gedächtnis', copyright © Deutsche Verlags-Anstalt, München, 1993. Reprinted by permission of W. W. Norton & Company, Inc., and Penguin Random House Verlagsgruppe GmbH. AMY CLAMPITT: 'A Procession at Candlemas' from *The Collected Poems of Amy Clampitt*, copyright © The Estate of Amy Clampitt, 1997. Reprinted by permission of Alfred A. Knopf, an imprint of the Knopf Doubleday Publishing Group, a division of Penguin Random House LLC. All rights reserved. LUCILLE CLIFTON: 'the lost baby poem' from *How to Carry Water: Selected Poems*, copyright © Lucille Clifton, 1972, 1987. Reprinted by permission of The Permissions Company, LLC on behalf of BOA Editions, Ltd, boaeditions. org. TONY CONNOR: 'Elegy for Alfred Hubbard' from *New and Selected Poems*, Anvil Press, 1982. Reprinted by permission of Carcanet Press. WALTER DE LA MARE: 'Fare Well' from *Motley and Other Poems*, 1918. Reprinted by permission of The Society of Authors. TOI DERRICOTTE: 'Elegy for My Husband' from '*I*': *New and Selected Poems* by Toi Derricotte, copyright © 2019. Reprinted by permission of the University of Pittsburgh

Press. EMILY DICKINSON: 'Because I could not stop for death;' 'Safe in their alabaster chambers' and 'I felt a funeral in my brain' from *The Poems of Emily Dickinson: Reading Edition* by Emily Dickinson, ed. Ralph W. Franklin, Cambridge, Mass.: The Belknap Press of Harvard University Press, copyright © The President and Fellows of Harvard College, 1998, 1999. Copyright © The President and Fellows of Harvard College, 1951, 1955. Renewed by the President and Fellows of Harvard College, 1979, 1983. Copyright © Martha Dickinson Bianchi, 1914, 1918, 1919, 1924, 1929, 1930, 1932, 1935, 1937, 1942. Copyright © Mary L. Hampson, 1952, 1957, 1958, 1963, 1965. Reprinted by permission. All rights reserved. MAURA DOOLEY: 'I've Been Thinking a Lot About Heaven' from *Five Fifty-Five*, Bloodaxe Books, 2023. Reprinted by permission of Bloodaxe Books, www.bloodaxebooks.com. DOUGLAS DUNN: 'The Kaleidoscope' From *Elegies*, Faber & Faber, 1985, copyright © Douglas Dunn, 1985. Reprinted by permission of Faber & Faber Ltd; and United Agents (www.unitedagents. co.uk) on behalf of Douglas Dunn. T. S. ELIOT: 'Death by Water' from *The Complete Poems and Plays, 1909-1950*, Faber & Faber, 1969, copyright © T.S. Eliot, 1950, 1943, 1939, 1930. Copyright © Harcourt Brace & Company, 1952, 1935, 1936. Renewed by T.S. Eliot, 1964, 1963, 1958. Renewed by Esme Valerie Eliot, 1980, 1978, 1971, 1967. Reprinted by permission of Faber & Faber Ltd; and HarperCollins Publishers. VICKI FEAVER: 'Gorilla' from *The Book of Blood* by Vicki Feaver, Jonathan Cape, copyright © Vicki Feaver, 2006. Reprinted by permission of The Random House Group Limited. CALEB FEMI: 'The Story of Damilola Taylor' from *Poor*, Penguin, 2020, copyright © Caleb Femi, 2020. Reprinted by permission of Penguin Books Limited; and Jo Unwin Literary Agency Limited. JAMES FENTON: 'At the Kerb' from *Yellow Tulips: Poems 1968-2011*, Faber & Faber, 2012. Reprinted by permission of Faber & Faber Ltd; and United Agents (www. unitedagents.co.uk) on behalf of James Fenton. ROBERT FROST: 'Nothing Gold Can Stay' from *The Collected Poems* by Robert Frost, Vintage Books, copyright © Holt Rinehart and Winston Inc., 1969; and *The Poetry of Robert Frost*, ed. Edward Connery Lathem, copyright © Henry Holt and Company, 1923, 1969. Copyright © Robert Frost, 1951. Reprinted by permission of The Random House Group Limited; and Henry Holt and Company. All Rights Reserved. ROBERT GARIOCH: 'Elegy' from *Collected Poems*, Birlinn Ltd, 2004. Reprinted by permission of the publisher through PLSCLear. ALLEN GINSBERG: Excerpt from 'Kaddish' from *Collected Poems 1947-1997* by Allen Ginsberg, copyright © Allen Ginsberg, 1961 and the Allen Ginsberg Trust, 2006. Reprinted by permission of The Wylie Agency (UK) Limited; and HarperCollins Publishers. LORNA GOODISON: 'For My Mother (May I inherit half her strength)' from *Tamarind Season*, Institute of Jamaica, 1980. Reprinted by kind permission of the author. W. S. GRAHAM: 'Lines on Roger Hilton's Watch' from *New Collected Poems*,

Faber & Faber, 2005. Reprinted by kind permission of the Estate of the author. ROBERT GRAVES: 'The Untidy Man' from *Complete Poems Vol I*, ed. Beryl Graves and Dunstan Ward, Penguin, 2015. Reprinted by permission of Carcanet Press. THOM GUNN: 'Lament' from *The Man with Night Sweats*, Faber & Faber, 2002; and *Collected Poems* by Thom Gunn, Farrar, Straus and Giroux, 1995, copyright © Thom Gunn, 1994. Reprinted by permission of Faber & Faber Ltd; and Farrar, Straus and Giroux. All Rights Reserved. TONY HARRISON: 'Book Ends' from *Collected Poems: Tony Harrison*, Penguin, 2016. Reprinted by permission of Faber & Faber Ltd. TERRANCE HAYES: Excerpt from 'American Sonnet for My Past and Future Assassin' from *American Sonnets for My Past and Future Assassin* by Terrance Hayes, Penguin, 2018, copyright © Terrance Hayes, 2018. Reprinted by permission of Penguin Books Limited; and Penguin Books, an imprint of Penguin Publishing Group, a division of Penguin Random House LLC. All rights reserved. SEAMUS HEANEY: 'The Strand at Lough Beg' from *Field Work*, Faber & Faber, 1979; and *Opened Ground: Selected Poems 1966-1996* by Seamus Heaney, copyright © Seamus Heaney. Reprinted by permission of Faber & Faber Ltd; and Farrar, Straus and Giroux. All Rights Reserved. GEOFFREY HILL: 'September Song' from *King Log*, 1968. Reprinted by kind permission of the Estate of the author. MICHAEL HOFMANN: 'For Gert Hofmann, died 1 July 1993' from *Approximately Nowhere* by Michael Hofmann, Faber & Faber, 1999, copyright © Michael Hofmann, 1999. Reprinted permission of Faber & Faber Ltd; and Farrar, Straus and Giroux. All Rights Reserved. LANGSTON HUGHES: 'Silhouette' from *The Collected Poems of Langston Hughes* by Langston Hughes, edited by Arnold Rampersad with David Roessel, Associate Editor, Alfred A Knopf Inc., copyright © the Estate of Langston Hughes, 1994. Reprinted by permission of David Higham Associates; and Alfred A. Knopf, an imprint of the Knopf Doubleday Publishing Group, a division of Penguin Random House LLC. All rights reserved. TED HUGHES: 'Sheep' from *Collected Poems* by Ted Hughes, Faber & Faber, 2005, copyright © The Estate of Ted Hughes, 2003. Reprinted by permission of Faber & Faber Ltd; and Farrar, Straus and Giroux. All Rights Reserved. MICK IMLAH: 'Stephen Boyd' from *The Lost Leader*, Faber & Faber Ltd, 2008. Reprinted by permission of the publisher. MAJOR JACKSON: 'Ferguson' from *Boston Review*, March 2016. https://www.bostonreview.net/articles/major-jackson-ferguson/. Reprinted by kind permission of the author. LINTON KWESI JOHNSON: 'Reggae fi Dada' from *Making History*, 1984, copyright © Linton Kwesi Johnson. Reprinted by kind permission of LKJ Music Publishers Ltd. JACKIE KAY: 'Burying My African Father' from *Fiere* by Jackie Kay, Picador, 2011, copyright © Jackie Kay, 2011. Reprinted by permission of The Wylie Agency (UK) Limited. YUSEF KOMUNYAKAA: 'Elegy for Thelonius' from *Copacetic*, Wesleyan University Press, 1984, copyright © Yusef Komunyakaa, 1984. Reprinted by permission of the publisher. PHILIP LARKIN: 'The Explosion' from *High Windows*, Faber & Faber, 2019; and *The Complete Poems of Philip Larkin*, edited by Archie Burnett, copyright © The Estate of Philip Larkin, 2012. Reprinted by permission of Faber & Faber Ltd; and Farrar, Straus and Giroux. All Rights Reserved. MICHAEL LONGLEY: 'Wounds' from *An Exploded View*, Little-hampton Book Services, 1973, copyright © Michael Longley, 1973. Reprinted by permission of The Soho Agency. ROBERT LOWELL: 'Sailing Home from Rapallo' from *Collected Poems* by Robert Lowell, copyright © Harriet Low-ell and Sheridan Lowell, 2003. Reprinted by permission of Farrar, Straus and Giroux. All Rights Reserved. LOUIS MACNEICE: 'The Suicide' from *Collected Poems*, Faber & Faber, 2016. Reprinted by permission of David Higham Associates. DEREK MAHON: 'A Disused Shed in County Wexford' from *The Poems: 1961-2020*, The Gallery Press, 2021. Reprinted by kind permission of the author's Estate and The Gallery Press, Loughcrew, Oldcas-tle, County Meath, Ireland. PAULA MEEHAN: 'Child Burial' From *The Man Who Was Marked by Winter*, Gallery Press, 1991. Reprinted by kind permis-sion of the author. MARIANNE MOORE: 'W.S. Landor' from *Tell Me, Tell Me* by Marianne Moore, Faber & Faber, 1966, copyright © Marianne Moore, 1966. Reprinted by permission of Faber & Faber Ltd; and Viking Books, an imprint of Penguin Publishing Group, a division of Penguin Random House LLC. All rights reserved. MOSCHUS: 'Lament for Bion' translated by Anthony Holden in *Greek Pastoral Poetry* by Anthony Holden, Penguin, 1973, copyright © Anthony Holden. Reprinted by permission of the author c/o Rogers, Coleridge & White Ltd., 20 Powis Mews, London W11 1JN. ANDREW MOTION: 'Serenade' from *Public Property*, Faber & Faber, 2002; and *The Mower: New and Selected Poems*, David R. Godine Publishers, Inc. 2009, copyright © Andrew Motion. Reprinted by permission of Faber & Faber Ltd; and The Permissions Company, LLC on behalf of David R. Godine, Publishers, Inc.. PAUL MULDOON: 'Incantata' from *Selected Poems 1968-2014* by Paul Muldoon, Faber & Faber, 2017, copyright © Paul Mul-doon, 2016. Reprinted by permission of Faber & Faber Ltd; and Farrar, Straus and Giroux. All Rights Reserved. LES MURRAY: 'Midsummer Ice' from *New Selected Poems* by Les Murray, Carcanet Press, 2012, copyright © Les Murray, 2007, 2012, 2014. Reprinted by permission of Carcanet Press; and Farrar, Straus and Giroux. All Rights Reserved. BERNARD O'DONOGHUE: 'The Day I Outlived My Father' from *Outliving*, Chatto & Windus, 2003. Reprinted by kind permission of the author. FRANK O'HARA: 'The Day Lady Died' from *Lunch Poems*, City Lights Publishers, 1964, copyright © Frank O'Hara, 1964. Reprinted by permission of The Permissions Company, LLC on behalf of City Lights Books, citylights.com. SHARON OLDS: 'The Exact Moment of His Death' from *The Father* by Sharon Olds, Secker, copyright © Sharon Olds, 1992, 1993. Reprinted by kind permission of the author; The Random House Group Limited; Aragi, Inc.; and Alfred A. Knopf, an imprint of the Knopf Doubleday Publishing Group, a division of Penguin Random House LLC. All rights reserved. ALICE OSWALD: Excerpt from 'Memorial' from *Memorial: An Excavation of the* Iliad by Alice Oswald, Faber & Faber, 2012; and *Memorial: A Version of Homer's* Iliad by Alice Oswald, W. W. Norton & Company, Inc., 2013, copyright © Alice Oswald, 2011. Reprinted by permission of Faber & Faber Ltd; and W. W. Norton & Company, Inc. TOM PICKARD: 'Spring Tide' from *Hoyoot: Collected Poems and Songs* by Tom Pickard, Carcanet Press, 2014. Reprinted by kind permission of the author; Carcanet Press; and United Agents (www.unitedagents.co.uk) on behalf of Tom Pickard. SYLVIA PLATH: 'Electra on Azalea Path' from *The Collected Poems* by Sylvia Plath, Faber & Faber, 1981, copyright © the Estate of Sylvia Plath, 1960, 1965, 1971, 1981. Reprinted by permission of Faber & Faber Ltd; and HarperCollins Publishers. PETER PORTER: 'An Exequy' from *Collected Poems* by Peter Porter, Oxford University Press, 1949, copyright © Peter Porter. Reprinted by permission of the Estate c/o Rogers, Coleridge & White Ltd., 20 Powis Mews, London W11 1JN. EZRA POUND: from 'Hugh Selwyn Mauberley' from *Hugh Selwyn Mauberley* first published in 1920; and *Personae*, copyright © Ezra Pound, 1926. Reprinted by permission of Faber & Faber Ltd; and New Directions Publishing Corp. PROPERTIUS: 'The Elegies (2.28)' translated by Christopher Childers in *The Penguin Book of Greek and Latin Lyric Verse,* Penguin Classics, translation copyright © Christopher Childers, 2023. Reprinted by permission of Penguin Books Limited. GARETH REEVES: 'The Great Fire' from *To Hell With Paradise: New and Selected Poems,* Carcanet Press, 2012. Reprinted by permission of the publisher. CHRISTOPHER REID: Excerpt from 'A Scattering' from *A Scattering* by Christopher Reid, Arete Books, 2009, copyright © Christopher Reid. Reprinted by permission of the author c/o Rogers, Coleridge & White Ltd., 20 Powis Mews, London W11 1JN. DENISE RILEY: 'A Part Song', first published in the *London Review of Books,* 09/02/2012. Published in *Say Something Back*, Picador, 2016, copyright © Denise Riley, 2012. Reprinted by kind permission of the author. RAINER MARIA RILKE: 'The Ninth Elegy' translated by J. B. Leishman and Stephen Spender in *Duino Elegies*, Hogarth Press, 1968. Reprinted by permission of Curtis Brown on behalf of the Estate of Stephen Spender. TADEUSZ RÓŻEWICZ: 'The Survivor' translated by Adam Czerniawski in *Selected Poems,* Penguin, 1995. Reprinted by kind permission of the translator. SONIA SANCHEZ: 'for our lady' from *We A BaddDDD People*, Broadside Lotus Press, 1970. Reprinted by permission of the publisher. SIEGFRIED SASSOON: 'Suicide in the Trenches' from *Counter-Attack and Other Poems*, 1918, copyright © Siegfried Sassoon. Reprinted by kind permission of the Estate of Siegfried Sassoon via Barbara Levy Literary Agency. ANNE SEXTON: 'The Truth the Dead Know' from *The Complete Poems of Anne Sexton,* Houghton Mifflin,

1981, copyright © Linda Gray Sexton and Loring Conant, Jr., 1981. Reprinted by the permission of SLL/Sterling Lord Literistic, Inc. STEVIE SMITH: 'Scorpion' from *Collected Poems and Drawings of Stevie Smith*, Faber & Faber, 2018, copyright © Stevie Smith, 1972. Reprinted by permission of Faber & Faber Ltd; and New Directions Publishing Corp. TRACY K. SMITH: 'Wade in the Water' from *Such Color: New and Selected Poems,* Penguin, 2018, copyright © Tracy K. Smith, 2018. Reprinted by permission of Penguin Books Limited; and The Permissions Company, LLC on behalf of Graywolf Press, Minneapolis, Minnesota, www.graywolfpress.org. LAYLI LONG SOLDIER: '38' from *Whereas*, Picador, 2017, copyright © Layli Long Soldier, 2017. Reprinted by permission of Picador through PLSClear; and The Permissions Company, LLC on behalf of Graywolf Press, Minneapolis, Minnesota, www.graywolfpress.org. WALLACE STEVENS: 'The Emperor of Ice Cream' from *The Collected Poems of Wallace Stevens*, Knopf, 2015. Reprinted by permission of Faber & Faber Ltd. ANNE STEVENSON: 'Orcop' from *Collected Poems*, Bloodaxe Books, 2023. Reprinted by permission of Bloodaxe Books, www.bloodaxebooks.com. HANNAH SULLIVAN: Excerpt from 'The Sandpit After Rain' from *Three Poems*, Faber & Faber Ltd, 2018. Reprinted by permission of the publisher. THEOCRITUS: 'Idyll 1 (Death of Daphnis)' translated by Anthony Holden in *Greek Pastoral Poetry* by Anthony Holden, Penguin, 1973, copyright © Anthony Holden. Reprinted by permission of the author c/o Rogers, Coleridge & White Ltd., 20 Powis Mews, London W11 1JN. DYLAN THOMAS: 'A Refusal to Mourn the Death, by Fire, of a Child in London' and 'Do Not Go Gentle Into That Good Night' from *The Poems of Dylan Thomas*, Weidenfeld & Nicholson, copyright © Dylan Thomas, 1952 and The Dylan Thomas Trust. Reprinted by permission of David Higham Associates; and New Directions Publishing Corp. TOMAS TRANSTRÖMER: 'After Someone's Death' from *New Collected Poems*, translated by Robin Fulton, Bloodaxe Books, 2011. Reprinted by permission of Bloodaxe Books, www.bloodaxebooks.com. DEREK WALCOTT: 'Sea Canes' from *The Poetry of Derek Walcott 1948-2013*, Faber & Faber, 2019, copyright © Derek Walcott, 2014. Reprinted by permission of Faber & Faber Ltd; and Farrar, Straus and Giroux. All Rights Reserved. MARGARET WALKER: 'For Malcolm X' from *Prophets for a New Day*, Broadside Lotus Press, 1970. Reprinted by permission of the publisher. WILLIAM CARLOS WILLIAMS: 'The Last Words of My English Grandmother' (First Version) from *The Collected Poems: Volume I, 1909-1939*, ed. Walton Litz & Christopher MacGowan, copyright © New Directions Publishing Corp, 1938. Reprinted by permission of Carcanet Press; and New Directions Publishing Corp. KIT WRIGHT: 'The Boys Bump-Starting the Hearse' from *Bump-starting the Hearse*, Hutchinson, 1983, copyright © Kit Wright. Reprinted by kind permission of the author.

ACKNOWLEDGEMENTS

ANDREW YOUNG: 'A Dead Mole' from *Selected Poems*, Carcanet Press, 1998. Reprinted by permission of Carcanet Press.

Every effort has been made to trace and contact the copyright-holders prior to publication. If notified, the publisher undertakes to rectify any errors or omissions in the next edition of this volume.

Index of First Lines

Index of Titles

THE PENGUIN BOOK OF
THE PROSE POEM

'A superb anthology . . . it is hard to know how it could possibly
be bettered' *Daily Telegraph*

This is the prose poem: a 'genre with an oxymoron for a name',
one of literature's great open secrets, and the home for over 150
years of extraordinary work by many of the world's most beloved
writers. This uniquely wide-ranging anthology gathers essential
pieces of writing from every stage of the form's evolution,
beginning with the great flowering of recent years before moving
in reverse order through the international experiments of the 20th
century and concluding with the prose poem's beginnings in
19th-century France.

Edited with an Introduction by Jeremy Noel-Tod

ISBN: 978 0 141 984 56 8

THE PENGUIN BOOK OF
IRISH POETRY

'And that moment when the bird sings very close
To the music of what happens'

The Penguin Book of Irish Poetry features the work of the greatest
Irish poets, from the monks of the ancient monasteries to the
Nobel laureates W.B. Yeats and Seamus Heaney, from Jonathan
Swift and Oliver Goldsmith to Eiléan Ní Chuilleanáin and Nuala
Ní Dhomhnaill, along with a profusion of lyrics, love poems,
satires, ballads and songs. Reflecting Ireland's complex past and
lively present, this collection of Irish verse is an indispensable
guide to the history, culture and romance of one of Europe's
oldest civilizations.

Edited with an Introduction by Patrick Crotty

ISBN: 978 0141 191 64 5

THE PENGUIN BOOK OF
JAPANESE VERSE

'The sea dark,
The call of the teal
Dimly white'

The Penguin Book of Japanese Verse contains over 700 poems from the third century to the twentieth, including both tanka ('short poem') and haiku, and covering such classic themes as nature, love, partings and time. Displaying the full wit, sadness and subtlety of Japanese poetry, this collection also illustrates the continued popularity of the poetic form in Japan. Introducing the more complex 'New-Style' verse, the anthology offers a complete picture of Japan and its culture through the centuries.

Translated with Introductions by Geoffrey Bownas
and Anthony Thwaite

ISBN: 978 0 14 119 094 5